Give Me My Spirit Back
The Last of the Buffalo Soldier

This book is autographed to:

Charles (chuck) E. Bussey,

I am The Buffalo Soldier of World War II. One of the greatest
results of World War II was the integration of the US Armed Forces.
My greatest contribution was to help to make it happen.

Cecil W. White

— CECIL W. WHITE

Dec. 2, 2006

Give Me My Spirit Back

The Last of the Buffalo Soldier

The Autobiography of Major Cecil Ward White, US Army, Ret.

This book is an autobiography of the life of the author in a segregated society during the greater part of the 20th Century. It depicts his sacrifice in the defense of his country and personal determined efforts in eradicating detrimental policies, attitudes and incorrect implementation of the Constitution of the United States guaranteeing justice and equal rights to all of its citizens.

Author
Cecil Ward White
First Edition, October 2000
Second Edition, October 2001
Third Edition, December 2002
Fourth Edition, December 2004

Cover Design: Cecil Ward White
Cover enhancement and book format by Hristo Vassilev
Edited by Carole J. Jarvis

ISBN 0-9764890-0-7 softcover (previously ISBN 1-930211-16-3)

Library of Congress Control Number: TX 5-947-725

White, Cecil Ward.

Give Me My Spirit Back: The Last of the Buffalo Soldier /
an autobiography / Cecil Ward White

p. cm.

1. Autobiography. 2. Education. 3. Civil Rights. 4. Racism. 5. World War II, Europe.
6. U. S. Army. 7. Segregation. 8. Court Decisions. 9. Integration. I. Title

Manufactured in the United States of America by Jones Printing Service
2 4 6 8 10 9 7 5 3 1 softcover

Cecil Ward White Book Company
Last of the Buffalo Soldier
3900 Elba Street
Virginia Beach, VA 23452

www.cecil.w.white@buffalo-soldier.com

US Army Retirement Photograph
September 01, 1965
Major Cecil Ward White

BRIEF HISTORY OF THE BUFFALO SOLDIER

Shortly after the Civil War on July 28, 1866 Congress authorized six black units to serve during peacetime. These units comprised Negro veterans of the Civil War and former slaves under this structure, the formation of the 9th and 10th (horse) Cavalry along with the 38th, 39th, 40th and 41st (foot soldier) Regiments.

Once the westward movement had begun, the 9th and 10th Cavalry conducted campaigns against warring Indians, bandits, cattle thieves, murderous gunmen, bootleggers, trespassers and Mexican revolutionaries. Their endeavors also including escorting, protecting settlers, cattle herds, railroad crews, building forts, telegraph lines, and mapping trails through the American west.

Throughout the era of the Indian Wars, approximately twenty percent of the of the U.S. Cavalry were black troops and they were in more than 177 engagements. The troopers won the respect of the American Indians which inspired them to be called "Buffalo Soldiers". The Indians believed the name symbolized their respect for the Buffalos for its bravery, tenaciousness and valor. The Buffalo Soldier down through the years have worn the name with pride.

For the next thirty years, these regiments campaigned on the Great Plains, along the Rio Grande, in New Mexico, Arizona, Colorado, Wyoming and as for north as the Dakotas. The Buffalo Soldier participated in many other American military campaigns including: The Spanish American War, Philippine Insurrection, The Mexican Expedition, World War I and World War II.

It was US 92nd Infantry Division (Buffalo Division) which fought in Italy during World War II, helping to win the war there which led to the integration of the United States Armed Forces by President Truman in July 1948. As a result of the success of the Buffalo Division in Italy and the integration of US Armed Forces an environment was created to change the civil rights laws within the United States, making this Country a better place helping America to make the world a better world.

PROLOGUE

Buffalo Soldier writes history

Retired man publishes book on role in Army integration

by Eric B. Pilgrim
"Stars and Stripes", Wednesday, January 17, 2001

WIESBADEN, Germany - Cecil Ward White points to a picture of himself: another time in another world. The younger man sitting beside White smiles admiringly at the World War II veteran. He looks at White's 79-year-old hands as his wrinkled, weathered black fingers find more pictures.

The two have never met before. Still, they sit talking like old friends, the pictures being brought to life for the young man.

This is White's book, his life, his spirit.

White's autobiography, titled *Give Me My Spirit Back: The Last of the Buffalo Soldier*, tells the story of a man who fought for a dream of racial equality long before Dr. Martin Luther King Jr. walked up steps to the Lincoln Memorial in Washington and delivered his famous *I Have a Dream* speech, long before Rosa Parks refused to move to the back of the bus in Alabama.

"I believe that I am the father of the Integrated Army," said White, a retired major now living near Mainz, Germany. "And I believe that my plan has led to the civil rights movement of the '60s and the rise of Dr. King."

White said his dream, his plan, began back in 1932, at the age of 10.

White, born in Selma, Ala., in 1921, said it was at that age that he heard about four black men whom the police charged with raping two white women. A friend told him the four would probably hang, whereas four white men facing similar charges would probably walk free.

Coming from one of a very few educated black families in the United States at that time, White said he understood, even at that age, that education was the key of freedom - for himself and his race.

"I felt education was most important way to combat the race problems," White said. "I felt God made education as an equalizer."

So White made a prediction that he would later believe to be a gift from God.

"I told my father that within 30 years all of this would end, that a black man would surface who would lead the charge for racial equality," White said.

Not only did he make the prediction, but White also made plans to do all he could to prepare for it. He attended and graduated from Tuskegee University in Tuskegee, Ala. The he joined the Army as a second lieutenant, with an underlying goal of integrating the black man into a white man's Army. His opportunity came quickly.

It was September 1944, and the nation was embroiled in World War II. U.S. troops were fighting tooth and nail for the liberation of Italy.

White was sent to the 92nd Infantry Division, an all-black unit known as the Buffalo Division at Fort Huachuca, Ariz. Shortly after arriving, he reported to Headquarters and Headquarters Company, 371st Infantry Regiment.

The 92nd, along with another all-black unit, the 93rd, was partly created by the Pentagon to provide justification for integrating the armed forces after the war, according to White. If they could fight as well as the white divisions, the military would integrate them after the war, he said. According to history, many white leaders felt the black man would throw down his weapons and run in the heat of battle.

The 92nd was considered a well-trained, highly motivated group ready for war. But after transferring to Virginia before shipping out to Italy, the Buffalo division soldiers had to wait a long time for transportation. During that long wait, White said, morale dropped.

"We received a letter from the Pentagon that said morale at the Buffalo Division was too low for them to go to war, " White said. "They gave us officers and senior [noncommissioned officers] 24 hours to find the reason why and fix it. I was concerned because [General Douglas] MacArthur had recently relieved the 93rd Division for it and was now looking at relieving us. "

Some of the officers suggested the soldiers were simply sad about leaving family and friends. White knew that was not the truth, but as the newest officer in the unit he felt strong pressure to agree with them. He knew the division was a real chance at integration, maybe even the only chance.

"The Buffalo Division was our last hope," wrote White in his book. "My mind was split between telling the truth and evading it. I decided to put my life on the line by telling the truth and putting my whole situation in God's hands."

He told the others what he thought was the real reason that the soldiers were going overseas to fight for democracy, a democracy that was there for everyone but the black man. In essence, the black man was fighting for somebody else's freedom while he remained enslaved. He said they had encountered blatant segregation problems on the base, some that led to fights and extreme frustration over why they should lay down their lives for a country that didn't care.

Then he told the officers that if the Army fixed the problem inside the gates of its bases, "there would be no morale problem."

His suggestion was accepted, and overnight, the base was fully integrated. Morale soared, and in a few days the soldiers shipped out to Italy.

As the book makes clear, the rest is history. The soldiers fought bravely, defeated the enemy and helped change the Army forever. Integration of the armed forces came shortly after the war. And a man did rise up in the '60s to lead the charge for integration of the black man into the fabric of America: Dr. Martin Luther King Jr.

As White sat at the Wiesbaden food court, signing the younger man's copy of his book, he looked to the future, to his spirit and the spirit of others around him. White and black stood in lines together waiting for food. White and black passed through the same door to the bathroom. White and black sat together at tables throughout the court.

"The white man wasn't necessarily responsible for the black man going to America. It was God's responsibility," White said. "Blacks wouldn't have come to America if it hadn't been for God. And now, the spirit of the white man and black man are intricately tied together."

In the preface to his 185-page book, White writes that his main purpose is to show how racism prevented the armed forces from realizing the full benefit of integration and how education gave it back. Lying within the pages are his hopes of a better future for the military, America and even the world.

"My greatest hope," he said, "is to eliminate all racism in the next 50 years."

PURPOSE

The purpose of my book is to provide information about my personal history for my family and friends. Most of my experiences are unknown to them because of my having to live away in the service of my country and the raising of my children. It is my wish to be a part of the family legend; and by my experiences I wish to inspire future generations to follow the examples and continue with the tradition established by the family. Further, I hope they improve on them as well.

Most importantly, I want to pay tribute to the Buffalo Division of World War II, the United States 92nd Infantry Division, a unit which I consider made the greatest contribution to our democracy than any of our World War II divisions. Its combat performance provided the basis for integrating the Armed Forces of the United State and the foundation for all civil rights achievements of the 1940s, 50s and 60s. Without its wartime contribution, these accomplishments would not have been realized at the time in which they occurred. The accomplishments played a major role in enhancing the post World War II image of the United States on the world scene, contributing to the winning of the cold war. Even though it is quite late, I recommend, and I am prepared to support the granting of a Presidential Unit Citation for the contribution of the Buffalo Division during the second World War.

One of the purposes of this book is to provide a view for all America into the minds of black people so that they can see themselves in the same mirror and realize that our democracy for them, as well as the for rest of the Americans, is very incomplete until we can see each other the same way. Every advance for one group is an advance for the whole group. We all suffer when any group is deprived of the opportunity to reach its full potential. Our progress and world leadership is based on the opportunity and encouragement of every individual to reach his and her full potential.

The main purpose of this book is to show how the sin of racism has prevented our armed forces from realizing the full benefit of the integration process. There were always enough racist commanders around, conspiracies formed for limiting integration, causing good people to leave the service. Black military personnel felt the racist pinch more than other minority groups. This past Thanksgiving, November 25, 1999, I took my family to the local military installation for dinner where I met the new battalion commander. This was where I served as the Education Officer over thirty-three years earlier. The battalion commander said to me, "I don't have a single black lieutenant in my command," a battalion which has between thiry-five and forty officers. Tears almost came to my eyes because I had predicted this forty years earlier. I had already commented that I was seeing fewer and fewer black junior officers around.

I was happy to see and hear of the recent survey concerning racism in the services. It came out just as I had finished this book. I cannot think of a better purpose this book can serve than for every officer in the Armed Forces to read and to use it as a guide. Many of them may not realize their shortcomings. Others may be afraid to do anything about them. There must be a strong integration policy with teeth which will enable good officers to take the leadership with respect to obtaining the maximum benefit from integration of an integrated Armed Force.

This book is dedicated to the making of a better Armed Forces, a better America, as we move forward into the 21st Century. Racism of the past four centuries as we celebrate the two thousandth birthday of Jesus Christ must be treated as the sins of the past. Let us pray that it will be so.

PREFACE

This book is about the plans which I made as a ten year old boy for solving the race problem in southwest Alabama where I lived in 1932. My plans were to do it through my education, the education of my family, and for our educational achievement to serve as examples for inspiring other members of my community to do likewise.

Even though I was not at all sure that my family would be able to accomplish the education goal I set for them during the Great Depression existing during this period., I did have faith that through hard work and prayer we would somehow accomplish it.

I felt our educational achievements would cause others to do likewise, to the extent, that by the 1960s, there would be enough educated black people to find a way to solve the civil rights problem(s). I had no vision, with the exception of faith in education. How this would be done was unclear, but I felt that if I stayed focused on my objectives, doors would open up to show the way.

I did stay focused and proceeded with my education until I completed three years of college before entering the military during World War II. The attained education enabled me to become a commissioned officer in the United States Army. I was an infantry officer when I made my greatest contribution toward achieving my goals.

In February 1942, under the pressure of civil rights leaders, President Roosevelt promised to look into integrating the Armed Forces after the war. The integration of the military, I felt, was one of the doors which was opened for correcting the civil rights problem, provided the performances of black soldiers in combat would be reasonable equal to those of white combat units.

Chapter 17 of this book (Appendix A), Silent Power, explains the role I played and the result of my efforts to achieve civil rights goals of the 50s and 60s. First, the integration of the Armed Forces, which caused a chain reaction for civil rights achievements. Secondly, the Supreme Court Decision of 1954 and 1955, eliminating segregation in public schools. Third, the Anti-Discrimination Act of 1964. Fourth, the Voters Right Act of 1965. And fifth, the US Supreme Court Decision banning discrimination laws dealing with marriage in 1969.

My objective in 1932 was to eliminate all laws which violated equal protection under the Constitution of the United States, which were accomplished in the 1960s. My book deals with the spiritual implementation of the integration of the Armed Forces, the lack of it, as well as application of civil rights laws in our civilian communities which are covered in more detail in Chapters 10 and 16. This book is about the elimination of racism everywhere.

Table of Contents

THE CIVIL RIGHTS BLUE PRINT OF 1932

Cecil Ward White established an education plan as a 10 year old boy in the cotton fields of Alabama in 1932 for correcting the civil rights problem facing African Americans. His plan to do so would be made possible by the education of himself and his family which would give incentives to black people to do likewise over a 30 year period which would enable them to figure out a way to solve the race problem. He visualized that a better educated black environment would cause a well educated black person to emerge as a civil rights leader to bring about changes in the civil rights laws.

He believes that God created education to be an equalizer that would help the down and out to rise up and be equal to the high and mighty; it would help the poor to become equal to the rich, and would help the blacks to become equal to the whites.

As a result of this education plan of the White family, Mr Whites education enabled him to become a commissioned officer in the United States Army during World War II and to become a member of the 92nd Infantry Buffalo Division which went to war in World War II in Italy. The fighting achievement of Mr White and the Buffalo Division provided sufficient evidence to enable the Armed Forces of the United States to become integrated in 1948. The integration of the Armed Forces together with education of black veterans of World War II and the Korean War who become educated under the GI bill would enable them to create the environment which led to the emerging of Dr Martin Luther King. Together with the effort of Mr. White, they where able to bring about the changes in the civil right laws which he predicted as a ten year old boy. The forces which brought about these changes remain in effect to bring about continuous improvement in racial and human relation.

Mr. White believes that he did more to change the Civil Rights within the United States than all the US Presidents since Abraham Lincoln.

Chapter 1
EARLY CHILDHOOD

I was born June 30, 1921, the fourth child of Clarence and Jennie T. White. I was born in Marion Junction, Alabama, on the Chisolem Place, approximately three and a half miles from Marion Junction. Our home was located on the Chisolem Road that was a connecting road. On one end, it stopped at the Marion, Alabama-Harold's Cross Road Highway, with the latter crossing Highway 80, which connects Selma and Marion Junction. The other end of the Chisolem Road ended at Pernell Road that ran parallel to the Cahaba River where it connected to the old Selma-Marion Junction Highway on the south. All three of my homes in the Pernell Community were located on these two connecting roads, Chisolem and Pernell Roads. My first home on the Chisolem Place existed through my first year of elementary school.

My memory goes back, I believe, to when I was three years of age. I remember traveling from Selma to my home in a horse-drawn buggy and a horse-drawn surrey. A surrey was a little bit like a car; the difference was that it was horse drawn. We sat inside protected from the weather like in a car. The driver sat outside in the open weather. One day my father drove us home in the heavy rain with his only protection being a rubberized raincoat and a rubberized rain hat. In 1926, when I was four or five years of age, my father bought his first car, a new Model T-Ford. This car cost my father $500; now my father was protected from weather when he was driving.

My two oldest brothers and my oldest sister were attending school in Selma, Alabama, boarding with my aunt and uncle. My aunt, my mother's oldest sister, was a teacher. I was the oldest child at home, with no other children to play with. My brother Ed was only two, and my sister Geneva was a new baby. I probably had to play with them, which must have kept me entertained until my brothers and sister came home from the city school. The only play which I can recall doing was hide and seek.

During my early years a high percentage of my time had to do with eating. I was accused of being a little on the greedy side. I believe a high percentage of my drive was due to the ingenious means I used to satisfy my appetite. I remember going to a little country store about a hundred and fifty yards from our house and asking the storeowner for sugar. Every time I went there, I asked him for sugar. One particular day, Mr. Paten, the storeowner, said, "I am going to gouge you from always begging me for sugar." He took a whole cup of sugar and packed it into my little mouth. I could not move my mouth at all due to the heavy packing. My instinct told me to keep my mouth closed and do nothing. In a minute or so, all the sugar had melted. I scraped my throat and swallowed the remaining sugar, which was still in my mouth. Soon as my mouth was sugar-free, I said, "That was good. Give me some more!" "I'll be damn if I will!" Mr. Paten replied.

I really did not want any more, but I did not want him to know it. This really did inflate my ego because I had won against this fifty-year-old man, and I was only four years old. He must have felt pretty bad being white and allowing this four-year old black boy to outsmart him. At this time, of course, I did not know anything about black or white, but I did know that I had won. I did not brag about it, but I never forgot it.

I had my eating problems with my mother. Every day about ten o'clock I went into the field where she was working and told her that I was hungry. My mother quit work, went home, and fed me. There was a time when I told my mother that I was hungry and she went home as before, but I did not eat which made her angry. When I insisted on eating after that, my mother gave it to me.

I had to look for another way. My great aunt and uncle who were about seventy lived in our house. My parents took good care of them, but generally left them alone. I decided to get chummy with them, being their boy in exchange for getting something to eat when I wanted it. We got alone fine! I do not know when they passed away, but I do remember when my father's cousin, cousin Scrap, and her daughter Arlene came to live with us. It must have been after the passing of Aunt Tilde and Uncle Tom. Although Arlene was several years older than me, we became close playmates. Her mother took care of my eating needs as well as those of her daughter.

When I became six years old, I began my education at the Pernell Primary School, walking some five miles on a wagon trail, passing through a creek that had no bridge. During times of high water, instead of traveling on this trail through the pasture, I had to travel along the Chisolem Road past the house where we moved to after my first year of schooling. I traveled to school with my cousin and a neighbor boy whom we called Pie Back. He was the son of a Mr. and Mrs. John Moore. This boy was several years older than me. As a six-year-old, these two provided protection for me.

After my first year of school, my family moved to Ham Place, about two miles to the east on the Chisolem Road. Now my family consisted of four boys and three girls. My sister Jewel was the last one of us who was born on Chisolem Place.

It was on the Ham Place where the foundation of my life was established. My drive for food on the Chisolem Place gave way to my drive for education and sports. It was not that I liked food less; but because of work, I ate morning, noon and evening, rather than between meals as it was when I was younger. I no longer went to the fields and asked for food or asked my mother to let me work. But now at seven, I had to work. I was given a hoe that would be my primary working tool for the next five years.

On Sundays, I went to Sunday school and church. I went to the public school from Monday through Friday. My first day in school, after moving to the Ham Place, I got into a fight. Therefore, I was forced to learn to fight also. I learned about racism and the injustices, which went with it. All of these experiences and others helped to shape my life. I got beat in my first fight and went home crying to my mother about it. The only fight that I knew about was that which I got from my mother. Naturally, I lost all of those. My mother told me if I lost my next fight, I would lose the next one after that which she would give me. I learned that the boy who had beaten me was afraid of blood. When he jumped me the next day, I bit him on his nose causing it to bleed. That time I won; and in the process, I learned better how to protect myself. I did not win all of my fights, but I did not tell my mother when I did not win.

My favorite subject in school was arithmetic. My father believed if I could master this subject that I could handle all the others. The others were geography and history. I guess I wanted to know about the world and what had happened in it. Often I talked to old people and asked them about their lives. Even though many of them had traveled only a few miles from where they were born, I wanted to know all that they were willing to tell me. I found the personal history conversations fascinating. I was very fortunate that my parents believed in education. My father wanted more education; but because he was limited to finishing the sixth grade, he was determined to do for his children that which he wished for himself. He therefore became an education father. My mother was more fortunate as she was a high school graduate. Her two older sisters were high school graduates also. Her father was a teacher and a preacher. Later, her oldest sister, my Aunt Willie, became a teacher as well.

My father believed that education made everyone better at whatever profession he chose, be it good or bad. He said that, "Doors of opportunity will open for those who become educated and will remain closed for those who are not." Education did not come cheap after elementary school. Where I lived, boarding in the city was necessary in order to go to junior high school and beyond. When the Depression set in, beginning in the late twenties, the cost of education looked prohibitive. Cotton, which had previously been sold for over $100 per bale and weighed between 500 and 600 pounds. (During the 1930's a bale of cotton sold for about fifteen dollars for the same size bale, which made going to the city school look impossible.) Without regard to the Depression, my sister and brothers continued their education in Selma. I did not know what would happen when I finished the sixth grade. This was a little way off.

Our one-room elementary school started in October when cotton picking was finished and closed in April when chopping cotton began. We did lots of reading out loud, had lots of spelling bees, and recited the multiplication tables. We must have done something else, but I cannot recall what else was taught us. Because my mother had finished high school, I had help with my homework in reading, spelling and arithmetic. Later, my Aunt Willie taught me mathematics, fractions, decimals, and other exercises, which would prepare me for the seventh grade in the city school.

Lots of farm work had to be done by us between the second and the seventh grades. I worked from sun to sun, sun up to sun down. The sun was hot, and the ground was hard. It looked so far away before I would go to school in town and get away from this hard work. I had to face reality and work hard so that my two oldest brothers and oldest sister could stay in the city school. If they did not stay, I would not be able to go beyond the sixth grade. I, therefore, had to work for them, in order to work for me.

In addition to raising cotton, we raised corn, melon, sugar cane, and many types of vegetables. We had cows for milk products and beef, hogs, chickens, and turkeys for other meats and poultry. In addition to consuming these products for our foods, we marketed them to customers whom we were able to acquire from already established customers. Money obtained from marketing our products supplemented cotton, which was our major means for obtaining cash. We produced hay for our mules and cows. In addition, we produced food products for our needs and marketing. We used it to pay the board for my sister and brothers, and later for my younger brother and sisters and me.

The hardest work I can remember was on the hill, the highest piece of ground that we farmed on the Ham Place. The ground was of prairie soil--lots of clay and rocks mixed together--making the ground a little like cement during the dry hot summer days. The ground became so hard the hoe would rebound like a ball when it was struck while removing grass from it. Not even the corner of the hoe could penetrate this hard ground, causing the grass to be broken off instead of being dug up by the roots. The hoe had to be filed often because its cutting edge was blunted and made dull by the hard ground. We pecked away at the grass, breaking it off instead of digging it up, as we moved to the end of the row where there was no shade. The return trip to the other end was where there were shade trees and cool water obtained from our well, which was about five hundred yards away. It gave us some comfort and something to hope for as we worked.

When noontime came, we went home where our mother always had a wide variety and more than enough food for our meal. After dinner, which we called it, we slept under a nice shade tree at our house for an hour. Then we headed back to the field until the sun was down. During the hour we slept, we kept cool by our clothing that was as wet as if we had jumped into a pool of water. This wetness was caused by the sweat of heavy work in a temperature at about one hundred degrees Fahrenheit.

The work during the afternoon was just as hard as it was during the morning. The only satisfaction we had was that we would have a night of rest before we started the work routine over again the following day. Before going to the table for our supper meal, we had to feed the cows, hogs, mules, and chickens and milk the cows as well. When this was all done, we had our evening meal; and we talked about our accomplishments of the day and announced our plans for the next day. We relaxed, joked, and went to bed to get a well-deserved night of rest.

Most workdays were similar, but the ground was not so hard as it was on that high hill. I must have achieved a level of managerial ability so that my father could put me in charge during his absence. One day my father, Mr. Matt, Miss (Mrs.) Lou, and I were hoeing cotton when my father had to leave to go to Selma to buy items for our country smokehouse store. We were out or in short supply of some items. I believe I was nine years of age at the time. My father left me in charge. Miss Lou had a dominating personality and did not like it at all having a nine-year-old boss. Mr. Matt, on the other hand, could deal with it.

I knew Miss Lou was going to cause me some problems, and I did not know how I would handle it. I was not afraid, however, to do that which my father had assigned me to do. As soon as my father had left the area and was no longer available to rescue me, Miss Lou left some grass around the cotton that she should have cut away. I said, "Miss Lou, you left some grass back here," pointing to it. She came back and removed it. One or two minutes later, she left some more grass. When I called it to her attention, she called me a "fresh ass" and did not remove it.

This was difficult for me because I had always been told to respect older people, and Miss Lou was about sixty. But this was business, and my father was depending on me to get the job done. I said, "Miss Lou, if you do not get that grass up, I am going to tell my father." She did not move. "But if you do get it up, I won't tell him." Miss Lou did not want to tangle with my father, especially about sloppy work. She very quietly removed the grass and did not leave any more grass the whole day. Miss Lou felt (like most people in this situation would feel) that I would tell my father anyway and get praise for a job well done. I kept my word by not telling him. I do not think I ever told him. She was nervous for about a week. She was surprised and delighted because I kept my promise and spared her from a chewing out. From that time on, Miss Lou thought I was the greatest.

This situation with Miss Lou, a controversial encounter, became a model, which I always followed. The job came first, and I had to use what power I had to get it done. I did not have much power in this case, but I knew she was afraid my father in this particular situation. When she did nothing, I sweetened the situation by saying that I would not tell my father if she removed the grass. I kind of let her off the hook, so to speak. Getting the job done and winning the admiration of Miss Lou in the process has always been a source of satisfaction to me. This became a model, which I would use throughout my life.

Either that same year or the year before I had this encounter with Miss Lou, my brother Clarence, who was six and a half years older than me, and my brother Frank, four and a half years older, decided to go into the chicken business on our farm. They excluded me, saying that I was too young. I set up my own chicken business, which was much better than theirs. They got disgusted and quit their business. My father was very disappointed with my older brothers for allowing me to put them out of business. Of course, I got my satisfaction from this victory.

We played sandlot baseball every opportunity we had--every time it rained, on holidays, during the rainy season, or during "lay by time" (July and early August when the crops were mature enough to make it without further work). The four brothers in my family and the five neighbor brothers of the Harrell family went at it. The fifth player on our team was Tom Edd Morrow, the only white boy in the neighborhood, who also was my playmate. We played knock-down drag-out baseball. Sometimes we lost, and sometimes we won; but they were usually well played games.

I was perhaps the most dedicated baseball player in the group. I kept all the equipment--used broomsticks, broken baseball bats, homemade bats, rubber balls, patched baseballs, tennis balls, and golf balls were among the items we used. Some of us had gloves and mitts, and the rest of us used our bare hands. We could hit and play error-free ball on relatively rough ground. Quite often we had an audience of ten to fifteen people. During our leisure, baseball was often the main topic of discussion. My father, mother, sisters, as well as brothers, played the game. Most of people in the community either played or had played. Everyone who did not play was a spectator. When the newspaper came, we turned to the sports page to see how the major leagues did, as well as the Southern League, which included Birmingham, Alabama, and the South Eastern League, which included Selma, Alabama. We were most interested in the major leagues, especially the New York Yankees and Philadelphia Athletics. My brother Clarence liked Philadelphia, and the rest of us favored the Yankees. We paid particular attention to Babe Ruth, Lou Gehrig, Bill Dickey, Lefty Gomez of the Yankees, and Jimmy Fox and Ty Cobb of the Athletics.

One day baseball taught me the most significant lesson of my life. We were having our normal sandlot baseball game while we were living on the Ham Place. I was nine or ten years old. That day my team lost. We lost because Tom Edd, my white playmate, played so badly; he could not hit that day and made all kind of errors. I did not mind losing so much if we played well, but I got all "shook up" when we lost by playing poorly. I went to Tom Edd and chewed him out. He felt pretty bad about playing bad and about me chewing him out; but I felt that he had it coming, and I gave it to him.

My oldest brother Clarence and the oldest of the Harrell boys, Buster, came to me saying, "You can't talk to that boy like that." I did feel a little bad about what I said to him, but I was not going to let them know it. Then I said, "Why can't I? He played bad, didn't he?" They said, "Because he is white, that's why." "What does white have to do with it?" I said. "Because he is white, he is better than we are," my brother Clarence said. "He is not better than me. Babe Ruth, Ty Cobb, Lou Gehrig, Bill Dickey, and Jimmy Fox are better than me, but he is not. Until he can play baseball as good as me, he will never be better than me," was my answer to my brother.

"Let's go to Mama," my brother said. I spoke first. "Mama, Clarence said Tom Edd is better than me because he is white." Mama said, "He is really not better than you, but the white people have control over us. The land, which we are renting, belongs to a white family. All the big stores and banks belong to white people. The judges, the sheriff, the police, and the man with the key to the jail are all white." I said, "I know that Mama, but that still doesn't make Tom Edd better than me." Then I walked away with my opinion never changing about this issue.

In 1932, Elsey Wells, a young man living and working with us, picked up the daily newspaper as it had just been left there by the mailman who traveled by automobile in the rural area. Sometimes he traveled by horse when the roads were too muddy for cars. Normally, the first thing we read about was the baseball news. This morning Elsey did not mention anything about baseball. I asked him, "What's the matter?" He said, "Four black men raped two white women in Scottsboro, Alabama." I said, "What's going to happen to the men?" He said, "They probably will get hung." I said, "What would happen if four white men had raped two black women?" "Nothing," he said. This was the first time that I had been confronted with the race issue since that baseball game with Tom Edd. I really had not thought anything about it since that time. Now for the first time I began to see the injustices which takes place in racial matters. This certainly did not fit the principles of the Ten Commandments, especially the one which says, "Do Unto Others As You Would Have Them To Do Unto You." I said to my father, "This race situation will never change until a black man is free to marry a blonde." My father said, "It may happen in your lifetime, but it will not happen in mine." I said, "It will happen in the 1960s." My education plan to solve the race problem was to educate my sisters and brothers who were older and younger than me in order for me to be educated. I would be the example for my family, and my family would be the example for the community. Our examples would, in my opinion, produce enough educated black people within thirty to forty years to figure out a way to solve the race problem and to create an environment to find a well educated black person to lead the way to complete the job.

During that same summer, I was sitting on the bench by the well house where we got our water. It was a little more than a hundred yards from where Elsey told me about the Scottsboro Boys and about two hundred yards from our house. This was the well from which we got our drinking water, watered our mules, and washed our clothes. This overflow well ran continuously, creating a little swamp before draining into the branch close by. The swamp and willow tree watered from the well created an air-conditioned area, which was ideal for chatting on a hot day. On this day I sat there with my brother Ed, Tutt, Charlie and Kenny, when Tutt was his usual self who always liked to praise the white man and tear down the black man. He said, "I hear black soldiers don't fight well. They are cowards, and they run away in battles." As usual, I got angry when he came up with something stupid like that. I said, "I don't believe it. The way we fight every Saturday night at the jook, we can fight as well as anyone. If I ever go to war, I will show everyone that we can fight as good as anyone else."

In the same timeframe, I went to visit Miss (Mrs.) Lou and Mr. Matt. I wanted to ask Miss Lou what she thought about the race issue. Most black people would not talk about it. When they did talk about it, they would come up with an answer that "we like it like it is." This was a nice safe answer, which the white man wanted to hear and because black people were afraid to say otherwise. I knew Miss Lou trusted me not to tell anyone; she would tell me the truth. She said right away, "It is not right the way white people treat us; but every time there is a war, things get better for us." Even Mr. Matt, who was usually quiet about everything, came out and supported Miss Lou's views. I felt pretty good about Miss Lou's answer.

During the fall of 1932, my father and his brother, Uncle Frank, with some friends proceeded to build our new home on the land which my father had been buying since I was one year old, 1922. It was located less than a mile due east of our home on the Ham Place. Boundaries lay on and to the west of the Cahaba River and on the Dallas side of the Dallas-Perry Counties line, the east side of the Pernell Road, and south by the Pernell Place from which the community got its name. The Pernell Community at this time consisted of about forty-five black families and two or three white families. The east-west limits of the community were about five miles and the north-south limit was about two and a half miles.

My father bought a keg of moonshine whiskey to celebrate when the construction of the house was completed. I began to sip away at this whiskey and gave away quite a bit of it. I took some to school where my friend and I drank it during recess. I even gave some of my father's money to people to whom I gave the whiskey. I believe in November of that year, I came home a little drunk. My mother, being a little afraid for me, said, "You better not let your daddy catch you like this." My father did find out about it, and he whipped my ass and made me tell everything. He was even hunting with his gun for the man who had talked me into stealing his money and whiskey. Every time my father thought about what I had done that week, he beat my ass again. It took him quite some time before he forgot about it, but I did not. That situation made me a tough negotiator. After that, nobody was ever able to talk me into doing something I did not want to do.

Those years on the Ham Place, between seven and twelve years of age, were my learning years. I wanted an education because I wanted to get off the farm, to get a professional career, and to correct the race problem. I wanted an education, not only for me, but for my sisters and brothers as well. I wanted it for my friends, but they did not have a chance. Neither they nor their parents ever talked about education. They talked about going to Birmingham and working in the steel mills, coal mines, and construction work; but they thought nothing about education. I remember Miss Lou stating that every time there was a war, things got better for us. I remember saying to her, "It looks as if we are going to wait a long time, because there is no war in sight."

In 1933, in our new home on our new land, we were in a big Depression. Mr. Roosevelt was giving us hope and that was about all. My father was always worried that his objective to educate his family would not be realized. We hung on to hope, worked hard to clear away the forest. At eleven years of age, I could do anything a man could do--cutting down trees for firewood and burning brushes until everything was cleared away except the roots. Those roots made plowing difficult. About every six inches, the sweep of the plow become stuck in the roots and had to be pulled free. This went on and on causing plowing to be hard and difficult. Each time the ground was plowed, it was a little easier as more and more of the roots were cleared away.

Our new land was sandy soil, which made plowing and hoeing easier. It was also highly fertile, as it had not been worked in a number of years. All of the 231 acres of our land was in use. That which was not being used for farming was used for pasture. Our cotton production was about twenty-two bales per year, earning us about five hundred dollars per year. Without consuming and selling just about everything we could raise and produce, we never would have made it. Most of our work was in cotton; it did not reach our economic needs. By paying the school board with food and by selling food items from the farm to produce cash on a continuing basis, we were able to make it. We needed workers on the farm.

My brother Frank was the only member of our family who was a school dropout. He was boarding with my Aunt Willie and Uncle Ned. My Uncle Ned was a cattle broker at the stockyard, working for his white father. In trading cattle, he was the best. He wheeled lots of power because of his powerful position and with the support of his father. He gambled and bootlegged whiskey with the knowledge of the law. My brother Frank, who followed the example of this uncle, bootlegged, gambled, and played hooky from school. My father brought him home where he was whipped a lot by both my mother and father. They were trying to make him break his ways and go back to school, but he would not do it. He was kept on the farm. Sometimes he left and went back to stay with Uncle Ned. Then my father brought him back again.

He taught me about smoking and drinking, but he had nothing to do with my stealing and drinking my father's whiskey and giving it away along with the money. My brother Frank did not have much influence on me because I did not agree with what he was doing either. Even though I wanted him to go back to school, his decision to stay on the farm did provide more help there and made it easier for me to go to school in Selma upon completion of the sixth grade.

During my twelve years, I learned lots about my community and the surrounding communities; and I continued to do so through my years in high school and college as I came home during the summer months to work on the farm. Black people in my community and in most of Dallas County were small cotton farmers who rented their land of five acres, more or less. This gave these farmers a high degree of independence as opposed to black people who were sharecroppers on a large plantation. On these small rented farms the farmers were limited to what they could earn by smallest of their farms and were therefore in an economic straight jacket. Sharecroppers were a little better off than slaves. The landowners provide them with a house, food, clothing, and provision for work. Many never quite paid off their debts, according to landowners' figures, regardless of how hard the sharecroppers worked. Some landowners beat their sharecropper when they felt that they were lazy and unproductive. There were a couple of cases I knew about where the sharecroppers left the land and went 160 miles away to Mobile, Alabama. The landowner went to Mobile, located the sharecroppers, beat them, and brought them back to the farm. This landowner was later tried in Federal Court for kidnapping, putting an end to this and other such civil rights violations.

My father had a large family farm and the vision and ability to use it to educate his family. Other black families closed their eyes and minds to this and never talked about it to us. They never said, "I wish that I could do it for my children."Their spirit and motivation were asleep from years of negativism. This is what the white people liked, as this was their way to maintain white supremacy. The landowners, to discourage too much initiative and ambitions, visited the small farmers. In this way black people were discouraged from thinking positively. My father was rocking the boat by attempting to provide a high school and college education for his children. Once my father received a message, "If you don't stop educating your children, you will find yourself floating in the Cahaba River." My father got angry with that, giving a response that the Cahaba River was big enough for more than one body. We knew who sent the message. We did not hear any more threats. My father had many good white friends and white relatives who kept him notified as to whom to watch out for.

Chapter 2
JUNIOR AND SENIOR HIGH SCHOOL

In September 1934, I left my county home on the Cahaba River in the Pernell Community for enrollment in Clark Middle School in Selma, Alabama. Life would certainly be different in this small city of about 25,OOO, county seat of Dallas County. There we had a different teacher for each subject as compared to my country elementary school, which had one teacher for the entire school. Here we had electric light instead of oil lamps, bathtubs instead of metal washtubs, hot and cold running water instead of pump water heated on the stove, and water closets instead of outhouses. City living was a world apart from my rural country living. Selma had two motion picture theaters compared to nothing in the country.

I thought about my mother and father whom I left behind to live in the relatively primitive lifestyle of the country, but they received great pleasure in meeting their goals to educate us, which previously seemed impossible. I still had a guilty feeling because they had to work hard to keep the rest of us in school. Every two years one more of us would be moving away from home for school in the city. On the other hand, this was their ambition and lifetime goal, educating their family.

My father gave me only fifteen cents per week and I wanted him to give me more, but he said this was all he could afford. Ten cents of that went for the cowboy movie every Saturday, which left five cent for one cinnamon bun for lunch at school. In order for me to have social status, I had to be able to buy one bun and one RC cola each school day. Therefore, I needed sixty cents per week or more. It became necessary for me to find work, which was selling a two-cent weekly newspaper, which came out every Saturday. I sold an average of twenty per week; one cent went to the publisher and one for me. This helped a little, allowing me to buy five buns per week but no drink. I was a good salesman and could even sell a blind man a newspaper.

Two or three months later, I started caddying, making an average of $2 per week. Now I could roam with the big shots during lunchtime, and my father no longer had to give me fifteen cents. From now on I was making my own spending money.

I was boarding with my Aunt Mable, along with my sister Erin. My brother Clarence, who had also lived with her, was now attending a teachers' college in Montgomery, Alabama. Both had previously lived with my Aunt Willie, but she and Uncle Ned had divorced because of his wildness. My Aunt Willie was now living with her father at the family home four miles northwest of Selma. Aunt Mable and I did not hit it off too well. I felt it and she felt it, but no one else did. Maybe it was due to the fact that my double first cousin, Frank, was spoiled by her. He was not as hard working as I, or maybe I was making him look a little bad in comparison. Frank and I were about the same age, in the same class, and were like brothers. Aunt Mable, being a little bit tight with her money, did not cook enough food to suit me. Since I was often a little hungry, I would slip back into the ice box and eat a little of the food which she was saving for the next meal. Although she never caught me, she knew that I was the culprit. All of this drew a wedge between us.

My sister Erin, who had always been a top 'A' student due to the tutoring by Aunt Willie, had skipped a couple classes and was going to college when I was in the tenth grade, although she was only two years older than I. We were all quite proud of her.

My cousin Frank, helped me a lot with my schoolwork because he knew the procedures better than I. I was good in mathematics because of the help that I previously received from my Aunt Willie. English was my biggest problem subject. I did not get a good background in this subject in elementary school, and I did not like my teacher who taught seventh grade English. I got a lot of lashes on my hand by the lady English teacher. I managed, however, to do quite well, both in school and my private work during my first school year away from home.

I went back home after school to help my father on the farm. As always, I was a good farm worker, wishing to help and encourage my parents to educate us. I never wanted to do anything that would discourage them. My objective to solve the civil rights problem through education was still my primary objective. I was still good with the plow and hoe and could perform all the chores on the farm. We played baseball on Saturdays and went to church on Sundays. Because we could not afford a full-time pastor, we sometimes had pastoral services one Sunday per month and other times twice per month. We often visited neighboring churches during our off Sundays, often looking for girls as well.

We left for school during the middle of the cotton picking season, leaving the work to be done by family members at home and hired hands. As always, I was happy to leave the hard farm work to the soft life in the city, even though I always had guilty feelings about it.

When my Uncle Frank told my father that Aunt Mable did not want me back, it did not come as a surprise to me. My father took me to Birmingham, Alabama, where I lived with my grandmother and step-grandfather. They treated me like a King, plenty of food and plenty of home brew, which my grandfather made. Every morning for breakfast, I had my bottle. A few mornings I felt a little tipsy, but the teacher never did notice it.

I made my own money as I remember working every afternoon in a white lady's flower yard for a dime. She paid me fifty cents when I worked a half-day on Saturday. When I worked for a black lady the same amount of time, she paid me seventy cents. The only expense I had was ten cents for the cowboy movie on Saturday. My grandmother did not like it because I was spending a dime every Saturday on what she called going to that cowboy show.

My grandmother was a bed patient because of her leg, and it was easy for me to go to the movie without her knowing it. No one was going to keep me from going to the movie every Saturday. The money that I was making I started saving for college five years ahead of time. My friends got angry with me for working because they wanted me to play baseball. Even though I liked baseball better than almost anything, I put making money first.

I enjoyed my schooling very much and living with my grandparents, and I believe that they enjoyed having me. I worked hard, was a good student, and did not cause any problems. I had lots of friends, old and young, and never got into a fight. Most of the relatives from my father's side lived in Birmingham. I visited often my great uncle Johnny Sturdivant and my great aunt who was his sister and others. Uncle Johnny and my aunt were younger than my father. This was understandable with my great-grandfather having between twenty and forty-five children. Uncle Johnny lived with his father and mother, and his sister lived one or two doors away. I was able to see all of them during the same visit, until my great- grandfather died at the age ninety-six.

My great-grandfather was born in the 1830s and was fathered by his white slave owner father. He became a slave supervisor under his father, thus having his way with the women. A great-aunt, whom I lived with one year later back in Selma, knew my great-grandfather very well, saying he had nine wives and forty-five children. Upon, the death of my Uncle Johnny in early 1996 at ninety years of age, it was written in his obituary that his father was married five times and that he had twenty-five children. I knew five or six of them. Although most of his family originated near Selma, Alabama, a high percentage of them lived in Birmingham, Alabama, moving there with my great-grandfather who worked most of his free life with the Southern Railroad. He was forced to retire at the age of ninety-six, and he died shortly afterward.

My Cousin Scrap and Cousin Arlene, her daughter, and Arlene's son lived not more than eight blocks from my grandmother in Birmingham, Alabama, and quite close to my school. This afforded me the opportunity to visit them quite often. I was very happy to visit them because Arlene was my playmate when she and her mother lived with us on the Chisolem Place when I was between four to six years of age and continued to live in the Pernell Community until I was about twelve years of age. The year with my grandmother was the last period that I saw Arlene and her mother. Arlene's son, Author Reese Junior, attended my mother's funeral in June 1972, stating that cousin Scrap had passed away. Airline, his mother, was still alive. His visit brought back happy memories to me. I was expecting to come back to Birmingham for the ninth grade, but because my brother Edd had finished elementary school, it became necessary for both of us to go to school in Selma for our middle school and high school education.

The only problem was that we did not have any place to stay; and Aunt Mable, whom I considered to be a little selfish, would not take us. I found a great cousin, a great-great aunt, and the daughter and grandson and granddaughter of my great cousin living in a two-bedroom shack. I told my father that I thought we could stay with them. They told my father that they would be happy to have my brother and me. Four generations lived in that house, and I think all four them were illegitimate children. They gave my brother and I one bedroom; four slept in two beds in the other bedroom. Aunt Bam, the great-great Aunt, slept in a bed in the kitchen. My father provided plenty of food. I was happier there than I was at my own home, because I was King there. I could do no wrong. I stayed there four years, and my brother Ed stayed there six years. They felt honored for us to stay with them, and we brought prestige to them. They had been lost from the family and now they were found.

I worked, went to school, and played high school varsity basketball. This time I had a paper route for selling the Birmingham News, the state's largest daily newspaper. I was making about three or four dollars per week. I bought my own bicycle, which was perfect transportation for a city the size of Selma. I proved again to be a super newspaper salesman as I had been two years earlier with that two-cent paper. I made more money than any of the paperboys. In fact, most of them lost money. The three Jeffrey boys who lived across the street from my Aunt Mable had this business for years. They gave it to me because they could not make it work. I made it work and I caddied, also making good money for a student. I helped my Cousin Fanny when she got into a jam, which was most of the time. They took in washing and ironing for income. Magi, her daughter, did domestic work. I could do no wrong, and I did no wrong. I was truly the man of the house. I was saving my money for college as I had started to do a year earlier in Birmingham--buying my own clothing, helping my brother Edd, my brother Son who was in college, and paying my own expenses. My father was quite happy with me, especially because I was paying my way. I did well in school; and in the summer time I went home, worked on the farm, and played baseball. As before, I kept the diamond in shape that was about one hundred yards from our house.

On Saturdays we were ready for baseball in a nearby community four or five miles away. We often walked there and back. The ones that were further, we went by car. My position was shortstop, second, or pitcher. Three of my brothers pitched; and when we were not pitching, we alternated on short and second. We were all good, winning most of our games. We liked to beat the Marion Junction team. We got our mail from there; we ginned our cotton in Marion Junction, and after that we had nothing to do with this place until we went there to play baseball. This village had a population of about five hundred houses. Ours had about forty-five. It was natural for them to look down on us. When we went there and beat them, both the black and white people were embarrassed. We rubbed it in and went home proudly with our bragging rights.

The summer after I finished high school, I stayed in Selma and played on the baseball team there. My brother Frank invited us to play the old team at home. My brother was pitching when I came to bat. I knew where he was going to throw the ball to me. He did. I made a homer. In fact, I got three straight home runs and a triple off him. My mother was a spectator that day, and she did not want to speak to me for what I had done against my old home team. When I told her I always try to play my best, it did not help much.

The manager of the Selma team wanted me to try out for the Kansas City Monarchs--Satchel Page, Jackie Robinson, and Hank Aaron's old team. I declined and decided to go to college because I did not see any future in the old Negro Base Ball League.

I returned to Selma for the tenth grade, this time going to Selma University High School, because Knox School where I went for the ninth grade provided the highest level of public school education for black students in Selma. I went to Selma University, a black Baptist college that also provided a high school education through the twelfth grade. I played only basketball there and would not play football. The coach got angry because my oldest brother had been a good football player, and he wanted me to play also. I decided that I did not want to get myself all banged up. I would not be pressured into playing.

I became more and more serious about my schoolwork as I was only three years from college. I took lots of mathematics, plane and solid trigonometry. I liked history because President Dinkins taught it. He was a very brilliant man who knew not only history, but he knew how to make it interesting. He was also the college president.

I was back in the newspaper business, taking over where I left off before I went to the farm. This time I applied for a job working at the post office during the Christmas season. I got the job and made about $160 during the holidays, carrying special delivery mail and working on the parcel post trucks. After working there during the next Christmas, I was allowed to work on weekdays after school and on weekends also. This permitted me to save more money for college.

I returned home after school upon completion of the eleventh grade and did the variety of farm work that I had always done before when working the cotton fields, the cornfields, and other types of farm work, including managing livestocks. My father worked the garden. My mother and father usually took care of the chickens and turkeys. We went to church on Sunday and played baseball on Saturday, like always. We played the usual community teams that bore the name of the churches or towns or villages. We normally played within a fifteen-mile radius. Some time we went beyond that. During this period, I was seventeen years of age. Several of our players were invited to play with a team near Marion, Alabama. Together, we went to play against a team at a coal mining camp north of Birmingham, Alabama, over one hundred miles away. We were the guests of this camp for the weekend. We stayed at the home of the players with whom we would be competing.

The first game was played on Saturday. I hit four for four times at bat, but my team lost 4-0. The next day, I hit three for four; and we won 7-4. I was the baseball hero for the weekend. The whole weekend was greatly enjoyed by everyone.

My brother Clarence finished college and had a job as coach of Walker County Training School in Jasper, Alabama. My sister Erin had finished two years of college at Tuskegee University in home economics. Her job was to provide us with the best food that she could put together, which she did. Ed, my youngest brother, was also home from Selma where he had finished the ninth grade. I caddied at a golf tournament at Selma Country Club earning about $30 that I gave to my brother Frank to get married. We had our usual productive year on our family-owned farm without getting much money for our efforts, as we were still in a Depression.

Ed and I returned to live on Union Street with our Great Aunt Bam, Great Cousin Fanny, Cousin Magi, Cousin Thomas Hays (nine years of age), and Cousin Bitty Girl (eight years of age). It would be another good year for me as I moved into the twelfth grade, preparing my way for college both educationally and financially. I would continue in the newspaper business and work at the post office. I continued to save my money and buy my clothing for college. I played some of our high school basketball games in Montgomery at the Alabama State Teachers College gym. The college scouted our players where some of my teammates, including me, were offered basketball college scholarships. I did not accept my offer as I was planning to go to Tuskegee University.

During the four years that I lived on Union Street, a Master Sergeant Davis lived two doors from Aunt Bam and Cousin Fanny's house. He had spent thirty years in the Army, joining about 1906. During World War I, he fought on the Mexican border. (This brought me back to the well house where my friend Tutt told me about the fighting ability of black soldiers-but I did not believe what he said.) I guessed Master Sergeant Davis must have been one of the old Buffalo Soldiers, a name which given by the American Indians to distinguish the black soldier from the white because of their hair, the clothing black soldiers wore, and the color of their skin. Following the United States Civil War, the Buffalo Soldier (the 9th and 10th Cavalry) played a major role in helping white settlers to establish the U.S. west, to protect those building railroads and telegraph lines, and to settle American Indians into Indian reservations. Master Sergeant Davis was a product of that proud tradition. I considered him second only to Geronimo - about six feet four, heavy but not fat, black complexion, soft spoken, and polite. He was well organized, neat, fitting all the images of a super soldier. His Chrysler car was clean and neatly polished; his house was like one would expect a military barracks to be. His lawn and flowers were neatly trimmed and well managed. Black people were proud to have a man of his stature in their midst. White people did not know how to deal with him, but they had to respect him.

During my last four years of high school, I was probably his best friend, spending much time with him. He and my father became good friends. My father had more respect for him perhaps than any other person, because he was the image of what a man should be like. Master Sergeant Davis liked me because I was the kind of boy he wished he had hard working, self supporting, putting work before pleasure, and saving money for college. We talked often about the fighting ability of black soldiers. He assured me, as I had always believed, that black soldiers could fight as well as anyone. He said, "I was fighting on the Mexican border side by side with white soldiers, using the same foxholes. I could be on top of them, or they could be on top of me. This was a matter of life and death, race made no difference. To stay alive was everything." They said to me, "When this war is over, we are going to help make things better for you." "When there was a break in battle and we had a little R and R (rest and rehabilitation) those same boys did not know me." I said, "I believe you." He helped me to confirm what I believed about the fighting quality of the black soldier.

My father had a profound influence in shaping me, even though I did my own thinking, and I was a little more outspoken. I agreed with him in education and that we could get it only by hard work, hope, faith, and prayer. We prayed because we needed help beyond ourselves to achieve our goals. My father was a completely honest man who loved his fellow man, black and white, without regard to their racial views. He was a patriot who loved the United States because he felt that all his dreams could be realized here, both for himself and other black people. He became disturbed and angry when injustices were committed to anyone, black or white. He felt that the things he wanted changed wouldn't change in his lifetime, but he was able to educate us so that changes could take place in our lifetime. I was very proud of both my mother and father and what they had done for the family and me as I headed for college. I was determined to make both of them proud, because being proud would be their only pay.

During the hungry years of the Depression, my father gave credit to his customers in his little country smokehouse store to both black and white neighbors at times when he thought they might not pay him. He had sympathy with the destitute situation of his friends and did not want to see them go hungry during the Depression years. Maybe he got the money later or maybe he did not. I remember the time when the wife of one of our white neighbors was sick. Her husband asked my father to take her to the doctor. The husband sat in back of our car, and his wife sat on the front seat. When she returned home, she apologized to her husband because she had to sit next to a nigger during her ride to and from the doctor. This was more than my father could stand. Her husband apologized to my father for his wife's stupidity.

What part did religion play in my early life? I went to church, as did the other boys of my age. I slept most of the time when the preacher was preaching. If he said something that was interesting, I stayed awake. Church was a little bit like the movies; I judged how good it was by my reaction. If I slept, it was not very good. If I did not sleep, it was good. I always knew that Miss (Mrs.) Lou Crenshaw was going to shout in the heat of the pastor's sermon, and she was not going to calm down until Mr. Woosey, one of the deacons of the church, held her. Church was a social event where members of the community got together to greet each other and talk about the news and gossip. It was always the place where boys hoped to meet girls.

Every August we had revival at our Baptist church. When the young people became eleven years old, they were expected to go on the mourners' bench where they prayed to God to help them become born again. During this period, everyone was picking cotton. Those who were praying to become a Christian did everything alone and made little or no communication with family and friends. I was trying as hard as I could to make it, but nothing was happening. I did not make it during my first year. I tried it again during my twelfth year. Toward the very end of the revival I made it. I was later baptized in the Cahaba River and became a confirmed Christian. Christianity always played a major role in my decision making, even before I became a Christian, following my favorite Golden Rule, "Do unto others as you would have them to do unto you." I always felt that someone was looking over my shoulders and that if I did something wrong, I would have to give an accounting for my discrepancies. This always made me be very careful about doing things for which I had no justification.

Chapter 3
I BECAME A COLLEGE STUDENT

In September 1940, I went by train from the L&N Railroad Station in Selma, Alabama, to Montgomery, Alabama, to Chewhaw, Alabama, then to the campus of Tuskegee University. I was sharp as a tack in my new plaid double-breasted, tailor-made tweed suit made from Australian wool and dressed a little bit like Cab Calloway. It did not take long for the upper classmates to make me feel like nobody as we were ushered to a bathhouse where we lived initially like soldiers in an Army barracks. While we were there, we got a few paddles on our buttocks to make us feel at home. This bathhouse had the advantage of bringing a lot of freshman together coming from all parts of the United States and one from Africa. After a week or so, we were all moved into dormitories.

It did not take me long to find out that I did not do well enough academically in high school. I had to take remedial English and remedial mathematics. I was not very good at my other subjects either. I also had to get a job on campus to help pay my way through college. My first job on campus was that of a night watchman. Because I was kind of a sleepy head, I missed some of my punches on the clock. Therefore, it was not long before I was looking for another job. I fared very well in the labor office because my sister was previously a student secretary there. This time I got a job as a student bus boy in the cafeteria. I cleaned up the dishes from the table and glasses from the water fountain. I was super at this work, and I do not believe any other student did this work better than I. I carried a tray a yard in diameter full of glasses and could maneuver them in the biggest crowds without ever breaking any of them. I was good at cleaning off tables too, almost making an art form at this busboy job. The best part about the job was that I could eat any thing I wanted, especially the desserts.

Chefs, hotel management, and catering services were among the courses taught in the cafeteria. All the fancy foods had to be prepared by the students as a part of their agenda. I benefited as they prepared all of my favorite desserts-- lemon pies, apple pies, potato pie, coconut pies, cakes, and all kinds of jelly. I was really in heaven in that cafeteria. I worked there for two school years, leaving there because I became manager for one of the morning newspaper delivery services in the Tuskegee community during my junior year.

I took my schoolwork seriously, giving up varsity sports, girlfriends, everything with the exception of studies. Studying was not easy for me. Out of six hours of study time, maybe I got in about two hours of productive study done. I just kept falling asleep. I would wake up and go at it again. I found my best study time around two and three o'clock in the morning, when everyone else was asleep. As I continued to work at it, I got better. After my first quarter, I finished my remedial work and was carrying a full academic load. At the end of my second quarter, I received a C in all subjects with the exception of biology. I flunked it twice and never took it again. Beginning with the third quarter, I moved to a C plus average in academic subjects.

During my freshman year, I participated in other activities that did not interfere with my studies, such as intramural basketball, tennis, and golf. Golf became my varsity sport because I could play alone, when I had time. I walked about a mile and a half to the golf course, played nine or eighteen holes and walked back to campus. I made some lifelong contacts on the golf course. Dr. Russell Brown, professor in bacteriology and later vice president of the University; Mike Rabb, business manager; Lt. Benjamin O. Davis who later took the 332d Fighter Group into Italy during World War II; and retired Lieutenant General from the United Air Force. I later became captain of the golf team and received my letter "T" in golf.

I was a great spectator in the many varsity sports held on campus. Tuskegee at one time dominated sports in black colleges and universities, but Tuskegee lost its dominant role as many of the state-supported black colleges had strong scholarship programs, which gave them an advantage in recruiting the best athletes. This prevented Tuskegee from maintaining its top position. It continued to be competitive, however. In the spring of each year Tuskegee held the Southeast Regional Invitational Basketball Tournament.

This was the biggest sport event of the year for the campus. Many alumni and sport fans near and far came to watch the highly spirited competition. I even visited this event after I graduated and became a career Army officer.

Lieutenant Benjamin O. Davis, a West Point graduate, commanded Tuskegee's junior ROTC program. He always impressed me--standing like a ramrod. He was handsome, very impressive, and highly respected. His father, who commanded the ROTC prior to him, become the first United States black general at the beginning of World War II. The things we did militarily were small unit drills and marches, indoor rifle range shooting, and parading to chapel each Sunday morning.

Members of the Dean of Men offices who had previous military experience supervised drills. When we drilled and paraded to chapel, we wore the university blue uniform, which we called the Booker T. The Booker T name was for the University's first president and founder, Booker T. Washington. The school band played as we paraded for Sunday's mandatory chapel service.

We had wonderful and educational chapel services. I do not think I ever slept as Dr. Richardson delivered his Sunday messages, the best I had heard so far in my life. We had to go to church again Sunday evening. This time the President of the University spoke or some other distinguished guest. There I heard Dr. Benjamin Mays, President of Morehouse College in Atlanta, Georgia; Walter White, Executive Secretary of the NAACP; Philip Randolph, President of the Sleeping Car Porters (later Vice President of the AFL-CIO); Thurgood Marshall, the Chief Civil Rights lawyer for the NAACP; and Roy Wilkinson, the next Executive Secretary of the NAACP among our distinguished guests. The mandatory chapel services were as educational to me as my regular college courses.

Shooting on the ROTC rifle range was not too exciting to me because of my previous experience at shooting at live moving targets on the farm. Occasionally I went to the range to try out the military technique for shooting. My enthusiasm for target shooting did not become exciting enough for me to join the rifle team. Drilling and parading were more interesting to me.

My first home on campus was Thrasher Hall, the dormitory for varsity athletes. My two roommates were sophomores--one was from Oakland, California, and the other one was from some city in Oklahoma. They were both good students and nice people. Davis from Oklahoma was very good in mathematics, and he helped me quite a bit when I needed it. Richie from Oakland, California, was a good student; but I did not need his help. It was an honor living with upper classmen on the upper end of the campus where most of the important buildings were located--the academic building, library, cafeteria, post office, bank, gymnasium, tennis courts, football stadium, and the President's office.

Most freshmen lived on the lower end of the campus in the buildings called Emorys. The four dormitories were donated by some rich family with that name. Students there had to walk a lot: to the cafeteria, post office, administration building, academic and science hall, library, gym and athletic field. All of the facilities were about fifteen minutes away for students who lived in the Emorys. I lived five minutes or less from all of these.

I chose Tuskegee for a number of reasons which I picked up on my own during a few years prior to going there. My grandfather knew and talked about what a great man Booker T. Washington was. Our farm demonstrator and my tailor were graduates of Tuskegee. Some of my acquaintances came home from Tuskegee wearing their uniform with such great pride that I was impressed. My sister went there until she got married after her third year. These little things, which I came by over a period of time, were enough for me to make Tuskegee my university of choice.

I was the only one from my Selma University High School graduating class who went there. After enrolling there, I became even more impressed. In the bath house were I first lived, some of the freshmen students enrolled in agriculture said: "Man we have a professor in agriculture who can name over one hundred forty local weeds and grasses by their common names and by their scientific names. This was when I first learned about Doctor George Washington Carver. I had a chance to see this distinguished professor sometime later in his laboratory when I was walking to and from my classes on the lower end of the campus. He was a black, skinny, gray haired man, bent forward due to his years; he was in his early 80s. Once or twice he spoke during the evening chapel services.

I learned that all the buildings on the campus had been built by student labor. Students carved the logs into lumber and made the bricks in the University kiln. In 1919 students built the University chapel--installing electricity for the first time in Macon County. This building was an architectural wonder. People were invited from far and near on the Sunday evening when the lights were turned on. This was a sight that had never been seen by most of the observers. When this spectacle event unfolded, the electric lights were turned on and the people shouted, "New Jerusalem!" (A Building from Heaven)

The cafeteria was built by student labor and looked like some state capitol with its dome. The cafeteria was located on the highest ground on the campus and could be seen from the main highway some five miles away. Whites were curious about Dr. Washington's intentions for having such a building constructed. They wanted to know what kind of capitol this Washington was trying to establish.

Doctor Washington was a personal friend of all Republican presidents and had visited President Theodore Roosevelt at the White House. He also controlled all of the philanthropic monies that were donated to black schools, colleges, universities, and private schools. They were becoming curious about him becoming President of black people.

The prestige of Tuskegee was so great that it was an inspiration to all of us. The philosophy of the founder: "I will let no man drag me down so low as to make me hate him." "You cannot keep a man in the ditch unless you get in the ditch with him." "We will prosper in proportion that we learn to dignify and glorify labor and put brains and skills into common occupations of life." "The difficult we do immediately; the impossible will take a little longer." The philosophies and achievements at this institution made Tuskegee once again my university of choice.

The black civil right leaders, all of whom were associated with the NAACP, inspired me. Work and education were their goals; and these were the same goals I had set for myself as a means of improving the civil rights for black people. Now I moved another step forward by joining this powerful civil rights organization. I joined the NAACP during my freshman year; and Mr. Gomillion, head of the Sociology Department, was President of the NAACP there. Civil rights efforts at this time involved racial discrimination in graduate school, law, and medicine. Progress was being made, chipping away at Ferguson vs. Plessy, equal but separate Supreme Court decision of 1896. Later we got involved with voter registration, paramount to any civil rights progress.

I learned a lot and got involved in many university activities during my freshman year. When the school year was over, I went back to the farm to help my father. Almost as soon as I got there, my first cousin Frank Blevins told me about the opportunity to work on a tobacco farm near Hartford, Connecticut. It appeared that I could make enough money for my sophomore year. My father allowed me to go. Now, for the first time in my life, I would be able to travel a distance--more than a hundred and fifty miles--from my home. On the way up there, I wrote down the names of every city with a population of 50,000 or more. I wanted everyone to know where I had been.

On Saturday morning after I got there, I begin sliding down the tobacco rows on my back. The ground was wet, and I looked a little bit like a hog when I reached the end of the first row. Right away, I did not like this kind of work. When I picked cotton, I crawled on my knees because my back got tired; but I did not lie on my back. I completed my first day of work, ate, and took a shower. I was determined not to do that again. I did not like the slop I ate. I did not like the unsanitary condition of the camp and the filthy looking people who cooked and ran the place. I believe my Cousin Frank knew some people in Hartford whom we visited on Sunday. We begin making plans to leave the camp. My Cousin Frank and one or two others made arrangements to return home. A non-college acquaintance from Montgomery, Alabama, and I decided to go to the labor office for a job.

Leaving this farm was not so easy because the tobacco farm owner had paid our way from Alabama. We packed our baggage and left. But, because some of our followers got cold feet and could not make up their minds, the owner was able to overtake us before we got away. I became the spokesman for the group, telling the owner that I did not know about this humiliating kind of work. We were not making enough money, the food was bad, and the camp was filthy. I told him that I would send him his money when I got home. He got rough saying, "I am going to call the sheriff." I got rough back and told him, "The sheriff cannot make me do that work." Some in our group decided to stay; four of us did not. The owner backed down, and we went to Hartford.

My friend and I went to the labor office and got a job working at a crippled children's hospital at Newington, Connecticut, just outside of Hartford. This was a truck garden type farm where vegetables were grown for workers and children at the hospital. We had to milk the cows at the dairy and harvest the hay in the hay field. It was nice there--good food and a nice room where we stayed. This type of work was similar to what I did on my father's farm. It was not exactly the type of work I wanted, but it was acceptable. We worked there until it was time for me to return to college.

We had regular bus service to Hartford. I cannot recall having much of a social life there. I bought a slide rule and spent much of my off-duty time mastering it. At the beginning of my sophomore year, I would be taking physics and chemistry. The physics teacher, Mr. McCormick, had a reputation of being very mean and he did not mind flunking his students if they did not meet his standards. I felt that the use of the slide rule would be quite helpful. Working with the slide rule was probably the reason I do not remember much of a social life. Again, I was saving my money for college. During my freshman year, I paid three-fourth of my expenses from my savings. My work on the farm was going to pay less than half my expenses during my second year. My father would have to come up with the rest

We left there with a good reputation and were invited to return the next year. Instead, I arranged for two of my schoolmates from the school of agriculture to go for us.

I began my sophomore year in good standing and got my old job back in the cafeteria. My study habits of the first year and my work with the slide rule elevated my grades to the "B" level. In my chemistry examination, I received the highest score--136 points out of 14O. The student who stole the examination got only 135. I was also one of the best students in physics. I did well in all my subjects. I also enrolled in the civil aviation program and received my private pilot's license.

On December 7 of that year the Japanese bombed Pearl Harbor bringing the United States into World War II. Lieutenant Davis made captain right away and was sent to the command and staff college after which he made major. Black aviation cadets were everywhere on campus, training to be combat aviation pilots. They were stealing all the girls. I did not know what my status would be, but I was informed that college students would be deferred. Because I was a licensed pilot, I received an application to become an aviation cadet. When Major Davis returned, he was promoted to Lt. Colonel and was made commander of the 99th Pursuit Squadron.

In January, 1942, Tuskegee University was authorized to have a senior ROTC Unit. Right away I was placed into the enlisted reserve taking me away from the jurisdiction of the draft board. Instead of just drilling and parading, we began to study military science and tactics. We had weapons, training with rifles and machine guns. I began to go down to the rifle range a little more often. I continued to play intramural basketball, a little tennis, and a little more golf. I continued to do well in my classes.

In February 1942, Mr. A. Phillip Randolph petitioned the President, Mr. Roosevelt, to integrate the Armed Forces of the United States. The President said no. As Mr. Randolph began to organize a march on Washington, D.C., the President issued an executive order requiring all industry doing business with the federal government to give fair employment to everyone without regard to race, color, or creed. He asked the civil rights leader to postpone the march on Washington and that integration consideration would be considered after the war.

The 99th Pursuit Squadron, the 92nd Infantry (Buffalo) Division, and the 93rd Infantry (Helmet Division)--all black units were established. I believe the two infantry divisions were established in June of 1942. I felt that these units were established to provide research to enable the President to determine the evidence for justifying whether or not integration of the forces would occur. If these black units performed at the same level as whites, the President could be justified in integrating the armed forces if he chose to do so. He could do so by issuing an executive order, authority that the Senate could not kill with a fili-buster; and the President could be held accountable politically, even If he did not do it. I felt that at this time this would provide a good opportunity for progress in civil rights. At the end of the sophomore year, thirty-four members of my ROTC class were enrolled in the advance ROTC, which allowed us one more year in college. Because of this, I did not apply to become an aviation cadet.

During my junior year, I became a newspaper boy again. This time I took over the management of the Montgomery Advertiser, a morning newspaper. I had three routes, and I employed two boys. But, I would soon fire both of them because of poor service; and I would do it all myself. Every morning--rain or shine, sleet or snow--I started delivering my papers at 0430 and finished in time for breakfast and class. I made about $300 per month, enough for all my school expenses plus a bank account. I remember one day a man asked the head of my department for some change; he told the man to see me because I had more money than any of them.

I became a sergeant in my ROTC platoon where I became very good at drilling. The ROTC suited me, but I was not so highly motivated as some of the others. The highest-ranking cadet in my class was ser-geant major. The student with this position was Louis A. Scipio, my roommate, whose father was a ser-geant major in the U. S. Army at Fort Benning, Georgia. All of the ROTC student officers came from the senior class. Major Welch, who was the director of the Architecture Department, was called to active duty and became Professor of Military Science and Tactics. He was also the University's Dean of Men. He was very efficient and did a good job getting us ready for military service. All thirty-four of us were promoted to cadet second lieutenants upon completing our junior year.

In addition to my newspaper business and regular class load, I took a government-sponsored class in electronics, dealing primarily with the radio. Because of my heavy load, I was pretty tired in the evening when this class was held and did lots of sleeping. I hung on to finish it, even though I missed lots of knowl-edge, which I wanted. I did the best I could and learned all that I could. Because I did not know where I would end up in the military services, I wanted to have maximum qualifications. I wanted to be a combat aviator. My plans were to finish three years of college, go to the Army officers' school, become an offi-cer, and then get transferred to the air corps to become a combat aviator. I did my schoolwork as if there were no war and did my ROTC work religiously because I felt it was necessary in order for me to become an officer.

My newspaper business was very important because I was making good money and was able to live a good life as a student. I used my contact with my customers to push voter registration. There were many doctors and managerial people at the all-black U.S. Veteran's Hospital and members of the faculty and administration at the university whom I would encourage to register for voting. I was the most productive member of the NAACP in getting people to register. This made me very close to Mr. Gomillion, the civil rights NAACP chapter president. I was so busy doing so many things that when I was going, I met myself coming, so to speak.

Chapter 4
WORLD WAR II AND ME

On June 9, 1943, all 34 members of my ROTC Class were called to active duty, but not at the same places. Instead of reporting to the induction station closest to the University, we went to the installation closest to our home. About ten in my group went to Fort Benning, Georgia, then to Camp Croft, South Carolina, just outside Spartenburg, South Carolina. There were ten basic training regiments there, nine were white and one was black. They were separate, but equal. I believe we were in a seventeen-week training cycle, learning all the things necessary for becoming a combat infantry soldier. In the barracks it was spit and polish, being ready for inspection at all times. We spent lots of time cleaning rifles, machine guns, and other infantry weapons. My ROTC group at Tuskegee could do the rifles and machine guns blindfolded. This was nothing for us. On our own time we were outside drilling. KP duty, peeling potatoes, washing dishes, scrubbing floors, and manicuring outside of the mess hall were routine duties performed by all of us.

Members of my group were trainee squad leaders and assistant squad leader. My extra duty was as an assistant in the supply room, plus being an assistant squad leader. After duty we went to the service club, snack bar, PX, and the movies. On Sundays I went to church on and off post. When I went to church off post, I went with a friend who was a student at Fisk University. We always were hoping to find some nice girls at the churches. We also went to different churches within the fifty miles travel limit authorized for us. My friend was more of a ladies' man than I and was therefore more successful. Nevertheless, I had a nice time.

There were ten baseball teams on post, one for each regiment. The team from my regiment was on top in the league. Many of the white players were draftees from the major league who were held there to play baseball. Trainees or recruits normally did not play in the league. The first one or two days after my arrival I went to the baseball field to watch my regimental team work out. I asked the white lieutenant who was coaching if I could practice with them. He put me on third base, a position that I had never played. I ate that position up; I played it error free. The Lieutenant got the Regimental Commander, who loved baseball, to allow me to play. He made an exception to the rule and put me on the team. All my friends in the company came out to watch me play. I remember one day when my company was on a twenty-mile hike, a captain, the Regimental S-3, came to my unit. He said, "Private White, the Regimental Commander wants you to get two hours' sleep before the game this afternoon." He drove me to the barracks, and I got my sleep. We won the game. My friends were a little envious, but they liked it. My team continued to dominate the league, ending the season in first place.

I was also a good soldier, shooting like Sergeant York with the M1 rifle; and I was also an expert with the automatic rifle and machine gun. I was as good as the drillmaster with a squad or platoon. I had learned these skills at the university. I had agreed to stay at Camp Croft and play baseball and to forget about officers' candidate school. The Department of the Army said no. My Platoon Leader interviewed me and recommended me for Officers' Candidate School. This was the end of baseball for me.

After basic training, those in my group who were recommended for having the prerequisites for becoming officers and who were under contract for that purpose were sent to A&T College in Greensboro, North Carolina, for enrollment into the Army's Specialized Training Program while waiting for the call to go to Officers' Candidate School. We were there for six weeks, two weeks in November and all of December 1943.

Across town was an all girls' college, Bennett College. The girls there were the most beautiful that I had ever seen. The rumors were that every applicant had to send a photo. If ugly, she would not be accepted. True or false, it certainly looked that way. This was during the party season, just before the holidays. All of our classmates from Tuskegee, including those who took basic training at camps different from ours, joined us at A&T College. A high percentage of us were country boys and could not dance. We felt that in order to get the girls we needed to learn to dance. A city friend of ours, James Hamlet from Buffalo, New York, became the dance teacher. Every day at noon we were in our dormitory counting to the jitter-bug beat. I learned to count, but it took me more than six weeks to get the beat. I tried to work with what I had learned in my dance class, but my performance did not qualify me to dance with any of the girls the second time.

I met and became attracted to one of the most beautiful girls that I had ever met, Edith Chandler from Wilmington, North Carolina, the daughter of a dentist. She was marriage material for me. We did very well at the reception where we met and did very well while I was there, but without any commitments. We had lots of parties and lots of fun. A girl at A&T College wanted to become romantic with me, but I could not trade her for the Bennett girls. There was another flashy girl at Bennett named Winfred Taylor, who was the sexiest girl that I had ever seen. She was from Marshall, Texas. We rode the same train from Greensboro, North Carolina, to Montgomery, Alabama. During that train ride, she made me forget about Edith Chandler. I proposed marriage to her when I graduated from officer's school, which she accepted.

At OCS, one of our schoolmates from A&T College knew Winfred. He said she was wild and that he had been out with her. They all kind of laughed at me for being in love with her. When she did not write and did not keep the promises she made, I called it quits.

My whole concentration now was to become an officer. My first challenge was that of drilling a pla-toon. No one was better at this than me. I was an expert at this before I got into the Army, and it was the same in basic training. Moving, controlling, and managing troops were absolutely essential for becoming an officer. Another one was physical condition. I practiced on the obstacle course until I broke the record. I was wrestling with an all-American football player in my class who weighed about 75 pounds more than me. I threw him. Everyone thought he slipped. I threw him two more times. In the country where I grew up, we wrestled a lot; and I was good at maintaining my balance. I even wrestled with cows as well. Right away, I made a big hit in officers' school.

Our real problem was that the school was a little hesitant about making black officers. Our first encounter was when our tactical officer/supervisor encouraged us to drop out by telling us how difficult if would be, using every means that he could think of to discourage us from trying to become officers. We got together to counter that effort, which was successful. No one volunteered to quit. Then the school threw a power mathematics examination at us. I worked the easiest ones first before returning to the more difficult ones. I thought I had flunked, and maybe I did, but I was passed. My leadership potential may have shined through, making the mathematics examination insignificant in my case. We lost thirteen of twenty-six black platoon members. About six were put back into a later class, and they later became offi-cers. The three white platoon candidates in our OCS company were surprised that we lost so many from our group. "We were given the test last night to review," the white students said to us." I said, "We did not see it." We knew that was a deliberate attempt to eliminate as many of us as possible. No one else in out platoon was washed out after that run. Some white candidates were washed out also, but for real reasons: leadership, physical conditioning, attitude, and not passing the map test.

In our group, our supervisors figured that they had the best as we were elevated to a higher standard than the white boys. There were many courses which we had to pass, such as shooting ability, passing the map-reading courses, and passing written examinations. Shooting came natural to me as I had shot all kinds of hunting weapons in the country where I grew up--sling shots, air rifles, caliber 22 rifles, single and double-barrel shot guns, as well as pump shot guns. I was not too good at shooting rabbits because they bounced around too much while they were running, but I could knock down squirrels, quail, and even ducks. Military stationary targets, bobbing targets and moving targets I could hit. I shot expert with all World War II Army rifles and machine guns. My country experience with the woods, rivers, lakes and grounds made it easy for me figure out distances and adjust mortal and artillery fire.

We had a class in adjusting artillery fire with mortar and artillery; it was necessary to establish a brack-et. That is, an attempt had to be made to have a long round and short round, with the target between them. When the long and short rounds were 100 yards apart, a 50-yard adjustment was supposed to be made; and the order to fire for effect would be made. This procedure would enable targets to be destroyed. In this class, I was called on to engage the target. When the 100-yard bracket was established, the school solution was to slip the bracket and fire for effect. This meant firing for effect should destroy the target. Instead of my doing this, I made another adjustment. The instructor stated that I did not follow the school's solution, but that he would put my adjustment on the guns and fired the mission. The target was a panel about 2,000 yards away. When the guns fired, the target was obliterated. The class gave me a standing ovation. One student stated, "I always wanted to see one of those targets panels destroyed:" The instructor said, "I cannot argue with perfection." I said to myself, "Boy, I was lucky."

On the Ml rifle range, I was shooting with three other classmates--one was a classmate from Tuskegee named John Suggs and two white students who were good friends of mine. All four of us were shooting nearly perfect scores. The school's marksmanship committee had seen one or two outstanding shooters on the same point, but never all four. The instructor in charge thought that maybe something was wrong. He put an officer on the target when I was firing at 500 yards. I fired ten shots at a distance of 500 yards. All ten shots were in the middle of the target - bull's eye. I shot 194 out of a possible 210; Suggs shot 196. My two white friends shot 197, 198 respectively. This was a record for the Infantry School, and we were given a write-up in The Infantry School's newspaper, The Bayonet.

Map reading was a must. I believe some students got washed out because of it, but no one from my platoon. I learned map reading very well in my ROTC classes before going into the Army, but not the out-of-doors application of it. I passed it without difficulty. We all had to do the compass course by following an azimuth, a straight magnet line measured with a pocket size compass. For example: an azimuth of seventy degrees must be followed to a creek some two miles, over varied terrain, woods and valleys, to a marked stake not visible from the starting point. I found the right stake, as did most of the students. Some had to take this class over; and if they failed, it would be a basis for them being washed out.

Each platoon member had a leadership-rating requirement in which his own buddies were the raters. In my platoon, I was rated number one during the first two rating sessions and number three during the last one. My friend John Suggs was rated number one during the last session, perhaps because he had shot two points better than I in the marksmanship class. I did not think he was better, but I figured my buddies did not want to give me all the glory. My tactical officer hit the ceiling and accused me of slipping. I told him that I did not think I was slipping, but that it was due to some of my classmates doing better than before. Anyway, I told him that I would bear down.

One of my best friends whose bed was next to mine and I had bets throughout the course. The one who was the best in any event received a pint of ice cream from the one who was less good. Out of ten events, I won at least seven from my friend Marshall D. Daughters. He was generally better with written examinations, but not always; and I was generally better at everything else.

After seventeen weeks of hard work and highly intensified mental concentration, I graduated with the rest of my classmates on May 16, 1944. My tactical officer, a white South Carolinian said, "Men, you are as good as the best, and I am damn proud of all of you." We said, "We made a believer out of him." I become a second lieutenant in the United States Army, competing with some of the best college students in the United States, coming from some of the best universities in the United States. This was the end of a long road for me … and it was the beginning of a new one. As a cotton-picking country farmer from deep in the country of southwest Alabama, I had my proof that God did not make any inferior people. I had competed with the best and was at the top. I believed it always, and now I had my proof. I did it for myself and also for my father. He put his faith in God, hard work, and education; and now he had his pay. I had achieved what only white people were supposed to achieve according to the thinking back home. I had changed things. The Lord had been with me. He, as I always believed, helps those who help themselves.

I saved money from my newspaper route, which I used to buy all of my uniforms. My first trip was to Greensboro, North Carolina, and Bennett College. I wanted to see Winfred Taylor, the girl who I wanted to marry during the past Christmas and who I broke up with because she did not keep her promises. I wanted to forget all that and renew our relationship. I was quite disappointed that she had been kicked out of college. I said, "Maybe I am blessed." My second choice was Edith Chandler whom I still had a relationship with, and she was still there. I visited her, and we had a warm reunion. I promised to write and maintain contact.

I left Greensboro to visit my parents in Marion Junction, Alabama, where both my mother and father were happy to see me and proud of my accomplishments. They were happy that I was going to Camp Breckenridge, Kentucky, and not to war. My Aunt Bam, Cousin Fanny, Master Sergeant (Ret) Davis, as well as all my friends in and around Selma, were proud of me. "You are the first black officer from Selma," they said. I also went by the post office where I had worked. Both whites and blacks with whom I worked during my high school and college years were not surprised at my achievement and congratulated me on my accomplishments. Barton, one of the owners of a Jewish department store, called me from a half block away to congratulate me on my accomplishment. The Selma newspaper carried the news about my becoming a commissioned officer. This news was not in the colored section of the paper, but in the white section. That news was very special with both white and black people. I was proud, because I had set an example. This was a goal I had set for myself when I was ten years old.

I reported for duty as Second Lieutenant Cecil W. White to 332d Infantry Regiment, a black National Guard regiment from Boston, Massachusetts, which had been relocated to Camp Breckenridge, Kentucky. I was assigned to the 3d Battalion, commanded by Lieutenant Colonel Lofton. He assigned me as assistant motor officer. I found this regiment was not well disciplined and was not the kind of unit that I would like to go to combat with. I went to work in the motor pool and achieved the highest rating among the three battalions of the regiment during a Fourth U.S. Army Corps vehicle maintenance test.

On weekends I went to Evansville, Indiana, and never visited Henderson, Kentucky, where the camp was located because Evansville did not have a segregated society. I enjoyed this environment, which I had not been a part of since I left Connecticut in the summer 1941. My stay there would be short lived, as I would soon be transferred to Fort Huachua, Arizona, as a member of the 92d Infantry (Buffalo) Division. In the meantime I worked for the battalion commander, Lieutenant Colonel Lofton, a nice man who was a probation officer in Boston, the brother-in-law of Colonel Gerdine, the regimental commander who was a judge in Boston. Lots of relatives were in The 372d Infantry, which meant lots of favors were shown. Lieutenant Colonel Barrower, the Regimental Executive Officer, was highly political. I was happy to leave this regiment because I was not impressed with it.

I did not have any time for leave because I got that upon graduation from officer's candidate school; but I did have travel time, which was about a week or ten days. Because I had never been to Chicago, I decided to go there. A schoolmate and my Regimental Commander in ROTC had finished OCS and had just got married. He invited me to visit his home. Unis Van Zandt and his mother were Tuskegee graduates. Mrs. Van Zandt, his mother, was the president of the Tuskegee Club in Chicago. She was a very powerful woman and considered all Tuskegee children as her own. That, plus the fact her son and I were friends made her home my home. Unis had just married a very pretty young lady from Mississippi and they were on their happy honeymoon.

The young Mrs. Van Zandt had a cousin named Yvonne, a very attractive girl from Fisk University in Nashville, Tennessee, a famous black college. Her father, Mr. Cornelius Davis, was a State Representative of Illinois, a big wheel. As a young Army lieutenant headed to the 92d Division, along with Unis, I hit it off very well with Yvonne and her parents. Because of the highly patriotic spirit and our recent commission as officers headed to war in Italy, nothing was too good for us. I, for one, had the best possible times. I had a chance to visit some of the sights, famous nightclubs, recreation facilities, and to see and hear some of the most famous entertainers of the time. All of this made my stay there unforgettable. Yvonne and I promised to write.

I left by train to Fort Huachua, Arizona, and to the 92d Division. I arrived in time and reported to my new unit, H Company, 37l Infantry. My company commander was a white 1st Lieutenant John Runyon. I was welcomed and given the 2d Machine Platoon. I met my men and begin to get them ready for combat. I remember running my men a lot because I wanted to keep them busy and in good condition. I do not remember now exactly what we did, but I know we kept busy. We did not have much work to do because everything was either packed or being packed for shipment to the port. A high percentage of the equipment had already been sent and maybe some of it was already on ships. I remember assembling with all the newly arrived officers to meet the Division Commander, Major General Almond. After I introduced myself, he asked me where I was from. I said, "Selma, Alabama, SIR!" He said, "I am from Anniston, Alabama. Do you know a lawyer in Selma? He told me his name." I told him that I did and that I had caddied for him at the Selma Country Club. I think I made a big hit with him. I said to myself later, "That was the way he probably wanted me to know his lawyer friend." Not knowing him very well, I was impressed with his sharpness.

A few days later I was assembled with most of the officers of the division for a class in adjusting artillery fire. The General was doing lots of talking, although he was not the instructor. He naturally had permission to interrupt any time he wanted to do so. One time an artillery round fell short, hitting the hill that we were on. Everybody hit the ground and no one was hurt. One of the officers commented, "Someone is trying to get him." Someone probably had it for this miscue. Training continued after the short round exploded.

I got a chance to visit Mexico, but I wasn't too impressed. Most of these border desert towns were poor. Nevertheless, I was happy to say that I had visited Mexico. Had I been there like some of the old timers, I probably would have had something better to say about the country. My stay in Arizona was short. About ten days or two weeks after my arrival, I was on my way to the port of debarkation.

The arrival of the E Company commander was one event I remembered as we both showed up at the same time. After I finished my reporting to H Company, I came out of the back door of the orderly room. At the same time three or four soldiers of E Company were coming out the back door of their orderly room. The soldiers said, "We are going to kill him; we are going to kill him." I said, "Who are you going to kill?" "That redneck Louisiana Captain. When we get to combat we are going to kill him." I was kind of glad they were going to wait until they got to combat. By that time I figured they would have another point of view. I thought they were blowing off lots of steam, and I did not get involved. This company commander was "a sight for sore eyes." He was drooped over like a mining prospector and had a long heavy red mustache. He did not look much like an officer. That was the end of my concerns about E Company and its red-headed company commander.

We traveled through Louisville, Kentucky; Cincinnati, Ohio; and through West Virginia to Camp Patrick Henry at Newport News, Virginia. The train hit a car that did not get out of the way as we went through West Virginia. About two hours was spent there before we proceeded to our destination. The port was crowded with Buffalo Soldiers when we arrived.

After two or three days I was on duty as KP supervisor. There were so many people there. This was necessary until things got better organized. It did not seem long before I did not have much to do, after about a week there. We were scheduled to go overseas by convoy. Most of our cargo was probably loaded on the ships; and I presumed that we had to wait until all the ships that were scheduled to travel together could be assembled. I was given a five-day leave, which I used to travel back to Chicago.

Unis was still there on his honeymoon. Yvonne Davis had gone back to college as it was September. This made it necessary for me to find another girl. I went shopping with Unis and his wife, and I shopped upon another girl. She kept me entertained during this trip to the windy city. Again, like most military personnel, I visited the nightspots. At the end of this leave, I flew back to Virginia. The convoy still was not ready to leave. I was not in any type of hurry as we were hoping that the war in Europe would soon be over.

During the latter part of September 1944, I was given another five-day leave. Again, I went back to Chicago, staying with Mrs. Van Zandt. This time Unis had left for overseas. His wife was there. I continued to visit the girl whom I met during my last visit. She plus the nightspots kept me busy. I returned to Virginia, with only a few days left in September. I figured that we would be leaving about the end of the month.

We were scheduled to ship out to Italy on Wednesday, September 30, 1944. Sunday evening, three days before time to ship out, officers and senior non-commissioned officers of H Company were assembled. I figured this was a meeting concerning our debarkation. Instead, Lieutenant Runyon read a TWX (message) from Washington, D.C. from the Office of the Secretary of War, Harry L. Stenson, and George C. Marshall, General, Chief of Staff. The morale of the 92d Infantry Division is unworthy for combat. They could not understand why the best-trained division of the war had lost its morale and was considered combat unworthy. The cause and solution to the morale problem must be determined within 24 hours. This was an order from the highest level and with the greatest urgency.

The first thing that came to my mind was that the 92d Division would be deactivated as was the case of the 93d Division which was deactivated by General Douglas MacArthur because he said it would not fight. I believed these divisions were activated in June 1942 to provide data for the promised decision by President Roosevelt to look into the integration of the Armed Forces after the war. There was great opposition by some members of Congress who were against civil rights to the activation of these divisions as well as the establishment of the 99th Pursuit Squadron and its expansion to the 332d Fighter Group. They too realized that if these units proved successful, that the President might integrate the Armed Forces; and they were against that. In addition to the above, I had been concerned about the fighting ability of black soldiers since I was ten years of age and became aware of what Miss Lou Crenshaw said about things getting better for black people every time there is a war. I knew this white supremacy theory was incorrect ever since my brother said my white playmate was better than I because he was white. Whites were using their economic, political, and legal power to force most black people to believe and accept this incorrect theory.

From the very beginning I knew that black people had to work hard and become educated and to use the strength of the Constitution and their economic power to change things. My theory and beliefs were reinforced by my conversations with retired Master Sergeant Davis from 1936 to 1944, by listening to civil rights leaders who spoke at Tuskegee, and by my involvement as a member of the NAACP there. To me, civil rights were important for blacks and whites as well. No one benefits from racism; and until racism is proven to be what it is, things would remain the same.

Many whites said they believed that blacks were cowards and that they would run away in battle as my friend had said when I was ten years old. But, I also felt that whites did not believe that as much as they pretended. Their worst scenario was that they were not completely sure of it, because blacks had fought well during the Civil War and the Revolutionary War. I believed that much of their good service during the Spanish American War and World War I had been discredited. White historians have stated that the Civil War would not have been won by the North without former black slaves and free men who were in the Union Army.

I felt that it was necessary for a black division to prove it in combat. A unit smaller than a division, in my opinion, would not do it. The Buffalo Division of approximately 40,000 soldiers, most of whom were from the Deep South and had less than a high school education, would do it. When these young men who had experienced or observed so many injustices could go to war to fight for their country, which had denied them so much, an everlasting impression would be made that would advance the cause of civil rights and democracy for them and everyone else. A black combat division, in my opinion, would do it.

To find the reasons for the low morale, all companies of the division (which I estimated to be about forty) were assembled to find the causes and solutions for it. My unit, Company H, 371st Infantry, met with five officers and five of its senior non-commissioned officers. The only white person in the unit was its commander, First Lieutenant John Runyon. Because he felt this was a black problem for which he had no answer, he called on the second-in-command and company executive officer, First Lieutenant Henderson. He stated, "Our men are going overseas to war for the first time, and they feel that they will not see their love ones again. They are a little sad about that; but once they get out into middle of the ocean, they will be over it and everything will be all right."

I expected everyone to have his own theory about this situation, but I was a little surprised when the third senior officer of the unit, First Lieutenant Butts, said, "I agree with Lieutenant Henderson." Lieutenant Gyles, senior second lieutenant, was the kind of officer to express his own point of view; but when he failed to do it and adopted Lieutenant Henderson's view as that of his own, I assumed that he did it as means of avoiding war. If we do not find the answer, the division will be deactivated; and it will not have to go to war. Lieutenant Henderson, who was chairman of this discussion, skipped me and went to NCOs (non-commission-officers). This discussion was a little controversial as it touched on the race issue, and it appears as if everyone so far was avoiding it. The NCOs found it safe to agree with the answer already provided, and all five of them adopted it.

While listening to the agreement, with which I did not agree, I had not yet decided on what my answer would be. I knew that blacks had not done anything to cause the low morale problem. Upon arrival at the camp the morale was high. But, because I had two vacations in Chicago during the month, I had not seen any evidence of low morale. To me, whatever caused the low morale had happened here since we arrived at the port. I was concerned about the impact on the integration of the Armed Forces because I had long assumed that the two black divisions were set up to provide evidence for the President, the Secretary of War, and the Chief of Staff of The Army to make their decisions for integration after the war as promised. Since the 93rd (Black) Division had been deactivated by General MacArthur because he said that it would not fight, the 92nd was the only one left. If it did not go to war and do a good job, integration and other civil rights benefits would be out of the window, so-to-speak. This was my opinion.

Like the others, I saw a chance to avoid war; but I could not go back on all those things that I felt so strongly about. I could not justify adopting the answers of the others, and by saying the cause of low morale was caused by whites without them being fully aware that they were guilty of it. If the cause of the morale problem is not found, the President and his administration would be in an embarrassing situation, with both black divisions being seen as unwilling to fight for their country. The biggest losers would be black people. The winners would be those southern senators and congressmen who opposed the establishment of the divisions in the first place. I was beginning to see the morale problem and its solution resting on my shoulders, a twenty-three year old junior second lieutenant who turned twenty-three on June 30, just a little less than three months earlier. I had a decision to make: Tell a lie and stay at home, or tell the truth and get myself killed. I felt the best thing for me to do was to tell the truth and put the matter into God's hands.

Because I was the only one left, Lieutenant Henderson said, "Junior, what do you think?" I said, "I do not believe that I have heard the right answer. We are going overseas to fight for democracy. Here at Camp Patrick Henry is the worse example of democracy that I have seen anywhere. I am from Alabama, and I have never seen anything there as bad as it is here. For example, my first night after my arrival here, I went to the service window at the Officer's Club and ordered some food and a drink. When I received them, I was not allowed to eat and drink what I had bought in the Officers' Club. I took it to my room and said to myself, 'I will not go back in that place again.' I also noticed at the non-commissioned (NCO) club about 25 whites in this plush facility. There are about 500 black NCOs here with no club, and they are not allowed to use the club used by whites. There are more than 20,000 low-ranking enlisted soldiers here with no service club, and they are not allowed to use the one used by white soldiers of similar ranks. It is true that some of us will die if we go to war. This will be the last bit of American soil which some of us will ever see. We need to see an example here on this soil, the last bit of American soil that some of us will ever see again--that for which we will be fighting and dying. The Army does not have the power to change this wrong in Mississippi and Alabama. It does not have the power to change that which is wrong outside these gates here in Virginia, but it does have the power to make this change at Camp Patrick Henry here in Virginia. If it does change these conditions, there will be no morale problem."

It sounded just like I had made a winning touchdown at a homecoming football game. JUNIOR IS RIGHT! JUNIOR IS RIGHT! JUNIOR IS RIGHT! These were statements of all the other black officers and NCOs who had previously given their answers. What I had said made all the sense in the world to

Lieutenant Runyon who saw perhaps for the first time that black soldiers were no different than white soldiers. I judged him to be a non-racist commander. I guess this was in the Lord's hand because Lieutenant Runyon's father-in-law was a Brigadier General and Assistant Division Commander, which allowed him to skip channels and go to the top--thus preventing some more racist commander from blocking what I had said. He knew that he had the right answer, and he headed out of there like a rabbit that had just been jumped by a dog. Major General Almond, the hand-picked commander of the Division, brother-in-law of General Marshall and also a graduate of Virginia Military Institute, received the answer which I had given. He passed it on to General Marshall. The only way the President, The Secretary of War, and The Chief of Staff could find out if my answer was correct was to try out what I had recommended. Apparently that was the answer they wanted, because the next morning the base was fully and completely integrated. The morale of the Buffalo Division "shot up" like a rocket. Whites who worked on the base were as happy as black people were. I just felt that I had done my duty as a soldier. It was a little bit like I felt when I swallowed that last bit from the cup of sugar that Mr. Patton had stuffed in my mouth when I was four years old. I had won. Everybody had won.

The Buffalo Division, with its newly-found morale, got its spirit back and shipped out on schedule--I believe it was Wednesday, September 3O, or October l, 1944--in a convoy of ships headed for Italy. The trip was for the most part a pleasant one. We sailed for 31 days, listening to the progress of the war in Europe on radio, in the West and in the South, with the hope that it would be over by the time we got there. We had lots of time to give troops the news, as they were spending lots of time cleaning and inspecting weapons. Lots of boxing matches went on for entertaining the troops. We had lots of movies: military, civilian and health films.

One time the soldiers wanted the officers to box. Because I was Junior, I got my calling. I did a little boxing in high school, and I believe I got beat every time; but I had learned one useful deceptive punch. I weighed about 150 pounds and was boxing with another lieutenant weighing about 185. I told him that we should do only some light boxing, because I was sure that he could beat me if he chose to do so. Right away that guy got rough. I decided to get rough back as I was not going to be his punching bag. I decided to use my secret weapon, a deceptive blow to his short ribs. After a few of those, the fight was called off. His company commander got angry with me because I beat him pretty good. It was about three hours before the lieutenant whom I boxed with became sociable again. I told his commander that his lieutenant was the one who started the rough stuff, and I just got the best of it. That was the end of the discussion about the fight.

One of my best buddies on the ship was Doctor Greenlee, First Lieutenant, Battalion Surgeon, from Homestead, Pennsylvania. I guess it was because of where he was from that made me become close to him. The Homestead Grays were considered the best Negro baseball team in the United States. It had played a game in my hometown (Selma, Alabama) either when I was in high school or college. I believe it was when I was in college. I remember Josh Gibson to be considered the best catcher in the United States, black or white. He was a great hitter as well. He later became a member of the Baseball Hall of Fame. Doc liked to talk about his team too. We talked about that and what I did back at Camp Patrick Henry. I might have even bragged about kicking the German's Ass when I get to Italy. "Maybe I will and maybe I won't," was his attitude. Most people were a little braggadocio on the ship but became a little quieter when the enemy started throwing the big stuff around.

One evening in the middle of the ocean we were notified that an enemy submarine had been spotted. Three blasts on the ship's whistle would be a notice to abandon ship. We got three blasts on my ship, and we put on our life-jackets. It just looked as if the ship was sinking. I said that I would wait until the ship sink a little more before I jumped off. A little after that we were notified that it was a false alarm because the ship's whistle had gotten stuck. We had to have a muster (roll call) to check if anyone was missing. Luckily, no one had jumped. We crossed the Atlantic without any further incidents, sailed through the strait of Gibraltar, into the Mediterranean Sea between Spain and Africa, south of Sicily, through the strait of

Messina to the Port of Naples where we anchored for one or two days. Then we sailed to the Port of Leghorn, where we got off the ship. There was a staging area where we camped for about a week. We hiked to Pisa where we walked up the Leaning Tower.

After this time we moved up on the front line where my machine guns went into a defensive position on a hill we named Florida. We gave hill names that everyone knew for easy memory. Every evening we had mail call, a few discussions, read the "Stars and Stripes," and drank coffee. It was here that I learned to drink coffee. I remember saying, "Coffee is the only thing I drink in the Army that I did not drink before I came in." These little get-togethers were good for our morale.

After about ten days my platoon was moved from a defensive position to an offensive one. Toward the end of November, I was given my first offensive combat order. Now everything I had talked about what I would do in war was about to become a reality. My job was to provide machine gunfire on Hill Georgia, another Italian mountain given an easy name to remember. My mission was to support F Company with machine gun fire beginning at H-10 and continue to fire until my fire was blocked by F Company, and then shift my fire to the enemy's hill position behind Georgia in support of F Company's reorganization on Georgia.

I issued my orders to my platoon and had my four machine gunners to man their guns. I made my first mistake by telling my platoon that the life of machine gunners in offensive combat, according to statistics, was five minutes and that I would rotate them to give every man a chance. H-10 was the time my guns were supposed to start firing on the enemy position, pinning the enemy down in his defensive position to prevent him from firing on F Company's platoon until it was in position to assault the enemy's defenses beginning approximately 25 yards from the crest of the hill. This meant my platoon must shift its fire to prevent it from hitting members of F Company whom my platoon was supporting. When I gave the order to commence firing, nothing happened. I gave it twice; I gave it three times. Not a single gun fired. Lots of things went through my mind, such as that which my friends said at the well when I was ten years old. In OCS it was stated that it may be justified to shoot your men under these circumstances. They can be court-martialed also. None of these things could help F Company, which would be moving out against the enemy without support. My machine gunners' hands were frozen, and they were unable to pull the trigger. Time was running out, and something had to be done. First, I rushed to one of the guns and started shooting it myself. Then I ordered one of the section sergeants to shoot one of the other guns. We both were on target. Then I ordered all the gunners back. Their hands were no longer frozen. I said, "They blew the top off the hill." F Company took Georgia, and my machine gunners broke up the enemy's counterattack, killing and wounding a number of them, and forcing the rest back where they came from. It continued firing for another 20 minutes.

Lieutenant Henderson called, "Cease firing. You did a good job." I thanked him and my men for doing a great job and did not say anything to the gunners for being unable to shoot at the beginning. I became a fast learner. I always seem to find the right answer in emergency situations, like some guardian angel is always there when I needed him. Maybe it was because I was always prepared to do my thing. When I did not have the answer, it came to me, like at that meeting concerning low morale at Camp Patrick Henry.

Not thinking anymore about the action of the day before, Lieutenant Runyon congratulated me the next morning on doing a good job. He said. "The Division Commander saw your platoon in action yesterday." He said, "That was the best machine gun fire that he had ever seen, including World War I (which he was in) and World War II." "You are authorized a Silver Star Medal, or a promotion to first lieutenant, combat Infantry badge and a R&R to Rome." I took the latter ones, giving up the Silver Star Medal. In the Staging Area back there in Leghorn, I made myself a promise, "Do not get medal happy; it can get you killed." I would have taken the medal too if it had been given it to me in addition to the other awards.

I took off for Rome on my R&R with my driver. I stopped by to see my brother who was the supply officer of a quartermaster battalion at Leghorn, where I got off the boat. His battalion had helped to unload the ship when we got to Italy from the States. He gave me a shelter half to wrap around my jeep as we traveled some 300 miles this cold night to the Holy City. It was the coldest night of my life, being not sure whether the shelter half helped to keep the cold out. We arrived at Rome the next morning, frozen and hungry and sleepy. We took a hot shower, got clean clothing, and ate a hot meal. Then I slept for six hours.

My first trip uptown Rome was to either the Red Cross or USO Club where a beautiful, young Italian girl met me, whom I judged to be about sixteen years old. She greeted me sucking her fingers. "What you mean by that?" I asked. "You should be at home sucking your mother's bottle, instead of being over here in the war," she said to me. I told her, "I just got promoted to first lieutenant for my fighting ability." She did not say any thing else about my youthful appearance. She invited me into the room where all kinds of snack were displayed and available for consumption. I consumed quite a bit. Then she invited me to the ping-pong room where she began to take me apart on the ping-pong table. I had considered myself to be pretty good at this game, but no one could tell that about the way she beat me. After I lost three sets to her, I left and never went back there. But I do not think that was due the fact that I was somewhat embarrassed by the way she defeated me. This girl later becomes known as Sophia Loren.

I left there and went to the Excelsior Hotel, which was an American Officers' Hotel and Officers' Club, where officers from Allied countries also were allowed to attend. There was a big band and ballroom dancing every night, attended by more than enough beautiful Italian girls. By this time I had become a very good dancer, practicing a lot since stumbling over those Bennett College girls in November and December 1943. Very shortly after I got there, I approached the first girl asking her for a dance; but she refused. "Any girl has a right to have a choice," I thought to myself. When the next two girls said no also, I began to smell something "fishy" about this situation. Then I looked around and saw several black officers sitting alone with their heads hanging down. I assumed that they had faced similar situations. Then I began to think that I came overseas to fight so that this kind of situation would be stopped. If I did not do something about it, I could not justify to myself that for which I was fighting. I decided to keep on asking, even if they kept on refusing. "Surely, I will be embarrassed," I said to myself, "but I will be more embarrassed and would be fighting for nothing if I did nothing." As long as I did something to expose this racism or try to stop it, I could justify my fighting for democracy. I asked numbers 4, 5, and 6; the answer was the same as the first three. Then I asked numbers 7 and 8. No changes. After that, a white lieutenant colonel gave me his girl to dance with as my partner. I felt vindicated and would continue to fight to change the racist environment, which always seemed to be there in such social events.

It is possible that the ballroom dancing was terminated after that because I cannot remember seeing dancing there any more after that night or any other night during this and my next R&R when I lived in this hotel. I do remember much more about my first visit to Rome. I had a nice time there, and I always want to go again as often as possible.

After the completion of this little vacation from Combat and to the Holy City, I returned to my unit. On the way there, I stopped by to see my brother at his quartermaster battalion where I was always treated very nice in an atmosphere of respect given me as a front line combat officer. They always sent me off feeling good and wishing all the best for me--happy that it was me and not one of them. I appreciated it very much and was not at all jealous of them living the life of relatively luxury. I did not get the feeling that they were at all jealous of me. My commander and my platoon were happy to have me back.

I did get a chance to reflect on my hero status based on the praise given to my platoon performance in attack on Hill Georgia, on November 27, 1944. The division commander praised the fire support given by my platoon in assisting F Company to take the Hill. More importantly, breaking up an enemy counterattack by inflicting heavy casualties on him was an equally important accomplishment by my platoon. Neither the general nor any of my superiors saw the action, which was most gratifying to me. It was the example I set by firing the machine gun when my machine gunners did not have the courage to do so. Even I did not know what to do, but I did the only thing I could do. That was enough. I mistakenly told them that the life of machine gunners in offensive combat, according to statistics, was only five minutes. Even though I told them I would rotate them every five minutes to give every man a chance, the thought of that apparently paralyzed them with fear. For some reason, I put myself on one of the guns and started firing and then required one of the section sergeants to do likewise. Bringing the gunners into action from the deep freeze cause by their fear was what made me proudest of all.

It is amazing how easy it becomes on the battlefield when one is considered a hero. The most important thing is that it enables one's subordinates to trust him and follow his leadership. None of the members of my platoon, nor I, would have thought a great deal about what we did if the Division Commander had not seen it and given it such great praise. Because of it, I was made a hero; and my job on the battlefield became easier as my men trusted me and followed my orders more willingly.

Some time later during the month of December, we went after Georgia again. We gave it up because the enemy had an observation position on the hill and could use direct fire with tanks dug into the mountain. I could not understand why it was decided to take that hill again, without first taking the hill behind it. We attacked Georgia again, taking it. I began making a reconnaissance forward for the purpose of being close to the forward element of F Company, which I was supporting. The enemy caught me out in the open and began firing at me with 88-millimeter tank shells, among the most dangerous shells used in the war. As soon as the first round fell, I knew that I was in trouble. I started running instantly, counting one to five and hitting the ground, waiting for the next shell to hit. As soon as it exploded, I ran counting one to five again and hitting the ground. I kept up this process until five more rounds fell. This tank was very accurate and the shells were falling very close; but because my counting allowed me to be on the ground when each shell arrived, the metal fragments thrown out by the exploding shell always went over my body. After the fifth shell landed, I arrived at some very big rock formations, where there was only a small crack between a portion of the rocks. I was able to wedge myself between them, but only sideways. Even then, my body was only a few inches below the crest. The tank fired three more rounds at me, hitting the rocks where I inserted myself; but the rocks protected me, and the tankers gave up. I crawled out from between the rocks and returned to my platoon where its guns were on the reverse slope of the mountain and where the enemy tanks could not reach my unit or me.

I did not tell anyone about it. On the battlefield, misses are never counted. This was routine. Each such situation was like driving down the highway when I missed an accident. I took it as a warning not to do it again. Hill Georgia was taken again; but it could not be held because that same tank, which was firing at me, fired on our troops each time it took the hill. We could not locate the tank because it was dug into the mountain. Georgia could not be held until the hill behind it where the tank was dug in was taken. That had to wait until the spring offensive for ending the war in Italy. Lots of the little winter attacks were made for intelligence and keeping the enemy honest, not permitting him to leave to support some other front or battle.

Shortly after this second attack on Georgia, my company commander was not pleased with the lieutenant commanding the first platoon, because it had not performed well in the two previous attacks. Because my platoon had done well and was now well trained from the successful battles that it had experienced, he switched the first platoon leader to my platoon and me to his platoon. I hated to leave my platoon, but the company commander had a right to do what he thought best for his company. I agreed to move over to the first platoon.

Upon arriving there, I liked the first platoon immediately because they liked me immediately. I was already benefiting from my heroic reputation. I got the impression that this platoon did not trust its old platoon leader and considered me a Godsend, which inspired them a lot. They knew from the outset that they could trust me and were willing to follow my leadership. I also suspected that the Company Commander of E Company did not like the old first platoon leader, which was supporting his company. And, as a result, he may have requested my company commander to make the change.

The company commander of E Company is the redheaded captain who reported to the battalion the same time I did back in Arizona. When I came out of the orderly room of my company, some of the enlisted men of his company came out the back door also, saying that they will kill him when they get into combat. As soon as I saw him wearing four pistols, I said to myself, "They haven't killed him yet. Maybe," I said jokingly, "they are afraid of his four pistols." When I looked at all those pistols I thought, "Boy, he is a real cowboy." He was one of the best combat company commanders, and he seemed to like to fight. Just about every day he went out to get a little piece of the enemy--his body, his weapons of various types. All his combat soldiers were highly decorated, wearing one or two silver stars. The ranks of soldiers in this company were higher than those in similar companies in our battalion and other battalions in the division. They were that good. I did not see any private or private first class in the company; they were E-4s and higher. I was happy to be working with E Company and the redheaded Captain.

His men who disliked him in the States may have even loved him in Italy. He was indeed a great commander on the battlefield. He was all that the soldiers under his command could want in a combat leader. The way his soldiers fought under his leadership proved to be what I had believed as a ten-year-old boy--black soldiers can fight as good as anyone when properly led. These soldiers of E Company, 371st Infantry are as good as they come

I tried to evaluate black soldiers as I got more and more combat experienced with them. In taking black soldiers to combat, they had to be evaluated from their point of view. Of all the soldiers who fought in the war, black soldiers had less to fight for than any other of our soldiers. They were subjected to injustices, abuses, lack of education, poor employment, and lynching. By forgetting the past and looking to the future, they could be motivated to fight as good as anyone else. They fought well for the same reason that Miss Lou Crenshaw said: "Things always get better for us after the war." The black man's fighting spirit can be turned off by injustices and racism, even on the front line. Black and white soldiers must have the spirit to fight, and that spirit is motivated when they believe in what they are fighting for. When Camp Patrick Henry was integrated, it gave members of the division the spirit to fight. As long as there is good and fair leadership, they will fight as well as anyone, whether the leader is black or white. I kept telling my men that if we fight well, the Armed Forces will be integrated at the end of the war; and this will help to bring about other civil right advances.

I liked my new platoon not only because they liked me, but also because they were good. We had a nice command post where we lived, better than the one my company commander had. We had a three-story stone building, previously owned by an Italian fascist, which meant that we did not have to treat his house with any respect. He had barrels of Italian wine in such quantity that we could never drink it all; but we tried, drinking red wine instead of water. We stayed on the ground floor where we slept and cooked, maintaining a skeleton crew on the guns 24 hours per day. We were able to prepare hot meals all the time, which I could not do with my old platoon. I made sure that my men did not forget that they were in combat; a little carelessness can cause the death rate to go up fast. The situation on the battlefield for my platoon for the Christmas holidays, New Year's, and January was defensive. Because defensive situations can sometimes be so peaceful on the battlefield, it can make one forget that a war is going on.

In February, everyone began to think about the offense, as this was the only way to get the war over. It was still winter. The ground was wet and frozen, with lots of snow on it. In Western Europe and the eastern front where the grounds were flat, offenses were more continuous. On February 14, 1945, my battalion had an offensive mission for taking a ridge extending down from the mountain toward the sea, beginning from Hill Georgia. This ridge was named Ohio.

The battalion plan was to attack on a two-company front with E and G Companies to take this ridge. My platoon was in general support of G Company. On February 13, my company commander gave the order: "Men, we are going up there and fight and win this battle for democracy." After he left, I said, "Men, I want to turn the commander's order around a little. Tomorrow, we are going up there to help win the war, and we are going home to fight for democracy." They were impressed. Black soldiers must feel that their effort in battle will benefit them as it will benefit other Americans.

On February 14, the battalion attack began in the mid-morning. After about three hours of light fighting, we seized the right half of Ohio Ridge and begin digging in to defend it. Our mission was a training exercise against a live enemy, to see if we could fight. Even though I was not impressed with that type of mission, I did my job. The training objective was completed, but we were required to remain on the objective until we were ordered to withdraw.

During the middle of the afternoon, I noticed Captain Cook, the commander of G Company, having a heated telephone conservation. I went to him to see what was the problem. By that time one of my boots began to act like it was in quicksand. I noticed the dirt being cut out from under it. About 300 yards to our right flank, I spotted a German machine gunner shooting at me. I quickly fired a shot from my M1 rifle and silenced the machine gun. Then the enemy ran five or six feet without his gun and fell dead. Without telling Captain Cook that I had just saved both of our lives, I asked instead what was all the excitement about. He said, "Our U.S. Navy wanted to get into the act by firing their big guns. It fired all right, killing eleven of my men. I told the battalion commander that if they fired, killing any more of my men, I will march my company off this hill." I expressed my regrets over the incident, feeling certain the battalion would stop the Navy's shooting.

I went back to my position. Fifteen or so minutes later, I saw Captain Cook marching his company off the hill. I said, "Captain Cook, what are you doing?" "I am taking my company off the Hill, The Navy has killed eight more of my men."

Because I was in general support of G Company, I should have left the hill with the company. I knew that he was making a mistake, even in this very tragic situation, and was playing in the hands of those who chose to discredit us. This begins to look like what my friend said to me at the well house--black soldiers are cowards. They run away in battle. Even though he was not running away from battle, nor was he a coward; but to those who would discredit us, this would be their allegation. I decided not to be a part of it. I said, "Tell the battalion commander that I hate to take this real estate and turn right around and give it back to the enemy. I will deploy my platoon to try to hold this hill until he sends reinforcements." He said that he would. I stayed.

I established a reverse slope defense with one of my sections up and one back. With the two guns up front, I separated them in depth about 100 yards. The rear section was on the next hill to the rear. All guns had their defensive mission. We waited all that afternoon without receiving reinforcement or instructions. We had to spend the night up there. I did not like it much because we were vulnerable to a night attack. I told my men to stay in their holes and shoot at anything outside of them. We got very heavy rain that night which made enemy patrolling on that mountain by the enemy unlikely because it made walking very slippery. That heavy rain may have stopped the enemy from attacking us.

The next morning the rain stopped. About ten o'clock in the morning, I met with my platoon sergeant and two machine gun section leaders. I divided a half-gallon of Sicilian whiskey between them so that they could give a little to each of their men. This would be the only food which they would have until we returned to my unit. We met at the Truce House in "no man's land" which was known for its good wine. The wine was so good that no one would shoot anyone at that house in fear of destroying that good wine. Because of this legend, we felt an element of safety there. I said, "We did not get the reinforcements I requested. If the enemy wants us, it will be over our dead bodies; they won't capture us. They will take us over there behind that mountain, line us up, and shoot us before a firing squad. That is no way for a soldier to die." They knew I meant it, and they were willing to follow my leadership.

After the meeting, each us went back to our positions. As soon as I got back to my trench, I noticed that I had a visitor. The enemy had visited my position with a mortar shell with a direct hit while I was at the meeting. I received so many of these. I just shook it off like water off a duck's back. They reminded me that I was not back home on easy street. Most of the day went by without contact from my unit. I did not wish to remain there another night because of our vulnerability to a night attack. About two hours before dark on February 15, I sent my platoon sergeant to lay a telephone wire to my company commander. It was completed in about an hour. My commander was surprised to hear my voice, because he thought that my entire platoon of 36 men were massacred by the Navy as was the case with G Company. Maybe it was not a massacre; but when nineteen men are killed, there must have been three times that many more men who were wounded. I told him that we were all here, holding Ohio Ridge with no one in my unit receiving as much as a scratch.

The Company Commander said, "E Company pulled back yesterday when G Company came down. You are out there all by yourself. Come back at first dark. I will alert the company on the front line to expect you and let your platoon come through." Immediately, I pulled the front gun back (which was with me) to the second gun that was also up front. Then we moved back to the rear section where we had to negotiate a deep ravine, which we wished to clear before dark. We did so under the protection of the rear section. At first dark, we moved quickly through the front line where we got a heroes' welcome.

It did not take me long to find out what had happened when G Company arrived to the rear without being ordered to do so. The Regimental Commander broke down and cried. I did not know that the whole U.S. press in Italy had been invited down to see the big show. When G Company got back, the curtains were pulled; the show had turned sour. Had I known this, I would have tried to talk Captain Cook out of withdrawing. However, it would have been hard to do when so many of his men had been killed and wounded by our Navy in this training exercise. Especially when I thought he was playing into the hands of those who would discredit us.

I did not think the press was there. The faults went three ways: Captain Cook withdrawing his company without orders, although he had told the Battalion Commander he would do so. I heard him say, "If the Navy kills any more of my men, I am going to march my men off this hill." The battalion was at fault for not controlling the Navy's fire. The big fault was the Navy. It did not practice proper safety procedures, by firing way out in front of friendly forces and creeping its fires in under observation to insure that its shells landed at a safe distance in front of friendly troops. Someone should have observed those fires, so that if something went wrong, another would not follow the first disaster. The Navy may have been a little careless because of the black soldiers. This I do not know.

The white press chose to blame everything on the blacks and protect the whites. Captain Cook, whose company had been incapacitated to an ineffective force, was blamed for everything. Not only was he blamed, I was blamed, E Company was blamed, the whole division was blamed. All the black people were blamed. We were back from where we started--black soldiers are cowards who run away in battle. The press covered up for the whites and blamed everything on the blacks. Because we always received criticism and never praise, this was another snow job to discredit us. I personally did not think that the press came up there to discredit us; but when things turned nasty, rather than tell the whole truth, it took a few facts and turned on the discrediting propaganda machine against us. I cried because of all those lies. The press did not know the complete story. No one knew the whole situation like me, and that is why I am writing about it now. Much of the outstanding work done by the Buffalo Division, before and after these highly distorting and discrediting stories, placed a damper on things, thus preventing the division from receiving proper recognition for its performances. I was made to understand that when these stories hit the streets in the U.S., many magazines carrying this story sold out. This was good news to those who wished to block the civil rights movement, which would enable them to say, "I told you so."

Because of my action on February 14 and 15, I was recommended for a promotion to captain and given a company of 200, in contrast to the 36 men that I was presently commanding. My company commander and battalion commander made this recommendation; but the regimental commander said no because he thought I was too young at twenty-three years of age. He looked at my youthful appearance instead of my performance. I looked much younger than my age as the Italian girl had noticed back in December when she started sucking her fingers when she first saw me. I was not offered a silver star or any other award-- which I felt that I deserved--because of all the bad publicity. The division did not want to produce any heroes in this conflict, to the extent that medals were not passed out. I deserved a silver star in this conflict more than the one offered during the 27th of November battle. I was given another R&R to Rome instead.

I went to the Division rear to take a shower and get a change of clothing en route to Rome. While I was taking a shower, a whole throng of Generals came to the shower section to see how the shower was working. They were not there to show any interest in me but to see what the shower was doing for me. These shower and change-of-clothing units were new innovations in combat, and the Chief of Staff wanted to see them in operation. Naturally, I was a bit nervous at being naked and seeing General of the Armies George C. Marshall, with his five stars; Lieutenant General McNauney, three stars, commanding general for U.S. Forces in Italy; Lieutenant General Mark Clark, Commanding General of the U.S. Fifth Army, another three-star general who was the Corps Commander; Major General Almond, Division Commander, and three one-star generals. General Marshall came over there because of all that bad publicity He was there on this "Top Secret" mission in about three days following that bad publicity.

When they left, I completed my shower, dressed, and got out of there fast and a little bit excited. All of that brass in the shower unit with me continued to flash through my mind as I drove up and down those hills and around those curves en route to the Holy City. I made the trip without incident, arriving at the Excelsior Hotel where I would be staying. This was much better than Campo Mussolini where I stayed the last time. I did not notice any ballroom dancing, which I observed and participated in on the first night of my visit in December. This appeared to me to be so narrow. In order to prevent black soldiers from dancing with Italians girls there, they closed the dancing events, denying everyone the pleasure that it provided. Maybe I put an end to all those dances, because I broke up its unenforceable segregation policies back in December.

I visited an Italian Club during my last two days in Rome, which became know as a Hill Billy Club. It operated like the Officers' Club at the Excelsior Hotel, which I visited during my first night back in December. It was owned by an Italian but controlled by a United States white officer through the use of economic power. White Americans visited this club in large numbers, bringing good business to the owner. These same Americans used economic power to pressure the owner to deny patronagé to black Americans, in this case to black officers. If the owner did not comply, they would take their business elsewhere. Because the owner needed and wanted the business, he complied with this economic pressure. I assumed this was a replacement for the unenforceable segregation policy, which previously existed at the Excelsior Hotel. I went into this club and faced the same situation which I faced the first night that I visited the officers' club at Hotel Excelsior during my first night's visit there in December. The difference here was that the American official, such as the military governor, when confronted with a complaint by a black officer, would simply say, "This is a civilian establishment over which we have no control." If one of the Italian girls danced with a black officer, they would be told not to come back. One such girl who danced with me my first night there got so nervous that she quit in the middle of the floor. I was embarrassed; but because I knew what was going on, I stayed there and drank at the bar. They had to serve me, but the girls could not be my guests there, even if they wanted to be.

The U.S. Army could have closed down this facility that discriminated or put it off limits; but this was unlikely because it gave silent sanction and looked the other way. I went there my last night of R&R and I did not ask any girls to dance with me. I stayed at the bar where I did some light drinking. Around ten o'clock, one of the girls who would not dance with me the night before went to the door and signaled for me to join her. She took me to her apartment and invited me to spend the night. There were two other girls who had a room in the same apartment. One of the two other girls was the one who quit dancing with me in the middle of the floor the night before. I asked her why she did that. She said that if she danced with me that she would not be allowed to come into the club again. One of the girls had a British officer, and the other one had a Canadian officer as their guests. Because all three of these girls wanted to be with me, these two officers came to me and said, "What is it that you have that we do not have?" I said, "I do not know. Whatever it is, they must think I have more of it." That was the end of that. These officers were nice.

I was very impressed by the non-racial attitudes shown by these Italian girls. Of course, I knew that anyway. The great compassion these girls showed to me made me feel quite proud, especially with my date. None of these girls were prostitutes. They were generally nice girls who went out to enjoy themselves, hoping to find a husband. If stationed in Rome, I would have been happy to have made my date my girlfriend; and she would have been happy to have me. The next morning when I had to leave to go to the front, she broke down and cried a lot. I had tears in my eyes, something which does not come easy for me. The great compassion she showed to me made me feel so grateful.

I left Rome, feeling quite happy about my second adventure there. I did not let the American-imported racism bother me. I was quite pleased with the way I dealt with it. Again, I stopped by to see my brother at Leghorn where I was given a nice meal before returning to my unit. My unit had moved to regimental reserve for training because of the "goof up" on February 14. I believe I attended some classes in mine training. Then I was informed that I was being transferred to the 370th Infantry Regiment.

The 370th Infantry was considered the best regiment in the division. It came to Italy in July 1944 and participated in offensive operations along the Arno River, connecting Florence, Pisa, and Leghorn. It advanced some forty miles to the north to the Italian Alps where the Germans anchored their defenses from sea to sea, and we were still there.

This regiment had been designated to spearhead the Fifth Army's Spring Offensives, the final major battle for ending the war in Italy. I believe that this arrangement was made with the approval of General Marshall who came to Italy to investigate the newspaper stories of February 15. The honor given to the division and to the 370th Infantry to make a break through the German defenses, initiating the spring offensive which was approved by the Chief of Staff of The United States Army was a vote of confidence for the Division, fully vindicating the division of all false information written by the newspapers on February 15 about Buffalo soldiers. I believed that the success of the division in the forthcoming campaign would determine the outcome of integrating the armed forces after the war. This could be the final test.

I was sent to D Company, 370th, and was assigned as platoon leader of the First Machine Gun Platoon, the same type of unit that I previously commanded. I joined my unit, which was on defensive duties, located on the south of a canal that ran from the mountain to the sea. We stayed there for a short period of time, before moving just south of Hill X, the location of the spearhead attack, which would begin the spring offensives. I believe I had about a month to become acquainted with my new platoon and prepare it for extensive combat. This would not be a one-hill attack and pull back. It would be continuous for about a hundred miles over some of the most rugged mountains in Italy.

My strategy for mental preparation for combat for my platoon was that we were fighting for the future. My men could not be motivated by the past. We talked about all the bad things which had happened to them--what they saw or heard, true or not true. My objective was to rid the subconscious of my men of thinking of the many bad things that could choke them in a critical battle situation.

Every morning at breakfast, my platoon came into my command house where we had a hot breakfast, with the exception of the crew, which had to stay on the guns. We had prayer before breakfast, then breakfast. After breakfast, we had our rap session when everyone was invited to talk about all the bad racial conflicts that they knew about. I began by telling about things I had heard about, about things which I had knowledge of, although none of those things had ever happened to me, even though I knew they could have. After about a week or so of this, I explained to them why we talked about all these things. I said we talked about these things because we want to stop them. The Constitution of the United States guarantees us all the same rights that it does for white people. We are fighting here to let everyone know that we have earned those rights and that we want them. If we fight well on the battlefield, we will fight well on the home front; and we will win. If we do not have the courage to fight here, we will probably not have the courage to demand and receive those rights to which we are entitled. I said that the best way to fight and win this war is for 100 percent participation by everyone in this platoon, no one acting cowardly. I also said that jeopardizing your own life and that of your friends would cause us to lose. I stressed that we must all do our part in order to win and to live. This war will be over pretty soon, and we must do our part to make sure that it will be over.

I did not know exactly what a spearhead meant at that time. I knew it meant that the spearhead unit was the first to attack. I thought that it would be on a much broader front instead of a narrow front like we did on Ohio Ridge, a battalion attacking with two companies abreast. I found out that we were attacking on a one-company front. Like attrition warfare, one company attacks behind the other until a breakthrough is created. This makes for rapid forward movement because the reserve would be ready to exploit the breakthrough. The spearhead was scheduled at daylight on April 5, 1945. The spearhead begin with A Company, 1st Battalion, 370th Infantry, and my machine gun platoon. We were the spearhead. If we fall, the company behind us would continue to push forward and as many units as necessary will follow our path until the spearhead succeeded. As I understood it, the whole regiment's spearhead was on the same 300-yard front, which we were attacking.

This 300-yard front consisted of three hills clustered on one ridge, which was the spearhead objective--Hills X, Y and Z. To the east of these hills was a reverse L-shaped valley which wrapped around Hill Y on the east and around Hill Z on the north. The grounds to the south of Hills X and Y were flat. All the grounds to the west of Hill X and Z were also flat, becoming a part of the beaches. Highway 1 north/south lay along this flat ground to the west of these two hills; X and Z, to the east. The flat ground to the south, which we would travel in order to reach Hill X, gave the enemy a tremendous advantage as we moved from our line of departure to our first objective, Hill X. We had to run as fast as possible on the flat ground about the length of three football fields long.

These three clusters of small hills were essential for gaining control of Highway 1 as a communication and logistical route north along the west coast of Italy to La Spezia and Genoa and to cutting off the escape route of the enemy in the mountains to east of this highway. A heavy volume of fire covered Hills X, Y and Z, including my machine gun fire. A Company took advantage of this cover firepower, which enabled it to move quickly to Hill X, the first spearhead objective. As soon as I could no long support Company A by fire, I ran as fast as I could with my platoon, taking advantage of Company A's assault fire to protect my platoon during its run for Hill X.

When I reached Hill X, I only saw five men from Company A who were stragglers. I asked them, "Where is the company commander?" They pointed to Hill Y, the key hill amongst the three. I did not know whether to believe those men or not, and I did not want to march my platoon up Hill Y on the words of those stragglers. I thought Company A must be on the forward slope of Hill Y. If it was not and something went wrong going up Hill Y, my platoon would be at the mercy of the enemy. I didn't like that, not knowing what had happened to Company A. Instead, I moved my platoon to the highest point on Hill X where it could engage the enemy on all three of the hills. I liked better the route to Hill Z, our final objective, thinking that Company A at the speed at which it was moving, may already be there.

I liked going to Hill Z better because I could be supported by a section of my machine guns, which I put on the western edge of Hill X. It could fire on the eastern part of Hill X, on Hill Y, and Hill Z and could see us all the way to the final objective; and it could help us if we ran into trouble. The other reason I liked going to Hill Z was because we could move along the edge of the mountains, which dropped down to Highway 1 below us. We could hang on to the edge or drop down to the highway below if necessary. I liked the options which I had going to Hill Z. I kept thinking Company A may have captured Hill Z also. It was embarrassing to me that I was out of contact with the company, which I was supporting. I moved along the rim of the mountain, skirting and marking the anti-tank mine field, which was placed about ten yards from the edge of my path. When I reached the left flank of Hill Z, I took one of the machine guns from the gunner and gave him my rifle and had it cradled over my shoulder with a canvass machine gun ammunition belt, balancing it with my left hand on the grip and my right hand on the trigger. I was beginning to think that Company A may not be on Hill Z after all. I was determined not to give the enemy the upper hand by surprising me if he was on Hill Z instead of Company A. I figured if anything happened, I was going to let the machine gun do the talking, as there would be no time for verbal orders. In a sudden situation, I knew what I would do; and I did not know how my men would react.

Just before we reached the crest of Hill Z, the enemy soldiers threw the lid open on their underground bunker and threw potato mashers, a grenade with a long handle. My men hit the ground, an automatic reaction when grenades are thrown. I notice that the grenades were thrown with such a force that they would be over our heads and down the side of the mountain. I dropped to my knees, squeezing on the trigger of my machine gun; and I liked the way it talked. As the enemy rose up to take advantage of the grenade, which he threw but didn't know where they landed, he ran into my blazing machine fire. He was finished. I had the final objective and still had not found Company A.

I would like to have been at division headquarters, Fifth Army Headquarters, or the Pentagon, when they found out that the Buffalo Division had achieved its spearhead objective in about two hours after it crossed the line of departure. It was done so quickly that they probably thought I was mistaken and was not sure of the objective that I had captured. When everything goes perfectly, it is easy. But the more imperfect it goes, the harder it becomes. The enemy was in his underground bunkers, not even visible, when we stood on top of them. The first enemy soldiers I saw all day were those who came out of the bunkers on Hill Z.

We had used one of the principles of war in achieving our objective, the element of surprise. Because we had shelled those hills all winter, the enemy apparently thought that his was just another shelling. Before he knew anything, we were standing on top of him. They did not come out to oppose us, with the exception of those on Hill Z. The element of surprise had allowed us to achieve a tremendous victory in a very short time. It was to our credit that I did not hesitate after taking the first objective, thus preventing the enemy from reacting in time to impede us. Nothing is more important in combat than achieving an objective so quickly that the cost in lives is minimized. No one in my platoon, again, had received a scratch. With that kind of success, I believed that my men would follow me anywhere.

To me, I had passed the integration test. As soon as I stood on Hill Z, I said, "I have passed General Marshall's Integration Test. Now the Armed Forces will be integrated.

I was happy to call my company commander to tell him that I was on the final objective. I imagine lots of people did not believe it. It took about four hours before my commander and the battalion commander moved to their observation post where I had placed the rear section of my platoon.

My company commander told me to pull back as soon as a friendly unit passed through our unit, because we had a similar spearhead mission on another front the next morning to the east. It came to my mind that all of a sudden we had achieved superman status.

A short time later, I noticed a black captain moving boldly from Hill Y, toward me on Hill Z, with his captain bars shinning like new money, standing up right like General Patton. I said, "Captain, you better get down and cover up those bars." I guess, he was not in any mood to listen to me, a lieutenant. He moved forward, and I moved backward toward Hill X where my other machine section was located. About two minutes later, a soldier from the company that had just passed through me came to me and said the captain was dead. I was not too surprised because he did not plan his movement into enemy territory skillfully. I told him that I had no authority to take over the company and that I was under orders to pull back and the commander must be found within its own chain of command.

I began to pull back as ordered. As I approached the area where I marked the minefield, I noticed those five stragglers from Company A--which I ordered to follow me--had drifted into the minefield. For some reason, I guess because I had placed them under my orders, I assumed responsibility for them. I went into the minefield to tell them which way to move, away from the enemy toward the friendly side. Instead, they moved toward the enemy setting off one or more mines. One of the mines close to me went off also. I broke one of my rules--do not do someone else's job and do not fight for medals. I guess I figured that I had some responsibility for these men, however.

I was blown unconscious, but I do not think it was for long. That I do not know. When I became conscious, I felt for my feet and legs, because I had no feelings in them. I found that I still had them; but the seams of my trousers had been blown loose, and I could not see. I managed to stand to my feet, but tumbled to the ground due to a lack of feeling in the lower part of my body. I lay there quietly and was ready to go to my maker. I gave up to die. I felt that I had been a perfect soldier in battle, more perfect than anything that I had ever done before. I had been as nearly perfect as possible in leading my men. It was my destiny to prove that black men in combat could fight as good as anyone. I had fought so that the life of people in the United States would be better for black people when the war was over. I felt within myself that I had done all these things. I was now unafraid of the mines, which were close by, or of the enemy who apparently had seen what happened. I was ready to leave this earth.

But because I believed that God owed me something and because my parents had prayed so much on my behalf, God gave me my life back. I have no divine proof of this, but this is my belief. My company commander had me picked up by the medics for evacuation to an aid station and beyond. When I left a few yards from where the commander was, the enemy opened up on me from Hill X with machine gun fire, trying to kill me on the stretcher. I had always heard that everything is fair in love and war. That which I had done to the enemy on Hill Z was fair in war; but the fact that he was trying to kill me, as I lay wounded on a stretcher, was not fair. I did not know how the enemy missed. I guess the Lord came to my rescue again. The men who were carrying me dropped me on the ground and took protective cover, leaving me in the enemy's line of fire. They tried to kill me as I lay wounded on the ground on the stretcher. Those bullets came so close to my stomach that I sucked it in to keep from getting hit. My company commander saw this and directed the medics to pull me back under cover, which they did. I had often wondered why the enemy wanted to kill me so badly on that stretcher. I thought they were seeking revenge for what I had done to them earlier on Hill Z. I figured that it was necessary to wait until dark before I could be taken to the aid station.

I had assumed until recently that this was the case. Reading the U.S. News and World Report in July 1996 I found out something about what happened as I lay there on the stretcher. The article was published May 6, 1996. Lieutenant Vernon Baker who was a platoon leader in C Company of my battalion, commanded by Captain John Runyon, my old commander, and which was in battalion reserve, came up to Hill X and knocked out those machine guns, which were trying to kill me. I read in this magazine that Lieutenant Baker would be awarded The Congressional Medal of Honor for knocking out those machine guns, which were trying to kill me. I did not know all of this at the time I was taken to the aid station.

I was given a hero's welcome at the aid station, but I could only hear it. People there knew all that I had done and what had happened to me. I heard Doctor Greenlee's voice. We spent lots of time on the ship talking together. I was telling him about my hopes and ambitions that he probably did not pay much attention to. Now that I had done just about everything, maybe more than those things we talked about, he was astounded. He had all the praise in the world for me as he laid the Purple Heart medal on my stretcher. I later felt it, held it in my hand. They apparently had heard everything on the radio, making this whole event appear like a scene in the movies. They sounded as if they wanted to give me the Congressional Medal of Honor. All this while, I was more worried about my platoon that I had left behind than I was for myself lying on the stretcher with no vision. I was given a shot, treated, and shipped out to the division clearing company where I got another shot, then to 171st Evacuation Hospital, where the next morning one of the doctors picked a piece of metal from the white part of my eye. I was given a few shots there before they sent me to the 64th General Hospital at Leghorn.

The first or second day after arriving there, the Red Cross director came to me and said, "I need your permission for me to authorize the doctor to operate on both of your eyes." I asked first, "What are the doctor's qualifications?" She said, "He is from the Mayo Clinic and is the third best eye doctor in the world." I said, "If he said that they need to be operated on, tell him to get with it." My brother, who was close by in a quartermaster battalion, could have given permission. I did not tell her to tell him that I was there in the hospital, nor did I tell the Red Cross director about him. I did not do it because he would have gotten too shook up over my situation.

The operation went off as scheduled and with great success. I was told that I would remain there a few days before being shipped to the 17th General Hospital in Naples, Italy. Almost the whole time that I was there, I was a bed patient, receiving penicillin shots every three hours. I slept well, but I woke up every time to receive the shots. Through all those days, I kept pace with the war--by radio or by talking with someone. I wanted so much to be with the Buffalo soldiers as they roamed over the Italian mountains going north to capture Genoa. I hoped that we fired them up when we took those spearhead objectives to move full speed ahead for final victory. Maybe we fired up the 11th Mountain Division, whose soldiers scaled the highest mountain along the eastern front leading to the fall of Bologna and opened the PO Valley for the final assault for Italy.

In the meantime, I was still in the hospital bed with bandages over my eyes and being punched with the needle ever three hours. I wanted so badly to be moved toward Genoa, but now for me the war was over. Maybe I should have been happy, but I was not. I just had to work on it.

According to the history book, victory in Italy was effective May 3, 1945.

A day or so before the War in Italy ended, the bandages were removed from my eyes, and a miracle occurred, according to my nurse. My eyes had cleared up; the Lord had blessed me once again. I was happy, because I felt that I deserved it. I celebrated at the hospital, drinking gin mixed with grapefruit juice. I believe I went to the Officers' Club and danced a little bit in downtown Naples on Via Roma. It was a happy and glorious celebration, but I did think about my friends who would never be here again. They had paid the ultimate price for the victory, which we were celebrating.

I got a chance to visit the Officers' Club on the Isle of Capri belonging to the Tuskegee Airmen, many of whom were my schoolmates at Tuskegee, commanded by Colonel Benjamin O. Davis, my first ROTC commander and golf partner when I was a student at Tuskegee. They all were some place else, and I cannot recall seeing anyone whom I knew. For them, the war was not over, as they were escorting bombers supporting the war on the western front.

Very shortly after that, I was placed on a hospital ship going home. Before I left, I received a letter from my girlfriend in Chicago, Yvonne Davis, expressing her sorrow over the loss of President Roosevelt, saying that our fight for civil rights may have gone with his death. I, too, shed some tears over the passing of the president, as he was the only president of the United States that I had ever known.

I will always remember my nurse telling me good-bye. "I have seen a miracle in the recovery of your eyes," she said.

The trip back was a little different than the one I had coming over. Maybe I went to Italy as a boy and was returning home as a man, too much growth in such a short time. I needed time to absorb all that had happened in my life. I faced death many times on the battlefield that never bothered me. Death was a little like golf, closeness does not count--only the real thing counts. Now all those near misses would plague me, and it would take some time for me to shake them off. The slow ride home should help. I had to be a little happy as the war for me in Europe was over. I remembered often when I gave up to die, after being hit by that mine, thinking that I would soon be in the bosom of Abraham. Feeling that way had to make me happy, because I felt I had done what the Almighty wanted me to do and that I had done it very well. Then I began to take some more delights because I believed that I had been spared because I had done my job, which was my destiny.

My objectives had always been to vindicate the black man's fighting ability and to pave the way for his full participation as a first-class American citizen. I took great delight in feeling this would be accomplished. I felt that our successes on the battlefield assured the achievement of integrated armed forces of the United States of America and that this would be the first link in the chain for achieving all of our civil rights.

Now, for the first time, I began to think about awards for all my achievements. I did not receive one Silver Star, even though I had been offered one among four choices as the result of first combat operation on Hill Georgia on November 27, 1944. I took the other three choices instead. I feel that I should still get it. As a result of my action on February 14 and 15, 1945, I was recommended to be given a company and promoted to captain, but not recommended for a silver star, due to all the bad publicity. The division would claim no heroes for that action; but my action was the only visible bright spot in that battle, which enabled the Chief of Staff of the Army to give the Division a clean bill of health during his investigation, shortly after the 15th of February 1945.

As a result of my action, both my company commander, Captain John Runyon, and I were considered among the best officers of the division; and we were transferred to the 370th Infantry to be a part of the force to spearhead the Fifth Army's spring campaign. I believe my action in the spearhead justified the award intimated by the medical personnel at the aid station who had followed my action on radio. They had high praise for acting as if I had won the Congressional Medal of Honor. I began to believe on the ship home that their reaction was correct and that I had earned the Congressional Medal of Honor. I did not think I would ever get it, regardless of how much I had earned it, because no black man had received this award during World War I or World War II. Whether or not I get it, I want my autobiography to show that I believe I earned it and should get it. My action in seizing Hill Z, besides what it would do for the civil rights movement, put a little fire under the campaign to end the war in Italy.

The role I played in bringing about integrated armed forces, in my opinion, deserves a Distinguished Service Medal. I realize that more people earn medals than those who get them. Many are not interested in medals; they just want to do their jobs and go home. Others get killed. Witnesses get killed. I believe General Marshall and I were on the same wavelength and that wavelength was the key, which helped him to recommend to President Truman that the Armed Forces of the United States should be integrated.

As in my case, I was wounded on the first day of the final campaign to end the war in Italy. I got wounded and no details of what I had done were fully known, with the exception of the members of my platoon. The war went on for nearly a month, covering thousands of square miles; other heroes emerged and the earlier ones were forgotten. I was expecting to receive an award while I was in the hospital, but I did not receive one. Captain John Runyon, who commanded C Company, had knowledge of my action on May 5, 1945; and he was my company commander during the time when I believe I earned the Distinguished Service Medal and the two Silver Star Medals.

He was the Commander of C Company when Lieutenant Baker received the Congressional Medal of Honor for knocking out those machine guns, which were trying to kill me on the stretcher.

I also had to begin to forget the past and to look toward the future. I was a reserve officer who had to finish another year of college. I wanted to become an automobile dealer after leaving the Army and finishing college. I wanted to visit General Motors, Ford, and Chrysler in Detroit to become a dealer at Tuskegee Institute, Alabama, a black community where most of the faculty and staff at the University as well as doctors, lawyers, and administrators at the all-black U.S. Veterans Hospital lived. I was planning to join the ROTC at Tuskegee University when the post-war ROTC programs were reestablished. This would give me a chance to finish college before leaving the Army. I wanted to have a little fun, too, by visiting my parents and relatives, girlfriends, places of entertainment, and just live it up a little. I felt that I deserved this. All these things would help me to shake off the past and start a bright new future. I had plenty of time to think about all these things plus talking with fellow passenger-patients on the ship about their plans and hopes. These were all good ideas for me to think about on the way home.

After about fifteen or so days on the ship, we made it home--even after fighting off a storm, sealing a few storm leaks, and fighting off seasickness (even though it did not happen to me). The hospital ship reached Newport News, Virginia, on schedule. Surprisingly, I returned to the place from which I departed--Newport News, Camp Patrick Henry, Virginia.

The happiest part about my return was that the integration, which we established in September 1944, was still in tact. I noticed that the whites were as happy as the blacks. Although the segregation society existed everywhere in Virginia, I was happy because I pointed out the problem and gave the solution to the race problem that caused this base to be integrated. I was happiest that the integration continued after the Buffalo Division departed for Italy. This made me feel that the integration, which we established, was a continuing example of what we hoped to achieve in the post-war period.

The Buffalo Division was responsible for this integration; and its achievements on the battlefield paved the way for the same results to be achieved throughout the country, which would result in great social change in the United States and the world, almost like the shot which was heard around the world.

Time marches on and so did I. I left Camp Patrick Henry in Virginia for William Beaumont General Hospital at El Paso, Texas. Traveling slowly by train along the deep south route made it seem like it would take as long as the return trip across the Atlantic. The places I remembered along the way were Shreveport, Louisiana, and Longview, Texas. I believe the reason I remember that Texas town was because one of the patients on the train was from there. I do not recall going through Marshall, Texas, the place where the girl lived that I wanted to marry after getting my commission. She was the first girl that I ever proposed to, but I cannot recall going through her town. I can recall going through Dallas and Fort Worth; but for some reason Longview, Texas, as small as it was, remains in my memory more than any of the places on this long journey to El Paso.

We did arrive at El Paso, Texas. I believe it took longer than the trip from Fort Huachuca, Arizona, to Newport News, Virginia, back in September. I was happy that the long train ride was over, and hopeful that I would remain at the hospital as short a time as possible. I wanted to go to Chicago; my home in Selma, Alabama; and to Washington, D.C., where the one girl who I ranked number one on my marriage list was residing for the summer.

I liked the hospital in Texas as the people were quite friendly. I like the Mexican girls most of all. I thought that they were more beautiful than the Italian girls. I remembered following one over all of El Paso to no avail. My first night there I went into a white club where dancing, drinking, and having a good time were going on, celebrating the end of the war in Europe. This was racial segregation city, but it was not as bad as Dallas or Forth Worth. One white man there did ask me if I were a Philippine. I said yes. He asked me to speak a little of it. I had learned a few words of Italian that I spoke. He accepted them as genuine Philippine language. After my first night out on the town, I went over to Juarez with the rest of them where I did not have to be a Philippine.

In about four or five days, I had all of my medical evaluations and was given sixty days of recuperation leave. I went to the airport at El Paso where I got a military flight, either to Dallas or Fort Worth to Montgomery, Alabama, and then to Chicago, which I called my second home. There I went to see my girlfriend, Yvonne. She and her parents were happy to see me, as I was among the very first European war veterans to return to the United States immediately after the war. In fact, I was on my way home before the war in Western Europe was over. Naturally, her father, being a State Representative of Illinois, wanted to know about the performance of the Buffalo Division. I believe that I was the right man to tell him, although I was not in any big mood to talk about the war, rather more in the mood to forget about it, but I felt compelled to do so. They were quite impressed with me when I told them about a few of the things which we did. Yvonne was too impressed, because she proposed to me, catching me really off guard. She was a very pretty girl, but not so much that I was going to say yes without thinking about it. My plans for the future did not include a wife at that time. I said to her that: "I wanted to talk it over with my mother." She said, "Here is the phone, call her." I said, "I want to talk to her in person about this, and I will be back here in about three weeks with my answer." I did not tell her that I was a country farm boy from rural Alabama and that we had no telephone, electricity, and hot and cold running water. We had outhouses.

Marrying Yvonne did not quite fit my mold. I did not like Chicago politics, and I did not want anyone controlling my life. Her father was a big wheel in Chicago, a State Representative. I presumed that he was a part of the political organization there. I knew that if I married Yvonne, the only daughter and child, I might end up being a part of the political machine which I wanted no part of it. If I had loved Yvonne enough, I would not have allowed her father's politics to control me. I had known Edith Chandler, who was in Washington D.C. longer; and she was one on my marriage list. I was a little doubtful about caving into Yvonne's marriage proposal.

One of my rules about marriage was to ask myself, "Should I marry that girl?" If my answer is no, I wouldn't marry her. I could somehow say no to marriage to Yvonne. I believe this was the case in point more than anything else. I went home after Chicago and never mentioned marriage to anyone. If I wanted to get married, I would tell my parents; and I would do so only if I was sure of my choice. Even if I became engaged to be married, I would have had to wait until I got my post-war career established

When I arrived home during the month of June 1945, after leaving Chicago, it was cotton-hoeing time. I went to the field where my mother and father were working. My father looked at me to see if I had any war damage. When I looked quite normal to him, he was even happier to see me, so were my mother and my sisters. All my brothers and brothers-in-law were still away in the military services. My father was a little disappointed that I went to Chicago before I came home. I had to make up something to justify that. We had a wonderful family reunion.

My brother Frank was in the Navy, stationed at Daytona Beach, Florida. He invited me to visit him and to travel there with his wife. I did. He was a bartender at the Navy Officers' Club. Being a bartender was about the best job for him because he was involved with bootlegging whiskey with our uncle, which contributed to him dropping out of school. He remembered 150 different drink combinations in his head, and he was fast. The people at the naval station loved him. One of the naval officers, who owned a big resort on one of the lakes in Minnesota, invited my brother to work for him after the war with Japan. My brother wanted to do it, but my father talked him out of it. I think that would have been the best post-war job for him.

I enjoyed seeing my family at home, as well as my brother stationed in the Navy. I believe that I stayed about two weeks. Craig Field was at Selma where I visited the Air Corps Officers' Clubs there. I went by the Red Cross office in Selma to thank the Red Cross people for asking me to write my parents a letter shortly after my operation at Leghorn, Italy. One of my first visits was to my Cousin Fanny and Aunt Bam, who loved me as much as anybody. I visited Master Sergeant Davis, the old Buffalo Soldier, and enjoyed a get-together only Buffalo Soldiers could understand. By this time, I had become his ideal officer. I visited the Veterans Club there in Selma, where I saw many of my friends who were in and out of uniform.

I wrote Edith Chandler at her home in Wilmington, North Carolina, about my return to the United States and expressed a desire to visit her. She was living in Washington, D.C., with her aunt and working for the Federal Government during the summer along with her younger sister. She invited me to visit her. I did so, staying a week or ten days, going out every night to the movies, dances, clubs, and restaurants. We had a wonderful time. She did not ask me to marry her as Yvonne did. If she had, I do not think I could have said no to myself. She fitted my mold, and it was looking like I was fitting her mold also. She stayed home from work on my last day in Washington, and she invited me to her house. My inexperience at being a playboy caused me to goof that opportunity for holding on to her. She and her sister came to the airport to say good-bye as I took off for Chicago.

Upon arriving in Chicago, I did not contact Yvonne right away. Like a greedy fool, I tried to date her girlfriend. It did not work; and after that, Yvonne did not want to see me. To me it was just as well, because I planned to say no to marriage. I dated and had a pretty hot romance in Chicago with a young lady who was a friend to Mrs. Van Zandt where I was staying. She was one or two years older than me. She too begin to think about marriage. I decided it was time to get out of Chicago.

I started hopping around the United States by going to air bases, flying to cities where I had never been, such as Saint Louis, Missouri; Denver, Colorado; Salt Lake City, Utah; Omaha, Nebraska; and the like. All the bases had USO lounges for sleeping and snack bars for eating and buses for tours. All of these services were free.

All good things must come to an end, sooner or later. I returned to El Paso, Texas, and to William Beaumont General Hospital upon completion of my sixty days' leave. I stayed there a few days and was assigned to Fort Sheridan, Illinois, just outside Chicago. I was released on August 15, 1945, VJ Day, the last day of the war because Japan surrendered to General MacArthur on the Battleship Missouri.

I was given about a week's travel time to go from the hospital to Fort Sheridan, Illinois. I went out to the commercial airport to get a hop, but no military planes were flying from there on this national holiday. I caught a ride on a private airplane, and the pilot asked me to fly it to Fort Worth some 600 miles. I had a flying license to fly a piper cub, but not a plane that size. I could keep the plane horizontal; I could maintain altitude and navigate it along the railroad tracks. The pilot slept as I flew it. The journey took about three hours. When I saw Fort Worth in the distance, I woke the owner. He took over and landed the airplane. I called the air base at Forth Worth for a hop to Maxwell Field at Montgomery, Alabama, fifty miles from my home at Selma, Alabama. I was told that a plane was leaving in a half hour. I got there and I believe air operations had to drive me to the runway to catch the plane. I traveled by bus to Selma from Montgomery. I stayed most of my travel time at home before heading to my new station. I believe I got a hop to O'Hara in Chicago, and I went to Mrs. Van Zandt's house where I stayed until it was time to report to Fort Sheridan, Illinois.

My last girlfriend in Chicago had departed for Los Angeles where she planned to stay and was not waiting for me because she figured that I did not have any matrimonial designs on her.

Chapter 5
THE INTEGRATION OF THE U.S. ARMED FORCES

The war was over and the future was in front of me. I began to think about finishing my fourth year of college, starting a business, where I would live, and even about marriage. In the meantime, I was in uniform where I planned to remain as long as possible and to save as much as possible, as this was the best way for preparing for the unknown that lay ahead. Now that I had a vision of what I wanted to do, I would continue to do my military duties and let things unfold. My first hope was to get an ROTC job at Tuskegee University, finish my last year of college, and go from there.

Upon reporting to Fort Sheridan I was given 15 days temporary duty at the Dennis Hotel on the Boardwalk in Atlantic City, New Jersey. This was a working vacation, more vacation than work. Most of the work I had to do was about the Soviet Union, post-war orientation, and the things the Soviets were already trying to do in East Germany and Eastern Europe that appeared to be their objective for the future. It was a little difficult for me to take, because two or three months ago the Soviets were our friends. And now, they appeared to be our adversaries. The man conducting the orientation was a southerner who had some difficulty in convincing me about anything. My experience in the South was that any man who talked about civil rights for black people were called communists, which made it difficult for me at that time to accept what he was discussing.

Later, when I read more about the action of the communists in Eastern Europe, my attitude came more in line with what this officer was talking about. Most of our time involved rest and rehabilitation with many programs and activities planned for us. The food was good, and the hotel accommodations were perfect. Our stay there was for fifteen days, and then I was reassigned to Fort McClellan, Alabama. I had about a week's travel time to my new station. On the way south I stopped by Greensboro, North Carolina, and Bennett College to see Edith Chandler, who was in her senior year.

The visit with Edith did not please me because she was dating an enlisted soldier stationed there in Greensboro, and she was not giving me any priority over him. I was really disappointed, because I was an old friend, an officer, and a war hero. None of this seemed to make any difference with her. There was another girl at Bennett College from Edith's hometown who was competitive with her for the campus beauty. I dropped in to see her. Edith just about went crazy when she found out about it, telling me that she never wanted to see me again. It did not bother her that she was seeing that other guy, but she could not accept the embarrassment when college friends began questioning her about losing out to her hometown competitor. I just about got on my knees to apologize to her, but she was playing hardball. I believe I got her to come around a little, and we may have gone to movies once before I left; but I certainly did not own her.

Upon graduation from Bennett, she was planning to attend graduate school at Atlanta University, which was less than 100 miles from Fort McClellan, Alabama, and about 150 miles from Tuskegee, Alabama. During this time, she would have finished college; and she would be a little bit more mature having a better vision about her future.

I left Greensboro and reported for duty at Fort McClellan, Alabama. It did not take me long to find that this was not the place where I wanted to be. It was a kind of officers' pool with no one knowing what his future would be--some would be leaving the service, some would be staying, and no one was sure about anything. The work there had no meaning. I was lucky, because I had come there through hospitalization, and I was authorized 15 more days of leave. I planned to use those 15 days to get out of there.

Even when I was in combat, my post-war objectives were to return to Tuskegee University, serve on the ROTC Staff, finish my fourth year in college there, stay in the Army as long as it would have me, save my money, and plan my civilian business when the Army no longer needed my services. To accomplish my objectives, I went to Seventh Army Headquarters in Atlanta, which was over all ROTC in the Army area and asked that I be considered for assignment on ROTC Duty at Tuskegee. I figured that the Army would reintroduce the post-war college military program at authorized institutions of higher learning. I got the impression there that they were glad to see me and that I was just the type of person that they were looking for. I was told to talk with the Professor of Military Science and Tactics at Tuskegee University about it and that I would hear from them in a few days.

I was very happy and went to talk with Major Welch at Tuskegee, my old military professor. He was a little angry that I had gone there and asked for such an assignment, and he felt that I should let the Army decide where I should go. I was not too happy either about his reaction. I just figured that if I want something, I have a right to ask for it. I returned to Fort McClellan forgetting about what I did. In less than a week after my leave ended, a first lieutenant came to me on the rifle range where I was working, asking me whom did I know. I asked him, "What are you talking about?" He said, "You have been assigned to ROTC duty at Tuskegee." I felt like jumping up to touch the sky with happiness. I did not talk to too many people about what I did because the superiors did not like it when one jumped channels to make assignment requests.

I reported to duty at Tuskegee University, which met with the delight of the whole faculty and administration. They were so happy to have one of their own on the military faculty. I was one of the very first war veterans assigned to an institution of higher learning. The freshman class when I left for the Army in 1943 was now the senior class. It was extremely difficult for the ROTC Cadets to accept me as anything other than as a student. I told them, "I am a commissioned officer in the United States Army, a war veteran, wounded in action, decorated for bravery. I have earned your respect; I am entitled to your respect, and I expect it." From that time on, I had no problems with discipline.

Tuskegee was very rigid about fraternization between faculty and students. This was a problem for me because the girls in the senior class were freshman when I left for the Army two years earlier, and they considered me as one of them and a most eligible bachelor. I stayed my distance, but it was not easy. I did not date the faculty either, because I did not want to be pinned down. I did not see anyone around whom I wanted to marry; therefore, I just continued to be the most eligible bachelor around.

I still had my eyes on Edith Chandler at Bennett College, and I was looking forward to the time when she would come to Atlanta University, which she would do after finishing Bennett College. I felt that my position for getting her had improved with my assignment on a college campus. I believe that I was still in touch with her, but I do not remember visiting her again while she was in Greensboro, North Carolina.

I worked quite hard on the ROTC staff because I was a product of the program. I believed in the program for what it provided for the students and the university. It was necessary for me to do lots of research to meet the criteria set forth in the military curriculum. New military texts had to be developed which would incorporate lessons learned in and during World War II. It was both hard and educational as I struggled the first two years--writing and rewriting lesson plans and doing more and more research.

Some parts of the curriculum that never changed included: drilling, parading, and marksmanship. This was the easy part. We had close order drill several times per week and every Sunday when the ROTC students paraded to chapel. The parade drew crowds from far and near to observe students who were in uniform marching to the music of the university band. It was necessary to do well.

In January or February 1946, Major Welch, my commander, suggested that we submit applications to apply for the regular Army. If we were selected, we would be the same as West Point officers-- timely promotions, travel to different parts of the world, and twenty years' retirement. He said the military probably would not select any black officers as the Army did not select any after the last world war, but we should be on record as having applied. I had not planned to stay in the military; but if I applied and was not selected, I would be able to claim racial injustice. With that in mind, I submitted my application.

The procedures required that all applicants be interviewed before a board of regular Army officers. Because I wanted to make a good impression during the interview, I studied a great deal about the principles of leadership. I was called before the board in Atlanta, Georgia, at Seventh Army Headquarters. Because I had not planned to stay in the Army anyway, I was more relaxed than I would have been if I really wanted to stay in the Army; and I think I did very well during the interview because of it.

Toward the end of June 1946, I got a telephone call from a former teacher of mine at Tuskegee, who had a business there, including a Western Union office. He called to tell me that he would bring a telegram to my office. This was a bit unusual, as he would normally call for me to come and get it. I was really astounded when I got it. "The President of the United States has selected you this day to be a member of the Regular Army of the United States of America. Will you accept it?" I was so proud that tears came into my eyes. I was congratulated by all of those who were around. I must make up my mind as to what my answer would be, because I had not planned to remain permanently in the military.

The Assistant Dean of Men who worked for my boss, who was also the University Students' Commandant, was a retired disabled Army Captain from World War I. I decided to show the telegram to him for the purpose of getting his advice. When he saw it, he jumped up, shouting, as it was the second coming of Jesus Christ. He advised me to accept it. I think he must have told all the important officials at the University about it.

I liked traveling and the twenty-year retirement. I could save my money, buy a new car, get married and go into business at forty-two years of age, with a retirement nest egg, so to speak. I took Captain Ecton's advice and sent a telegram to the Pentagon that I accepted the regular Army appointment. This made me a super hero around the campus, getting congratulations from the University President, the dean and just about everybody else. This was considered not only an honor for me, but for the Tuskegee University, which helped me to qualify for this honor. This also enhanced my status as "the most eligible bachelor" around there. There were many officers at Tuskegee Air Base who applied, were not accepted, and had to leave the service. This made my appointment even more significant. My wartime commanders had to recommend me. I knew that they would give me the strongest possible recommendation. My war record was paramount in this selection.

My career now would begin anew, a regular military career, with everything possible. I was still interested in Edith Chandler. I felt that my regular Army appointment would help. I do not remember now whether I wrote her about my appointment or whether I waited until September when she enrolled at Atlanta University. Shortly after my appointment, Major Welch, who had been at Tuskegee throughout the war, was now on orders to go the Far East. He was not selected, maybe because he was too old and did not have any war experience. Major Welch's transfer made me the commanding officer of the ROTC. Many on the faculty were hoping that it would stay that way, but that was not possible.

Shortly after my appointment, I had to attend a PMS&T (Professor of Military Science and Tactics) Orientation Course at Fort Benning, Georgia, because the post-war ROTC program at all authorized colleges and universities would commence during the fall of 1946. This course defined the U.S. Army's policy with respect to the role the ROTC would play in military strategy. Subject matters which would help the military meet its strategic objective were defined in as much detail as possible during this course. As soon as the course was over, I had to rush back to Tuskegee to develop the schedules, both academic and practical, for the school year.

The ROTC program expanded during school year 1946-47 to include Air Force and Army ROTC, consisting of six officers--three for the Army and three for the Air Force. My new boss, Lieutenant Colonel Barrow (the former executive officer of the 372d Infantry at Camp Breckenridge, Kentucky, my first regiment upon becoming an officer) took command over both units until the Air Force ROTC was established later in 1947. After that, two co-equal departments existed: Army ROTC and Air Force ROTC. Lieutenant Colonel "Spanky" Roberts, formerly second in command of the Tuskegee Flyers in Italy, became commander of the Air ROTC program.

Captain Johnson and I completed the Army officers' staff. Captains Perry and Hutchings completed the Air Forces officers' staff. With the exception of LTC (Lieutenant Colonel) Barrow, the rest of us had active World War II war experiences. LTC Barrow became a little jealous of me, as I was the only officer there with a regular Army appointment. All five of the other officers had applied for it but did not receive it. In fact, very few black officers were selected. Out of 9,800, only 11 blacks officers from the Army and 11 black officers from the Air Force received regular service appointments by the President. I was the only combat officer from the whole 92nd (Buffalo Division) Infantry Division selected and the only combat arms black officer who was appointed with white commanders' recommendations in the Army or Air Force.

If the other officers were jealous of me, they did not show it. On the contrary! I believed that they were happy for me. Maybe LTC Roberts may have been somewhat envious, but the three captains were on my side. Colonel Roberts was sharp, and I personally felt that he deserved one. Through his political connections and after a number of trips to Washington, he did get a regular Air Force officer's appointment; none of the others were so fortunate.

LTC Barrow was a little suspicious of me because of my popularity on the campus. Many members of the administration called me when they wanted information, rather than going through him. They were civilians who took the easiest way and the one of least resistance. Colonel Barrow was more of a politician from Boston than a soldier. Little by little he found out that I was not working behind his back and that I was a correct officer with him, although his character was a little bit questionable. My being a regular Army officer may have continued to bother him. Of all the officers there, he was the only who did not have the qualifications, education, and active war experience. And I do not believe that any of his former commanders ever recommended him for a regular Army appointment. He had the EGO of a superman, which in my opinion he did not measure up to. He also went to Washington with LTC Roberts to use politics to get a Presidential appointment, but he did not get it.

In February 1947, a military directive came out authorizing that all officers who had been wounded in action since their last promotion would be promoted to the next higher grade. LTC Barrow did not submit my name, even though I was eligible. I had not seen that regulation. General Charles Palmer, Chief of Staff of the Seventh Army in Atlanta, was in my corner. A red-bordered letter came to my boss giving him three days to submit my name for promotion. He called me in and told me about it. I was promoted promptly to captain after he was forced to recommend me for my new rank. In less than three years after becoming an officer, I made captain in two years and nine months. I had been recommended for this grade about two years earlier, during the war, after being commissioned for nine months, but was denied it because the Regimental Commander thought I was too young.

During September 1946, I started visiting Edith Chandler who had enrolled in graduate school at Atlanta University. I was there most weekends, going with her on Sunday morning to the Catholic Church, even though I was a Baptist. She was elated over my being assigned to the ROTC staff at Tuskegee University and being selected by the President to be a member of the regular Army. Then after I made captain, I bought my first car, a new maroon Pontiac, which she liked. Now for the first time I said to her, "If you marry me, I will work hard to become a colonel and later a general in the Army". She did not accept it. That, I could not understand. Eventually, she even stopped seeing me. There were a lot of rich black families in Atlanta with their sons driving around with big cars who were available to take her out and show her a good time. I felt that her father, being a doctor, wanted Edith to marry a doctor, as black people with the most money were usually doctors. She was a super beautiful girl who could get most anyone she wanted. She was never excited by military rank. Later she married a doctor in Chicago, which I felt was a planned event.

Every Saturday and Sunday evening I went dancing at the Tuskegee Air Base Officers' Club or a night club at Tuskegee where big named black bands played often such as Duke Ellington, Count Basey, Dizzy Gillespie, and the like. I worked on my dancing, and I considered myself to be an amateur Fred Astaire. Like Tony Bennett said, "Dancing is a good way to get the ladies." It certainly was a good way to get dances, but not always the ladies. There were nice ladies on the faculty and staff at Tuskegee, but my standards for beauty were so high; and I was afraid to date them unless I had some matrimonial design on them. I was considered the number one eligible bachelor around there, and I did not want to give anyone a false impression about my romantic intentions. I always wanted to be free in the event the right girl came along.

One day I was driving up Franklin Road, one of the nicest streets in Greenwood, the black community of Tuskegee University. I saw two nice high school girls whom I had known for a long time when I was a paperboy during my junior year in college (the year before going into the Army). These girls were quite a bit smaller then. Because I knew them and I had a nice new car, I offered them a ride to take them where they were going. They accepted. The larger of the two, Lolla, sat next to her younger sister and me; Carol sat next to the door. Then I felt Lolla curling up to me, catching me a bit surprised and not knowing how to react. She was a senior in high school, eighteen; and I was twenty-six. Eight years between us was large, but not too large. I did not exactly know how I would respond to that, but I was cautious.

She was not a student at the University, and I did not have to worry about that; but I did think about it. I remember a Doctor Wilkinson who was on the faculty when I was a student. He was sixteen years old with a Ph.D. degree, and he dated a high school student.

Very shortly I found that her mother was all for the relationship. We started hitting it hot and heavy. I was doing everything except sleeping at her house. I had all my meals there. I took her and her sister to high school every morning. I loved it. Lolla met all of my criteria for marriage, and this was becoming a foregone conclusion. This hot romance continued during her senior year and her freshman year at Talladega College, Alabama, which was close to 100 miles away. We even went on vacation together with her parents. Our relationship was perfect and was highly respected in the community. While she was in college at Talladega, I was there most weekends with permission to take her off campus.

One of the reasons I wanted to return to Tuskegee in the first place was so that I could finish college while on active duty. When I was in the war in Italy, this was on my wish list. Now, it had come to be. Beginning with the academic year 46-47, the Army allowed me to go college as long as it did not interfere with my military duties. Colonel Barrow permitted it. I did my college work, taught my ROTC classes, and spent all my spare time with Lolla, either on weekends when she was in Talladega or continuously when she was at home.

I did take time off from my work, academic requirements, and romantic life to play sports. My favorite sport was golf. I received a letter "T" for being captain of the golf team when I was a student. Dr. Russell Brown and Mike Rabb, who were my partners when I was a student, were still my partners when I joined the faculty, because the only place where we could play golf was on the University's course with sand green. I could play on the Air Force golf course at Maxwell Field at Montgomery or the officers' golf course at Fort Benning, Georgia. They could play on these military courses as my guest, which we did quite often. Besides golf, I played on the faculty all-star baseball team during the summer, which consisted of faculty and student members. We were very good. Because baseball was my first sport and because I was considered major league baseball material, I was happy again to put on that baseball uniform.

Our faculty, students, former students, and some Tuskegee Air Force players who also were former students made up the team membership. I do not remember any other baseball team ever defeating us. One of our pitchers, a former student and an officer at the air base, was released from active duty; and he returned to his home at Houston, Texas. We needed a pitcher. On my team at the Pernell Community where I grew up, I was a pitcher and so were my three brothers. I agreed to work on my pitching for two weeks to go against an all-star team from Fort Benning, Georgia. On the mound that day, the weather was hot and my curve ball was dancing. I was a strike out artist, but a little wild with my dancing curve ball. I walked the bases full several times and then struck out the side. Because the rules had changed, I made lots of balks. One time the bases were full and the catcher called for a pitch, which I did not like. I threw it, and the batter hit a single up the middle scoring two runs. After the twelfth inning, those were the only runs and the only hits the Fort Benning team got. The game was called due to darkness after twelve innings, ending in a 2-2 tie.

I could very well have pitched a no-hitter that day, but had to settle for a one hitter. I continued to play the whole summer, pitching only one additional game, which I did not do as well as the first one, but we won nevertheless. This ended my baseball career because in my future organization my commander would not allow me to play because he felt that team sports, such as baseball, football and basketball should consist of enlisted personnel and that officers did not have time for them.

In spring 1948, my father passed away at the age of 61 because of a heart attack, one of the saddest times of my life. He had worked giving his life for his family. He believed in education, feeling it would solve the economic and social problems facing black and white people in the south. He did the impossible by giving all of his nine children the opportunity to go to high school and college, something no one else whom we knew were doing. How lucky we were to have had a father like him. He not only was a great father, he was a great neighbor who helped blacks and whites alike. He had lived to see me make officer and become a regular Army officer, become captain at twenty-five years of age, and become a faculty member at Tuskegee University. His oldest son was a high school principal, his oldest daughter was married and working on her doctorate degree, his youngest daughter was in high school, and the next youngest one was in college at Tuskegee University. He must have died a very happy man; because when God judged my father by his works, he should be up there with the best of them.

In June or July, I received orders for West Germany. This kind of put an end to my romantic closeness because I did not want to take Lolla out of college. We agreed to get married when I returned from Germany in three years. I would save my money for that purpose, and I would visit her in eighteen months with an engagement ring. I was dead serious about my promises. I left Tuskegee for Camp Kilmer, New Jersey. Because I had some time there, I was allowed to return to Tuskegee to get my college degree at the summer commencement. This would complete an objective I had set for myself when I was on the front lines in Italy. I had an opportunity to say good-bye to Lolla again before finally leaving for Germany.

Upon the death of my father, I more or less became the father of my family. My fourth sister, Mable, was enrolled in nursing school at Tuskegee; and I assumed financial responsibility for her education. I was also partially supporting my mother, my third sister who was handicapped, and my youngest sister Jean who was attending high school in Selma. I spent quite a bit of time trying to get rural electrification at our country home in the Pernell Community, but I did not achieve it upon my departure for Germany. It had to wait until I returned to the United States in three years.

In 1946, the U.S. Senate began hearings concerning integrating the United States Armed Forces. Many of the top generals, including Eisenhower and Patton, opposed it. The President, as Commander-in-Chief, did not need congressional approval to do it. Mr. A. Phillip Randolph asked Mr. Roosevelt to integrate the Armed Forces in early 1942 and threatened to march on Washington if he did not do so. He backed off when the President issued an executive order requiring fair employment in businesses and industries doing business with the federal government and promised to look at integrating the Armed Forces after the war. Mr. Randolph was back on the integration track. He asked Mr. Truman to live up to the promise made by Mr. Roosevelt. When he believed that the Mr. Truman was dragging his feet on the issue, he threatened to march on Washington, again. The President let it be known that he would not be intimidated by this proposed march on Washington, but his move to integrate the forces seemed to have picked up a little speed. Secretary of State Jimmy Burns parted company with Mr. Truman over the issue and resigned his cabinet post. General of the Armies George C. Marshall took over as Secretary of State. All of this was in the mill as I departed for my overseas assignment. Even though the President issued his Executive Order to integrate in 1948, almost no movement took place for several years before showing a genuine move to integrate. The Korean War, which started in the beginning of 1950, began with segregated units.

Chapter 6
THE BEGINNING OF THE COLD WAR

I arrived in Germany in late September and was placed on temporary duty at Frankfurt serving the Berlin Air Lift. The Russians had cut off ground transportation to Berlin in an effort to take over the whole city, hoping to starve the Germans into submission of the city to East German Communists controlled by the Soviet Union. The United States and Great Britain began the airlift to meet the needs of West Berliners, thus preventing the Communists from taking over the city. To carry out the supply mission there were three principal types of transportation--airplanes, trucks, and trains. The freight trains brought bulk supplies to the railheads, where they were picked up by five-ton trucks with ten-ton trailers, then to the air base where they were escorted to the transport aircraft, loaded and flown to the Tempelhof Airport in Berlin. There were ships bringing supplies from Britain and the United States, which would be taken by trucks and trains. Trucks carried all the supplies being loaded up on the airplanes.

I was on temporary duty with the 67th Transportation Truck Company (Heavy), which was also on a temporary assignment to the 24th Transportation Truck Battalion in Frankfurt, commanded by Lieutenant Colonel Hymann Y. Chase, a black man. Colonel Chase was a doctor and Professor of Zoology and a military dictator. I reported to him at his battalion where I also met a Major Sorrell, the battalion executive officer and brother of one of the department directors at Tuskegee University. Because of that, Major Sorrell and I became instant friends. He also was one of the six black combat arms Army officers who were given regular Army appointments by President Truman. Colonel Chase was known to envy the black officers who got Presidential appointments because he was not appointed, even with all his qualifications and combat experiences during World War II.

I was sent to the billeting office where I was given an apartment in the best residential area of Frankfurt. It was perfect in that it enabled me to keep my social life private, which is quite necessary for single officers, and more than necessary under Colonel Chase.

The Sunday after I arrived there, I met Colonel Chase who took me for a ride in his Chrysler to look at ground transportation operations and the Frankfurt and Wiesbaden Airports from which all U.S. airlift planes departed for Berlin. The British planes flew out of Hamburg, Germany. He wanted to impress me with his genius in planning and conducting his supporting role for the airlift. After looking at the organization at each airport, he took me to his house where I met his wife and had dinner. This would be the last time that he would treat me like a guest.

Sometime later he told Captain Walker who commanded the company where I was temporally assigned, "That damn White thinks he has it made because I drove him in my Chrysler to see my operation at Wiesbaden and Frankfurt and to my house for dinner. He'd better watch his step because I will mess him up. He did make a good impression with my wife, however." Later he told me, "You are on a three-years' probation because of your federal appointment. You better be careful because I will mess you up." I knew he was that kind of man if I played into his hands. I did have an ace in the hole in that I was under Captain Walker who would make out my efficiency report, and not him. I did not tell him that, of course. His threats were not as direct as he wanted me to believe.

My main function was operations officer at the airport when the 67th Transportation Company was working. Every day the 67th supplied 40 heavy trucks, which were used for work at one of the two airports for 12 hours. This meant the truck drivers worked 14 hours per day, seven days per week. Twelve hours working on the airlift and one hour each way driving to and returning from the airports was the daily routine for our drivers.

I was given other duties in addition to that of operations officer. One of those duties was that of a prosecutor or trial council for the Battalion Special Court Martial Board. This was my first job as a member of a military court martial board and as a prosecutor. I conducted a very complicated court case in which a sergeant sold one of the five-ton trucks with two ten-ton trailers full of supplies on the black market. This sergeant, who had returned to the United States, was arrested and brought back to Germany as a prisoner on a ship. I had to investigate the crime, develop the charges, and prosecute the case. The only court cases that I had seen were in the movies. Major Sorrell would become my friend and coach, recognizing the assignment as one of the monkey wrenches that Colonel Chase would throw at me. The Major schooled me in all the things I needed to know and do. The first step was to conduct the investigation, which became very useful during the conduct of the trial. The procedures of the trial were outlined in the court martial manual, which I memorized. I even wrote the scenario of the court case and rehearsed it until I knew every detail of the trial and how to conduct it. Everything went off without a hitch. I got no reaction from the Colonel.

He and I did not make it as summary court officers. Every Saturday he had between five and ten men up for summary court trial. He called his court officers in and told each one how much of a sentence to give soldiers being tried. This did not go off with me too well, because I gave the men that I tried the sentence they deserved and not the one the battalion commander said I should give them. He never called me in about it, but he put me on one of his summary court officers' list. This was illegal, which I could not be commanded to do.

I had my connection and protection against him, if necessary. One, I was on temporary duty controlled by a Colonel Ray who was the advisor on Negro Military Affairs to the Commanding General for U.S. Army Europe. He did not like Colonel Chase very much, because Chase was trying to undermine him with the top brass in Germany. If he did something incorrect to me, I could take it to Colonel Ray and ask him to take me off temporary duty and away from his command.

As a regular Army officer, I could not afford to allow myself to be subjected to unscrupulous dealings. I liked living in Frankfurt, and I did not want to leave unless it was absolutely necessary. Therefore I was managing to stay clear of Colonel Chase and to have as few dealings with him as possible.

After about a month my company left Frankfurt and moved to a suburb of either Wiesbaden or Mainz, called Mainz-Kastel. It rested on the west side of the Rhein and north of the Main Rivers. There we had a nice stone building that supported two heavy truck companies. This area was under the control of the United States Air Force located in Wiesbaden. Captain Walker asked me develop a club for the men of the two companies. Because we were supporting the airlift, the Air Force gave us everything we needed. I was able to put the club about 100 yards from the men's barracks, which met all their social needs. This was especially good because our truck drivers had only ten hours for themselves after working fourteen hours.

Girls! Girls! They were everywhere. Every afternoon about 1600 train loads of German girls arriving from Frankfurt lined up at the front gates to be picked up by their boyfriends and taken to the new club I had arranged. This club was good for the soldier's morale and contributed to the efficiency with which we operated at the air bases. During this time in Germany, there were about eight girls to every man, which meant that there was no shortage of women, thereby causing so many girls showing up every day. The soldiers were not complaining because of the nice club to which they could take their guests.

I had a little "run in" with Colonel Chase at the Rhein-Main Air Base at Frankfurt. He found the men on the waiting line sleeping. He came to me asking why. I said because I told them to sleep while they wait for the airplanes to become available for loading. Our men work fourteen hours per day, with ten hours for bathing, eating, recreation, and sleeping. Sometimes they wait long periods of time before they are required to take their supplies to the airplane for loading. Another reason, sleepy soldiers cause accidents and may even damage one of the airplanes. If one of our drivers backs into one those planes and damages it due to fatigue, we would have lots of explaining to do. He overruled me demanding that the soldiers not sleep in the trucks, even though an Air Force loading sergeant goes to each truck and drives it to the airplane when required.

Later, there was an accident; and I had to investigate it. I found the soldier not at fault due to being fatigued. After that, I had no more trouble with the Colonel about men sleeping in the trucks.

I was still in love with Lolla, my girlfriend back home, and was working hard to prevent the German girls from getting between us. The first girl whom I met in Frankfurt was visiting the home of one of the officers who lived near me. This was a very beautiful and intelligent German girl who had an African father. She was considering herself to be the perfect mate for me. When I told her about my girlfriend back home, she just could not accept that. I did flirt around with her a bit before she finally gave up.

I liked dancing and was happy to go dancing at the best nightclubs in Frankfurt. Lieutenant Lyles, a black officer who was pretty ugly, had one of the most beautiful lady friends that I had ever seen. If I had been free, I think I would have tried to get her. I went out dancing with her and the Lieutenant to nightclubs. Even though I wished that she were mine, I never responded to her flirtations when we happened to be alone in the officers' barracks. We continued to go to the best nightclubs together in Frankfurt. Because she was always the most beautiful one among the many beauties, I had no problems getting dances with the girls that I admired.

I was verbally engaged and thus was not a candidate for serious relationships; I limited my activities with girls. As I became more suspicious that my girl back home was not living up to her promises, I began to loosen up with other girls when I found the right one. I was a little patient at first with Lolla because she was in college and was a serious student. But it did appear to me that she could have done better. I called and wrote her about it, but nothing changed. My Mother wrote me that she was playing around (according to a neighbor boy who was a student at Talladega). When she failed to send me a Christmas greeting or present, I quit her. I knew the boy she was dating and would have said nothing about it under normal circumstances, but this was not normal circumstances to me because she was supposed to belong to me. I was not going to break with her because of what my mother said. But when I received her Christmas present in February, sent by her mother instead of her, this was just too much for me to take.

I told her, however, that I would return to the United States in Christmas 1949 as I had promised before leaving for Germany. If we decided to renew our relationship, we could start over again. Her mother did not appreciate the fact that we had broken up and that she was dating this white boy. She pulled her out of Talladega and brought her back to Tuskegee and enrolled her there.

When I broke up with Lolla, I was still in Frankfurt working for Colonel Hymann Y. Chase on the Air Lift. For no reason at all, I think, he would have been very happy to give me an impossible mission thinking I could not accomplish it. He just liked to destroy people, or make them think so. I think it was a little of both. He gave me the job of rehabilitating ten of the worst soldiers in the twelve truck companies supporting the Berlin Air Lift. Many had been rounded-up from AWOL and desertion status. Some came out of jail. During this time soldiers could take off with their German girlfriends and live a whole month on a cartoon of cigarettes. I was given a cool, damp attic floor for living quarters for my rehabilitates. How was I to do it? I did not know because I had never been trained for this type of work nor had I had any experience at it.

Confucius said, "A journey of a thousand miles began with the first step." My first step, I knew what to do. That was to explain my mission to them. I said, "They said to me that you are the worst ten soldiers in your company and that it is my job to rehabilitate you. I will do my best to do that. I do not want to know what you did, and I do not want you to tell me. Your life starts anew today. If you do a good job, you can make the Army a profitable and rewarding career. If you do not, out you go. I promise to do my best to make you good soldiers. We are going to take this damp, cool, and dingy place and make it into the best possible place to live. We are going to arrange our clothing into perfect order. Our bathroom is going to be clean and free of odor. We are going to be an example for all the other soldiers at this installation. We are going to start by arranging your clothing in your footlockers the best way you know how. I am going to inspect them. We can determine the best one, which will be sketched on a stencil, printed, and glued to the top of your locker as the standards which we will follow."

I set up a six-week training program during which four hours were devoted to civilian subjects and four to military subjects. Since I had a free hand to do it my way, this is the way I wanted it done. I felt that soldiers with a good civilian education would make better soldiers. Military subjects become boring to the soldier with the feeling that they are not doing anything for themselves. The Army was already setting up the United States Armed Forces Institute to help soldiers with their high school and college education. I was already enrolled in a course in German and music, learning to play the piano. In our civilian program, we dealt mostly with English and mathematics. My assistant, a lieutenant, had a degree in English. I taught mathematics. In our English classes the soldiers were helped in writing letters to their parents, girlfriends, or anyone else whom they chose to write. In our military class we conducted drills, correct dress, discipline, good behavior, first aid, sanitation, and basic subjects which could be correctly taught in the classroom, in the barracks, or on the parade grounds.

In rehabilitating the soldiers, I also realized that many of them had been driven into bad behaviors not only by the temptation about the shortage of men, eight girls to every man, but also by poor military leadership (non-commissioned officers who were not trained leaders and were also poorly educated). They set bad examples for the soldiers. Soldiers were often harassed and abused because many leaders thought that was the way to go. Many leaders played favors. Their problems had their roots in the military and civilian environment. None of these things existed in our training program. I kept my promise to do my best in developing these men to become assets to themselves and the Army. When the program was completed in six weeks, each of the 81 men received a rating of excellent. .

I often learned a great deal from the men that I led. By having good intentions and doing what I knew, I always found my answers. A person has to be humble, realizing that he does not know it all; and he can learn something from everyone. Answers often come from unknown sources and maybe they come from God. Teaching these soldiers English and mathematics in the morning and basic military subjects in the afternoon captured their interests, and they tried very hard to do the things that we required of them. Not one infraction occurred within this group. Each of the 81 men received an excellent rating. Colonel Chase told everyone that his idea for rehabilitating those soldiers was a good idea of his that worked. He never said one word to me about it. I said to myself, "He won't be able to get me for this one either." It started out with all those bad boys, but ended up with all those good soldiers. I did not have one infraction. I had given those soldiers their spirit back. They all received excellent ratings. I believe in doing unto others as I would have them do unto me.

Colonel Chase was one who did not give up. He wanted to make me company commander of one of the truck companies which continued to provide unsatisfactory performance on the Berlin Air Lift, providing six to eight trucks per day when it was supposed to provide forty. He showed me one of his letters of destruction, which he wrote concerning the white company commander (written by Major Sorrell who had a master's degree in English). He said to me, "That letter is written in perfect English." His great delight was writing those letters of destruction. He wrote most of them against black officers. To do it against white officers, he had to have overwhelming evidence against them so that his white superiors wouldn't get upset. Destruction of black officers is all right, but go careful on white officers. We were told that Colonel Chase went to Frankfurt Post Headquarters and said to BG Duff (Brigadier General), "Sir! Let me handle the niggers." The General would say, "Handle it your way, Colonel Chase. I know you can do it." He had a way of finding out everything that was going on. I never characterized him as an Uncle Tom but as a brilliant person who wanted all the credit for himself and did not much care about whom he hurt in the process.

My best characterization of Colonel Chase would be that of a foreman over black slaves chosen by his master for great leadership in the mold of the slave owner. He would give him complete freedom to handle the slaves because he knew how to handle them in a manner that would be pleasing to the owners. He would periodically brutalize some of the slaves because his master felt this was necessary to insure discipline. The Colonel was well liked by General Hubner and General Clay, who was the supreme commander in Europe. One from Kentucky and one from Georgia, each believed in plantation type leadership when dealing with black soldiers.

Colonel Chase's last shot at me was to make me company commander of one of those dilapidated truck companies, which was doing less than twenty percent of its mission. Should I take this company, he would no longer be my endorsing officer. He would become my rating officer, pretty close to where I could be a target for his destruction. Major Sorrell, Captain Walker, and all my friends advised me to leave Frankfurt. They felt that Chase would give me that company and do all in his power to guarantee my failure. I believed them. I called Colonel Ray in Heidelberg, who wanted me for his assistant at U.S. Army Headquarters, but he could not get the authorization approved. I requested that my temporary duty status be terminated and the reason for it. He invited me to come to his office to talk about it. Colonel Chase was trying to undermine his authority with the top commanders in Germany. I went there and told him about things he had done and what I had done. I was advised by everyone not to stay there under Chase's command. Colonel Ray was on my side, terminating my temporary extension and sending me to Kitzingen Training Center, 22 kilometers from Wuerzberg and about 80 kilometers from Nuernberg, Germany. All of these places were on Highway 8. Kitzingen and Wuerzburg were on the Main River. All of the places were in northern Bavaria. Frankfurt was about 150 kilometers to the west from Wuerzburg.

Kitzingen Training Center was a former German air base, with a nice long runway and nice stone buildings. The U.S. Army was using it to train black truck units for post-war service in Germany. Soldiers have a tendency to be a little wild and undisciplined following a great victory in a war and when serving as an occupying Army. The wildest people around were the German girls who liked American men, black and white. They had little respect for German and returning German soldiers. There were about eight girls to every man, no private transportation, and not very good jobs. Those that had jobs were not paid very much money. U.S. soldiers had more money than the British and French and were friendlier. Black soldiers were more accustomed to harder times than the white were and were more sympathetic to the plight of the German people. In the snack bar in Kitzingen, I often saw the soldier and his girlfriend gazing in the Sears Roebuck catalogue in the fashion section where the girl picked out the dress or other item that she wanted. The soldiers ordered them. I often thought it was soldiers ordering things for their foreign girlfriends that made Sears and Roebuck the world's biggest department store.

I was reassigned from the 370th Infantry Battalion whose headquarters was located at Kitzingen Training Center to the Training Center itself. I was first assigned as the general subjects instructor. The instruction there was outstanding, requiring one to be an actor to qualify. All the officers there were college graduates and beyond. The commander, Colonel Newton, was not required to teach; but he did it because he liked it, and he set the standard for the teaching quality. I taught three years on ROTC duty, but not at the level required here.

Colonel Newton decided to set up an NCO (non-commissioned officers) school for promising young black soldiers, preparing them to get promoted to the position of sergeant. I was the tactical officer over this school with responsibility for leadership training, housekeeping, and leadership management. All classroom subjects were taught by the training center. It was a little bit like my job in Frankfurt with my rehabilitation unit in housekeeping. Also, it was a little bit like officer candidate training in leadership training. This was down my alley. I was given a nice two-story wing of a large building with a nice attic. Again I turned the students loose to arrange their clothing and clean up their quarters on their own. I looked around, watching each one to see how they did things. I was capitalizing on their knowledge to set up standard operating procedures, learning the procedures from my students. They used shoe wax to shine the floors and brass polish to shine the metal in the bathrooms; and they used the attic to hang their fatigues.

Cigarettes were a semi-legal exchange method for getting things done because no military money or supplies were provided. Each student gave one package of cigarettes per week to pay a German to press his fatigues, because they were required to change dress each day. We had a few cigarettes left over with which we bought paint and had the presser paint the interior of the building. I also used cigarettes to buy wax and brass polish. Through our efforts we made the interior of our building look like it had been renovated. The floors were waxed and all metal in the bathroom and showers looked like new money. The arrangement of the student lockers and clothing left no room for improvements, thus setting standards that the students could follow upon returning to their units.

This school became an outstanding success. It was the only one of its type in the United States Army. All the VIPs coming to Germany--including the Secretary of Defense, Secretary of the Army, and top

Army Generals--came to Kitzingen Training Center and to the NCO School when it began. The Inspector General of The United States Army said, "This is a little West Point."

Major General I. D. White, Commanding General of The United States Constabulary--those units which manned the borders against the Soviet Union, East Germans, Czechoslovakia--and later the Commanding General of The Seventh United States Army, spoke at one of the graduating classes and decided to set up such a school for non-commissioned officers at Munich, Germany, moving later to Bad Folz, Germany. This school became the Seventh Army NCO Academy and the United States Army's most outstanding NCO School. Following this, similar schools were started throughout Germany and later in the United States and around the world. After a year, a regular Army lieutenant who was an instructor took over my job.

I took over command of Headquarters and Headquarters Company, 7871 Training and Education Group, which had failed the Annual Command Inspection. I had to get the company ready for re-inspection in two weeks. I found the company to be in bad shape and everyone had to work day and night, including the weekends, in order to get ready for the next inspection.

The first Saturday after I took command of the company, I issued an order for everyone to report for duty. This was a Saturday when the Training Center's football team had an important game at nearby Wuerzburg. I found myself there alone. All my officers, non-commissioned, took off for the game. The next Monday morning I read the riot act to the officers, non-commissioned officers, and enlisted members of my company. I ended up by firing the executive officer and approving his transfer from the unit. I gave my first sergeant one more chance. We were having midnight curfew, and I noticed that the first sergeant was shacking-up somewhere and was showing up just ten minutes before reveille, which all the men could see. I fired him and got another first sergeant that I hand picked. That Monday evening when everyone was supposed to show up for work, only a part of the men were there. I went to the snack bar (making everyone get up and leave his food), to the gym, service club, library, craft shop, and closed the movies, rounding up everyone and taking them to the company and putting them to work.

This time I said, "Any man who does not show up will be court-martialed; everyone is restricted to the company, included married personnel." This time everybody got the message. They knew I meant business. They worked, worked, and worked doing those things that I required. When the Commanding General showed up for re-inspection, he looked around for about twenty minutes. The inspection ended, and we were given a superior rating. One of my best basketball players, who was not known for being one the best soldiers in the company, came to me and said, "Sir, I don't think we have ever had a superior rating before." Even he had pride!

When I closed down the theater, some of the ladies and wives at the Officers' Club gave me a hard time. They could not figure out what kind of person I was. "My company failed the last command inspection, and I have only two weeks to get ready for the next one. I must do that which I think is necessary to prepare for it. If I don't do it, I am going to be blamed. I am going to do my thing, regardless of the criticism." They had to accept my method because I was going to do it my way. Upon receiving a superior rating, none of the women congratulated me.

In my Headquarters and Headquarters Company, most of my men worked for officers who were Majors, Lieutenant Colonels, and even the Colonel who commanded the center. I required all of my men to soldier regardless of whom they worked for, and I would not hesitate to see whoever was necessary to make sure of it. Every Saturday I taught the information hour--not only the news, but also company policy on discipline, behavior, and justice. I said at one of my meetings, "If any man in this company thinks I have mistreated anyone, you can state your case before the company. I will give him a three-day pass and will apologize to him before the company if it is proven that I am guilty." Some soldier stated, "I think that is a trick." "It's no trick," I said. "The whole company is a witness." One soldier said, "Why did you court-martial Joe Bloe when he missed curfew by only one minute?" "When the MPs caught him, he was going in the wrong direction." I said. Just about everyone in the company laughed. This was again the application of my policy: Do unto others.

There was another case dealing with discipline involving one of my soldiers on whom I received a delinquency report from the military police. In an endorsement to me from my commander, I was instructed to investigate the incident and to report back what action or actions I planned to take. I found that this soldier had gotten into a fight at a gasthaus with three German men in which the soldier used his knife in the fight. I noted that no one was seriously hurt and that the knife used by the soldier was four inches long, not the illegal knife which was six inches long. I was under pressure from the boss to take firm disciplinary action, and I had a responsibility to make sure justice was done. I sought advice from an administrative officer, a warrant officer, W-3, who was pretty smooth about such matters. He read the regulations and said to me, "You are the only man that the soldier can look to for justice." I said to myself, "You are not much help. I already knew that." My conclusion was that the soldier had a right to self-defense. No one was seriously hurt. Three men attacked him, and the knife that he was carrying was not an illegal weapon. He may have prevented himself from being seriously hurt. I decided to take no action.

Colonel Bigelow, the new commander at Kitzingen Training Center, was hand picked by the U.S. Army Europe Commander, General Hubner. He was considered a tough disciplinarian who knew how to handle black troops, a plantation type commander. I was also a plantation sort of guy who could stand up to a plantation type commander when I considered myself to be right. I endorsed his endorsement that I had investigated the case and came to the correct conclusions, which I hand carried to him. I debated with him the reason behind my conclusions. When I saw that he wanted me to retract my views, I said, "Sir, my conscience will not allow me to court-martial this man. You are in the chain of command. If you feel that he should be court-martialed, you should prefer charges against him." He said, "Leave the papers here, and I will look into it." This was the end of it. I was already proven to be a capable commander. He had to support me or fire me. He did support me by dropping the case. Again, this was a case of "Do unto others."

I gave the soldier a long lecture warning him to watch his step and avoid places where he could get into trouble.

In addition to my military duties, I founded and became President of the Tuskegee Club, Europe. Our mission was to provide social communication to graduates, former students, and former faculty members of Tuskegee University. We also sponsored and supported the United Negro College Fund Drive, which was founded by Tuskegee University's President, Doctor Frederick Douglas Patterson. We met monthly at different members' residences in Germany, which not only provided good fellowship between members; but we became acquainted with the different environments in which they lived. In November 1950, Doctor Patterson had a command invitation to visit a military installation on the VIP selected list. Captain Stewart, representing Headquarters, U.S. Army Europe and I met Dr. Patterson in Hamburg, Germany, and took him to the VIP Castle in Krongberg, Germany, just outside of Frankfurt. We took him to Kitzingen Training Center where he visited the military installation there and the Tuskegee Club. We later took him to Heidelberg, Germany, where he met the U.S. Army European Commander. We also took him to Munich, Germany, where he met Brigadier General Bruce Clarke, who commanded the 2d Brigade, a Constabulary Unit that patrolled the borders. He explained his unit mission. He also had the NCO School which I had helped set up there in Munich before it moved to Bad Folz. He showed Doctor Patterson a little bit of the Army's new integration in effect in the school, explaining that it was working fine. The General's home, which was near Watertown, New York, accepted the new integration policy without any reservation. This new move to integrate the Armed Forces was the most pleasing part of Doctor Patterson's trip.

When I came to Kitzingen in the early spring of 1949, Lieutenant Colonel Chase was undergoing an investigation because of his highhanded methods of commanding his unit. I gave Colonel Raye, the advisor of Negro Affairs to the U.S. Army, European Command, the reason I wanted to leave Frankfurt. My reason for wanting to leave triggered the investigation. I did testify at the investigation, telling the investigators what I had told Colonel Raye. Many more people were called also. I went back to check with Captain Walker, my commander there. He told me that he had given me a "7" on my efficiency report, the highest possible numerical rating. He said that Colonel Chase tried to get him to change it, saying that I talked behind his back and said all sorts of thing against him. The Captain knew me better and did not change his report on me, even though Colonel Chase may have given him a lower report because he would not change mine. That was the kind of guy he was. Colonel Chase was found guilty by the investigators. His promotion and his request to have his tour in Germany extended were both withdrawn.

In spite of all of this, Colonel Chase had much support among white Generals. When he went to the United States, Howard University ROTC was on probation. The University was informed that if Chase was accepted as the Professor over the ROTC, it would be able to keep its ROTC and the probation would be removed. The University President bit his tongue and accepted Chase as the ROTC director. The whole time that I worked for the 24th Transportation Battalion, I got the impression that Colonel Chase was trying to put the whammy on me; but in the end, in order to avoid his whammy, I was able to put the whammy on him.

Lolla and I broke up early in 1949. I was therefore morally free to look around. My high standards for beauty and quality made finding the women I wanted extremely difficult. Another quality I possessed was not to misuse or abuse women, because I never wanted anyone to use or abuse any of my five sisters, my relatives, or my friends. My conscience required me to do unto others as I would have them to do unto me. That was a little bit hard to do in Germany with so many women coming after me. I knew that if I married to a German girl, my career in the military would fall apart sometime later. If I sacrificed my career for a white wife, she would have to be worth it. I felt a little indebted also to U.S. women, which prevented me from getting too serious with European women.

One day a lieutenant friend of mine was traveling with me in my Pontiac from Kitzingen to Frankfurt. Just outside of Kitzingen we were flagged down by a young lady, which was done quite often by men and women during this period when almost no German cars were seen on the streets. Hitler took most of the personal cars. Some people buried their cars. Hitchhiking was the rule, not the exception. This young lady was very pretty. She said, "I am Princess Blank (name protection). My friend just passed here on a motorcycle; please catch him for me." At first I thought her name was Princess. Therefore I said, "Hi, Princess." She said, "I am Princess Blank." I could see that we had a real princess on our hands, and I was not going to try to catch her friend. I had a flat spare tire and there was an American service station a few miles down the road. I stopped there and got the tire fixed. By this time we were sure that her friend had gotten lost. She told us she was from Heidelberg, which was not too much out of the way en route to Frankfurt, where we were going. We took the high road around the Wuerzburg Castle and her friend took the low road; where they converged; we met. I thought fast, saying, "Tell your friend to leave his motorcycle here and we will drive both of you to Heidelberg." She convinced him to do so when I told her that I would return to Heidelberg to pick him up and take him back to his motorcycle at the time he wished to return. That did it.

We drove along the Nectar River valley to University City where they lived. We were served some cookies and I danced with the princess by her cranked-up record player. Then the lieutenant and I took off for Frankfurt. We talked a lot about what we hoped our new contact would do for us in the social arena.

That next Tuesday was some kind of an American holiday, the day I had to go back to Heidelberg to pick up the friend of the princess. My lieutenant friend was the assistant PIO, public information officer. On this day some Norwegian officers came to visit our area in connection with the establishment of NATO. My friend got tied up because his boss was away, which required him to stay at home to cover this newsworthy event. I took off without him to pick up the Princess's friend, the doctor.

I went there, picked him up, and drove him to where his motorcycle was left. Before we left Heidelberg, the doctor said he had a dog, which he wished could be brought to his home. I said, "I am free on Thursday, and I can pick the dog up and drive him here." This I did. The Princess said when I brought her the dog, "If it wasn't an imposition, I would like to drive with you to see my friend." This caught me by surprise as I was not expecting it, but I saw something in her remarks as if she was coming after me. The temptation was too much for me to push aside. So I said to her, "It is not an imposition. I can take you to see your friend." She conferred with her maid, packed up a few items, and got into my car. I decided to take the long way along the Main River valley and through the Spessarts Forest. We stopped at the snack bar on the Autobahn between Heidelberg and Frankfurt, and then turned northeast toward Aschaffenburg.

She said, "I would like to drive your car." I let her put her hands on the stirring wheel so she could control the car. After we passed through Aschaffenburg, I put her under the wheel. Accidentally, on purpose, I placed my arms around her and then apologized. She said, "I don't mind." I took control of the car and continued through the forest. In the middle of the forest, I took one of the forest roads to the right where I parked my car some distance from the main highway. Some MPs from the Big Red One, 1st U.S. Infantry Division, known to be the big rednecks, followed me. I had my uniform on with my captain's bars. I asked them why they were following me? They gave a sharp salute and got out of there. Now, the Princess belonged to me or I belonged to her.

We finally reached her boyfriend who had called about the dog, and the maid told him that I was bringing her to him. When it took us so long to get there, he was a little suspicious. We had our alibi made up that I went by Frankfurt to see my girlfriend on the way there. He probably would not believe us, but he could not prove otherwise. She was there two or three days, at which time I time picked her up so that she could hitchhike back to Heidelberg. When I picked her up after duty hours in the evening, her boyfriend wanted to follow us to see where she was staying; but his motorcycle would not start. So he had to take my word, when I stated that she would be staying with one of my married friends. Instead, I took her to my quarters.

Early the next morning, I took her to the highway on the north side of Wuerzburg where she could catch a ride directly to Heidelberg. The next time she came there, the motorcycle did work. He followed us on his motorcycle to Kitzingen. A lieutenant and his wife in my company lived on the highway to Wuerzburg. I asked his wife if the Princess could spend the night. They were happy to have her and got me off the hook; and it made her boyfriend feel a little better. Maybe he would think she stayed there the last time.

One Saturday evening they decided to give a party for me at their home. I was not in much of a mood for a party, and I called to back out of it. The Princess said, "No, this party is for you." We had princesses, princes, dukes, counts, barons from the Black Forest and France. I took off for this grand royal affair where I was the featured guest. The doctor was a little suspicious of me, and he began eyeing a younger blonde. This kind of gave the Princess and me a little breathing room. When the doctor was there, I stayed in the guest room. I always signed the guest book whenever I visited the house, whether he was there or not. I began to think the Princess wanted to hook me, and I did not quite know the way out. Her boyfriend was beginning to look elsewhere, and she began to look toward me. Even though she was royalty, her royal riches had not been returned to her, but it would be. I did not want to give up my career in the military and be at the mercy of the Princess, although I felt that she loved me a lot. She was pretty and famous, but I was trying to find a way out.

Later, I was at umpire school getting ready for maneuvers at Oberammergau, Germany, in the Southern Alps of Bavaria, when an MP came to my quarters. "Captain White," he said, "a Princess is at the gate for you." I went out there, and there she was. She said, "I was on my way to my friend's, but I wanted to see you first." I took her to Garmisch, where I had to find a hotel with a side entrance because she was so well known. I found one and sneaked her into the side door where she stayed two nights. The first morning she wanted to go to the "Passion Play," which is put on every ten years. I said to her that she couldn't attend without a reservation. Americans need three months and Germans need six months. "Just take me there," she said. She walked in there and told the people who she was. The receiver stepped aside, and she walked in. "I told you that I could go to the Passion Play." She made a believer out of me. After the second day she headed to visit her friend.

In December 1949, I kept my promise to visit Lolla Patterson by returning to the United States for the Christmas and New Year's holidays. I made this promise before I left the States in September 1948, and I told her I would keep my promise to return after we broke up the previous February. When I found that she was no longer at Talladega, but was enrolled at Tuskegee, I was surprised. Because she was dating the

President's son at Talladega who was white, her mother brought her home for that and perhaps because she had caused our relationship to deteriorate. My old girlfriend was still upset about what had happened to her, and maybe she blamed me also. I was surprised at what happened and assured her that I played no part in her removal from Talladega and that I had returned to keep the promises that I made to her. Even when I showed her the 3/4-carat diamond engagement ring, she showed no interest at reconciliation. I tried to use all the influence at my disposal to get her to change her mind. Her lawyer brother talked to her; her mother, aunt, father, and powerful friends, all tried to persuade her that she was making a big mistake. She held on to her stubborn views. "This is the real end," I said to her. "I will make no further effort to renew our relationship. If you choose to do so, you better do so before I return to the United States. If you do not do that, I will not renew our relationship under any circumstances."

I was happy to be home with my mother, brothers and sisters, aunts, cousins, and friends. They were all happy to see me and to wish me the best during the rest of my overseas assignment.

I returned to Kitzingen Training Center without a bride. Everyone began to suspect that I just wanted to go home and did not plan to get married in the first place. I would have married her and brought her back to Germany had she agreed to it. Leaving from Germany for the United States during this time was normally not granted, except for matrimonial purposes. Maybe the undercurrent was that I had pulled a slick deal. My intentions were good, but it took two to tango.

Before and after my trip to the States, I traveled extensively in Europe. My first leave was to Luxembourg, Belgium, Holland, England and France. This was lots of traveling for fifteen days' leave. I first drove to Luxembourg where I spent a couple nights at one of the best hotels. There I toured around the capitol city with my Pontiac and visited restaurants and nightclubs where I went dancing. I had become an accomplished dancer, putting on a floorshow, especially with rock-and-roll dances. An Englishman said to me there, "If I could dance like you, I could make a better living." I traveled through Bastion where the Battle of the Bulge was fought, through Liege, Belgium, and to Brussels, Belgium.

I was told that Americans were well received there. In Brussels, I stayed at Hotel Metro Pole, one of the biggest and nicest ones. I danced there too and enjoyed it as I had in Luxembourg. The next morning, Sunday, I saw a pretty young lady giving me a look as she went into a tourist office to sign up for a bus tour to Holland. I decided to sign up also. During the trip, she sat at one end of the bus, and I sat at the other. We kept glancing at each other as we moved deeper and deeper into Holland. I knew that it was just a matter of time before we came together, language barrier or not. About midway through the tour we managed to sit together at one of the tables where we did a little eating and drinking. From then on, it was a little lovey-dovey. We became quite close as we drove around many points of interest such as Brogue, Waterloo. I drove down the coast of Belgium where I left my car and took a ferry and train to a London hotel, where I had a reservation.

My trip in London was educational, where I took a lot of tours around the city and took lots of photo shots. I visited Buckingham Palace, where I watched the changing of the guards. I did no clubbing or dancing there. I was saving that for Paris. After two or three days, I crossed the channel the way I came, picked up my car, and drove to Paris.

In Paris, I saw a policeman talking to a lady. I asked him the location of the Grand Hotel. The lady interrupted, saying that she had a grand hotel. This ended my search for the night. The next day I went down where I found another hotel where I stayed for several days. There I met a North African who lived in Paris and was somewhat acquainted with American ways. He volunteered his services to show me around. He became my chauffeur, showing me the famous places in and around Paris, arranging my dates and showing me various places of entertainment. I stayed as long as my money allowed. He also took me to the palace at Versailles. I promised my new girlfriend in Brussels that I would stop by and spend my last few days of leave visiting her.

Because I was a little short of money, she helped foot the bills. We became pretty close. I came to see her several times later on three-day passes. She got a little angry when I stopped visiting her at a later period in our relationship. Because I did not have any plans to marry her, I did not want to be using her. Therefore, I concluded my visits. This was before the Princess.

My next big vacation was in 1950, when I visited Vienna and Rome. I stayed several days in Vienna where I did some clubbing, dancing, and golfing. The social life was good, but not too exciting. I did enjoy playing golf and observing the horse races on the track, which bordered on the golf course. At the end of my visit there, I traveled to Innsbruck, Brenner Pass to Bolzono where I met a young lady who took me to a very nice Italian club in the mountains where I saw some of the most beautiful women I had ever seen. I only wished that I had found the place alone, but I was stuck with the girl I had. She was nice to me, but I was more interested in those girls at that club.

My next stop was at Genoa, the World War II final objective of my division, the Buffalo Division. Because I was wounded on the first day of the campaign during which this city was taken, I wanted to visit it. My hotel was one of the tallest buildings in the city. There were a few young Nazis trying to go to Argentina and were enjoying looking at the beautiful Italian girls as I was. My final and most important objective was Rome where I had been twice on R&R during the war.

This time I did not stay at the Excelsior Hotel, but at another one across the street from it. Down the street, not so far from the hotel where I was staying, I visited a cellar club, which was there during the war. I went to take a look to see if it was still there. It was, and I found it filled with beautiful girls, dancing and waiting to dance. There was no imported U.S. racism like I found there during the war. They were so pretty that I could not make up my mind which one to ask for a dance. I danced with number one, and I saw another girl who I named number two. I went to her. Then I went to number three and number four. When I asked number five for a dance, she said, "Why are you going from one girl to another one?" "I am only trying to find the right one," I said. "I have found her. She is you." She became my date during my stay in Rome.

She was traveling with her sister who was in an entertainment company, performing at Europe's biggest clubs including North Africa. She spoke good English and knew some Americans. A man in this company became my chauffeur and drove my date and me in and around Rome. At nights, I went to where her sister and her company were performing which was at the best and biggest nightclubs in the Holy City. Every night we went there. Several Hollywood movie stars were there that my date knew. The music and dancing there was the best that I had experienced in Europe, including the Cassa Carioca at Garmisch, Germany. At this club, there were pretty girls working there to provide dance partners for guests.

Before I left Rome, my date and her girlfriend gave me the name of a girlfriend who lived in Genoa. They gave me the address where she worked and said I should contact her. I took the name, but I had no intention of visiting the girl at the address that they gave me. But, when I found things in Genoa were not quite like Rome and if was a little harder to find someone to go out with, I decided to contact the girl. I contacted the headwaiter at the place where she worked and told him that I wished to talk to her. I noticed an elderly white couple that I took to be Americans who seemed to have been a little concerned about me being there with their faces turning a little red. I could see that they were a little racist, but that didn't disturb me. The waiter returned, asking me if I was looking for someone to go to bed with. I said, "No, I want someone to go out dancing with me." He returned and a very pretty girl came to me and said, "Lets go." I took another look at the elderly couple when I walked out with this very beautiful girl. They were looking as if they were saying, "I wish we had him back in Mississippi."

We went to the roof club at the high-rise hotel where I was staying. This girl was a super dancer and entertainer, who made my evening most enjoyable. She was very a nice young lady who limited her activity as my date and dance partner. She gave me her address and invited me to visit her, should I return to Genoa again. It was my intention to do just that, because she required a little more investigation by me because I saw some matrimonial qualities in her. I wrote her and she wrote me, extending further an invitation to come to Genoa as her guest; but I was unable to do so because I had to return to the United States to attend a required career officer course at Fort Benning, Georgia.

I also had the opportunity to visit Amsterdam in the Netherlands; Hamburg, Germany; and Copenhagen, Denmark. Of all these places, I liked Rome best. I had not been to Berlin. I spent my first six months in Germany feeding and taking care of the people in Berlin, and I felt that I owed it a visit to in order to satisfy my self-interest.

In the fall of 1950, I bought a car, a 1950 Buick Special, dynaflow automatic transmission, four-door sedan. It was light blue, one of the most beautiful cars that I had ever seen. The Princess fell in love with it. Shortly after I bought the car, Kitzingen Training Center was closing due to pending integration of U.S. Armed Forces. My new assignment would be with the 370th Armored Infantry Battalion, the original unit to which I was assigned when I went on temporary duty on the Berlin Air Lift. But I did not serve with this battalion when my temporary duty status ended. I was transferred to the Training Center. Previously, the 370th Infantry was a regiment of the 92d Infantry Division in Italy, and I was a member of its spearhead unit during the final campaign that ended the war there. I was wounded in that campaign as a member of this regiment. During the post-war period, this regiment was reorganized and became the 370th Armored Infantry Battalion.

It was a great honor for me to return to the 370th Infantry, even though it had been down graded to a battalion. I was assigned as the S-3 of this unit, which was a part of the 2nd Brigade, a unit of the U.S. Constabulary, which patrolled the eastern borders against Czechoslovakia. Although my battalion did not perform border duties, it did train with the armored cavalry regiment that did. My duty with the battalion headquarters was in Munich, Germany. I was given nice quarters in Schwabing, the area where the University of Munich is located. This reassignment helped to make my duties most enjoyable. When I went to this Bavarian capitol city, I had already been in Germany two and a half years. The Department of the Army sent me a letter asking me if I were available to attend the advance officers' course at Fort Benning, Georgia. I informed it that I was not because of my important job as S-3 of the battalion.

After I informed the Army that I would not be available to attend this course, I took leave to Berlin, Germany. I went by Heidelberg to see the Princess and inform her of my leave to Berlin. She wanted to go with me and asked me to wait for her to get the necessary papers that would allow her to go. Even though I did not want to take her, I could not say no. I said that she had to be ready to go by a certain time, or I would have to go without her because it was necessary for me to be at Himstedt, Germany, where the Soviet checkpoint was located in order for them to clear the way for me to travel through the Soviet Zone to West Berlin. She did not get back in time. Therefore, I took off without her. I was there about ten days learning about the city, going through Check Point Charlie on a tour to the Soviet Memorial. I was able to visit some officer friends there who showed me around, making my visit pleasant and educational.

Upon completion of this, my last vacation, I headed back to Heidelberg to see the Princess. She was hopping mad with me, because she returned with all the necessary papers to travel with me ten minutes after I left. My apologies were not lightly accepted. After we had lunch and a little time together, she came around. She said, "I have permission to visit Bavaria for a six months' period." I expressed my delight to her about that, but I did not mean it. She had designs on me, and I did not know how I was going to wiggle out of it. I returned to Munich to worry about this pressure situation. When I got there, I had orders to return to the United States to attend the advanced infantry officers' course at Fort Benning, Georgia.

Major Freddie Davis, who had finished the previous such course there, became my replacement. I had one delight. I would escape the Princess's charge. On my way to Bremerhaven, I stopped by Heidelberg to give her the bad news, but she was not in. I told the maid about my departure and informed her that I would write the Princess explaining what happened. I did write her, but I got no answer. This was my last contact with her, and I was unable to find her during my next tour of duty to Germany. It was not until 1967, after I retired, that I had knowledge of her whereabouts; but I decided not to visit her again. She had regained her royal status and was one of Germany's richest families.

Chapter 7
INFANTRY SCHOOL AND FORT DIX

I departed Bremerhaven by ship July 1951 for New York City. It was the year 1951 that the Army officially initiated its integration program in Germany, although it went into effect in 1948. The segregated Army in Germany during the past three years did not change. In Frankfurt, I went to a dance at a German club where white Americans were and found everyone quite courteous. Black and white units had their own clubs and areas and had no reason to cause racial friction. In Kitzingen we had one Officers' Club where white officers and their wives sat on one end and black on the other; but we all danced on the floor together. Occasionally, one or two of the white officers would dance with some of the black women. None of the black officers danced with the American white women, but those who had German girlfriends brought them there and danced with them. I cannot recall any racial problems during my two years there. White commanders normally accepted German women who dated black officers. When one or two married officers came there with a German date, everybody looked the other way.

The First Infantry Division, the Big Red One, was often called the big red neck. Black soldiers knew not to visit those areas. I did not experience any situation during my three years there when I saw justification to initiate a racial complaint. My efficiency report by white and black commanders alike were at the highest level. Racism existed, but I did not experience any. I could find it if I went looking for it, because it was there. But for the most part, it was avoided.

On the boat back across the Atlantic, there were two dances scheduled. I wanted to see how integration would work at these two dances. There was no commanding authority that could prevent it, and each person and families were on their own. This was a very delicate situation, which had not been tried before: How would I do it? I knew that I was one of the best when it came to dancing. My first plan was to dance with black women to demonstrate my skill at dancing. There were two German young ladies who were going to the States to get married. I targeted them to be the first white women whom I would ask to dance, then a young American white college student who was with the German girls, then the nicest white who I had observed. It worked. Then I asked the ones whom I thought might say no. They did not. I was really astounded at this relationship. One hundred percent of the white and black women on that boat accepted my invitation to dance with them. In the absence of command pressure, integrated dance would work, making integration a working reality. I always felt that it would be on the dance floor where there would be integration problems. To deny this is to deny the true spirit of integrated armed forces.

Picking up my car after my arrival at New York City, I headed home to Alabama. I had one or two girlfriends to visit, after my return from Italy after World War II. It was too late for Lolla because I told her that she would have to contact me before I returned to the United States if she wanted to renew our relationship. My reason being, she failed the absentee test. A wife in the military must be able to accept her husband being away on assignment, especially in restricted areas during conflicts. Lolla had failed that test as far as I was concerned. I had lost a high percent of interest in reestablishing our relationship. I arrived on the campus at Tuskegee University during my 30 days' leave before reporting for duty at the Infantry School at Fort Benning, Georgia. Lolla came looking for me with her friend who was a member of the faculty at Tuskegee University; she was a student in graduate school there. I thought it was quite strange for her to greet me with her friend, although it was quite all right. Had she came alone, maybe I might have had another point of view, without regard to my "no reconciliation" stand. Maybe, just maybe, I might have turned soft, even against my will. Coming to see me with that friend hardened my resolve even more.

I went to my home at Selma, Alabama. My father had been dead a little over three years. I was determined to modernize my mother's home with hot and cold running water, electricity, water closet, and telephone, and to repair and enlarge the house. I could make the necessary loan, payable within two years, to get all this work done. I was also financing my youngest sister's college education. Having a nine-month school assignment at Fort Benning, Georgia, would allow me to visit home every month. My mother would now have a refrigerator instead of an icebox, TV instead of a battery-operated radio. No longer would she have to cut wood for her fireplace to keep her warm during the winters. Now she could wash her clothing with a washing machine, instead of pumped water and the use of a rubbing board. Now the benefits of city life, long denied to her, were all there to make her burdens lighter, one of my lifetime dreams.

At Tuskegee, I had two sisters and a brother. I had already financed my sisters Mabel's college education, and she was now serving as a graduate nurse at the United States Veterans Hospital there. Both my two sisters were living in a house with my brother who was attending Tuskegee under the GI Bill and who was enrolled in the Air Force ROTC Program. My brother was married, and his wife was also a veteran. This meant that I had a family close by, about fifty miles from Fort Benning, Georgia.

My two old golf partners, Doctor Russell Brown and Mike Rabb, were available once again to play as my guests at Fort Benning, Georgia, and at Maxwell Field in Montgomery. Doctor Brown was director of the George Washington Carver Research Foundation and was working with the March of Dimes Polio Foundation to develop the polio vaccine. My old girlfriend Lolla was a graduate student in his department. He was not only interested in playing golf with me, but he was also interested in Lolla and I getting together again. There were lots of undercurrents around there to get that old romance recharged.

I knew most of the members of the ROTC Staff at Tuskegee. One Captain and his wife were members of the Officers' Club at Kitzingen, Captain and Mrs. Allen. He was a big poker player. Every week after bingo at Kitzingen, there was a dance. I kept the wives busy dancing while their husbands were playing poker, including Mrs. Allen. An Air Force Major with ROTC and his wife were also good friends of mine. His wife was the Secretary to Dr. Patterson, the President of Tuskegee University. I was able to walk into the President's office to see him whenever I was on campus. The Major's wife and Captain Allen's wife and Lolla were in the same sorority. Lolla was using them to renew our relationship. I was not giving in.

I spent one weekend at Doctor Brown's house as a guest. The Sunday morning while I was there, I called Lolla's house and reached her mother. When I asked to speak to Lolla, her mother said she was asleep and that I should call later. I never did. This was the end. I never tried again to get our relationship going. It was forever finished.

While I was at Fort Benning, I dated one or two students on the campus at Tuskegee, some school teachers who attended the University, and a local lady in Columbus. Later I dated a student from my hometown and a staff member, both at Alabama State Teachers College at Montgomery. The one that got closest was Jean from my hometown at Selma. Neither one reached marriage level, but I did give some thought to the girl from my hometown. Later she was trying to choose between a local dentist and me. I bowed out of the competition and allowed the doctor to have the upper hand.

The Advanced Officers Course at Fort Benning, Georgia, was required for all regular Army infantry officers. Students in my class ranged from first lieutenant to lieutenant colonels. These courses were designed to teach officers to function at any level within an infantry regiment, including the regimental commander level, who was a full colonel. The course included everything from shooting, map reading, physical training, tactics, and strategy. We played a variety of sports--basketball, touch football, softball, and soccer. Many of us played golf, which I did on weekends and sometimes during the weekdays.

There was a wife of a white sergeant who worked at the bar at the Officers' Golf Club who followed the civil rights movements. Every time I went there she was asking me questions about school integration. These cases were now before the Supreme Court of The United States. She was asking me how did I think it would work out. I told her that I thought that it would work out all right. It had been estimated that about seventy percent of affected people felt that it would be accepted. It would be that 30 percent who would cause all of the trouble. I told her that a secret survey had been made in and around Tuskegee, and it was found that a vast majority of the people thought it would be acceptable.

While I was there, Attorney General Patterson of the State of Alabama, was investigating Tuskegee for Communist activity, which was the racist propaganda line directed at us by whites when black people were trying to get their civil rights. He was targeting Mr. Gomillion, the head of the NAACP there and the leader of the civil rights movements. We worked very closely together when I was a student. I went to Tuskegee to talk him about the investigation. He told me not to get involved in it. I told him that I was not planning to, but I wanted to inform him that the Attorney General was using the investigation to fan the race issue so that he could become the next governor of Alabama. He said he could handle it and that I should not get involved.

Toward the end of our course, representatives from the Pentagon came to Fort Benning to give us our assignments. My assignment was Fort Leonard Wood, Missouri. No one wanted to go there. I had previously requested Fort Dix, New Jersey. When I talked to the assignment representative, I told him that I had asked for Fort Dix. I asked him if there were vacancies there. He said yes. I told him that I wanted to establish my home in that area and that was the reason that I wanted to be assigned there. He said that he would look into it. He kept his promise and reassigned me to Fort Dix, New Jersey.

Fort Dix was the home of the 9th Infantry Division with a mission to conduct basic training for draftees from the northeastern part of the United States. I was assigned to the G-3 Section of the division headquarters. I was made range officer with control over twenty-six live fire ranges. My job was control, construction, maintenance, and safety. Ranges had to be marked off, and in some cases fenced off. Warning signs had to be posted alerting everyone to stay off the ranges unless permission was cleared through my office. This work was very useful for me in a future assignment involving live fire exercises and designing live fire ranges.

All basic training companies were fully integrated. Some of the trainees were not acquainted with being mixed with black soldiers. On one occasion when some new trainees entered the barracks and saw only black soldiers, one said, "Sergeant, where are we going to stay?" The answer was, "You can stay in here or you can pitch tents outside." That just about set the stage for the integrated Army. There were no problems once the new soldiers knew the policy. I had the opportunity to inspect just about all of the basic training companies because I made daily checks on the twenty-six ranges I controlled. Both on duty and in the military clubs, integration was working well.

Integration worked well among regular Army personnel while on duty. At the clubs, blacks danced with blacks and whites danced with whites unless three were integrated marriages. Naturally, if a black man had a white wife, no one could stop him from dancing with his wife. In most cases, integrated couples did not go to the clubs frequently. They were probably concerned about their efficiency reports, especially officers. More integration took place in non-commissioned officers' clubs because efficient reports were not made in enlisted ranks as they were in officer ranks. At the Officers' Club integrated couples kept a low profile.

In my section, I was a member of the bowling league. We had a party with dancing; I asked one of the white ladies whom I knew quite well to dance with me. She declined. I assumed there was a secret policy among whites not to dance with black officers. I did not feel bad about it, because everyone had a right to say yes or no. It just pointed out that integration had its limitations.

At first, I spent lots of time in New York City. Major Sorrell, my battalion executive officer in Frankfurt when I worked on the Berlin Airlift, lived in New York. He gave me a standing invitation to stay at his home whenever I visited the Big Apple. His home was on Sugar Hill in Harlem where most well-to-do black people lived. His wife treated me like a member of the family, and I felt as comfortable there as in my own home. I also stayed at the Theresa Hotel, which during this time was a very nice place to stay. I visited the Apollo Theater where I saw many of the top black musicians and entertainers. During all of my visits to the City, I had only one girlfriend there that I kept seeing for a short time.

Beginning in the middle of the summer, I went to Atlantic City. I slept until 3 a.m. in my quarters at Fort Dix. Then I got up and drove there, where I visited the Harlem Night Club, which was quite famous and had nice shows that were attended by famous people from New York City including Milton Beryl's wife. The audience consisted of as many whites as there were blacks. The bar was likewise. At the bar one could not see daylight until about ten o'clock in the morning, when the curtains were drawn open.

The opening of the curtains announced breakfast time. After breakfast, most everyone went to the beach where they slept in the sand until about four o'clock in the afternoon. Then everyone drifted back, eating something, and started partying all over again. This was before the days of the casinos. I liked old Atlantic City better. The boardwalk was just like Fifth Avenue in Manhattan, the best of everything. The steel pier was one of the most famous sites. Just about everything first class was on the boardwalk.

Many of the people visiting Atlantic City came from Philadelphia. As I began establishing friends in Philadelphia, I rented a penthouse apartment off Broad Street called the Flamingo. It was the first such integrated place in Philadelphia. It was quite famous during that time. My old buddy who was my next bunkmate in Officers' Candidate School lived in Philadelphia. He had left the military and was attending dental school at the University of Pennsylvania. I spent a few weekends with him at his home before I got my apartment. He spent lots of time trying to find me a wife, but all the girls wanted to marry him because they knew he would become a doctor. That did not bother me because the girls he was giving me were not wife material for me. With my penthouse apartment, finding girls became a little easier; but I still did not find a wife.

In July 1952, while I was in my section at the division headquarters at Fort Dix, one of the enlisted clerks there asked me if I wanted to go to Las Vegas to observe an atomic explosion. I was told that it was safe. I agreed to go. We had our own private Air Force passenger plane, which left McGuire Air Force Base, adjacent to Fort Dix, flew to Washington to pick up some passengers, then to Amarillo, Texas, to pick up some passengers from Fort Leavenworth. The next stop was El Paso, Texas, where the passengers wanted to do a little shopping in Mexico, then to Las Vegas, where we ended up at Frenchman's Flat. We had transportation to Las Vegas, where I put five silver dollars in the slot machine. Then I said, "That's my donation to this city." I did not gamble any more.

A master sergeant assigned to Frenchman's Flat loaned me his convertible Oldsmobile while I was there. I used it to drive to the country club to play golf.

At the atomic explosion, our military trainers briefed us on what to expect and the safety features to observe. Before the explosion took place, we got down in our trenches. We felt the earth shaking like Jell-O when the explosion took place. We went a safe distance from where the explosion occurred, observing some of the damages that were caused by it. Afterward, we headed home over the same route we previously traveled.

Professionally, I benefited a great deal from being a range officer. It is on the ranges where the best experiences for combat occurs. Any time training involves live ammunition it's a little bit of combat. The only difference is there is no enemy firing ammunition our way. Throwing hand grenades, crawling under machine gun fire, adjusting mortar and artillery fire are examples. Setting and controlling ranges where this type of firing takes place is an ongoing requirement in military training.

Chapter 8
THE KOREAN WAR

During early spring 1953, I received orders to go to Korea where the war there was still going own. I had over a month of leave and travel time. I wanted to go to Canada and Detroit, where I had never been, and to Chicago where I had been a number of times. Also, I wanted to go home to Alabama where I would leave my car with my mother. Then I planned to fly to Los Angeles, to San Francisco, and to Camp Storneman, California, where I would get orders for travel to Korea. I spent a week in Montreal, Canada, where my friend Vaughters from Philadelphia lined me up with a date that made my stay a little more enjoyable.

One of my girlfriends from Tuskegee invited me to Detroit. I had four first cousins in Detroit whom I wanted to see also. I traveled nonstop from Montreal, leaving about nine o'clock in the morning and arriving in the Motor City the next morning at two o'clock. Even though I had not been there before, I found my cousin's home (where I wished to stay) with very little difficulty. I made all my visits and had a nice time there.

I always stayed with Mrs. Van Zandt whenever I was in Chicago. This time I could tell her about her son who visited me while I was in Germany. She was happy to get the news that he was living in Italy; he did not visit home because he and his mother did not get along well. She was very domineering, and he could not accept it with any grace. I do not believe that I did any dating during this stop in Chicago due to my short visit there.

Leaving Chicago, I headed for my home in Alabama, which took a little over eight hours. I spent ten days or so there in my new room which my mother had built for me during our home renovation. It now had electricity and hot and cold running water. The renovation was one of the great pleasures that I provided for my mother. Now I would leave her my car. I had a good time at home playing golf with my brothers and friends. I visited the Veterans Club, where I met with my old school and community friends, who always made my home visits enjoyable. Completing my vacation, I left Selma for Los Angeles, California.

I stayed at a nice hotel in L.A. and met some interesting people, including a nice girl. I gave some thought about getting married to her. However, there was a small complication; she had a young daughter. That did not bother me too much while I was there, but it did while I was in the Far East. I also had met a girl at Bennett College while traveling from Fort Benning, Georgia, to Fort Dix, New Jersey, a year earlier. She was marriage material for me. She had enrolled in Law School at the University of Iowa. We promised to correspond during my tour in Korea.

I stopped by the Military District Headquarters in Los Angeles to see if I got promoted to major. I had a major friend who was from Los Angeles who was stationed with me in Kitzingen, Germany, in 1951. He looked at his order file, then took his major leaf off his collar and pinned it on mine, congratulating me for being promoted. This would change things for me, because I was on orders to go to Korea as a captain and now I am a major. I decided to let the Army worry about that. I celebrated in L.A. one more night.

I reported to Camp Storeman at the end of my leave. I do not believe they had received word of my promotion. Now instead of flying to Korea, I would go by ship. I spent a few more days in the bay area, but did not have the fun that I had down south because Storeman was a little distance from the bay area and the weather was somewhat uncomfortable during this time. By this time, I think that I was also ready to take it easy.

We sailed to Yokohama, Japan, from Oakland, California. The trip took about fifteen days. We had thirteen dances, plus two days of seasickness. The sea was rough near San Francisco due to undersea mountains, making a high percentage of the passengers seasick. I never got seasick, but it was difficult to avoid it after smelling all of those who were seasick. After two days, it was smooth sailing all the way.

The ship that we sailed on belonged to the U.S. Navy, but the passengers were under the jurisdiction of the senior Army officer on board who was a major. There were only two Army majors on the ship, which made me second in command. Most of the passengers on the ship were women and children of military personnel stationed in Japan and some who had relocated from Korea. There were dances every night. I integrated these dances as I did in 1951 when I traveled from Bremerhaven, Germany, to New York City. The results were the same; everyone whom I asked accepted my dance invitation. As always, I was a gentleman. After fifteen days, we reached our destination. My next stop was Tokyo, Japan, where I remained for about five days.

I went out to one of the Japanese Clubs that American officers frequented. I ran into the same problem I had in Rome during my second R&R during World War II. Because the U.S. Army had political domination over Japan at this time and economic superiority, the white officers pressured the Japanese owners to prevent Japanese girls from accepting invitations from black officers. I did not like that any more than I did in Rome. I wrote a complaint to the Inspector General of the U.S. Central Command. I was told that this was a civilian establishment over which the Army had no control. I planned to tell the IG that it could put the place off limits. I had made my point and decided to drop it, because I would soon be going to Korea. I soon found nicer clubs that were attended by the general public, which were far better than the hillbilly clubs that I complained about.

I left Tokyo for Seoul, South Korea, and was station at Young Dong Po, just outside Seoul. Because I was a major, the Army did not give me an assignment right away, which gave me a little more time to look around this capitol city. I ran into Lieutenant Maxey, a former ROTC student of mine, who was stationed there. He invited me to a party at his house where I met a young Korean college student who worked for the Army's main PX in Seoul. She became my girlfriend during my stay in Korea, even though I did not see her too often because I was soon assigned to a front line unit.

Seoul was as peaceful as Tokyo. There I had nice meals and played a round or two of golf. Because this capitol city was only about fifty miles from the front, the pressure of the war could be felt. I stayed at Yung Dong Po for about three weeks, which pleased me fine. I was just hoping the war would end during my stay there. I was assigned to KMAG (Korean Military Advisory Group), which meant that I would be an advisor in a combat division. I was sent to the 3rd ROK (Republic of Korea) Division. When I joined this unit, it was in reserve and licking its wounds, because it had just got its pants kicked off by the Chinese Communists. I was back there where the big artillery guns were shooting like crazy, supporting the counter offensives pushing the enemy back.

I did some work up there, but not very much. My first job was to make a reconnaissance of the U.S. Corps defensive line, which was about sixteen miles long, and determine if its use would permit our forces to stop the Chinese if it became necessary. I walked this sixteen miles mountain ridge for two days, directing the Korean engineers to give me a study of the minefields and defensive barriers already installed. The mountain barriers were pretty strong in itself, due to the very steep slope that the enemy would have to negotiate should he attack us. But it was made stronger by the minefields that helped prevent surprises and reinforce the defensibility of the mountain ridge. I determined that we had ten to one advantage over the enemy on this mountain ridge and that it should hold when properly defended. I prepared this urgent report quickly, sending it to Eighties Army Headquarters where it was accepted. This line was never used since the Chinese and North Koreans were pushed back to the 38th Parallel where the war ended.

My unit, the 3rd Republic of Korea Infantry Division was already in training, preparing to move back into the front lines if the war had continued. Instead, it moved to a post-war defensive position on the central front north of the Warschon Reservoir, east of the Puchon River, in the area of Christmas Hill and the Punch Bowl. The names were given to the places where big battles were fought. The Punch Bowl looked like a big stadium that could seat ten million or more people. I had to approve many battle plans for the Punch Bowl Area.

My commander was a National Guard colonel who was a postmaster in some Mississippi village. I was a little concerned about my military career, not knowing his racial views. The other officers were all white and drinking buddies of the Colonel and perhaps a little jealous of me because I was the only regular Army officer there. I concentrated on doing my job and helping to make the Korean Army the best that it could be while letting the race issue take care of itself. Whenever the Colonel came in my area, I was in the field with my unit, supervising training, with a plan in my hand showing him what we were doing and what we were trying to accomplish. He never saw me sitting in my hut drinking. The Korean Colonel and General soon began to compliment me on the way in which I was helping their soldiers, giving them confidence in their abilities and the courage to use them. My boss soon begin to appreciate what I was doing and was learning something as well.

During this time, I lived in the Korean Regiment. Soon all advisors were removed from the regiment and consolidated at the division level. Before this reorganization, we had three regimental advisors: G1-G4, G2-G3, a communication advisor and a Division Advisor, who was the Colonel. The G1-G4 Advisor took care of personnel matters, supplies and transportation; G2- took care of matters dealing with enemy information and counter intelligence, G-3 training, combat planning and operations. The G2-G3 was the most important staff position. In this reorganization, I was given the G2-G3 position.

The colonel was pleased with me in my position because his most important work fell under my jurisdiction, and I had already proved to him that I could take care of business in a highly efficient manner. Shortly after the reorganization was completed, we had the mission of working with the Chinese Communist on the removal of dead bodies from the demilitarized zone. This was a personnel matter given to the Korean G-1 and our G1-G4 advisor. Our part of the mission was completely bungled, drawing criticism over the communist propaganda radio. A Korean General was court-martialed, and my boss was in trouble. He asked me to take over the job. I worked with the Korean G2, the most efficient staff officer in the Division, and a little bit with the G3. Working day and night, we pulled off the next operation without a hitch, receiving not one bit of criticism from the enemy. Higher headquarters was pleased, and my boss was happy because I had gotten him off the hook, so to speak. He immediately recommended me for promotion to lieutenant colonel, but it was not allowed because I had been major only about three months. The regulations required majors to be in grade at least six months in order to be eligible for promotion. This looked good on my record, however.

The war was over, and my boss would be leaving soon for the United States. He gave me the highest possible efficiency report, a "7", which was outstanding. Since the fighting was over, permission to exchange prisoners of war was granted and most U.S. divisions could return to the United States. I felt that we should give strong emphasis to unit sports of all types, to keep our soldiers busy with the things they liked. This would keep them strong physically, make them happy, and keep them out of the cities. I got two trucks for collecting sports equipment from the two division in my area, which was leaving for Korea. I returned to my unit where I built a tennis court, a swimming pool, a volleyball court, a basketball goal, and a softball park, all constructed by Korean engineers. I did this for only twenty-two people in our detachment. Our soldiers had high morale due to the provisions that we provided for their welfare. In our Officers' Club dining room facility we had a ping-pong table, which was always in use because Korean senior officers visited us for playing ping-pong, a favorite sport in the Far East. I was invited to play in some high-level Korean military ping-pong tournaments.

Every Thursday afternoon our new colonel gave us a half-day off to watch the softball game. We played against teams that had a population of 200 against our 22. We won most of our games. Previously, I had played every position on a baseball team, with the exception of first base and behind the bat. This time I became the catcher. We had one of the best pitchers on our team, which was one of our secret weapons. I made his job easier by becoming a good catcher. I even had my golf clubs sent over from the States. For my driving range, I used the mountain as a backstop; and my Korean aides picked up the golf balls for me. Play did not stop our work, but we did make good use of our off time. We were still in combat, even though the war had stopped. We still occupied the front line position, continued making our position stronger, and trained the Korean troops in order for them to assume more and more responsibilities.

The Korean Division commander would not accept any combat operation plans without my signature. I was pleased with the expression of confidence that both the Korean commander and my U.S. commander showed in me. Because all of our plans were accepted when reviewed by higher headquarters, I was more acceptable and valuable to my boss. Work was duty and play was duty. Both kept us ready for any kind of emergency.

During the war, the best U.S. officers were assigned to U.S. divisions; these included regular Army career officers, those from West Point, and those with Presidential appointments. When the war ended and emphasis was put on building the Korean Army, the best officers came to KMAG. All of our officers were regular Army officers, majors who were senior to me. I told my boss to give the more senior officers, who were better trained than I, my position. He said that did not make them better, and he wanted me to stay where I was. I think I was more interested in helping the Koreans than the other officers. They worked hard also, but they did not have the fire in them that they would have in a U.S. unit.

Periodically, the Koreans pitched a party in one of the nearby large cities, kind of like a banquet, with plenty of food and drinks. Afterward, everybody had to sing solo. It did not matter how bad we sang. We had to sing, no excuses. This was a must. Each time before one of these events, we began to figure out what songs we would sing. Old McDonald was a good one. Koreans sing and Americans sing. After these parties, dates were lined up for us. There were some who looked down on the Koreans and did not take any dates. There were others who were married and were faithful to their wives. The rest of us accepted the invitations.

I went on my first R&R to Tokyo, some time in the fall of 1953, after the war had been over for several months. I ran into a white Lieutenant Colonel whom I knew from Kitzingen, Germany, about four years earlier. He told me where diplomats got their dates. I was quite pleasantly surprised because white officers did not normally tell black officers where they could fine nice ladies. This was a plus. I called there and made arrangements. The girls were called 'Gicey' girls who were professional entertainers, a tradition in Japan. We went out dancing every night in the Latin Quarters and the best other places in Tokyo. The first night my date dressed in a western dress; the second night, a Chinese dress; and the third night, a Japanese costume. These three days were enjoyable.

Wherever I went, I looked for a woman whom I could marry. Since I was selective, I looked everywhere all the time. I just thought one day I would find one that I could not say "no" to. I figured I had the whole world at my fingertips and that I should take advantage of it. Most of the time when I thought I had found that person, someone else had already taken her. This was the price I had to pay when I went for the best, the most visible best.

I returned to Korea and back to the old grind. About once a month, I went to Seoul where I saw my girlfriend who worked at the PX. For some reason, she was always available. I told one of two of the Koreans officers up at the division about Yu Son He. Then she disappeared for about three months. I did not know what happened. Later, she showed up again. I asked her where had she been during the past three months. She said, "Do you know a Captain Kim?" I said, "Yes". She indicated that he had caused her much trouble. When I went back to the division, I told my interpreters about it. Captain Kim was transferred from the Regiment. He had lost faith. The Koreans did not want us dating their college or university girls. I could understand them not wanting their best girls being loved and left by us.

During the second half of my eighteen-month tour, I was placed on temporary duty at Eighth Army Headquarters in Seoul for the purpose of serving on a board to evaluate the equipment that the Korean Combat Divisions needed for combat. There were three members--the President, the G-1 G-4, and the G-2 G-3. I was the G-2 G-3. There were also advisors that represented the technical equipment branches of the Army. We had to develop a table of equipment, which was needed for the Korean infantry divisions. The board consisted of three members plus supporting members. The President was a colonel from the G3 Department at Army Headquarters. We worked a whole month developing the table of equipment. Some time later, even after I returned to the States, General Taylor received a Congressional Commendation for the money that this reorganization board saved for the United States Government.

During the rest of my tour in Korea, I continued to participate in training exercises of various kinds, keeping the morale of our people high and watching the time roll by. My four efficiency ratings were two 6s and two 7s. I would have gotten three 7s; but one commander dropped it from a 7 to a 6, because I helped a major whom he wanted to sack. He did not like it and he told me about it. I said this is the first time a white man ever asked me for help. I felt obliged to help him. I did. I respected the Colonel's views in the matter, and I believe he respected mine,

I had a little fun on the side, as there were Korean officers whose job it was to take care of our morale. Sometimes there were group parties, and other times it was individual parties. I did date a couple of Seoul University students who worked at the U.S. PX. I visited Tokyo three times where dating was better organized, beautiful girls were easier to find, and more sophisticated places to go were available. I think that Japan was the world's best. One of my Korean girls wanted to marry me, but I decided not to do it. She was a nice girl, but I had not met a girl there whom I wanted to marry. I am sure there were some there, but I did not meet one of them. I felt that it was better to break a few hearts by not getting married than getting married and break the heart of my wife.

I was given an opportunity to go to Japan at the end of my Korean tour. I thought long and hard about it. I felt that if I relocated to Japan that I would end up marrying a Japanese girl. Because I am sure that there were some there that I could not say "no" to, I decided to look for a western girl for a wife, which was the main reason I did not choose to accept a transfer to Japan.

In May 1954, the headline in the Stars and Stripes was that the United States Supreme Court had ruled to desegregate public schools. This was one of the happiest moments in my life. The first one was to integrate the U.S. Armed Forces. I was happy because I felt that I was one of the principals who played a major role in the integration of the forces. Integration of the armed forces was the link that led to the Supreme Court's decision. I talked about this many times with the bar maid at the Golf Club at Fort Benning. I fought for this during World War II. It was my belief that if the Buffalo Division went to combat and fought well, all of this would come to pass. This Supreme Court decision had just about given me the answer to all my prayers, works, and hopes for correcting race problems in the 1960s, which I predicted in 1932 as a ten-year-old.

Equality and an integrated society is what we are supposed to be. So many of our people are not happy unless someone is under their feet and do not seem to be happy unless they are the ones stepping on them. We are all children of God and He is not pleased with so much unnecessary narrow mindedness. The Book of Mark in the Bible, states: "We are all of one blood." Booker T. Washington stated, "You cannot keep a man in the ditch unless you are in it with him."

Chapter 9
ROTC DUTY AND THE CIVIL RIGHTS MOVEMENT

In November 1954, the good Lord had me assigned to ROTC Duty at South Carolina State College in Orangeburg, South Carolina, in a state where the major decision case in the desegregation decision took place.

I returned to the San Francisco by ship from Yokohoma, Japan. This time the sea was calm until we reached the mountains near the west coast of the U.S. This time we had families with husbands returning home. I planned to integrate the dances as I did when I crossed the Atlantic in July 1951, and again across the Pacific in April 1953. It worked. I danced every dance for thirteen nights with no refusals. Not one said no. That meant to me that if there were no consequences from some dictatorial commander when one engaged in integrated dancing, no one seemed to mind. If there was some kind of conspiracy that may hurt a person's career, the person subjected to that conspiracy might refuse to participate in mixed dances. I must admit I was the only one integrating, but everyone seemed to have enjoyed it. I believe it took about fifteen days to sail back to the west coast of the U.S.

We were all happy to see the Golden Gate Bridge again as we sailed under it to the Oakland Harbor for debarkation. There were many happy faces on the ship. Some of the married men saw their wives waiting at the harbor. I spent one or two nights in San Francisco, where I ordered some Japanese food with chop sticks. I went to a club where I saw Louis Armstrong playing. This was a sweet homecoming.

I departed San Francisco for Los Angeles. I looked for the lady whom I had dated there. I was informed that she had moved to Hollywood. I said that she was good enough to be there. I visited a couple that lived in Los Angles who were in Korea as a part of an entertainment group. They invited me to visit them when I returned State side. They gave me a nice welcome at their home.

I left Los Angeles for Atlanta, Georgia, because the smog there hurt my eyes. Upon reaching Atlanta, I went to a clinic at Fort McPherson to get some drops for my eyes. Then I believe I flew to Chicago and on to Cedar Rapids, Iowa. I rented a car and drove to see Barbara Crutchfield, a law student at the University, a good friend, and a possible candidate for marriage. I was not sure that our career fields and interests were mutual, but it was worth looking into. We had a nice friendly get together and we went out a little, but I soon found out that our relationship had no future. Upon finishing law school, she planned to go to Hawaii to teach in the law school there. This visit was more of an inquiry than a commitment. There were no losses and no gains. I believe I saw her later at her home in Virginia, before and after she married. She did not seem as happy after she married as she was before it. She had moved to the mainland where she and her husband practiced law in San Diego, California.

I left Iowa and headed for home through Chicago. I wanted to get my wheels from my mother and spend a little time at home before heading for Orangeburg, South Carolina. My mother was happy as always to see me, as well as my sisters and brothers, friends, and other relatives. Again, I was happy to be in my home with electricity, gas heat, hot and cold running water, refrigerator, electric stove, TV and all the conveniences of the city, a boyhood dream which I had provided for my mother. Now, I am about to provide her with something that I had not even counted on … my car. She had gotten use to it and I did not have the heart to take it. I went to the Chevrolet dealer and looked at the prices of a car that I liked. Then I went to my bank and drew out enough money to pay cash for a new Chevrolet. My Mother was happier and I was little broker.

I knew that I had to stop by Tuskegee on my way to South Carolina to see my two sisters, Mable and Jean. My sister Mable was a graduate nurse working at the VA hospital there, and my sister Jean was a college student. I was planning on stopping at SC State College and then drive to Washington to get my orders changed, because I did not want another ROTC tour. When I got there, I ran into my first commander, Lieutenant Colonel Lofton. He said he needed me very badly as he was short of officers and the program was on its last year of probation. Because I liked him, I decided to cancel the rest of my leave and settle down there for the next three years.

The first problem the colonel talked about was the college losing the ROTC program due to the inability to get interested students to achieve the minimum IQ score of 110. The University must have at least ten students each year for the advanced program, which was the junior year. I had heard lots of theories about IQs that I did not believe, especially when there was a common saying that white people were more intelligent than black people. Northern whites were more intelligent than northern blacks and that southern whites were more intelligent than southern blacks. To me this seemed to be a propaganda theory designed to make black people feel inferior to white or the white people did not know what they talking about.

As a country boy from rural Alabama, I did not believe any of these IQ theories. The items tested on the IQ test were about subjects taught in school, elementary schools, junior high schools, senior high schools and colleges. The subjects were English, mathematics, reading comprehension, vocabulary, and puzzles. An "A" student in the areas would do very well on an IQ test in these subject areas; a "C" student would have more difficulty. If a student had inferior schooling with poorly qualified teachers, as in black southern schools, especially in South Carolina, these students could be expected to do worse than white students in the same subjects in better schools. This was my conclusion about this low IQ business. I recommended that we give our students some reinforced training in these areas.

The University accepted my recommendations, spending some $50,000 buying visual aids to enhance the students' knowledge in the areas of deficiencies pointed out by the IQ tests. I monitored this program during the six months that it was conducted. During the next advanced ROTC IQ qualification test, we produced more students than we needed. It worked, and the University was taken off probation.

I had a better background than most officers in the ROTC program, because I was a ROTC student before coming into the Army and then I had an ROTC assignment from 1945 to 1948. I made it my mission to use my experience to make it the best possible program. It was necessary for me to work late each evening and on weekends to build lesson plan files, which we could continue to improve each year. My first year was all work and little play. I taught military law, military history, and subjects dealing with infantry tactics. My experience was quite adequate in military law and infantry tactics because of my work in military courts and combat.

In military law, I received experience as a self-made prosecutor in the grand larceny case in Frankfurt in 1948. I was also a summary court officer there. I served on the general court martial in the Frankfurt Post during the entire period that I served on the Berlin Airlift. During the next twenty months, I was a member of the special court martial court at Kitzingen, Germany. I conducted Article 32 proceedings in a murder case at Mainz-Castle, Germany, while serving on the Berlin Airlift. The experiences gave me a substantial background for teaching military law. My classes included simulated court martial cases. Upon completion of the course, our students had a good understanding of how military courts work, plus a good knowledge of federal law, upon which the court martial manual was based.

In military tactics and strategy, my knowledge and experience was quite adequate. I taught squad tactics in ROTC. It was expanded to platoon and company size units in basic training and Officers' Candidate School, plus some battalion tactics in Officers' Candidate School. I had nearly six months' war experience in an infantry division, serving in combat in two different infantry regiments, plus getting wounded in action. During my last six months, as the S-3 I was responsible for training, plans, and combat operation, in Munich, Germany, from January to July, 1951.

From August 1951 to April 1952, I was a student in the infantry officers advance course, dealing with all manners of training at the regimental level. In Korea, I was an advisor to a Korean Regimental commander for several months; later I became the G2-G3 advisor at the Division level, dealing with all matters of training, combat planning, and combat operations in a division of more than 20,000.

As executive officer and associate professor of military science and tactics, I was in a position to move full speed ahead in updating the instruction at the university. My boss was a reserve officer who did not know how long he would remain on active duty, which gave me a free hand to run the program. When he wanted something done, he let me handle it. I developed a drill team that put on shows around the campus, which delighted the President of the University. At the end of the year, during our annual inspection, we received a superior rating and so did I from my boss.

During my last ROTC tour of duty at Tuskegee University, I completed my senior year of college, because I was called to active duty at the end of my junior year. Now, because of the work that I did during the year just passed, I found enough time to enroll in the graduate program at the University. I enrolled with a major in education and a minor in social studies with a high percentage of subjects in American history. I took extra subjects dealing with the United States Civil War, which I found to be the most interesting part. My objective was not only to enhance my military career, but also to prepare myself for a civilian career. Most of all, I always wanted to be independent and to make my own decisions. Should I leave the Army before retirement?

Being independent to me is the most important thing in my life. Education is one way to help achieve it, and money is another way. Independence would allow me to make my own decisions, stand up for the right things, and not be pressured or blackmailed to do something that is not right. That was one of the things that I liked about being a farmer, being my own boss, and making my own decisions. In combat, as a platoon leader during World War II, I was my own boss. Because I did my job well, I was never told how to do it. As a result, I won all my conflicts and did not get any of my men killed. I was given a mission, but was never told how to perform it. I made sure that I knew more about my work than anyone else. In this way, I have always been independent

Up to my assignment at South Carolina State University, my life in the Army had been just great. I always did my job and got the best ratings from both black and white superiors. Even in the segregated Army, I had a feeling that somewhere, down the line, things would be different. Education would put me into a better position to deal with problems, whatever they might be. I always followed my conscience, which meant I must continue to have the ability to make decisions based on justice and independence.

I joined the NAACP shortly after I arrived in South Carolina. The United States Supreme Court had ruled during May 1954 to outlaw segregation in public schools. Lots of action was being taken by local whites to go after those who were most active in advancing the causes created by this decision. The Reverend Delaney of Clarenden County, South Carolina, was the principal in the most important case, which helped the federal court to arrive at its decision. He was forced to leave the State because of the threats made against his life. Federal Judge Waites Warren, white, from Charleston, South Carolina, was also forced to leave the State for his safety because he had ruled on the side supporting school desegregation. The NAACP was taking steps to protect the rights of blacks and to advance the cause of the Supreme Court ruling. Both sides were waiting for the court's decree, a judicial order for desegregating public schools.

One of the strategies of those opposing desegregation was to create fear in black people so that they would not petition for integration, regardless of the court's decision. The Supreme Court ruled in May 1955 that desegregation in public schools would proceed with all deliberate speed, meaning right away. In June 1955, I went to ROTC summer camp at Fort Benning, Georgia. When I returned in August, the first move to integrate schools under the Supreme Court order was in Orangeburg County where I was stationed. A petition to integrate the public schools was made by five members of the NAACP. Those whites opposing the petition organized into a group known as the White Citizens Council, with half of the businesses in the City of Orange, S.C., belonging to the Council. This group identified themselves as charter members. One of the banks, which was a charter member, denied services to a teacher who was one of the desegregation petitioners. The Mayor of the City, who had the Coca Cola franchise, refused to deliver the product to one of the "black brothers" who owned an Esso service station. He was also a petitioner. The local Esso distributor refused to deliver petroleum products to his station, but Esso brought in their products from North Carolina, not wanting to get involved in the Civil Rights issue.

The NAACP established a planning committee of five people. The only one that was known by the public was the president, the pastor of the Methodist church there. The other four were top secret. Some people said black people could not keep secrets. No one ever knew who the other four were. I was one of them, and this is probably the first time this has ever been revealed. The planning committee decided what measures would be taken by blacks or what counter measures would be taken against some of the actions of the White Citizens Council. We were always catching them by surprise because we could not be penetrated. The most effective measures were the boycott of the businesses owned by the charter members of the White Citizens Council.

These businesses needed black trade in this black belt county having two black universities. A number of black teachers, living within 100 miles of Orangeburg, lived there, returning home on weekends. Whites could not take economic measures against black teachers, because they wanted to keep black teachers in black schools, thus causing black teachers to be protected by members of the White Citizens Council who were boycotting their business.

There were no wins for the Council. It cried to the State for help. People in the State Assembly stated there were lots of communists down there in the State Teachers' College. The State highway patrol paraded through the campus, and the students went on strike. Life and Look magazines stated that the civil rights movement would be fought out in Orangeburg, S.C. The President of the University called the executive council in to advise him on what moves he should take with respect to the students' strike. The black president, B.C. Turner, was the whites' man in Orangeburg. I did not believe that there was a white man in the whole city who was as white as this African American and his wife with a 100 percent white face. He was not an Uncle Tom, but a traitor to black civil rights issues.

At this meeting, members of the Council were afraid to offer suggestions. My boss, Lieutenant Colonel Lofton, was away on leave; and I had to serve on the executive council in his absence. I was not afraid of the President. Also, he liked me a lot because I had saved his ROTC, which he also liked very much. He and I had helped it to achieve a superior rating during the Army's annual inspection. I had established an honor guard and a girls' drill team. So, at this time, I could do no wrong. I suggested to the President that since the whole thing was caused by the State, let the students express their dissatisfaction and then call them in and tell them you have expressed your dissatisfaction. Now let's call off the strike and go back to class. Everybody agreed that this was a good and workable idea. I had to take the ROTC up to Fort Jackson for a military orientation, when at the same time a newspaper from Charleston came out against the student strike. The President jumped scared and expelled the student leader. When I returned, I got very angry with the President for the double cross. I did not express it to him, however.

The faculty got into the act drawing up a proclamation to the Governor of South Carolina and the State Assembly stating that if they think the faculty is infested with communists at South Carolina State College that it was the duty of the State to close down this institution and enroll its students in the University of South Carolina and Clemson University. This document was signed by all of the faculty members and staff with the exception of the President and members of the ROTC Staff. After this, I did not hear any more comments from the State Government and the State Assembly. They seemed to have drawn the conclusion that the best way to win was to do and say nothing.

In the meantime, the students got restless and angry with the President for championing the cause of the White Citizens Council and working against the civil rights interests of the black people. They began to inflict damages to the building and school property, and there was nothing the Dean of Men could do because the students allied him with the President. The President wanted me to move into the student dormitory because I had their respect, and he figured that I could stop their riotous actions. I refused to get involved because the President had brought it on himself. I did go to him and offer my suggestions as to what action he should take, which I figured would save face on both sides and quell the disturbance. This was now my third year.

After this visit, the President and I became bitter enemies. When I left his office, he seemed to have agreed with me; but he later had second thoughts. Since I was already in my third year, I was ready to leave anyway. I called my friend in the Pentagon and told him that I would like to leave in September 1957. He said it could be done.

Our Civil Rights Movement in Orangeburg had been a great success. Black people who now had the law on their side were not about to let anyone scare them out of their constitutional rights. Whites had lost the battle of fear. Blacks had won the economic pressure battle, causing a national boycott against Coca Cola and thus forcing their stock to drop on the stock exchange. The most important part of this movement was that it inspired duplicate movements elsewhere. After Orangeburg began, it started in Rock Hill, South Carolina, then the walk-ins in Greensboro, North Carolina, and the sit-ins at the Woolworth Department Store. On December 1, 1955, Mrs. Rosa Parks refused to move back in the bus, thus setting the boycott movement and bringing out the leadership of Doctor Martin Luther King.

I believe the Good Lord brought me to Orangeburg to help initiate the Civil Rights Movement of the 1950s and '60s in a timeframe I presented to my father back in 1932 when I was 10 years of age. My plan to bring this about was to help my father educate the family. I wanted my family to inspire other families to push education for their children. By the 1960s, I thought then that enough blacks would be educated to figure out a way to correct the civil right problems. It was beginning to look as if my prediction would come true. If there was no war, civil rights movements would have depended more upon the U.S. Supreme Courts. The Supreme Court would have had to take the education achievements of black people under consideration. Education played a major role in the integration of the Armed Forces. The war, along with education, speeded up the integration process.

World War II, however, was a major factor because more blacks became educated because of it; and it helped them to overcome their fear in pressing for their civil rights. The war also helped by causing more blacks to stand firm and not break and run each time the white man said, "BOO."

When the President promised to look into integrating the Armed Forces after the war and establishing the 92d and 93d Division, to me this could produce the foundation for the integration. Over the years, I had prepared myself for solving the morale problem, which prevented the 92d Division from being deactivated at Patrick Henry, Virginia; and I had implemented some key performances on the battlefield in Italy to pass what I believed was the "Spearhead Test" on April 5 for the integration of the Armed Forces. The Supreme Court decisions of 1954 and 1955 were the legal steps in the Civil Rights Revolution of the '50s and '60s, which began in Orangeburg, South Carolina, in August 1955. I was happy to have been a part of the whole thing. Because everything fell into place like a completed puzzle, I felt that I had carried out the plans God had established for me.

At the time the State of South Carolina was accusing communists for starting all the trouble at Orangeburg, the Army sent a CIC representative to our office. He always talked to me. I assured him that there were no communists there. If one were there, he would be chased away. I told him that this was a movement by black people to achieve their civil rights. I told him that I was a member of the NAACP and that I attended all their meetings; and I knew at all times what was going on. The only thing I did not tell him was that I was one of the planners.

I did almost expose myself to an Army captain working under me who was in danger of being released from the Army. The new military district commander invited him to spy on me in order for him to save his Army job. I almost told him that I was on the planning committee of the NAACP. Had I done so, the Army would probably have transferred me, even though I was not violating Army laws. I felt that my civil rights involvement was in the best interest of the United States and the world; after all, I had paved the way for the movement.

I continued to be the most eligible bachelor as I had been at Tuskegee University years ago. Then I was a young Captain. Here I was a relatively young Major. It was as difficult at this University as it was at Tuskegee. Here, faculty and students could fraternize, but they had to keep it quiet. About the only person who opposed it was the President. No one was going to tell him. As always, I was trying to find the one who I could not say "no" to. Then I would marry her. This meant that I had to examine lots of girls and had to keep my activities a secret--not because of the President, but because of the envy and jealousy of other girls.

The first girl I dated was a student who lived with her parents in the City of Orangeburg. I did it with her parents' approval. No one could object to that. I dated other students, only with the student's approval. As long as there was no scandal, everything was fine. I made sure there were no scandals. Socially, it could not have been any better unless I had found a wife. That would have been perfect. I stayed away from young faculty members because all these women were looking for husbands, and I did not see one of them with whom I wanted a permanent involvement.

In Ebony magazine, February 1956, I saw a very pretty girl from Birmingham, Alabama, at her debutante ball; she was a student at Tuskegee University. I went to Alabama to meet her. We hit it off hot and heavy and were talking about get married. Her mother, a schoolteacher, was a little apprehensive about her daughter talking marriage with an Army major. After she met me, she was in favor of our relationship. I visited this new girlfriend in Birmingham and went to her church, the famous Civil Rights Church, the 16th Street Baptist Church where those four young girls were later killed during the civil rights struggle in Birmingham. I also met a beautiful girl from Charleston, S.C, on whom I had matrimonial designs. She was named Edith, a super beautiful young lady who had a black mother and a Chinese father. Her father ran a Chinese restaurant in Charleston that served only white customers during this time of the racially segregated south. She had the Chinese color hair and facial features, but the physical features of her mother. She possessed the best features from her parents and was one of the most beautiful women in the city. Her father's restaurant provided free food to the Charleston Police Department. Edith sometimes helped her father out as a waitress and knew all the policemen. She was also legal secretary for a black lawyer.

It was through a court case in Columbia, S.C., that caused her and her lawyer to stop by a restaurant in Orangeburg, which enabled us to meet. Even when she was in court, the white judge focused on her constantly. One day I was in Charleston with my new 98 Oldsmobile Star Fire convertible. Edith pulled up beside a police car with a white policeman. She said, "I will race you." She and the police went down the street racing each other. She had that kind of power in Charleston and was spoiled rotten by everyone. This background, plus the fact that I was being transferred to Germany, caused us to decide against marriage. It was just beginning to look as if I would never get married. I do not think anyone wanted to get married more than I did. Something always went wrong. This was the second time that going overseas broke up a potential marriage for me.

I was a thirty-three year old major when I went to South Carolina. To me this was the perfect time to get married. I had gone to Atlanta looking. I met another young lady there from Birmingham who was attending Spelman College. A cousin of mine, Erin Gooser, introduced her to me. This cousin of mine later married this girl's brother. I visited her in Birmingham. Her father was a big shot doctor there. I visited my girlfriend Joan and went to the 16th Street Baptist Church with her and her mother. This girl's mother also went to the same church.

Gwynn's mother and Joan's mother kind of began to develop a little competitive friction because I had been the boyfriend of Gwynn. I certainly was getting lots of attention there. An old high school classmate of mine, who had previously lived in the neighborhood and was now back in our hometown of Selma, said, "Both of those mothers were fighting over you and neither of their daughters got you." I had to laugh a little bit about it myself.

During my visit to Joan in Birmingham, I came in contact with Lawyer Shores who lived across the street from her. I became very interested in him because he was the leading black civil rights lawyer there. I told him about my involvement with the movement in Orangeburg. There had been some shootouts in Birmingham between black people in his neighborhood and the Ku Klux Klan, during which the Klan got the worst of the deal. He said the Klan did not come back after it lost that battle. I was involved in Orangeburg and did not choose to get involved in Birmingham. I wished him good luck and said to keep up the good work. But I did brief Mr. Shores and Mr. Gasden about the role I played in the 92nd Division; in Orangeburg, South Carolina, and in the civil rights evolution during and since World War II. I pointed out to them that we must stand tall; the law is on our side. I continued to stress this with them during the year and a half that I visited Birmingham.

Besides Gwynn, I had previously looked for wife material in Atlanta. Each time I found someone, I lost out to competition. During the Christmas of 1956, my fraternity had its conclave, annual ball, in Atlanta. Dizzy Gillespie's Orchestra played a variety of the best music that I had ever danced to. I met a very charming young lady from Philadelphia, Pennsylvania, who was trying to get hooked by a doctor's son there. I danced quite a few dances with this charming young lady without seeing her friend. I tried to get her address in the city of "Brotherly Love," but she did not give it to me. I got it somehow. I wrote her but got no reply. I did give not up on her, however.

I visited Bennett College in Greensboro, North Carolina, where I tried to marry three girls, starting in 1943. Before I came to Orangeburg, I went to Iowa State University to see the law student whom I had previously met when she was a student at Bennett College. I met a fourth girl at Bennett College who attended a ROTC Ball at A and T College, also in Greensboro. We had a pretty hot romance and were talking marriage. Her mother was for it and her twin sister was for it; but she was not. She ended up marrying some private soldier who was drafted into the Army.

This was hard to take. It just looked like some unknown force was against me getting married.

In September 1957, I left Orangeburg with a highly successful military tour, as well as achieving great success in the civil rights movement. I do believe that if it had not been God's will for me to be so involved in the civil rights movement, it could not have happened. Of all my successes, no one knew much about them. This was perhaps as I wanted it--getting the job done was more important than getting the credit. I was quite pleased, and I believe God was also. I somehow believe that God did not want me to get married. I must admit that I had no words from on High, but it just appeared that way.

I left Orangeburg, S.C., on my way to Washington, D.C., passing all of those nice restaurants on Highway 301 in my beautiful white and red striped 98 Oldsmobile Star Fire convertible and was unable to stop at any of them. I was hoping that when I come back through this area in three years that this would no longer be the case. My greatest regret was that I did not marry my Charleston, S.C., girlfriend; but I knew that not marrying her was the best thing for me. I do not think we would have made it.

Going to Europe as a single began to make me think about a twenty-year military career. I did not want to be in the Army thirty years as a bachelor. Now for the first time, I began to think very seriously about marrying a European lady. When this happened, my efficiency report rating would begin to fall. Because I had just been promoted to Major in the regular Army with fourteen years of service, my retirement was pretty well assured. My master's degree in education would help me to achieve a great degree of independence, something I always wanted.

I went by the career management branch at the Pentagon to check on my career standing. I had achieved a position in the top ten percent of all the majors in the Army. My future was already planned for me. I could not be in a better position to reach the top in military circles. I was proud of this standing which I had earned by being dedicated to duty and trying to make the Army the best that it could be--putting duty and country before me. My friend Lieutenant Colonel Freddie Davis said, "You are going to Europe on a designated tour. When you return, you are scheduled to go to the Command and General Staff College at Fort Leavenworth, Kansas." I began to rethink my twenty-year retirement. I had achieved too much to give it up. I decided that as long as things went all right that I would stay in the military.

In the spring of 1956, I went to Tuskegee to see the annual regional basketball tournament, which I had seen many times as a student and as a member of the ROTC faculty. I went to the latrine; and to my surprise was joined by Lieutenant Colonel (Chappy) Daniel James, a former schoolmate, a member of the University's aviation program. He said, "Cecil, I want you to make general in the Army. I am going to do it in the Air Force." I said, "OK, Chappy." Again, I felt that there might be some obstacles that I may not want to accept. I knew Chappy was a more easygoing in Civil Rights than I. I figured that I would have to wait and see. If my spirit was willing, I believed that I could do most anything. Up to this time, I had my spirit. I was hoping I would be able to keep it.

I reported to Fort Dix, where I waited for my orders to go to Germany. I contacted the young lady I met at the fraternity ball in Atlanta. She did not get the doctor's son she was trying to get when I met her in Atlanta. She was in her second year at Temple University. We went out together all the days that I was there. I promised to write and call her from Germany, which I did for a while. We did not have a hot relationship, and we were free to do our thing after I left for Germany.

Chapter 10
THE ARMY AND INTEGRATION

For the first time, I went overseas by air. My beautiful car was traveling by ship. I cannot recall now how I got to my assigned unit, the 1st Battle Group, 13th Infantry station at Neu Ulm, Germany. I am sure I was told how to get there when I arrived at Rhein Main Air Base in Frankfurt. It must to have been by rail. When I arrived, my unit was in the field; however, it returned the next day. This was in October, about ten days before the end of the month. One week later on Saturday, we had the Halloween dance. I was welcomed the next day by my new commander, Colonel Ellis Williamson. I was given a reception at the Officers' Club, and I was introduced to officers and wives of the unit as the new S-2 intelligence officer.

When the reception was over, a 1st Lieutenant, the S-1 and his wife, and another 1st Lieutenant and his wife invited me to the Friday night dance. Dancing is one of my favorite hobbies; therefore, I was quite happy to be there. I danced a few times with each of the wives at my table. Then I danced with the S-4's wife who was also white and who seemed to be one of the nicest ladies to me at the reception. She seemed like she was the boss of the ladies, because she had me dance with each one of them. I was very happy to see this integration on the dance floor. This was the first time that I had been assigned to a regimental type unit since the Army became integrated. I had a nice time, and it was beginning to look like I would go all the way in the Army. I was expecting to see something a little colder, but it could not have been better.

During the following week, I became familiar with the people working in the headquarters of the 13th Infantry, especially in my S-2 shop. I was responsible for all classified documents, from confidential to top secret. To lose one of these documents could mean the end of a career or even going to jail. I had to get involved in intelligence training. Most commanders pay little attention to intelligence matters, including mine, which is the reason so many U.S. military and governmental actives get spied on by foreign agents who put their top people in intelligence activities. Most S2 advisors are ignored, and they are subjected to getting low efficiency reports. Commanders do not pay much attention to what the S2 does or do not even listen to their recommendations. I got most of the jobs which had nothing to do with military intelligence, such as major accident investigations, Article 32 investigations (Grand Jury), president a of court martial board, 369 and 368 boards for eliminating soldiers from the Army for inaptitude, or not being fit for military service because of attitude or involvement in frequent disciplinary infractions.

On Saturday morning, eight days after my reception and all those dances, we had the weekly staff meeting. Just before the meeting, the Colonel went into another room where he called me aside for a private meeting. I did not have the slightest idea why we would be talking alone, until we had conversed a little. Colonel Williamson did not seem to know how to bring up that which he wished to talk with me about. My instinct as normal suggested that he might want to talk about my dancing with all those white women the evening after the reception. I asked him if that was what he wanted to talk about. I said, "We are in an in an integrated Army, and this is a part of integration." But I always think of what my grandfather in North Carolina would say about this. I said, "We are moving forward, not backward. We cannot practice mixing during duty hours and segregation after duty hours. Integration provides our military an unbeatable spirit. It is what democracy is all about. It was the spirit of democracy that made Alexander the Great and Napoleon's armies so much greater than their foes. It will give our Army the power to make us superior to anything the Soviets have to throw at us. I integrated every dance on the boat going from Germany to New York in 1951, and the entire dance when I went across the Pacific to and from Korea. I must have done 500 integrated dances without a single refusal. I believe the Army is ready for integrated dances."

The Colonel said, "I believe that all the Americans (meaning blacks) who marry foreign women will have to leave the United States and live in the foreign country from which their wives came." I said, "That will never happen; and if it does I will not wish to be a United States citizen. I am the one who helped to integrate the Armed Forces of the United States as a member of the all-black 92nd Infantry (Buffalo)

77

Division."

The Colonel was not about to win a debate with me on this issue, and I was not about to step down to his level of thinking. I suggested. "Do you wish that I be very careful with whom I dance (meaning with only black women) or that I don't dance with anyone at all?" He said, "I prefer that you don't dance with anyone at all." I said, "I will do my best to comply with your wishes." That was the end of the meeting.

We had the regular staff meeting, but I was too angry to remember what was said there.

The rest of the day was a "decision day" for me. I could have done lots of things, among them to call my friend at the Pentagon and tell him to get me the hell out of here. I could have gone to the Army Commander, Lieutenant General Bruce Clarke, whom I knew from Munich in 1951 and in Korea from 1953 and 54. I could have gone to General Bruce Palmer, Chief of Staff of NATO, and sort of a sponsor for me since I received my regular Army commission in 1946. I could have gone to the Division Commander who already had the Colonel on the hot seat over his extreme racism, because I thought most of the generals were against integrated dancing; and I was not planning to stop integrating them. I decided to stay there and fight it out with the Colonel and retire after twenty years.

Integrating dancing was not the problem, but a part of the problem of limiting integration without authority to do so. The Army was Southern oriented and, to some extent, it was still fighting the Civil War. Many of the commanders wanted to do as little as they could get away with when it came to integration. Integrated dances just exposed it. This Colonel was an extreme racist.

All the minority officers-including the Spanish and oriental--cried to me for help. I was even worried about an Italian officer who worked for me. I told them that I was in the same boat as they were; but if they had some concrete information on the Colonel, I would act on it. The difference was that I was planning to get out at twenty, and there was not much his racism could do about that. I was not afraid to stand up to him. My first decision then was to resign my commission or stay and retire in the grade of Major. If I resigned my commission, I was planning to take the Colonel to the highest tribunal for his extreme racism.

I decided to think about it over the weekend. I talked with a black Major friend who was over sub-post transportation, but he was a reserve officer. He was a little weak in this area, was married, and needed that monthly check. Talking to him was a waste of time.

I went to the Officers' Club for dinner that evening and sat alone, not wanting to talk with anyone. Then a white first lieutenant invited me to have dinner with him and his wife. He was so nice that I decided to join them. He said, "I am Lieutenant Boris, and this is my wife. We are the forward element of the 4th Armored Division from Fort Hood, Texas. We are replacing your unit that is moving. I am the new club officer." I was happy to meet him and almost anyone else who was not from the 13th Infantry.

He invited me to join him and his wife at the Halloween Costume Dance in the ballroom. I decided to do so. One thing I will not do is to go to a dance and not dance. He danced the first three dances with his wife, and I danced the second three. This continued for some time. Then the Colonel and his wife came. I continued to dance. I said to myself, "I did not promise him that I would not dance. I merely said that I would do my best to comply with your wishes." This was the best that I could do. I continued to dance. This officer was not under the Colonel's command; and as far as I was concerned, this was not the Colonel's dance. Maybe it was, or maybe it was not. I took it not to be; therefore, he had nothing to say about my dancing.

Later, Lieutenant Boris went to the Colonel to give him the honor to judge the best costumes. He came back to the table. "What's the matter with that Colonel? I asked him to be the chief judge for determining costume winners, and he chewed me out." I said, "I don't have the slightest idea of what the matter is with him." Lieutenant Boris asked, "Major White, will you be the chief judge?" I said, "OK." I did my job successfully, and everyone seemed to be happy.

A 1st Lieutenant's wife from Augusta, Georgia, a dance teacher and a pretty blonde, came to my table and asked me for a dance. I accepted. We put on a floor show. I had a very nice time, and I was happy that I had answered all of the Colonel's questions on the dance floor. He never said anything to me again about my dancing. I knew I was going to get it on my efficiency report. I had already decided to stay in and retire as a Major. His future bad efficiency report would only contribute to my twenty-year retirement. This was true because at this time there were articles in the Stars and Stripe, the Armed Forces newspaper which said that regular Army officers may not be allowed to retire after completing twenty years of service. I was going to do my duty, but I was not going to bow to his racism.

I decided to complete my twenty years and retire as a Major. I was firm, because I was not rich enough to resign. I thought that I was stepping down by not resigning. But, I was not stepping down on the issue of integrating dances at official military functions, because no one had a legal right to tell me whom I could dance with or date. Because we were moving to Mannheim, Germany, to the north, having our Infantry Division replaced by an armored division, all the families of our units moved to bachelors' quarters, including the Colonel and his wife.

One morning I was having breakfast with two service club ladies, one was white and the other was black. The Colonel came in and saw this white lady at the same table with me. His face turned as red as fully heated charcoal. I said, "Man, does he have it bad."

The black major in transportation introduced me to the nicest German young lady. I dated her and did not tell her that I was moving, because she would not have dated me if she knew it. I invited her to my quarters, which was right over the quarters where the Colonel and his wife were staying. As I walked the girl quietly by the door where he was staying, I was hoping that he would not open his door while I was going upstairs, because it might complicate things. Coming down, I would not have cared. We missed him going and coming. That prevented World War III.

Another reason I decided not to leave the unit was because I liked my unit's new home in Mannheim, even with my racist commander. I believed the other four colonels who commanded similar units in the division would not be much better. I do not think that I could go any where in the 8th Infantry Division, whether I danced or not and be treated like a first-class citizen all the time. This was the real Army, too many rednecks. With my high level of efficiency standings, in the upper ten percent of all majors in the Army, I could have done many things to protect my career. Integrated dancing would get me shot down just about everywhere.

During the early nineties, I told a white friend who married a German lady friend of my wife about my dance experience when I first came to the 13th Infantry. He said, "You should have expected that back in 1957." I said, "How about in July 1991?" I told a young black captain who had just returned from the war in the Persian Gulf about this dance experience. He said, "It's that way right now. I am getting out of the service because of it." I said, "Racism has to be attacked, whenever and wherever you find it."

My unit moved in our new home at Mannheim on the Rhein River. I had to check to be sure that I did not lose any classified documents during the move. When It was all over and every item was accounted for, I assumed my duties as courts and boards officer, German-American Relationship officer, and every other type of duty that came up which did not fall under the duties of one of the other staff sections. The Colonel and I did not see eye to eye on the amount of punishment during court-martial proceedings. It was the duty of the court to do that; but when my court did not give the accused the maximum punishment, he got all fired up. I was a man of justice, and I would not let his attitude influence my decisions. He did not like my sentences, but he would dare not discuss them with me. I was always willing to talk to him about them but not willing for him to tell me what I should do. I would just have told him to put someone else on the court. This is one of the reasons the Army later took court martial authority out from under the chain of command.

Even though he expected me to be an expert in intelligence, when we went on the field, he never gave me a chance to practice my trade. Had I fallen short of the mark, I certainly would have told him. I respected him; I had no fear of him; and I did not like him. I would have told him if he asked me. I loved my country. I was patriotic, but I could not stand officers who somehow associated racism with patriotism. I always covered my flanks, so to speak, so that he could never accuse me of not doing my job. One thing he knew was that I always tried to be correct. When I am correct, I can stand up to any man, tall and unafraid.

We had our own unit Officers' Club at Coleman Barracks. We stopped in for meals and a beer or so after duty. Most of the time I went to the main Officers' Club in Benjamin Franklin Village, across the street from where I lived. Other times, I stopped at a German gasthaus. Periodically, we had our unit dances at Coleman Barracks Officers' Club. Each time we had our unit dance there, the Colonel gave me a seat at the command table next to his wife, making sure that I did have someone to dance with at the table. His wife was always nice to me, but I would not dare ask her for a dance. He would either kill me or her, or both of us, if she defied him and danced with me. I did not wish to have further confrontation with the Colonel about his dance policy at his official dances. It would have been a little bit like mutiny. I merely went to the bar, drank a beer, and got lost. I had places where I could have much more fun than I could ever have there.

One Saturday, we were having a pretty big affair planned for that evening. I went by the Coleman Officers' Club to see how things were going. All of a sudden each of the five subordinate commanders with their wives cornered me. The wife of Captain Burke, a Congressional Medal of Honor winner in Korea, led the delegation. "Major White, we want to know why you stopped dancing with us." Boy, I was a little bit shocked about this! I said, "I am a bachelor, and I do not want your husbands to think that I am trying to be a little fresh." "We don't buy that; we know you are a gentleman," this Arkansas lady said. I said, "The Colonel asked me not to." "That's what we thought. We want you to know in the presence of our husbands that you can dance with us any time you like." I thanked them and really appreciated their feelings over the matter. I said, "The Colonel is leaving within a month or two. After that, I do not care who the commander is, I am going to dance with whom I please as long as you are willing to dance with me."

The new commander was Colonel Chiccolella, an Italian from Brooklyn, New York. This was better than North Carolina. His wife was from Birmingham, Alabama, however. She looked Italian, but I never asked her. Right away, I made all the dances in our unit; and he never said anything about them. I think he was smart enough and decent enough to know that I was within my legal right, even though he must have known that this was a "hot potato issue" for the Army. I think he might have been aware that our West Point Brigadier General Train from Georgia did not like it and that he makes out his efficiency report.

I had to help our new colonel get the Battle Group ready for its combat test. This was the first time that the Army had required a combat test for such a large unit. We ran lots of practice tests to make sure that we had the correct procedures and that we were following them. Before we had our test, members of my units were judges for the tests of other units similar to ours. This helped me to get ready for my test. Colonel Williamson, the previous commander, had recommended that I be relieved of my duties as S2; but my new boss did not do it. I would not have cared, because I had not practiced as S2 under Colonel Williamson; and he had no knowledge of my ability in the fields as an S2. This was not a big deal for me because I had trained people at the division level in Korea.

I gave my previous Colonel good intelligence on maneuvers, but he did not listen. In a real combat situation the enemy would have destroyed our unit. He never would have admitted that, of course. He never thanked me or apologized for his stupidity.

When we started our Battle Group Test, those who were judging me started giving me the whammy. Then the assistant division commander realized that giving me the whammy was also going to whammy him a little bit also. All of a sudden, I became a very famous S2 and received a good grade. Then my Colonel said, "I am glad that I did not follow Colonel Williamson's advice by relieving you." I was happy to do my job without the hope of realizing any benefits from it.

The German-American friendship program was among the many different jobs I had. I dealt with the German press and apologized for any trouble the soldiers may have caused the Germans. I had no problems in this job. I was superman, the best one for the job. I arranged soccer games between church, village, and non-league teams. One weekend a village about 100 miles away invited us from our installation. We met the villagers during one of our maneuvers. All villages have annual festivals. We were invited to this village during the summer of 1958.

To arrange for the visit, I flew to the village in a helicopter, meeting with the village Mayor and other civic leaders, giving the Mayor a ride over his area in the helicopter. We traveled by bus with a band, the soccer team, and a few other soldiers. I drove in my car. I made arrangements for our soldiers to sleep and eat at a nearby local U.S. military installation. After we arrived and played the soccer game, which we won, the villagers decided to board us in their homes. We partied until after midnight in the beer and dance tents. Many people came from nearby villages to participate in the festival. We left sometime in the early evening on Sunday. Our soldiers wanted more of these types of events.

Colonel Williamson was commander then. He played this up big by telling the general what he was doing to enhance German-American friendship, without of course giving me any thanks. The only time I got any comment was when things went wrong, such as not hanging soldiers each time they were court-martialed.

Next door to our installation was a small town known as Lampertsheim, The "Sparagel Stadt." This means 'sparagel city.' 'Sparagel' is considered royal vegetation that grows underground and is very delicious and expensive. It only grows between April 15 and June 15. This city was our friendship city in which I arranged social events through the mayor's office and through the mayor's secretary. The secretary was a little attracted to me, inviting me to visit her a few times. At one of these lunches she expressed an interest in me to my executive officer, a white lieutenant colonel. He said to her, "Don't get your heart all built up because he is leaving." She came to me all excited, "Where are you going? Where are you going?" I said, "I am not going anywhere." She told me, "The Lieutenant Colonel said that you are leaving." I said, "Don't pay any attention to him." This was during Colonel Williamson's tour with the 13th Infantry.

In the German Relationship Program there were also some local menaces trying to play big by suggesting something for stimulating friendship. Most of the times my commanders fell for it, giving me the job to develop whatever was proposed. One of these programs was a kite-flying program for German kids. I was so angry that I was about tell the Colonel that I was not going to do it and suggesting that he give the job to someone else. I thought it was beneath the dignity of an officer with the rank of Major to run a kite-flying contest for children. To me that was a lieutenant's job. I could not think of anything worse to do than going out flying kites.

The boss, Colonel Chiccolella, called a big press conference announcing this contest without conferring with me about the feasibility of the program. I figured that I had better try before telling the Colonel that I could not do it. Again, I was given an impossible job for which I would not get any credit. The only place available was a flat area under our control that had bomb craters from the second war. If I could not get the ground leveled off, that would be a basis for calling it off or getting it postponed. I called the post engineers, and they agreed to do it. That excuse was gone. I had big bolts of target cloths that I could use to form movable flying lanes, yet another excuse was lost. When I got two lowboy trucks to provide platforms for the band and VIPs, I decided that I had better do it. It turned out to be a great success, being published in fourteen German newspapers as far north as Hamburg, Germany. Again, I did not get any thanks, but the Colonel was pleased at the success. It did cost the U.S. taxpayers some money for this event.

A big flange was being given at the Coleman Officers' Club, this time during the command of Chiccolella. The Adjutant went around asking everyone how many guests. I never took any guest, always going alone. He asked me if I was going to bring a guest. He almost dropped dead when I said yes. Then he wanted to know who I was bringing. He almost went crazy when I told him that the girl was a blonde. Not only did he nearly go crazy, but just about every one else did also. No one could sit still in his seat until I brought my date, a local American black schoolteacher who was quite charming and well dressed. Man, I was the hero of the night, and I was never loved so. The Colonel's wife wanted to invite us over to her house for dinner. I began to feel that if they could get me married off to a black woman, half of their troubles would be over.

My teacher friend had her own agenda, going on ski trips on weekends and dating European men. We played the game very well together. I imagine if I had been married, my life in the military would have been different. Maybe, I would have fought for it more. I certainly would have left the unit when I first got there instead of giving up and going for a twenty-year retirement. I would have still pushed for integrated dancing. My reasons for integrated dances had nothing do with the white ladies within our units or anywhere else. For my personal life, I had more women than I needed. Segregated dances to me meant that the Army was not integrated. It was only mixed. In an integrated Army, everyone must be equal. It was purely an attempt to maintain some form of segregation. All of this racism was damaging the fighting spirit of our Army. I was very concerned about how much our soldiers would risk their lives for each other in the event of war. I was sure that we would pay a dear price for racism if war came. These commanders were too blind to see it.

I never let my personal life interfere with my military duties. I knew the advantage of fighting power of an integrated Army probably more than any one in it. After all, I feel I did more than anyone else to help to bring it about. I was afraid our soldiers would shoot the enemy and sometime each other, because it may become difficult to separate love for country and hate for one another.

The first weekend that I came to Mannheim, the first Saturday night; I went to a nightclub called Maxim. I was alone. Across from me were seven Germans, men and women. They invited me to join them. The leader of the group was named Leo Kaufmann. He wined and dined me, picking up all the tabs. He gave me his address, inviting me to visit him in his home village called Roedersheim, not far from the wine city of Bad Duerkheim. All this was wine country, and it was only a half hour from Mannheim.

Visiting Leo helped me to forget the military environment and made my stay there enjoyable. Leo was a building master or a building engineer. He built houses and small hotels, the kinds that were needed in the local area along with the Wine Street (Wine Strasse in Germany), which extended throughout this Rhein River Valley region. He was the fifth generation of builders, quite independent and quite wealthy. Right away he took a liking to me, extending to me permanent visitation rights to his house. When I visited him, he never allowed me to pay for anything. To spend $450 a night was no problem for him. He was a very quiet, simple, and non-boastful man, but highly respected as the head of his family (which included his wife and daughter, two sisters, and his mother, a village leader. I could knock on his door any time of day or night. He welcomed me and had his guest room waiting for me.

To his six-year-old daughter, I was Uncle Cecil. I remember when I was at the Army's Intelligence School at Oberammergau, Germany, down in Southern Bavaria in the Alps near Austria. His daughter, named Cecilia, wanted to see me. He drove there for four or five hundred miles, saying hello and spending one hour; then they left for home.

Leo was trying his best to find me a local wife, but found that to be an impossible task, thinking that I would never get married. Had I done so, I believe he would have built me a house on his land and given it to me. I spent a high percent of my time at his house during my stay in Mannheim and continued to visit his family, even though he passed away about ten years ago in his late fifties. Nice people like Leo helped me forget some of the Army narrow mindedness. I did not need lots of help because I had lived with it all my life anyway.

Toward the end of 1958, the l3th Infantry, being a Gyro unit, was scheduled to rotate back to the United States and to Fort Riley, Kansas. Those of us who came over to our unit after it came to Germany would be transferred elsewhere in Germany. My boss, Colonel Chiccolella, was the first to go. His new assignment was as Commanding Officer of the 2nd Armored Calvary Regiment in Nuernberg, Germany. The unit's mission was to patrol the borders of East Germany and Czechoslovakia in its zone of responsibility.

A new Colonel came over from U.S. Army Headquarters, Europe, to take over command of the l3th Infantry and take it back to Fort Riley, Kansas. He too was a hanging Colonel, wanting to give the maximum in court martial cases and wanting to kick every soldier out of the Army who came before the 369 Board or the 368 Board. I did not kick him out one of the soldiers coming before my 369 Board. The Colonel let it be known that this was against his policy. It was my job to follow Army regulation even if it was against his policy. I had independent authority to do what I did, and that is what I did. He was the same way about court martial cases. We didn't quite agree on that either. I know what justice is, and I always act accordingly. I was always willing to discuss my judgment with anyone, but I was not going to change it. No one ever called me in anyway.

Before the unit and I departed company. I was going to Nuernberg, Germany, and my unit State side; and another command dance was held. This was the farewell dance. Before I asked that nice lady from Arkansas for a dance, she came to me and said, "Major White, dancing with you tonight is 'Taboo.' What happened? Did the new Colonel issue the riot act?" "I am afraid so," I said. I was hopping mad and went to have a showdown with this Colonel. Issuing illegal orders by telling someone whom he or she could dance with compromised the position and authority of his rank and qualified him for no respect. As I approached him, he kept spinning around like a top and wouldn't face me. I gave up and let the matter drop.

During this timeframe I got a call from one of my counterparts from another Gyro unit of the division who had been transferred to personnel at U.S. Army, Europe, telling me that because of my accounting background, my new job would be in the Comptroller Division of Army Headquarters. He told me that my new boss was General Train. I said, "The General and I don't hit it off well. How about getting me a job in Munich?" He called me back. "We don't have anything in Munich. How about a Special Service Officer's job in Nuernberg?" I said, "I will take it."

My problem with Brigadier General Train took place in Hohenfels Training Area. I am sure that Colonel Williamson had painted a poor picture of me about integrated dancing, causing him to endorse those low efficiency reports that I had received for racial reasons. I was a member of a team of umpires from the 8th Infantry Division whose job was to umpire the five Battle Groups of 3rd Infantry Division. General Train was the chief umpire. I umpired all of the mortar batteries of the 3rd Infantry Division.

The division sent its best battle group first, and the mortar battery of that unit was very good. I gave it a high rating. The 8th Division had had its battle groups tested; and as a result, this division was rated as the best in the United States Army for which General Train got credit. When the high test scores came in on the 3rd Division with mortar battery rated very high, General Train said to me that he thought I rated my unit too high. I asked him what part of the test of the mortar battery I tested had he observed. He said, "I didn't see any of it." Then I said, "SIR! How can you say that I rate the unit too high? This unit worked very hard for its scores, and I called it as I saw it." He said, "I still think you rated it too high." I said, "Sir, I call what I see. If you don't like my work, you should contact my unit commander and get me replaced, because I can only call what I see."

At the end of the test, I went back to my unit in Mannheim for a week; then I returned with the other umpires to test the second battle group. Before I returned, the General flew down to Mannheim to talk to my boss. When he left, my Colonel said to me, "You better watch General Train." I told him what happened. Then I said to him, "What should I have done?" He said, "You better watch General Train." I said, "I will watch him." All the umpires were on my side. They were angry with General Train because no one is supposed to tamper with the judgment of the umpires, without cause. I had quite a bit of experience at umpiring at this time.

During the next test, the general said to all the umpires, "I can see the whole picture, and I think all the scores should be lowered by a certain amount." We umpires decided not to change anything. When we met again, he congratulated us for not changing our scores because he had made a miscalculation; and he would have been in much trouble had we done so. In the meantime, the 3rd Division Commander got wind of what General Train was doing. This quieted things down. After that, our General made no further attempt to get involved with the performance of us umpires. He did not bother to apologize to me either when he found out that subsequent units of the 3rd Division did not change the Army-wide rating of the 8th Infantry Division. He was, I believe, in a conspiracy to give me a low efficiency report for integrating dances, because he was the endorsing officer on my efficiency report.

That airplane trip pressured my boss to give me a lower rating on my efficiency report than he had planned. If he gave me a high report after that plane trip, my Colonel would surely have gotten a low one from the General. I did not blame him, because I did not need a high efficiency report as I had already decided to leave the Army upon receiving twenty years of service. I did not feel bad about the low reports because I knew I had never earned one. I would never allow a narrow-minded commander cause me to do a sloppy job.

I found more segregation in the integrated Army than I did in the segregated Army. Because black and whites were bunched together, some means had to be found to enforce social segregation. White soldiers set up Hillbilly Clubs, using high dollars and mass concentrations of white soldiers with command sanction to keep black soldiers away. If black soldiers went to one of the Hillbilly Clubs and an incident occurred, the black soldier would be blamed just by being there. They would have been told they should not have gone there in the first place. I investigated these clubs in uniform, but I would not dare do so in civilian clothes. The soldiers knew me and knew I was the Military Court Judge in my unit. Therefore, they were very nice to me, even willing to buy me a beer, which I did not accept. If a black soldier had been there and a fight occurred and an investigation followed, then the black soldier would be to blame. All of this had command sanction; even a fool could see what this would do to our Army if we had gotten into a fight with the Soviet Union.

When I brought this matter to the attention of the commander as the S-2, it fell on deaf ears. I was just saying racism was supplanting patriotism. I continued to complain that these Hillbilly Clubs violate the sprit of the integrated Army. Commanders brushed this off as being a way to keep down incidents. I was happy that we did not get in a fight. When it came to racism, black soldiers have memories like elephants.

When Chappy James said to me in 1956 that he was going to make General in the Air Force and he wanted me to make it in the Army, I told him that I would. But I had my doubts--not about my ability--but because of all the racism in the Army, which I knew was too deep to go away so easily. I am proudest of all by the way I stood up to it. I am sure I had the ability, the know-how, and the contacts to move very high in the military. For me to do so, I would have had to accept the racist policy that was a part of the Army. This would have been out of character for me, the "Father of the Integrated Army." I think it is better to be right than to be president is a statement by a Senator from Alabama made in 1924 which I adopted.

Chapter 11
SPECIAL SERVICES OFFICER

I arrived in Nuernberg in March 1959, meeting Colonel Chandler, the Nuernberg Military Post Commander. He gave me my job as Special Service Officer. The previous such officer was now the post housing officer. He lost this job because of too much red ink. The golf club and the entertainment fund were losing money. The entertainment fund had recently been embezzled, which was reason for his removal. In spite of all the red ink, I was happy to have the job. I was happy because I wanted to do something for the soldier. I had come to feel that special services activity was falling short of its mark, and I was welcoming the opportunity to do something about it.

I mentioned earlier that I did some special service activities when the war ended in Korea, by going to two U.S. Divisions that were rotating back to the States. I filled two 2-1/2 ton trucks with athletic supplies and used them to set up a variety of programs for the 22 enlisted men and officers in our detachment. The men were so happy with our programs that they left the large Capitol City of Seoul, with all the girls, to come back to our unit, where the nearest girls were ten miles away. This, to me, was the ultimate success in morale activity programs.

The big problem with these programs was that commanders gave lip service to them, always stressing training and combat operations. To me, the soldiers' needs should be addressed as well as those of the commanders in order to achieve the best total results. The Air Force was always out in front of the Army, which accounted in part for it having a higher quality personnel and retention rate. In my opinion, the non-combat program should be given adequate attention in order to make training and combat readiness more effective. Too much training and too much fieldwork can burn soldiers out, bore them, and make all that work less productive. I remember on the Berlin Airlift back in 1948, our soldiers were working fourteen hours daily, seven days per week. I prevailed upon the Air Force to give us the means for establishing a first-class club for our soldiers close to their barracks. We got it, and it made all the difference. Even our working men were able to spend one or two hours a day in it. They knew that this was the best that we could do, and they appreciated it. Because of this program, we had no morale problem or work problem.

Too often the commanders tried to make an impact on their superiors by staying in the field and most often failed to consider the soldiers who had to carry the heavy work burden from one commander to the next without relief. I interviewed so many soldiers who said when they got to the field, they'd sit around and do little, and not learn very much. Or, they'd say it was boring. It takes lot of preparation to get the maximum out of field training, a little bit like making a move. It should be designed to develop individual skills and unit skills, specifically skills which prepared men to be future leaders, which are need in the rapid turnover of personnel in combat.

After the Korean War, I was hoping that the Army would set strong morale programs designed to keep the soldiers happy and in place, as I was able to do. Because the enemy was just over the hill, the activity was training and training and more training. This was 1953, and the enemy was still just over the hill. We have to live with the enemy being just over the hill and try to live as normal a lifestyle as possible. Well thought out and balanced programs not only enhance morale, it helps the military keep high quality personnel in the services.

When I accepted the Special Services job at the Nuernberg Post, I knew the Army's attitude about special services officers, just a job that should be given to some sergeant. Do not put your best officers in special services; the same in S2 assignments. The old saying, "you get what you pay for." When good work is wanted, it is necessary to have good people to do it. The fact that I nose dived from the upper ten percent among Majors to a low ten percent in such a short time was very illogical. That did bother me because I know who I am. I welcomed this special services work because it would give me an operational opportunity to prove myself, doing activities that could be measured.

My responsibility as Special Services Officer included 18 military installations and facilities, which also included 18 clubs, 13 bowling alleys, 36 athletic facilities, plus a soldiers' field that was created by Hitler for his parades, sports activities, races, and military maneuvers. I had 16 libraries and a special service supply totaling more than $600,000.

All my sections were doing well with the exception of the entertainment section and the golf courses. Because professional entertainment and golf were in the red, the whole area of responsibility was considered to be in a messy situation. My first job was to take on golf, which was close to my heart. I had been playing golf since I was eleven years, received a letter in golf in college, and was captain of the golf team. I had seen many military golf courses operate at standards that I considered inadequate. I liked the Special Service Officer's job. I accepted the opportunity to place my brand of efficiency on its programs.

Prior to my arrival, all golf had operated under the Special Services Officer in Munich, under the authority of Southern Area Command, which was the superior headquarters to the Nuernberg Post. This command had losses over a quarter of a million dollars in golf. The new Commanding General in Munich dumped all golf courses on the military posts subordinated to the Southern Area Command. This included the Nuernberg Post, Stuttgart Post and Munich Post, with the exception of a nine-hole course at Dachau, just outside of Munich. Four of the golf courses that were dumped were in my area. I dumped three of my courses, turning them over to local commanders in the area where these courses were located. One was at Grafenwohr, another one at Arnsbach, and the last one was located at Herzo Base, near Nuernberg.

I took the nine-hole golf course at Montieth Barracks in Fuerth, which served the greater Nuernberg area. Not only did the golf courses get dumped, we were made a private association, which did not allow us to be supported by appropriated or non-appropriated funds. We were given a building, the ground, electricity, and water and was loaned the golf equipment for one year, all of which was the property of the Special Service Fund in Munich. The only thing we owned was a donated salvaged jeep that we used to pull fairway mowers. This belonged to Munich Special Services.

My first task was to write a constitution that would fit into my plans to operate the golf course. One of the requirements of the constitution was to require each installation served by the golf course to provide a regular golfer to serve on the golf council. A person who was not a regular golfer was not acceptable. I needed help and support from each installation to provide a council member who loved the game. I considered this necessary for the club to succeed. One of the problems that placed the club in the red was the small golf population of only 150 members. Normally, only about one-fourth of the membership plays golf on any good day. It was considered that a nine-hole course needed about 300 members to support it, and about 600 members to support an eighteen-hole course. To complicate the situation further, we had a general who wanted to expand the course to an eighteen-hole facility, still with only 150 members. The only way in the world that I could operate was to have one or two millionaires to pick up the tabs. However, it looked like I must find a way to operate with no millionaires.

I adopted an impossible strategy to run the course and to get it in the black. One was to charge family members $150dollars per year and single members $100 per year, perhaps the world's lowest annual membership rate. My next strategy was to charge only 10 percent profit mark-up on all of our new equipment and supplies, the world's cheapest. Everyone said this was economic suicide because we were operating without a profit. The General gave me a Master Sergeant who was a professional golfer, food services specialist, and former manager of the military golf club at Fort Hood, Texas. Later, I was given a Sergeant First Class whom I gave pro status.

Just what were my plans for making money? I figured that I did not have enough members to make enough money by charging high membership fees or from high profit mark-ups on equipment. I had to make money by maximum participation, which could be done by making everything so cheap that everyone could afford it. On a normal eighteen-hole course with 600 members, only about 150 of the 600 played on a daily basis. Keeping dues and equipment cheap, the golf population would expand; and the regular members would play more often. I was able to increase the golf playing population by using my assistant pro to give free lessons to beginners, with maximum emphasis on dependent wives. I would use the low cost of playing golf as the focus of my advertising campaign, reinforced by regular playing members of the golf council.

This was an experiment, and it worked. When husbands came from the field, they had to come to the golf course to find their wives. They were happy to find them engaged in praiseworthy activity rather than fooling around, shopping, and spending lots of money. The wives with this new, challenging activity ended up influencing their husbands to become involved. Once a month, we had a tournament with a buffet involving the family.

Every month at a scheduled council meeting, the constitution required each council member to play the course before the meeting's commencement in order to provide suggestions for improving the quality of golf and conditions of the course.

The Head Pro and Manager was a career food service supervisor. He used his knowledge to provide high-quality food and service at the club. Using his technique as club manager at Fort Hood and my knowledge in accounting, we set up a highly sophisticated accounting system, which showed cash received, level of profit, and the inventory balance after each sale. After every sale, we knew how much cash we had, how much profit we had, and the supply balance. It could not get any better than that. We required gentlemanly conduct, friendly relationships, and no rank pulling on the course.

We started constructing the second nine holes toward the end of May 1959. At the end of September 1959, we had an 18-hole playable golf course. I shot 68 for 18 holes on the first day of the tournament, establishing the first club record. At the end of the season, we returned all the golf equipment that belonged to the Special Service Fund in Munich. We had ordered and received all new equipment from a German factory in the Ruhr Industrial District. We ordered a full inventory of golf supplies and equipment for the next year, everything paid in cash. With the golf course expanded to 18 holes, all equipment and property paid for, and the club with a healthy cash balance, I looked back at my accomplishment. I considered it a stroke of genius, and luck, although I never considered myself a genius. I viewed it as such because it was such a success, yet it appeared so simple that it was not recognized. Not even my boss noticed that I took this defunct golf course and bankrupt fund that had been in the red since its establishment 1953 and put it in the black during my second month of operation. The golf course became the best place in the Nuernberg area where our people could truly enjoy themselves at the cheapest possible prices. I had grown used to not being praised for good work during this tour in Germany, but I was always satisfied when I knew I had done a good job.

Now that the Golf Course was functioning successfully, I turned my attention to the entertainment fund. Every month we had auditions at the U.S. Army Hotel in downtown Nuernberg. Custodians of the eighteen clubs in the Nuernberg Post area arranged contracts with my offices on the times and dates when the various acts contracted would appear in their clubs and the cost of each act. My office paid the entertainers and received ten percent of the cost price. The entertainment fund, of which I was president, was netting about $10,000 per month, which did not meet the expenses of the office, causing us to be in the red.

I quizzed the club manager as to the reason why they were not contracting for more entertainment. They said the quality was low. I contacted the agents in Frankfurt and Munich about this low-quality entertainment. I was informed that nobody wanted to come to Nuernberg. It was the worst place in Germany. Over half the time the entertainers were sitting around with nothing to do. I said to the agents, "Send me good quality entertainment, and I will keep them busy seven days per week." I got together with the club managers, telling them to keep these entertainers busy four nights a week regardless of the quality for two months. After that, I would guarantee quality. They did it. The service clubs had money for entertainment. I got the entertainers to perform on Monday, Tuesdays, and Wednesdays for half price. Both the entertainers and the service clubs agreed to it. The entertainment profit began to increase to $20,000 per month. When I left Nuernberg in July 1960, the fund had reached $50,000 per month. The arrangements which I established before leaving Nuernberg allowed the fund to reach $100,000 per month, enabling Nuernberg to become the first military post in Europe bringing live entertainment from the United States.

Beside the golf courses and entertainment fund, activities such as athletic events, service clubs, bowling alleys, establishing and servicing athletic facilities, serving on the German-American Council, the post welfare office, entertainment production crafts and photo, special service supplies, and other activities, everything was very successful. I had many German civilian employees and US Civil Service employees working for me who were doing outstanding work. I had a total of over 160 personnel working for me. If my special service activities were a private business, I would have earned a great deal of money.

Each time we had a Golf Council meeting, I was able show a profit each month of 2 to 4 percent above income and profit budgeted for the month and planned for the next month. Everything was so perfect each time; the council never had any business to take care of. All recommendations and proposals were approved. We played a round of golf required by the constitution, signed the minutes, and adjourned.

I had to organize and manage the U.S. Army Track and Field Meet at Soldiers Field, the largest such facility in Germany, which was under my jurisdiction. I had to set up food and drinks for VIPs attending these meets, including one three-star general, one two-star general, one-star generals, colonels, The Lord Mayor of Nuernberg, and other German military and civilian dignitaries. . Because U.S. Army Special Service was under the PX manager for Europe and was located at that time in Nuernberg, I had to do their work. They just paid the bills. I got the funds I needed to provide VIP entertainment in all major European sports activities, such as CISM sports and boxing championships. I had to sponsor all of the athletic clinics supervised by top college and professional coaches from the United States.

Because of my involvement in sports, I was the American Sports Officer for Nuernberg to the Germans. I was made an honorary member of the entire German sports club in Nuernberg and Fuerth (which were connecting cities). I was also a member of the German-American Advisory Council, which included the General, my boss; The Lord Mayor of Nuernberg, other German dignitaries, and me.

As Special Services Officer, I was also the welfare officer and was authorized to requisition welfare money to support morale activities. We maintained a file of projects, by priority, which needed funding. As welfare money become available, the Colonel and I traveled to Munich to the Welfare Council meetings with our projects. If a million dollars were available to distributed to the posts, each project was considered based on its need and priority. The Council made awards accordingly. I was able to give some nice grants to my old boss, Colonel Chiccolella from Mannheim, who now commanded the 2nd Armored Cavalry Regiment, which patrolled the border of East Germany and Czechoslovakia. Due to the nature of their work, the Council was generous with awards supporting this unit. This generous support from me probably gave my old boss a guilty feeling for giving me a low efficiency report. I knew he did not want to lower his report of me but was pressured in doing so by the general. I never took Army business personal.

Later this Colonel went to Frankfurt to be G3 of the 5th U.S. Army Corps on his way to become general. He asked me to go with him. I took that to mean he was going to correct the damage he and Colonel Williams unjustly did to me in the 1st Battle Group of the 13th Infantry. I still felt that I was too good for the Army or that the Army was not good enough for me. I declined. I told him I liked my special service job, which I knew would not get me anywhere, regardless to how good I might be. There was still too much segregation in this supposedly integrated Army. I was not having any race problems in Nuernberg as my colonel was from Boston, Massachusetts, which helped.

Besides taking care of Colonel Chiccolella's troops which operated on the borders, I built a little league park for the children in his housing area. I repaired his service club at Merrill Barracks; installed an automatic pin setter in his bowling center, and built an Entertainment Center which hosted Nuernberg Post entertainment's contest, Southern Area Command entertainment contest, and the All European Entertainment Contests (which were attended and judged by Olivia De Havilland, one of the stars in Gone With The Wind). During the same time, my craft section sponsored the All-Army Photo Exhibition in the City of Nuernberg, also attended by Olivia De Havilland during the same period when the Entertainment Contest was being held.

I did not have the unit dancing problems, because we did not have organization dances. Under the Post Commander, I would not have had any problems anyway. Several times Colonel Chandler and Mrs. Chandler appeared with me at some of the service club events where dance music was played, and dancing was going on. It was not a situation in which I would normally dance. I would ask Mrs. Chandler for a dance if the Colonel danced with her. But she always came over to me like she wanted to dance. I danced with her. I did not worry about the Colonel making any comments, because she was the boss in their relationship. One time on one of our welfare meetings, the Colonel was invited to the Regina Hotel in Munich to meet with a member of a military organization from Boston called Ancient Military Society. President Kennedy, I understand, was a member of that organization. Every year members would fly from around the world in a chartered jet to meet with members of the military. He invited me along, even though I insisted on staying at the bar downstairs where there was dancing. I knew the people there. I went with the Colonel at his request.

We were in a millionaire's suite where he had his own small dance band. Both men danced with their wives. When they sat down, I danced with Mrs. Chandler and later with the other man's wife. I guess I did it two or three times. The next time I asked his wife for a dance, he would not let her. I danced with Mrs. Chandler. I was not going to be embarrassed by that guy, not caring how much money he had. On the way home, I was in the front seat with the driver. I heard Mrs. Chandler say to the colonel, "We are not prejudiced." I always took Mrs. Chandler to be a fine lady. They were both from Boston, which helped.

The general wanted me to give honorary membership to our golf course to the German big wigs in the Nuernberg area. I gave one to Mr. Gustav Schickedanz, the owner of Quelle, who later became one of Germany's billionaires. I met Mrs. Grete Schickedanz and daughter at their work place in Fuerth and Mr. Schickedanz at his guarded home in Fuerth. I visited the home of the owner of Mann Motors, Germany's largest heavy truck company. His wife invited me to coffee on her back yard lawn. We chatted about golf and other things before I presented her with the honorary membership. I visited the toy factory in Fuerth, the world's largest at that time. The owner took me on a tour of the factory, complaining about a shortage of labor at that time in Germany and about the Japanese stealing some of his patented creations. We gave membership to the Siemens Electric Company owner, Germany's General Electric, and a few other VIPs that the General considered pro-American. None of the VIPs ever played there, possibly because they did not play golf.

At this time most Germans played tennis. It did start them thinking golf, because the Germans soon begin building a German Nuernberg Golf Club. I was an honorary member of all the sport clubs in Nuernberg, but I only visited the Blue-White Tennis Club in Fuerth. One reason was because the membership consisted of a number of pretty German girls whom I was looking at for a possible wife. The first two were blondes, who were friendly; but they were not too interested in a close romance with me. I still remained friends with them. The brunette, who was a close friend of the blondes, was a good possibility. I saw her on the street not too far from where I lived. I offered her a ride, and she took it. Her attitude to me was most encouraging, a little bit like Lolla at Tuskegee, where I gave her and her sister Carol a ride, which led to our friendship. My extension to remain in Germany six months beyond my three-year tour was disapproved, killing any hope of developing a romance with this girl whom I was interested in.

A mother in Fuerth who gave me massages every week was interested in me establishing friendly relations with her middle daughter. She was a very nice girl who did not appeal to me. I was more interested in the older daughter, but not for marriage. The oldest one was not interested in me. Her best daughter was her youngest one, but she was too young. Her mother said that when she got old enough, she would bring her to me. When I had retired from the Army and was teaching history in Princeton, New Jersey, her mother invited me to Cincinnati, because her youngest daughter was old enough. Because I was planning to return to Germany, I did not make the visit to Cincinnati.

In romantic circles I always traveled alone and dated alone. I was not trying to hide my social life from my military superiors. I was trying to hide them from my other relationships, but my social life was never a military problem. When I was in love, I had only one girl. When I was not, I had more than one; and I almost never got caught.

I played golf just about every day when I was the special service officer. When I was in the 8th Infantry Division, I very seldom played golf. Golf in Nuernberg was both business and pleasure. I was the boss of the golf course; and by being there every day, I kept things going smoothly and efficiently. Every night I went dancing, but I went alone. Besides having a good time doing my beloved hobbies, I was always looking for the girl to whom I would be unable to say "no." This was a never-ending adventure without success, a bit like playing lotto--hoping that if I try it long enough and often enough, I will some day succeed.

One of the sub-organizations in my Special Service Company (section) was the little theater section. I had one of the best producers in Europe. He organized a play "View From The Bridge", by Arthur Miller. Before these plays could be presented, permission of the writer was necessary. Our request was submitted through command channel in Europe to the Department of the Army and on to Miller. The approval was not received. We tried over and over again. We received word that Arthur Miller was in seclusion due to his break up with Marilyn Monroe, and he was not seeing anyone. All the other plays went off as scheduled, but Nuernberg Little Theater Group play did not go on because clearance was not received. This was published in the Stars and Stripes.

Colonel Chandler read this in the paper and became hopping mad. He called me over to his office to quiz me on what happened. I explained it. It was unacceptable. I told him to check with Munich, check with Heidelberg. "Why did you use Arthur Miller in the first place? Don't you know that he is being investigated by the House Un-American Activity Committee as a Communist?" I said, "Yes. They are still investigating and have not proved him to be one." I said, "This committee is often accused of witch hunting." I felt that the Colonel was a little off his rocker on this matter. There was not anything that could be done. We eventually got approval, and the play was presented and was found to be just as outstanding as everyone expected it to be. The Colonel never quite forgave me for this. It didn't bother me because I had no guilt over it.

The Colonel sent one of his Executive Officers over to inspect the Little Theater after a rehearsal the night before and found costumes scattered all over the place. He called me in about that. I told him that I had no requirement for them to stand by for inspection the next morning following rehearsal. All those working in the show were students and volunteers, and sometime they would leave things in place until the next day when the rehearsals were finished late in evening. To me, the Colonel was getting a little impossible.

He went out to the golf course about two o'clock one afternoon. "Where is Major White? Where is Major White?" One of the ladies that he did wife swapping with said, "Colonel, Major White does not play golf during duty hours." He was disappointed. One weekend after that, we were having a golf tournament with men and women, followed by a buffet. I had a German assistant manager who always catered to rank. Because I knew it, I called Walter aside and said, "Walter, I don't care if Jesus Christ comes out here, he is going to have to wait his turn. No one must be allowed to interfere with this tournament." I was away for a short time. The Colonel showed up wanting to "T" off. Walter said, "Colonel, Major White said he didn't give a damn if Jesus Christ showed up here, he could not tee off in the middle of the tournament." When he told me, I said, "Congratulations, Walter. That one time you did what I told you." The Colonel got mad and stomped off; but he never said a word to me about it. I was waiting for him.

When his son, Chip, went out to the golf club and met people at their cars to let him caddy for them, he was violating the caddie rules. He was doing it again and bragging about it to the German Caddies who had been there the whole day without work. One of the German boys beat Chip's ass.

When I came in from play, my golf pro had investigated it and reported to me in detail as to what happened. I was happy to have the news before Chip's parents. He was a mother's boy, and I knew the Colonel was going to call me in about that. The next morning he said, "Five German boys beat Chip." I said, "No, colonel, one boy beat him. We have already expelled him from the golf course." I did not, however. I was kind of glad he did Chip in. It was bad enough to violate the rules, but he also bragged about it. If that boy had whipped him, I might have expelled Chip from caddying. Anyway, Chip did not caddy out there anymore.

There was a German Gasthaus where I occasionally stopped by after work for a beer. The owner was married and had two daughters. Several other Germans were usually there. We chatted and had friendly conversations. I never stayed there very long. One evening I went there and for the first time there were a number of white soldiers. I sat at the bar with high bar stools next to a soldier who was in civilian clothes. He said to me, "You are leaving." I said, "I am, but only when I get ready." He said, "You are leaving before then." I said, "I am a Major." As I reached for my wallet to get my ID card, he said. "Ain`t that a bunch of shit?" He proceeded to flick the hot ashes of his cigarette on the back of my left hand. When he did that, I pushed him off the high stool to the floor. Then I picked that big soldier up and threw him against his three buddies who were coming to help him. Then I pushed a swing door against them when they got up and came after me again. At that time the oldest daughter of the owner asked me to leave, because I was grossly outnumbered. They followed me to my car and hit on it. I drove away to get the MPs.

A black left-handed MP gave that soldier who put the hot ashes on my hand a good beating. The Germans testified and identified the soldiers who caused the problems. They were court martialed, of course.

The next day the Colonel called me into his office about the incident, asking me why I was in a club where soldiers go. I said, "this time the soldiers went to a club where I go". I said, "it is a disgrace how these hillbilly soldiers caused so many problems with command sanction. I get all kinds of complaints when black athletic officials come to Nuernberg from all over Europe to attend sport clinics about these hillbillies around here causing all kinds of problems when they go to places of entertainment." This gave me first-hand experience about these hillbilly clubs that I had been complaining about for three years. This is one time that the white soldiers were tried in the military court.

The colonel was hard to figure out--even though I did not work at it very hard. I went to Munich when his daughter got kicked out of The University of Maryland for staying out overnight without permission. He brought her home with us. Sometime after that, he and his wife were out of town; and he placed his daughter in my custody. I picked her up, took her to the golf course, and told the Pro to give her some golf lessons. After I finished playing golf, some lieutenant was entertaining her. His face really turned red when he found out that I was in charge of her. I sent her home with a next-door neighbor of her parents. Everything worked out all right.

The Commanding General of the Southern Area Command was interested in three hotels, one at each of the military posts under his jurisdiction--The Columbia in Munich, the U.S. Army Hotel in Nuernberg, and another Army Hotel in Stuttgart. These were the general's high priority projects. This gave the captain who managed the Nuernberg Hotel all the encouragement he needed to do almost anything he wanted to in order to make money, even violate Army regulations. I did not care which regulations he violated as long as he did not violate the regulations that were my duty to enforce. All entertainment used by any club or military facility had to be rehearsed and approved and contracted by my office before they could per-form. The hotel commander, Captain Faulks, had a habit of hiring his own entertainment, not coming through my office, nor paying his ten per cent fees. I called it to the attention to the Colonel. He reduced me to Assistant Specials Special Officer, placed a lieutenant colonel over me, and appointed Faulks to entertainment fund council, packing the committee against me.

I wrote an announcement to be placed into the bulletin coming out of Munich as if it were coming from the general to stop violating these regulations. It came as I wrote it. The Colonel called me to ask if I had seen it. I told him that I had. He said, "Make sure you comply with it." I told him that I was already doing it.

We had our first meeting of the new Entertainment Fund Council. Earlier I was the president, and this time I was the custodian. The president called the meeting. I then read the minutes of the last meeting. Immediately Captain Faulks accused my German entertainment manager of violating Army regulations and recommended that the CID investigate him. I objected to it but got overruled by the new president and Captain Faulks. As custodian, I was the writer of the minutes, and I made sure that the overruling of my objections was noted. I noted that the Hotel was violating Army Regulations by not bring its entertainment through this office. My motion was overruled, but I recorded it also. Captain Faulks said, "Everything I did was approved by Homer (The Colonel). What's good enough for Homer is good enough for me." Lt. Colonel Smith said; "Me, too!" I said, "What is good enough for Homer is not necessarily good enough for me." If something happens which is detrimental to the Colonel, he is not going to take responsibility for it. It is going to fall on you." They did not believe me. The minutes went to the Colonel, and he approved them with all my objections, but did nothing about them. That was fine with me, because I had those approved minutes under lock and key. They were my protection.

The Chief of the CID (Criminal Investigation Division), a friend of mine, called me and informed me that he would be investigating my German Entertainment Manager. I said; "Come on; we are as clean as hound's teeth." After four or five days had passed, I called him asking what happened and that I had been waiting for him. He said, "I am investigating the Hotel." The Colonel called me about the investigation. I said, "Sir, I warned you and you disapproved my objections which are in the minutes which I have right here in my hands. Do you want me to come over and show them to you." He said, "No, no. That won't be necessary."

The investigation was from the Inspector General, U.S. Army Europe. When it was finished, the Commanding General Southern Area Command forced Lieutenant Colonel Smith, my new boss, to sign the papers to retire from the Army or be court-martialed. When he came to work saying he really wanted to make full colonel before he retired. I said, "I warned you. Any man who will tell you to violate a regulation will not back you when something goes wrong." Anyway, I was pretty sure he would never make full colonel under any circumstances.

I received my efficiency report the Colonel made out on me and sent it through channels for the General to endorse. Before the General put his endorsement on it, he wanted me to see it. He probably showed it to Lieutenant Colonel Sullivan who thought my ratings were too low. I got hopping mad when I saw that report. I wrote a three-page rebuttal against it because it showed downright dishonesty. Even it he had given me the highest possible report, it would not have made any difference. Because I had done the best job of my life in that special service job, I was entitled to the truth and did not get it. I think he rated me only about that little theater group, the best and most efficient section I had.

I later checked and found that the golf course stayed in the black for two years after I left. The entertainment fund rose to $100,000.00 per month. The Nuernberg post was the first one in Europe to bring stateside entertainment to the Continent to entertain in military clubs.

The General withdrew my six-month extension to stay in Germany after I wrote the rebuttal against Colonel Chandler's efficiency report on me. I, therefore, contacted a friend of mine in the Pentagon, requesting that I be sent to Fort Dix, New Jersey. It was arranged.

Chapter 12
THE CIVIL RIGHTS REVOLUTION

I arrived in New York sometime in July 1960 by airplane. My automobile was coming by ship, which meant that I would have to wait approximately ten days for it. A lifelong friend of mine, Lieutenant Colonel Harold Johnson, asked me to visit his family in Boston and tell them how he was doing. He visited me often when traveling from Wuerzburg, Germany, where he was stationed. I decided to go there and spend about a week. I traveled by an airbus from Newark, New Jersey. His wife met me at Logan International Airport. She took me to her home with her two children who were about twelve and fourteen. The oldest one was a girl.

Knowing that soldiers like to eat, she had a nice meal prepared for me. Then she took me around to meet her parents and friend.

I was happy that she did not try to get me married to someone, because both she and Harold wanted me to move to Boston upon retirement. I got a chance to visit Cape Cod and Plymouth Rock while I was there, focusing much attention on the Cape because of the forthcoming Presidential election. I was able to get some first-hand knowledge of the place. I also got a chance to play some golf. I believe I played two different courses. Because I played golf nearly every day during my stay in Nuernberg, it was difficult for me to go someplace without playing golf. I also took her son to see the Boston Red Sox play at Fenway Park where Ted Williams hit a homerun. My stay in Boston was very enjoyable, and I had a chance to meet many of Harold's friends whom I would see later when he returned from Germany for retirement.

I left Boston for New York on a very unreliable train called the New England Express. It slowly poked its way to New York City. It did get there, but my car did not. Now I wished that I had remained a little longer in Boston. I went out to Fort Hamilton in Brooklyn where I stayed until my car arrived. It came in several days later. I visited a girlfriend over at Staten Island that I met in Mannheim and whom I had communicated with after she left Germany. I remained there a couple days before heading south on my thirty-day leave.

My first stop on my way to Selma, Alabama, was at Orangeburg, South Carolina. Because this was in July 1960, the regular session for the University was out, but the summer semester was going on. The University had another president, an old friend. When I first went to the University, this president was in charge of the ROTC Armory. Later he became the director of the Student Center. Before I left, he was the assistant business manager. Afterwards, he became the business manager. The previous president (who was there when I left) was anti-civil rights. The political pressure got too hot for him and even for his white supporters. They told him he had to retire.

The business manager, Maceo Nancy, became the new president. The man who was the treasurer when I arrived there was the man at the University with the political power and was the father-in-law of President Nancy and was responsible for all of his promotions. I wanted to see the new President because I was close to him and his wife, but he was off to a university working for his Ph.D. which was a requirement for his new position as president. I saw many of my old friends in civil rights movement and others before heading for Alabama.

My greatest satisfaction upon reaching South Carolina was when I stopped at a restaurant on Highway 301 and had breakfast. When I left there three years before, I could have been killed, arrested or put in jail for going into that place. This time I was served as though it had always been done that way. No one paid any attention to me as I sat there enjoying my breakfast. This was much of a surprise! It was so easy that it was hard to take, because my friends had fought so hard to bring this about during the beginning of the Civil Rights movement. It was a pleasure sitting and eating there.

My mother and family were happy to see me home and to know that I probably would not have to go overseas before my retirement from the military. I played lots of golf in Selma and in Jasper, Alabama, where my oldest brother resides. I visited my old friends and professors at Tuskegee University. I went by Birmingham to see my old girlfriend and her mother. When I first went to her house, I only saw her mother. Joan was married and had two children, but her marriage was on the rocks. Her mother did not want my presence to make things worse. I stayed there a short time and headed northwest to Jasper, which was thirty-five or forty miles away.

At the end of my leave I returned to Fort Dix, New Jersey, where I lived initially in the BOQ (bachelor officers' quarters). My first job was that of a Battalion Commander, 3rd Battalion, 4th Training Regiment. This was one of the easiest jobs I'd ever had thus far in the Army. Basic trainees were sent to the four companies of my battalion at different times. This meant housing, training, and other basic trainee activities were managed at the company level, leaving only supervisory duties for me. Everything was so repetitious that even the lowest ranking enlisted manager was an expert in his position. Efficiency was competitive statistically. Performance and testing were all compared with previously established standards. The companies were under pressure to equal or beat the established standards. The cadre was very efficient and everyone knew his job, thus putting me in a position where I was always thanking everyone for a job well done. I inspected the soldiers' barracks in the morning and then inspected the companies in the fields and on the ranges.

Often in the afternoon, after training, there were weapons cleaning and maintenance activities in the company areas. Companies in the later stages of training were in bivouac. Every night I visited all troops who were camping out. In the afternoon I played golf, giving the company commander freedoms to run their own companies.

While I was commanding this Battalion I was dating Jacquelyn Willis, who lived in Philadelphia. I met Jackie at the Kappa Alpha PSI fraternity dance in Atlanta during the Christmas of 1956, as I had previously written. She was interested in a doctor's son at that time; but I danced with her a number of times and learned to like her. I did not make any progress with her then. During my brief stay at Fort Dix prior to going to Germany in September 1957, we dated the whole time while I waited for my shipping orders. As previously mentioned, her interest in the doctor's son did not work out.

When I returned in 1960, I called her at her home and told her that I was back. I asked if she was available to see me. She said that she would be happy to see me again. We began dating steadily, and I even brought her out to my battalion where I introduced her to my executive officer, a black major, whom I had know for some time. "Boy, you are crazy if you do not marry her," he said. She ate that up, which is the reason I never again brought my dates around the military. I even took her to my quarters (with her sister, of course) for only a short time. I did not bring her out there anymore, because my friend was always trying to get us married. She was all for that, but I was not so sure about it myself.

She was pretty, young, and had just finished Temple University and would become a teacher in Philadelphia in September. It was a perfect marriage situation, but I still was not ready for it. Aside from my military duties, my second mission was trading on the stock exchange. All my money was in the stock market--that which I had and that which I could borrow. I wanted to be a millionaire. I studied the market up one side and down the other and should have reached my goal, but it just did not happen. I learned a great deal about the stock market from a major friend of mine who was my second boss at South Carolina State University. His father had been in the market since the Depression year of the early thirties. He had General Motors' stocks when they were selling at $1.50 per share. He knew all the good stocks; he knew when to buy and sell.

I called my broker several times per day on what was like an 800 number. During my period at Fort Dix, I must have bought between fifty and one hundred different stocks. I probably would have been successful if my broker had advised me correctly. He always had me to buy on good news, when the professional investors were selling on good news. When I bought on good news, I helped to keep the stock up, which helped those who had the stocks to take a profit and get out. This always created a small loss for me, because I lost when the stock went down due to profit taking and due to the price of the commission for buying and selling. These kinds of losses milked me to death, so to speak.

Every Thursday night was happy hour night at the Officers' Club, which meant cheap drinks and dancing, which kept the crowds there longer. Like always, where there was dancing, I danced. I always integrated the dance, but only with those who wanted to do so. I found that other black officers were reluctant to do so. They were afraid of their efficiency reports. Because I came to Fort Dix to retire, I did not worry about efficiency reports. To me, my efficiency report should reflect my duty performance and not whom I danced with. This is why I decided on a twenty-year retirement. To indicate in anyway who a person should or should not dance with is segregation and not integration. Integration did not say partial integration and partial segregation. It said integration, and that is what I was doing. To try to force segregation on a dance floor in any form or any way is segregation. I would continue to do it every Thursday night.

During World War II, I fought and almost died in a segregated Army so that the Army could end its segregation. For some racist commander to impose his own form of segregation on his troops was illegal and not binding. I do not believe anyone in the Army participated in integrated dances more than I did since 1951. In 1958, when the white wives and their husbands of the 13th Infantry asked why I quit dancing with them, I told them because I did not want their husbands to think that I might try something ungentlemanly. They said, "We do not buy that. We know you are a gentleman. That is why we brought our husbands with us." This was a true assessment of my character at every dance that I integrated. My objective was to end this form of segregation. It was illegal but was condoned because of a southern attitude that governed the policy of the Army; and it was enforced by the Army's most potent secret weapon, the efficiency report.

I was so happy when I returned to the United States and saw quite a bit of progress had been made on the civil rights front, but much had yet to be done. The campaign for the President of The United States could not ignore the civil rights movement. Dr. Martin Luther King was on the sidelines to remind the candidates that civil rights must be considered. The total civil rights effort included the elimination of all forms of segregation and providing full constitutional rights for everyone, which included the right to vote and to end all forms of discrimination

Upon retirement, I wanted to become a schoolteacher because I believed so strongly in education all my life. Like my father said, "Education makes a person better at whatever he is doing." Civil rights' achievements would not mean much to those who obtained it if they did not have the ability to take advantage of it.

As long as I can remember, I believed in education. Even when I was quite small, educated people impressed me. By 1960, I had paid my youngest sister's way through college; and she was now a schoolteacher. I would pay the college expenses for a nephew at the request of my brother, who was unable to do so. He was the only high school dropout and was unable to command a job that would enable him to send his children to college.

I pushed all of my sisters and brothers to send their children to college; and they did it for all of those who wanted it, which was about 70 percent. This would not only enable my family to support the civil rights movement, they would be in a position to take advantage of all the progress made because of it. My whole life had been characterized by work and education. I took college courses continuously at the education center during my five years at Fort Dix. I took courses in abnormal psychology, three quarters of French, one in German, Spanish, European history, geography, computer programs, and others. Even though I had my master's degree in education and social studies, I took subjects to get a teacher's certificate in American history and world history in the State of New Jersey.

I also became a scratch golfer in Nuernberg and continued to be one at Fort Dix, as this was my biggest hobby. I even considered becoming a professional golfer. The other hobby was dancing. There was no conflict as I did one during the day and the other one at night (as I had done in Nuernberg). As a golfer, I played in the military golf league between Fort Dix, McGuire, Lake Hurst and Fort Mammoth, all in New Jersey. We held our own within the league. My love for golf, however, did not stop me from showing up each Thursday night for happy hour. No one at Fort Dix ever said anything about integrated dancing, as this was not a part of the country where segregation was a problem. But, there were those who were from the South who were stationed at Fort Dix who did not like it. That was no problem for me.

After my first year as Battalion Commander of the 3rd Battalion, 4th Training Regiment, I was transferred to Special Troops for a short time, but later went to Troop Commander of the U.S. Army Personnel Center. The Commander of my second job and I did not make it on racial grounds. The Personnel Center was the nicest job that I ever had in terms of racial harmony. This unit practiced integration at its best, from the commander downward. A white lieutenant called me every Thursday to see if I was going to happy hour because his wife liked to dance and he did not. If I did not come, he would not come. I danced with his wife every Thursday night, as well as with other ladies.

My first commander in the Personnel Center, as well as everyone else, was just wonderful racially. It was in those combat divisions where the race problems existed. I was called up in the middle of the night and invited to pajama parties. I liked parties, but not getting up at two or three in the morning and going to them in my pajamas. But I did, because I liked the integration nature of them. I always managed to keep by best foot forward as I did not want to give someone an excuse to say I was using integration for ungentlemanly conduct. There was never the slightest move in that direction. One lieutenant apologized to me for not creating the opportunity for me to date his widow mother, which was very nice of him. I am glad he did not, because I was interested in younger woman, not one close to my age. If she had been willing, I probably would have dated her, but I never would have wanted a serious relationship with her. Because I would have been afraid of that possibility, I am glad it did not happen; however, I thanked him his for non-racist attitude.

I had command authority over four overseas companies, one transfer company, three reception companies, along with one headquarters company and two consolidated mess halls at the Personnel Center in this new job. Everything there went just perfect. Because all company duties were repetitious, the work was easy for the personnel in these companies. This made my workload light, which allowed me to play golf every afternoon. In fact, the work in my new job was much easier than it was at the basic training battalion I commanded.

During the Cuban crisis, I had about 6,000 soldiers who were not going anyplace, because the ship designated to send them to Europe was diverted to support the planned invasion of Cuba. I converted one of my large buildings into a gym and put in basketball goals, so we could have continuous basketball tournaments. I was able to grant a few short leaves for those soldiers who had semi-emergency cases. My mess hall provided good food, which was great for maintaining high morale. I was very fortunate by not having any disciplinary infractions on the part of the soldiers who were stuck there approximately eight weeks. I was aware of this possibility, which caused me to provide additional recreational activities to avoid this difficulty.

I was very happy in 1960 when John F. Kennedy was elected President. I knew then that civil rights would be on the front burner because the President and Doctor King were on the same wavelength for making progress. Dr. King was going to make sure of it. Mr. Kennedy moved to get a judge in Decatur, Georgia, to free Dr. King from one of those high profile prisons believed to have given then Senator Kennedy the edge over Vice President Nixon, thus propelling him to election victory. Doctor King was not about to let our new President forget it, even when he said he was elected by a small mandate.

Doctor King felt that the President owed him something and he was planning to collect. When I went to my hometown of Selma, Alabama, during Christmas of 1960, I dated one of the civil rights young ladies who was a part of his marching group. After Christmas, Doctor King went to Albany, Georgia, to help the local civil rights organization organize a demonstration to end discrimination in public facilities there. The young lady called me at my quarters at Fort Dix, New Jersey, every night, telling me what took place. I also watched the demonstrations on TV. I eventually told her that the movement in Albany was poorly organized, not supported, and that It was not a part of Dr. King's program. He only went there to help out. I advised my friend that the movement there was not going anywhere, and I advised her to tell Dr. King to call it off, return to Atlanta, and plan his next move elsewhere, profiting by the lesson learned at Albany. It was called off

The next one, which I had nothing to say about, took place in Birmingham, Alabama; but I had laid lots of groundwork for a future civil rights movement in Birmingham in 1956-57, which I believed helped Doctor King. I watched it with great intensity and pleasure on my TV at my newly acquired bachelor hut near the golf course and hospital at Fort Dix. Bringing young people into the movement was a stroke of genius. Even I did not think it would work, but it turned out to be perfect. I played golf in the afternoon and watched the news about Birmingham marches each night. Golf had nothing to do with civil rights, but it did help to reduce the great tension in me--although I wanted to be there with Doctor King. .

During this movement I was reminded of what I had said to my platoon, in preparation for the spear-head attack on Hills X, Y and Z, prior to April, 1945. I said, "Regardless of how hard we fight and how successful we become, no one will gives us our civil rights. We will have to fight for it on the home front. Also, if we fight well on the battlefield, we will fight well on the home front." With all the forces brought to bear against the marchers--vicious dogs, police clubs, cattle prodders, water hoses--they continued to march. I was so proud of them. I sat there hoping and wondering if they could hold out. I prayed, of course, hoping that they would. They did. Even though the fighting we did during the war brought about the movement, the inspiration and leadership of Doctor King motivated the fights in Birmingham.

At noontime I practiced on my driving range in front of my quarters and played from the Seventh Tee to the clubhouse. Then, I was ready to meet my friends. We played for a little money. This allowed me to concentrate a little more on my golf while I waited for each night to watch the news in and about Birmingham. All of this was part of the prediction I made as a ten-year-old when I said to my father, "This race problem will not stop until a black man is free to marry a blonde. My Father said, "It may happen in your lifetime, but not in mine." I said, "It will happen in the 1960s." By this I meant all legal segregation based on race would be eliminated. The white woman was not the cause of the race; the Ku Klux Klan and racist white men made it that way. Every time we talk about voting, they were saying that if the black man voted he would be marrying some white man's daughter. This was nonsense, but the Klan raised the white man's emotions over these issues.

The U.S. Supreme Court took the barrier on interracial marriage down in 1969, but there has not been any noticeable increase in them since. In fact, a white man who was married to a black woman initiated this court case, which removed the barrier to interracial marriages in the South. This was a case in Richmond, Virginia. This ruling took the adventure out of interracial marriage, in my opin-ion; and I believe it raised the stature of black women. The same is the case with interracial dances at Officers' Clubs. Wherever there is a barrier, racial or otherwise, it becomes the nature of a person to remove it, especially when it is directed at him. Such barriers are an insult and are embarrassing to black people, and a disgrace to our democracy. Any commander who takes it on himself to go against the legal wishes of those who desire to express their friendly relationship with co-workers by dancing with them is going beyond his authority. President Truman stated in the beginning that those who could not serve in integrated Armed Forces should retire, resign, or be removed from the services.

Many Officers' Clubs, even in 1998, are closed because of hidden racism and because commanders use their dictatorial power and the efficiency report to maintain social barriers between black and white fami-lies at official dances. This type of discrimination is difficult to prove, but it exists. In December 1996, I met a retired (white) Lieutenant General at Ramstein Air Base. He was an Air Force or military academy graduate and was in Europe to visit his two sons--one was an Air Force captain stationed in Ramstein and the other one, also a captain, was stationed in London. I had the first draft copy of my autobiography with me. Because he was so nice, I allowed him to look at it, starting with his wife, who was a speed reader. She said, "It's so exciting I can't stop reading it. I think it might make the movies." Then her husband grabbed the book and started turning pages; and he stopped at the part where I was complaining about inte-grated dances. Although he did not elaborate on it, I got the impression he did not advocate it; but he went along with it and was quite surprised that I recognized it. I knew that the Army was guilty of this type of discrimination, but I was quite surprised that it went on in the Air Force as well.

If there is one issue that will prevent the services from being fully integrated, it is integrated dancing.

This book is full of it. Senior white commanders should break down this barrier by setting an example, by dancing with a black woman who is a part of his command. When this is done, his subordinates will not be afraid to do likewise. This one issue would integrate the Armed Forces. Until it happens, it will not be integrated. The spirit will not be in it.

At Fort Dix, there was a Colonel from Dothan Alabama who was my second commander. He was very much opposed to integrated dancing. Since I retired from the Army, I have had the feeling that this Colonel and the lady Captain who commanded he WACs were trying to trap me with the women in her company. She was always at Happy Hour and may have told the Colonel about me integrating dances when I was in his command. The Colonel had a black Captain, an Adjutant, to tell me that he had a secret letter from the Department of The Army that was against integrated dances. I told the Captain I did not believe such a letter existed; and if it did, I would not obey it. And, if I saw it, it would not be secret long because I would have it published in the New York Times. I believe this WAC Captain was later dismissed from the Army for having inappropriate sexual activities with the women in her company.

It was a little difficult for me to understand the Army's policy about the relationship of officers and enlisted men and women. There was a white couple on base who were married--the man was a staff ser-geant and his major wife was his commanding officer. This was written up in the Fort Dix newspaper stat-ing that his wife was the boss during duty hours and the staff sergeant husband was boss after duty hours. There were other cases when single officers who dated enlisted women had no problem at all.

One Saturday night there was a command ball at the Fort Dix Officers' Club in which the two generals, the colonels, the general staff, and the top brass were in attendance. Other officers who were not in atten-dance with the invited participants of the ball were free to participate at the dance. I did not know about it, and I was not invited and would not have gone there if I had known about the ball. But, I just happened to be there for dinner. Those who were in formal dress were sitting at a long table on the opposite side of the ballroom from where I was sitting. I had finished my dinner and was about to leave when a white lieu-tenant colonel from my organization came to my table with his wife, his seventeen-year-old daughter, her date, and an unescorted white lady friend of theirs. Colonel Yates was Jewish, and he was not at all racist. At the command table there were at least two racist colonels whom I knew, maybe others.

Then the dance started. I was not going to leave, and I was not going to dance during the first round. Then Colonel Yates came back to our table and asked his lady friend why was she not dancing. She said, "I am waiting for him (meaning me)." I jumped up and started dancing, and probably danced every dance after that, including all the women at my table. Dancing is one of my specialties. I am sure that I was rub-bing the necks of the two most racist colonels at the command table. That did not bother me. In fact, I was happy to have done so in front of those two racist colonels. I am sure there were those who appreci-ated me breaking down barriers that the colonels opposed but could do nothing about.

Early the following week, my commanding officer, Colonel Shelton from Mississippi, said to me that Colonel Harrington, the most racist one at Fort Dix, asked me, "Do you have anything on Major White?" I told him, "No. You better watch him," Colonel Shelton said to me. Colonel Shelton was from Mississippi, but he was one Southerner who was not a racist. It did not bother me even though this was the only such dance I participated in during my five years at Fort Dix, New Jersey; but I am glad I did. The reason was that none of my units had command dances.

Prior to this dance event, the Commanding General and I played golf together every Thursday in a four-officer group. The Thursday after the dance, I did not get my usual invitation to participate in this group. I made a few telephone calls to find out what happened. The General's secretary said that someone else was invited to play with the General. I do not feel that the General knew why I was not with his group. I believe his Chief of Staff, one of the other racist colonels, made the change in our foursome, perhaps telling the General that I was not available. My conclusion was that they did not want the General and me to be too chummy, just in case they could plan something up on me to get me into trouble. That did not bother me, because I did not think I was going to do anything so stupid to fall into any traps.

Since I retired from the Army, I came to suspect that Colonel Harrington could have been the plotter for me to accept six T-bones which one of my sergeants brought from the Army's dining facilities. It was similar to what he had previously done against Army women. But, he was barking up the wrong tree. I was always avoiding temptations, whether they were natural or conspired.

I sat on a General Court Martial Board, which tried a black warrant officer with 22 years service. He was waiting for retirement, and was perhaps causing a few problems due to the red tape associated with the retirement. A conspiracy was organized against him, saying that he had taken one bottle of hot sauce and a small salt and pepper shaker from the mess hall (which cost less than $5). Also, he was accused of having a homosexual affair with a gay man. The gay man was given immunity for his testimony. A sergeant, a witness to the homosexual act, described to the court the nature of the homosexual act. The president of the court was just about as racist as Colonel Harrington who always tried to throw the book at blacks. At the same time, he showed mercy for whites for similar incidents. I accused the president of that during closed sessions. I voted "not guilty" because these were obviously trumped up charges, even though they may have been true. But, the other members found him guilty and gave him a dishonorable discharge. His uniform was taken, and he was escorted off the post in civilian clothes. Tears came from my eyes. He, of course, was angry with me and accused me of conspiring with the others to deny him an honorable discharge. Even though I told him that I voted him "not guilty," I could understand his anger. I considered this was a planned conspiracy by Colonel Harrington. He was a master at using soldier spies to set traps of those he wanted to get.

I went to Camp Drum, New York, three out of the five summers that I was stationed at Fort Dix. It was my job there to evaluate the National Guard Divisions of New York and New England. There were three majors working for me doing this evaluation work. These were long working hours along dusty roads and grounds. Not only did I have to evaluate the training and the efficiency of the units, I had to escort VIPs (including Governor Rockefeller, the Army Commander, and dignitaries of all types). The work, although hard, was necessary and enjoyable.

There is a VIP house, the vacation house of the Army commander, which was built for Napoleon, where he was scheduled to go if he should except from Corsica. It is a huge stone mansion with four tall and imposing stone columns. I had the honor to escort General Bruce Clark and some German General who were involved in producing the motion picture the "Battle of the Bulge." I did just about everything at the camp other people could not handle.

I played lots of golf during my summers in Watertown, New York, both on the U.S. side of the border and the Canadian side. I played most of my weekday games at a public course in and around Watertown, but I played other more distant courses on weekends. Most of my civilian and military friends played at the public courses where we had Saturday night dances. These were integrated and causing no problems. Most of my weekend games were played in Kingston, Canada, although I played other nearby Canadian and U.S. courses. I played three courses at Ottawa, the Canadian Capital City, and at Montreal, the Capitol of Quebec, Canada.

One of the Canadian courses that I enjoyed most was at Cornwall. It was a beautiful course, which I saw on the side of the highway between Montreal and Toronto. It was too beautiful to pass up. This was Saturday morning when I stopped by asking to play. "Only members are allowed to play on weekends," I was told. "Let me check." "OK, we are going to let you play." This man will play with you." These were the comments of the starter. At the end of nine, another man played with me. When I finished, the boards of governors of the club--who invited me into the clubhouse as their guest--met me and said, "Joe Louis played here, and we are extending you the Joe Louis courtesy. You can come back and play any time you like." My food and drinks were on the house. All my contacts with the Canadians were wonderful; but this one at Cornwall, Canada, was the best yet.

This was what I called the Royal Canadian treatment. Although I did not go back, I will always remember it. From a racial point of view, I found the Canadians people to be amongst the best people in the World.

There was another very hospitable reception, which I received from the Canadians in Kingston, which is the city where most of the Canadian military schools are located. One Saturday, after I had played a round of golf at the Kingston Country Club, I went to a wall which includes installation where the officers school was located. I knocked on the door of the house, which was a part of the wall, and asked the occupant where the Officers' Club was. He said, "Come in. We are going to the Officers' Club. You can go with us." I was taken to the Officers' Club where everything was on the house. He took me back to his house after we left the club. He said, "It is too late to go back to New York. You better spend the night here." The next morning I had breakfast. The officer said, "I am in the Canadian Navy. I must go to London on some Navy business, but when I come back you are welcome to stop by." I really like the Canadian people. I did not go back because this was my last summer at Camp Drum, now Fort Drum, New York.

We played a golf tournament against the Canadians in Kingston, Canada. It was called the Saint Lawrence Cup. I was the Captain for the U.S. Team. The Canadians beat us, but we had lots of fun. After the tournament, they had a nice reception for us.

During my five years at Fort Dix, I spent three summers at Camp Drum, now Fort Drum.

One summer I spent at Fort Dix. In 1962, I was involved in Swift Strike II, a maneuver exercise with the strategic Army Command, known as the Carolina Maneuvers. A week before I was supposed to go, I shot a 31 on the first nine of the Fort Dix Golf Course and a 37 on the back nine. With this round of 68, I asked the Commanding General, whom I played golf with every week, to allow me to go to Pebble Beach, California, to play in the National Left-Handed Golf Association Tournament which was being held there. I told him that I had been awarded a membership with this organization. He said, "If you had also shot 31 on the back nine, I would let you go." I could only say I tried. I did go to work for the Carolina Military Maneuvers Headquarters.

When I returned from Germany to the United States, the "Black Brass" down at Washington, D.C., said I must have messed up in Germany due to womanizing. I was expected to be number one among black stars of the future. I was a little bit sorry that I did not meet their expectations, but none of them asked me what happened. I always womanized, but it was never a problem. None of my superiors ever accused me of being a womanizer. Some my women may have called me a Casanova, but they had no proof of that either. I kept my women from my women and from the military. In any event, I spent less time with women than married men spent with their families. Women never interfered with my work. Even though, I had given up on a military career beyond a twenty-year retirement, all due to inequality with some of my commanders, and racism in the military.

I was in the in the top ten percent of majors in the Regular Army in September 1957, fourteen years after I came in the Army. To me, this meant that I was first class. I could not let segregation in an integrated Army make me second-class, because I was not; and I was not going to stoop to a level of second-class citizen in order to move ahead. I did not do that on the cotton farms in Alabama; I did not do it at Camp Patrick Henry in Virginia in 1944; I did not do it when I seized the final spearhead objective on April 5, 1945, which was the beginning of the final campaign for ending the war in Italy,

The saddest day for me in the Army was on November 22, 1963. I went into my headquarters at the United States Army Personnel Center where the secretary told me that President Kennedy was shot in Dallas, Texas. I went to my car and listened on the radio for two hours, at which time it was announced that the President had died. I watch the TV coverage of this event from that time on and off for the next several days, after which time the President was laid to rest.

President Johnson used the death of the President and the Civil Rights movement in Birmingham to push the Anti-Discrimination Act of 1964 through Congress. Before my retirement in August 1965, Doctor King had moved into my hometown of Selma, Alabama, at the surrounding four black-belt counties, to help bring about the Voters Rights Act of 1965. It was quite appropriate that the final bill giving black people their fundamental rights guaranteed by the Constitution took place in my hometown before my retirement, both occurring in 1965. I could call myself, with some justification, the "father of the post-war civil rights movement," beginning with the integration of the Armed Forces, followed by the Supreme Court decisions of 1954 and 1955, which gave legal status to the movement. I felt somehow the Lord was doing this for me for the role I had played in the Civil Rights Movement by have the last major battle in my hometown of Selma, Alabama.

Naturally, I watched the movement in my hometown with the greatest interest. I saw on TV when Sheriff Clark slapped Doctor King when he attempted to register people for voting. I saw where some of the hoodlums had murdered a white clergyman. I noticed when a black man was killed in Marion, Alabama, about 15 miles from my country home. I was quite proud when the black people of Pernell Community, my birth community, stood up against the landowner when he threatened to evict them from their homes. They continued to follow Doctor King, and they became refugees in their own community. They bought land from an adjacent plantation to our land and built what I called a new Martin Luther King Village. The action of the landlord became a blessing to the Pernell Community. I could not help but believe that the examples set by my family and me over the years prepared them to stand tall for the Civil Rights movement.

I was greatly upset when a cavalry charge was directed against the first attempted civil rights march from Selma, Alabama to Montgomery, Alabama, some 50 miles away. This attack was lead by Sheriff Clark and the Director of the Highway Patrol for the State of Alabama. They ordered the cavalry charge against the civil rights marchers on Edmond Winston Pettus Alabama River Bridge.

I was greatly disturbed by this incident; therefore, I requested and received a leave of absence from the Army to go to Selma, Alabama. I was concerned about my family and the Civil Rights Movement. My four nieces and nephew met me, and they were quite proud of their stand against Mr. Clark. They said, "Uncle Cecil, you are nobody around here unless you have been in the Sheriff's jail four or five times." They had been locked up collectively between 20 and 25 times. Their morale was high, and nothing was going to stop them from marching to Montgomery. My mother was sixty-nine and could hardly walk, but she was planning to walk those 50 miles. My brother-in-law said to his son, "Junior, I do not mind you marching with Doctor King, but why must you always be at the front of the line?" "Daddy, I can't be on TV at the back of the line," was his reply.

The next day I was hoping to see and talk with Doctor King, but he had gone to Detroit, Michigan, to raise some money. Malcolm X was there. He said, "I did not come here to interfere with Doctor King, but to show them who they must deal with it they don't treat him right." I was at the Brown Chapel Church, the headquarters of Doctor King, where I talked to some of my friends about the morale of the people. I was assured that they were more than ready to go on the second march than the first one. I was concerned about the logistics, security, and rest sights along the way. I checked their arrangements and gave my assurance that they were workable. I returned to Fort Dix to watch the march proceed on Highway 80 to Montgomery. I regret with great sorrow the murder of a white lady from Detroit by a member of the Ku Klux Klan who was later arrested by the FBI in Bessemer, Alabama,

After President Johnson signed the Anti-Discrimination Act of 1964; he informed Doctor King that he had to do something equally as dramatic if he wished to get the Voters' Rights Act through Congress. Selma was picked because it was the hub of five Black Belt Counties, where blacks outnumbered whites. These would be the counties where his greatest resistance would take place. Whites did not want black people to have political domination. When the Selma-to-Montgomery march reached the State Capitol, Doctor King had produced all the drama needed to push the Voters' Right Acts through Congress as requested by President Johnson.

Chapter 13
MILITARY RETIREMENT

During the period 9 June 1943 and 1 September 1965, I feel that my accomplishments were tremendous. My most important role was the integration of the Armed Forces, first by solving the morale problem of the 92nd (Buffalo) Division at Camp Patrick Henry Virginia in September 1944, which not only prevented its deactivation, but also pointed out to the War Department the reason why black soldiers would or would not fight. This led to the integration of this southern base. This act enhanced the morale of black soldiers to such a high level, convincing the Pentagon that if you give black soldiers a reason to fight, they will fight as good as all other soldiers of the United States. Further accomplishment of the 92nd Division in combat provided enough proof for justification of the integration of the services. The integration of the services provided the foundation for the Anti-Discrimination Act of 1964 and the Voters Right Act of 1965. As I left the Army, I had helped it to achieve the accomplishments I predicted as a ten-year-old boy back in 1932.

The last barrier to legal racial discrimination, which prevented integrated marriages, took place in 1969. This was not done by any of the Black Civil Rights organizations, but by a white man who married a black woman in Virginia. They were not allowed to come home together. This really made my prediction come true. This Supreme Court Decision was based in part on its decision of May 1954 and '55 and also on the Anti-Discrimination Act of 1964 and the Voters' Rights Act of 1965.

I was pleased with the role I played in educating my family, which was my first plan for ending discrimination in the South, which I planned as a ten-year-old boy. I assisted in the education of my sisters and brothers who are college graduates and beyond. Out of eight members of my family who had college potential, six became college graduates. Of the two who did not go to college, one sister, Geneva, got married after high school to her high school sweetheart, Fred Martin, who went into the Navy during World War II. One brother was the only high school dropout. One sister was handicapped. I paid for the college education for my two youngest sisters and a son of my brother who was the high school dropout. The standards that were established for my sisters and brother would be applied to their children and grandchildren. There are about 50 people in the three generations of my family, and approximately 70 percent are college graduates.

Before retiring, I gave some thought of going into politics. I knew the county in which I was born was a part of five black belt counties from which the U.S. representative came. After making some inquiries, I found all the black people were angry and wanted to fight. They had supported Doctor King and received their civil rights, but their economic status had not changed. They were not willing to support my views that revenge got us nowhere. I, therefore, decided against politics. I also wanted to take a little vacation away from racism.

Because I felt that it would take 20 years for me to be successful in politics, I decided to be a schoolteacher.

My military career had not been as successful during the last eight and half years as it was in the first fourteen years. At fourteen years of service, I was promoted from the temporary rank of major to the permanent rank of major which was a statutory promotion. I was also ranked in the upper 10 percent of all majors in the Army, and I was on the career ladder for moving to higher positions in the military. Upon getting this information, I planned to go all the way in the military, changing my mind about getting a 20-year retirement because I had not gotten married. There were always question marks in my mind, even when I talked to Chappy James in the spring of 1956. Being a man from Alabama, I knew how deep racism ran there. My service since the end of the World War II had not been in a combat division. In the segregated Army, white officers were picked or volunteered to serve in black units. There were always white officers who refused to and did not serve in black units because of their racism; but in the integrated Army, these officers did not have that choice.

All my life in the South, I had been humiliated and embarrassed by all the racism. I had worked hard up to this time to bring about integration in the Armed Forces, not only because it was authorized under our Constitution but because it was in the best interest of combat efficiency and in the retention of the best black and white personnel in the service. Knowing that a zebra will not change his stripes, I knew that hard-core racist commanders did not leave the service as requested by President Truman if they could not serve in an integrated armed forces. I knew they would do as little as they could get away with on the integration front. I had paid a heavy price for all of it, but I had no choice. I would not have thought much of myself if I had caved into the illegal and unjustified racism I faced. I served under racist commanders who put their racism ahead of their patriotism and their oath of office. I would never be one who would permit myself to be discriminated against when the law was against it, especially in order to satisfy the racist view of my commanders.

My views were based on my belief in democracy and my belief in the power that integration would bring to our Armed Forces. I would never let a racist command make be bow to their level of thinking and the application of their views.

I decided that I wanted to be a history teacher. I learned to like history when I was in high school. The president of the Baptist College was a brilliant man, Dean William H. Dinkins, a brilliant history teacher. As a small boy I always wanted the older people to tell me about their lives. I had taught military history in the two ROTC jobs. When I studied for my Master's Degree in Education, I took American History.

I applied for and obtained a job as a teacher for American and World History at Witherspoon Junior High School in Princeton, New Jersey. I had to take two 3-credit hour courses, one in European History and one in Geography. This qualified me for a teaching license in the above two subjects in the State of New Jersey. I was given six years' seniority for six years of ROTC instructing at two universities. Now, for the first time, I was receiving two paychecks, which was a very good feeling.

I worked hard as a teacher, but I was not as accomplished as I wanted to be. That would take at least three years. I knew that I would make a great and effective teacher, and I would do all that I had to do to make it happen. I had a sort of Southern accent. I spoke fast, and my diction had to improve. This people of this district, the educational elite, were very observant. They wanted only the best for their students. They liked me and my background; and they were tolerant. I was best liked for leadership and the ability to handle the poor and least gifted students. I had the ability to motivate them. But in Princeton the greatest concern was with the elite, and there was a lower priority given to those in the C group or the lowest achievers. Nevertheless, they saw greatness in my potential.

There was one black student in the C Group that I tried to turn around. He was a football player, basketball player, and all-around super athlete. He could probably beat any of the male students there. He was well liked and respected because of his physical power and personality. He would be the first to admit that he was a poor student and a little bit proud of it. I worked on him, asking him what he would like to do when he became a man. "I will be happy to do what my father does. He makes lots of money." "What does he do?" I asked. "He works in the sanitary department." "Why not become the first black president of Princeton University? Then you could become the President of the United States. One Princeton president was President. Do you know who he was?" "No, sir." "Woodrow Wilson," I said.

I continued to work on him.

Two years later, after I left Princeton and returned there from Germany, I asked him how was he doing in football and basketball. He said, "I am not playing sports anymore." "What are you doing?" "I am getting my lessons. I have a B average." I almost broke down in tears. I thought what I said to him had fallen on deaf ears when he was in my seventh grade class. My example as a retired officer from the Army and as a teacher impressed him more after I left than it did when I was there.

While I was there, I tried to change the three academic groupings of the students--A, B, and C groups. They were all right for the two upper groups, but they were kind of a disaster for the lowest group. I believe the recommendations of my "research committee" to stop this type of academic grouping was adopted. The conclusion of our committee was that the grouping arrangement gave the upper two groups a feeling of superiority and the lower one a feeling of inferiority. By changing the attitude, working with the parents, and giving tutoring assistance, this could help elevate the lower achievement level student to move gradually to the upper level. That would prevent them from being written off as poor achievers and would help them to feel that they could achieve as well as anyone else. This, to me, was the role of education and the one the teachers should work to accomplish. The school's role, in my opinion, was to help every student, and not to lose anyone. I liked the teaching job and the students, but realized that I had much work to do to help me realize my potential.

I was pretty well accepted into the Princeton University community. For some reason, teachers were highly respected there. When I went to the bank that I used there, everyone was very polite and showed great appreciation for me using their bank. They even spoke when they saw me on the street. My politics were a little different from that of a typical Princetonian, which was conservative Republicanism. Mine was democratic, or a member of the Democratic Party.

Bill Bradley, who was a former Democratic senator from New Jersey, was a student at the University and a member of the basketball team. His politics were the same as mine. He was very popular with the students at my school. He came to us with some of his fellow basketball teammates and did some shooting and made a few demonstration shots for our students. They were given a big standing ovation for their performance. Later he became a professional basketball player with the New York Nicks and became a world champion.

The School Superintendent asked me to appear with him before the Chamber of Commerce, whose members were surely all Republicans. I was their guest along with one of the U.S. diplomats who returned from Cambodia. He gave the Chamber of Commerce his assessment of the situation there and its prognosis for the future. Because of the fluidity of the situation there, any guess would be about as good as another. About the only thing we could discuss was the existing situation and the hope of people for the future.

We talked a bit about Vietnam; I had my own philosophy about that war. The bad thing was that it was a no-win war mission and another was the high number of casualties experienced because of the policy there. The U.S. Army was not allowed to attack the enemy across the North Vietnam border. The containment policy prevented a further expansion of communism into Thailand and Indonesia, which was the good part about that war. The bad part was that it was a no-win war like Korea. This was my attitude about that war. And everyone there seemed to have been in general agreement with me on that issue. The fact that I appeared at the Chamber of Commerce meeting was an indication of the great respect afforded teachers in Princeton.

I remember sitting at a bar with a Princeton lawyer at one of the golf courses, and he was discussing his opposition to interracial marriages. I said marriage is a private matter. It is complicated enough for those who must marry and live together, without someone else telling them whom they can or cannot marry. Marriage, to me, is the most private of business. There has always been integration, and there will always be integration. This is healthy. The worst thing is for someone going around telling others what he or she can or cannot do. I am not so sure whether I changed his mind; I know that he did not change mine.

The people in Princeton still worship George Washington. The first U.S. victory in the American Revolution took place at Trenton and Princeton. A professor of history at the University, who had a son in my class, took my class on a field trip where the battle of Princeton took place. He explained first the battle of Trenton and showed how it led to the Battle of Princeton, and the personal role that General Washington performed in that battle. The fact that the United States Capitol was temporarily established in Princeton is one the highlights of Princeton history. The Colonial Government had to leave Philadelphia. It was established temporarily in Princeton and later it was moved to Morristown, New Jersey.

I was in the market for a wife, and I found the pickings around Princeton were not too promising. I decided to resign my teaching position and go to Germany and teach in American military schools there. I went first in July 1946, where I talked to a black principal who lived in Darmstadt. He gave me hope that a position could be found if I returned in August. I went back to New Jersey and made arrangements to return by U.S. aircraft and had my belongings shipped by military transportation. This was my retirement move paid by the U.S. Government, which it gives each retiree one year to decide where he wishes to establish his retirement home. My things were sent to Darmstadt, Germany, where I was hoping to teach.

My massage lady in Nuernberg with those three daughters, who wanted me to marry one of them, sent me a letter at Princeton to visit her in Cincinnati as her youngest daughter was apparently eligible for me. I had planned to visit her if I made some money in the stock market. Because I did not, I did not make the trip. I left for Germany on my permanent move, landing in Frankfurt, and went by train to Mannheim, Germany; where my golfing buddy from Fort Dix, a Major Borden, had moved with his family. I got a room in the bachelor officers' quarters in Benjamin Franklin Village where I lived in 1957-1959. Within a day or so I was on the phone calling about jobs.

One of my first calls was to the Education Agency located at the Southern Area Command in Munich, Germany, the same higher headquarters that I had when I was located in Nuernberg as Special Service Officer. I kind of hit the jackpot. The agency had a temporary GS9 job as Education Officer. It would be necessary for me to go to Munich to fill out an application and take a physical examination. I did all this and I was in. I was assigned as Education Officer for Wackernheim, McCully Barracks and Fin then Air Field in Mainz, Germany. Because of that job, I have lived in Mainz for 32 years, even though the job lasted for only three years.

The job I wanted as a schoolteacher was out because General deGaulle had required NATO to close down its operation in France, making it necessary to relocate elsewhere. This meant teachers in France had seniority rights over new teachers coming over from the States. This required me and other new teachers to look elsewhere or go back to the States. My mission now was to work and look for a wife. The work I had, but there was no wife in sight. Being an education officer was like being a special service officer, in that they were jobs that I liked. Helping soldiers get educated was always close to my heart. I had done a little of this back in Frankfurt in 1948, and I had pushed academic education while I was on active duty.

I finished the last year of college while I was on ROTC at Tuskegee. I got my master's degree during the three years that I was at South Carolina State University. There was not anyone, I believe, who felt that soldiers needed more civilian education in order to be a better soldier than I.

Most education officers were afraid of their commanders, but I was not. When I went out to my center at McCully Barracks at Wackernheim, I read the Army regulation on education dealing with the commanders' mission for the education of his soldiers. Every soldier must have a high school education; every warrant officer, two years of college; and every officer, four years of college. The commander at McCully was in the field when I got there, which gave me time to get organized and to work out a formula for carrying out the mandate in the regulation. When he returned, I introduced myself. I told him that I had acquainted myself with my job, his educational responsibility under Army regulations, and my recommendation on how I planned to help him to meet his educational obligations. I explained that when he goes to the field, my program would stop; and it would start again when he returned. Right away he gave full approval to my plans.

The U.S. Army Europe Commander said there would be no civilian education during duty hours, meaning during the day. Because my people were working on shift, some were always off and some were all ways on. Therefore, under the definition of the Army Commander, I could have my classes any time I wanted for serving those soldiers not working. As a result, my center and another center serving the higher headquarters of my unit fell into that category. Right away I had to find additional classrooms for serving my soldiers. We soon had the best education program in Germany. I was very forceful with my conviction with the battalion commander by showing him how he would benefit by my education program. We developed a perfect team to help him accomplish his mission. Even when he had some problems with his military program, I would develop programs to help him with his problem. I had more experience and knowledge for being a battalion commander than he had, and I could use it to help him. I do not believe any of the education officers in Europe were as strong as I for making the Army education more workable for helping the Army.

When I came to the Mainz area, Major General Cassidy was the commanding General of the 8th

Infantry Division at Bad Kreuznach, Germany. I was a member of this Division from October 1957 until February 1959. I was in it when it moved from the area near Stuttgart and Nuernberg to its present location. Maybe I had every right to hate this Division, because it was here where I was treated so unjustly; but I held no grudges. The General was given his second star when he left the 101st Airborne Division where he served as the assistant division commander. While he was there, he became knowledgeable with the new computerized maintenance program, which had been developed for the Army. He had already put it in place within his division and had set up courses at the Non-commissioned Officers' School at Baumholder to implement this maintenance program. He was concerned with a continuous loss of his instructors in this program due to them being transferred to Vietnam.

General O'Mera, the U.S. Army Europe Commander, had forbid the education center to teach academic classes during duty hours, virtually shutting down the education centers throughout his command, with the exception of the night classes taught by the University of Maryland. General Cassidy noticed this. He called in my boss, Mr. Holt, Education Supervisor for General Education Development (GED) District Number 2, which was located also at Bad Kreuznach. Mr. Holt contacted his superiors in Munich, which saw a new mission for the Education Agency. The Agency sent one of their Education Officers to the Army Readiness School in Murnau, Germany, to become acquainted with the program. He was sent to the NCO School at Baumholder with a bunch of slides for the purpose of briefing some twenty to thirty education officers in Germany coming from each of the Educational districts.

After the first hour, all of the permanent education officers in Germany disappeared because they saw a mission impossible for them; and they wanted no part of it. When Mr. Holt, District No. 2 Education Supervision, returned to the classroom after the first period of instruction, he found only three of us there. He saw me, a twenty-two year old wife, and another temporary education officer who was in Germany with his wife, who was on a year's leave from Tulane University in New Orleans. He said to the three of us, "You are in charge!" I just about thought the guy was crazy because none of us had any knowledge of nor had ever heard about this program before.

He gave us a TM 38-750, the technical manual written for one of the programs, called TAERS, The Army Equipment Record System. The motor officers called this book a manual written by PhDs to be read by PFCs (which meant it could not be read with any understanding by the soldiers). Others said it was written by geniuses to read by idiots. In reality, it seemed more like the last statement was correct. When Mr. Holt said, "You are in charge," I knew that if this program was ever going to be developed, it had to be done using my initiative. First I looked at the forms to be taught, recognizing only two of more than twenty forms. The two which I recognized were the DA Form 2400, the old trip ticket which may have been used with horses, and DA Form 2401, Dispatchers Record which showed all the equipment in use, the time of dispatch, and the user. The rest of the forms were all newly developed. We had to teach the use of these forms in the manual dealing with motor vehicles. We had to teach about 15 such forms in a 40-hour instructional period.

I counted the forms and the number of pages of instruction in the manual given to each of them, divided the total number of pages given to the 15 forms, and divided that into 40 hours of instruction. Then each form had a ratio of the total time required to teach it by the pages in the manual allotted to each of them. I developed a time schedule for each form during the 40 hours of the instructional period for the TAERS course. I decided to spread the forty hours of academic instruction over a two-week period, four hours in the morning for classroom work and four hours in the afternoon for practical work. I figured practical work would complement the classroom instruction and provide more time for writing lesson plans. My teachers would visit the motor pool to see what their students were doing.

When Mr. Holt came back into the classroom, I showed him my plans for teaching the course. Then he said to me "You are in charge." I guess this was the best thing for a bad situation. I assigned each of us a lesson plan development assignment. I took the first day, the lady the second day, and the other temporary GS9, the third day. When the first class started the next Monday, we had developed and rehearsed for four days of instruction. I wrote the first and fourth days, and I would write the fifth day.

I discovered the two sergeants who had previously taught the TAERS program. I got permission from the Commandant of the NCO Academy to let the sergeants sit in on my instructors during the first course for the purpose of correcting their mistakes. When the first class started that following Monday, I said to the new students that we are new at this and will probably make mistakes but that I had two sergeants in the rear of the room who will correct our instructor mistakes. I said that, "I don't know how many mistakes will be made, but everyone will work to make sure that the instruction you get will be correct. "

The General Education Development Agency (GED) had a book writer to work with us to collect information for writing our first text book. When this class ended two weeks' later, my teachers received a standing ovation for their efforts. While my two instructors were teaching TAERS, I was supervising them and writing a forty-hour program for MILSTRIP, Military Supply and Requisitioning System. This was a supply, requisitioning, and inventory control system, which the Army got from Sears, Roebuck and Company. The TAERS instructors used the two sergeants to coach them. I got the Command Maintenance Inspector for MILSTRIP to coach and correct me. I was able to teach these 40 hours with little difficulty.

After the first class, my other two instructors could teach the TAERS program without assistance. The lady became the permanent TAERS teacher for the Baumholder area. The man, who was the temporary Education Officer for Baumholder, would now work only at that job, and would not be used any more as a TAERS teacher. I would teach a Maintenance Supervisors Course, consisting of both TAERS and MILSTRIP for officers, motor officers, motor sergeants and senior non-commissioned officers. The officers I taught went as high as battalion commanders and could have been quite useful for brigade commanders as well. My college education in automotive science and my computer program training at IBM in Philadelphia while I was at Fort Dix made me an ideal for the computerized maintenance programs.

The Battalion Commander of the 8th Medical Battalion sent his Adjutant (S-1), and a first lieutenant to my Maintenance Supervisor Class. Both officers achieved an average grade of 96 for the course, but they would not take the honor student award, but instead allowed it to be given to an enlisted student with the highest grade.

The adjutant made his lieutenant classmate the motor officer and he loaded my maintenance supervisor courses after that with officers and non-commissioned officers from his battalion. This battalion would soon achieve the highest maintenance average in Europe, a rating of 98. It was so good that after the battalion commander left, the next battalion rested on his laurels and did nothing for two years and still had the best maintenance in Europe. He was a little drunk most of the time, but he was the untouchable. He sent no one to school. My efforts to get him to maintain the standards, which he inherited, fell on deaf ears. When I said to him that his replacement would fall on his face when he leaves, he just laughed.

My prediction did occur, and I told his replacement about it. He did not believe me.

After I taught several classes in the 8th Division, I was invited by a Mr. Coffee at Kaiserslautern to teach a TAERS class to the Air Defense Command maintenance personnel there at his education center. These air defense students were super smart and they knew a great deal about the system, but they did not know it all. I learned a lot from them without letting them know it. The class was a great success and from then on I included missile batteries, a part of the Air Defense Command, which were scattered over the hills throughout the state of Rheinland-Pfalz in my teaching areas of responsibility.

Mr. Coffee, one of the Education Officers who ran away after the first briefing before his program started, had to be impressed with how this program had developed. There were seventeen education centers in GED District No. 2. I would eventually get to every one of them and train teachers for some of them.

Just about every weekend I went down to Mannheim where I visited my old golfing buddy, Major Borden. When I first talked to him about how his maintenance was doing at the heavy truck battalion at Turley Barracks, he indicated it was going good and that he had a good motor sergeant. I later told him that I bet his motor sergeant was not as good as he thinks he is. I said, "How do you know how good he is?" He stated that he just believed he is good. I began to educate him about maintenance. The more I taught him, the more he checked. He finally told his motor sergeant that he was going to send him to school, because he did not know his job. Soon my friend got all superior ratings in maintenance and combat readiness programs. His battalion thought he was a superman, giving him all 7's on his efficiency report. The maintenance and combat readiness of his heavy truck battalion was best of all heavy truck battalions in Germany. He had no trouble getting promoted later to Lieutenant Colonel after he was transferred to Korea.

When I first started teaching these maintenance classes, I estimated the maintenance level in Europe to be about 30 percent. Maintenance personnel were working to 2300-2400 hours. At nights, getting ready for inspection, including weekends, then failing maintenance inspection, and doing it again and again, still failing. Six months after these classes were started, there were almost no failures and no overtimes getting ready for them.

In the beginning Colonel Horton, Brigade Commander in Mainz where I lived, failed a maintenance inspection. He asked the Education Center secretary to locate me and ask me to schedule a maintenance class for his Brigade. I did, and he passed the next inspection.

In December 1966, I went to Munich where I received a hero's welcome for developing this program and giving the Education Agency a new mission. I was asked to develop an instructional book for the program, which I did. Later I was given orders to come to Munich and become the European Director for this program. General Cassidy became aware of it. He called his buddy, the Commanding General of the Southern Area Command, blocking my transfer. He apologized to me for it, but he felt that since it was he who started this program that he should receive the benefit of my service. I told him that he was correct and that I had no objection to him blocking my move. His 8th Division had the best maintenance of any of the divisions in Germany, which I am sure helped him later to become a four-star general in Korea.

General Cassidy had great confidence in my ability to find the problems with his maintenance and correct them. He directed his brigade commanders to utilize my services whenever they had maintenance problems. This is what Colonel Hotrod did. The General told his Chief of Staff to give me whatever I wanted, although I did not bother the Chief; but I worked with the G-3, telling him whom I wanted for students and in what order. First, the motor officers who thought they knew everything. I took great pleasure shooting their EGOs down and showing them where they were making mistakes. I did not find a single motor officer who did not improve 30 percent after taking my Maintenance Supervisors Course.

I had a perfect background for this course. I had a college degree in automotive science. My first job as an officer was battalion motor officer. Before retiring from the Army, I took computer programming with IBM though Temple University in Philadelphia, Pennsylvania. My knowledge of the program made me an authority in the computer-related maintenance within six months. I corrected maintenance inspectors when they made inspection errors, which required them to work more closely with me for the benefit of all concerned. The three maintenance programs, which I played a major role in developing, raised the maintenance level in Europe 40 percent during the first six months these programs were taught. The 8th Medical Battalion at McCully Barracks in Mainz Germany, the installation where my Education Center was located, raised its maintenance level from approximately 30 percent to 98 percent, the highest in Europe.

I later wanted to raise the maintenance to the level so that the United Army Europe Commander could push a button, at his Headquarters in Heidelberg, Germany; and he could receive the exact maintenance status of any company size unit in his command, and that I could guarantee it. They could not conceive of it, much less to feel that I could do it. At that time the maintenance was so good that everyone wanted it to continue in the manner it was going. One of the missile battalions, which had its headquarters at the Wiesbaden Air Base, would not honor a requisition for spare parts unless the signer of the requisition had a maintenance certificate signed by me. I had a warrant officer, newly assigned to this battalion, who signed a requisition while he was still a student. I had to sign a temporary certificate so that he could get the parts that he needed.

In 1966 when I returned to Germany, General deGaulle was already having the NATO force to relocate out of France. A petroleum command unit, which had not passed an inspection in two years, sent their mortar sergeant to a TAERS class, which I held in Neubruecken, Germany, just south of Baumholder. The next week he took a MILSTRIP or PLL (prescribed load list) class. He passed both classes. Two weeks later he told me that he passed his first CMMI (Command Maintenance Inspection) in two years.

Chapter 14
FINDING A WIFE

To me finding a wife, the right wife, was perhaps the most important post- retirement mission for me. One lady said to me, shortly after World War II, "You will never get married. Your standards are too high." I agreed on the standards issue. I liked beautiful women with character, which did not always go together. And when I found one, the competition was fierce. I already mentioned some of the girls whom I wanted to marry; but for reasons I could not understand, some unknown something always prevented it. It appeared to me that God did not want me to get married at those times and with the ladies whom I wished to marry.

This time I returned to Europe to find her. Why? One reason, I did not have any prejudice. Another one was that I was not going to let someone else's prejudice determine who she would be. As a small boy, in 1932, I said to my father, "All this racism will not end until a black man is free to marry a blonde. It appeared that all the prejudice projected against the black man was blonde related. Just about all the prejudice projected against me and my military career was blonde related, even though I never dated an American blonde. This was a great barrier directed against black men. The white man had no barrier as such.

One of the great characteristics of man is that he does not like barriers. When King George III said to the American colonists that they should not go beyond the Alleghenies, they did. Man climbs mountains because they are there. They learn to sail the seas, under the seas, fly in the air, orbit the earth, and land on the moon. Men do not like barriers. In 1969, the U.S. Supreme Court lifted the last legal racist barrier by outlawing state statues preventing interracial marriages. Now that the barrier is lifted, the adventure is gone. The black man did not rush to the altar with his white bride when that barrier was lifted.

My most important mission for coming to Germany was to find a wife. This would be my fourth trip to Europe. Because of the amount of time I spent in Europe, most of my dates were with European women. I had never been married and I wanted a nice young wife. European women married older men more traditionally than American women. I first started looking for a wife in Mainz, where I resided. I went to clubs in Mainz and nearby Wiesbaden. Often I could not even get a dance, much less find a girl. The German girls were not as hot on Americans as they once were. The German men had moved up in the world and had taken control of their women. In Mainz, it was often thought that the Germans were hostile to us for all of the bombs that fell on Mainz during the war. Some of the reasoning was due to the parachute units that were stationed here. They had a reputation of messing up things for us.

Wiesbaden at the Park Cafe was the nicest place around, a little expensive, but it was wonderful. I had lots of dances there; but I did not meet or have a relationship with a girl that I considered wife material. When I was Special Services Officer in Nuernberg, I had more girls than I knew what to do with; and I was always looking for more. Now in Mainz, I did not have one.

I did have a girl left over from Nuernberg who lived in Garmisch. She came to Nuernberg at the invitation of my German Assistant Craft Director when I was there in the military. When I met her, I offered to show her around. I showed her where I lived. I visited her in Garmisch where she lived. She was the widow of a doctor who had died more than twelve years earlier, and she had remained very pious since his death. I guess my sudden and surprise action took away her guilt because she could not resist me. I went to the United States about a year after I met her, even though I visited her only a few times during that one year. When I visited her after six years later in 1966, without writing or contacting her, she acted as if she had been waiting all these years. She was a very fine woman who in all probability had been pious since our previous relations. I liked being with her, but not for marriage, because her age was too close to mine; and I wanted a much younger wife.

At no time did I have a steady girlfriend in Mainz. I was forty-five when I returned to Germany, and time was looking like it was running out on me for marriage. I was doing quite well financially, making good money from my job and retirement income. The exchange rate between the dollar and the DM was better than four to one, gasoline was twenty cents per gallon, and board was free. I could afford to go out and live it up every night.

I went to Munich, Holland, Hamburg and Denmark; but I was still not finding a girl that I wished to marry. In May or June 1967, I was driving down the German autobahn, driving from Mannheim in the direction of Frankfurt, when a car passed me with three people in it--a man, a woman, and a young lady. They waved at me. I passed them and waved backed. There was a German rest area with a restaurant. I waved for them to follow me. They did. We had coffee, cake, beer and drinks of choice. I invited them by my apartment where I served some more drinks of choice and whatever else I had that they accepted. I told them that the following weekend I was going to Garmisch to play in a golf tournament, and I would like to take the young lady as my guest. They agreed to it.

She lived about 100 miles away. She traveled by train to the Mainz train station where I picked her up. We departed immediately for Garmisch, driving by Nuernberg where we spent the night. This young lady would not sleep in the room with me, requiring me to buy her a separate room. I did not like it and hoped things would change in Garmisch. When I got to Garmisch, things did not change. After playing the first day of the tournament, I took her out to eat and returned to the hotel, where she still would not stay in my room. I was a little peeved and was about to send her back to her mother.

The next day on my way to the hotel, two pretty fresh young ladies wanted to hitch a ride from me. I stopped. They said, "We are from Berlin. We are living at that big hotel. We would like to go to the Sternberg See (Lake Sternberg)." I said, "I cannot do that because I have a date waiting for me." "Let her wait. We want to go to Sternberg See." I began thinking that letting her wait was a good idea because she had not been very cooperative. We drove to Sternberg where we walked along the beaches of the lake stopping at some of the inns where we ate and drank a bit. Then I drove them back to the Golf Hotel, the biggest one in Garmisch. I had stayed there many times. I put them out at the hotel, making a date for the next evening.

I was planning to send the girl home who came down with me. When I got to my hotel she was steaming mad, wanting to know where I had been. I just told her I did not rush home because of the way she had been acting. She decided that she was going home on her own, which was all right with me.

A Mexican-American soldier friend of mine who was leading the tournament was my guest the next evening. I invited him to join me with the two young ladies from Berlin. He agreed to it. I picked them up, but the girls were disappointed that I had brought him along. Anyway, we went out and wined and dined and danced. Then I took them back to their hotel. I did not make a date with them for the next night because it looked as if they were using me to pay the bills and entertain them; and they were not putting down anything, not even a kiss. The next evening after my third round of golf, I decided to look around Garmisch on my own and see whom I could find. I was not having any luck; then those two Berlin girls came along. They were better than nothing. I took them out again--wining, dining and dancing. I took them out four times before heading back to Mainz and work.

I was back in Garmisch again in July. At this time they were working at the hotel. Later they went to Yugoslavia on vacation, before heading back to Berlin. In the fall they flew to Frankfurt and to my place. That weekend we drove to Tegern See (Lake) a resort area east of Munich. I kept trying to get an invitation from them to visit Berlin, but they would not give me one. They were using me and I was going to use them to help me find a wife; but I was not having much success at it. The next time they came we stayed in the Mainz area where we visited some of the nice clubs in Mainz and the Park Cafe in Wiesbaden. I figured that by advertising myself with these pretty chicks, I would improve my standing in the area for finding a local girl who fit my standards. That did not work either.

We made another trip back to Garmisch. This time we went out with another beautiful girl. I tried to play up to her as we danced. I thought I made good progress with her. When I sent the two Berlins back home, I wrote this girl a letter and told her that I was coming to Garmisch to see her. I went to the hotel where she worked, but the owner did not want to let me see her. I did see her, but she was not interested.

I thought the lady hotel owner who always had a crush on me had something to do with it. This was the first time I met the hotel owner. I found him to be an epileptic, and he died very shortly after I met him.

During the same period I met my old lady friend in Garmisch. I do not know if she knew of my previous visits to Garmisch without seeing her. She would not have mentioned it, even if she knew I was there. Previously when I visited her, I had to leave sometime around midnight, because she did not want her neighbors to know that she had someone there other than visiting friends and no one staying there overnight. Because she had some knowledge that the lady owner of the hotel had an interest in me, she began to allow me to spend the night at her house so that I would not stay at the hotel. Once when she knew I was staying there, she invited me to her house, saying that I no longer had to stay at the hotel when I came to visit her.

She was happy when the daughter of Dean Rusk, the Secretary of State, married a black man. She let me know that she approved of mixed marriages. My old assistant craft director was there during one of my visits, suggesting marriage, asking me how old I was. First, I wanted to know the age of my friend. When she gave it, I gave mine as six years younger, even though I was four years older. She said to me that the Commanding General of the German Air Force wanted to marry her, but he was too old. He was fifty-eight, and she was forty-two. When I told her what my age was, it kind of dimmed her hope of marrying me. I felt bad when I always had to wiggle out of marrying women who wanted to marry me, but I always felt that it was much better to do it before marriage than after marriage. .

In the summer of 1968, those two Berlin beauties wanted to fly down to Mainz because they wanted once again to drive to Garmisch to see their lady friend who owned the Golf hotel. By this time I was becoming a little sick of these girls who were using me, without me being able to use them. Therefore, I told them that this would be the last time that they could come as my guest. They agreed, permitting us to make the trip. The lady at the hotel gave us two rooms across the hall from each other. One of the ladies, speaking in German, told the owner that I wanted one of them to spend the night with me; but that they were not going to do it. We had a nice time. That Sunday evening I took them back to Frankfurt for their return flight to Berlin. I told them that I was going on vacation to Stockholm, Sweden.

Because I had not had any luck finding a wife elsewhere in several European countries, I decided to try my luck in Stockholm. Before I went to Sweden, I spent a few days in Copenhagen, Denmark, going to a nightclub called the Christian Pearl, only a short ferry ride from Sweden. I met a group there from Stockholm. One of the girls invited me to call her when I got to Stockholm. I went there by train because I wanted to see the Swedish countryside with all those red barns. I guess the barns were painted this color because they become more visible when the snow starts falling in the winter. I arrived at the main train station at the capital city, where I got a taxi to my hotel, which I arranged through the American Express in Copenhagen. This was a very exclusive place.

Later, I caught a streetcar downtown where I could see the parliament building where the Swedes present their Nobel prizes. On the way back to the hotel, I made some inquiries as to where I should get off. One nice lady agreed to show me. I invited her to get off with me for a drink, showing my appreciation for her kindness. She agreed to do so. She told me that she was involved with the Vietnam deserters who were refugees there. Once at my hotel, I made some romantic overtures to her, which she accepted. I went up to my room and got a bottle of Scotch, which I took with me. We dated for three days. When I left during my third evening, she told me not to go into the underground club at my hotel because there were too many wild young people there. This was one of the places in Stockholm that I was looking for. When I got there, I found some super beautiful girls. One of the Swedes said to me, "If you want a girl you must fight for her." As each round started, there was a mad scramble to get a girl for the next round. I was never able to catch the one I liked, but I managed to get a girl every time. I said that I was going to come back to Stockholm, because I feel that I can find a wife up here. I flew back to Copenhagen, with a fond memory of Stockholm.

The girl who invited me to call her when I came back to Stockholm could not get away because of her boyfriend.

I spent a couple nights in Copenhagen going to one of the nicest clubs there, where it had some super beautiful prostitutes. They were too expensive for me, but I did get free dances from them. Before going back to Mainz, I spent a night at Hamburg, visiting the Reeperbahn, the wildest street in the world. When a person goes into one of those nightclubs, a girl would come to his table and begin pulling his pants down right there in the club. I said this is too much. When you accept it, they take you back into a private booth in the club, followed by very expensive champagne. I was there before, I was short of money, and I did not take the bait.

I drove back to Mainz again, failing to find a girl to marry. The girls in Berlin knew when I was returning from my vacation. One of them called me, saying they would like to visit me one more time. I said no. She said, "Sesso (Cecil), we have a girlfriend in Freiburg (Germany) whom me met last summer in Yugoslavia. We told her about you, and she said that it is all right with her parents if you come with us to visit her." I said, "OK, but this is the last time that you can visit me for sure." They agreed that this would be the last time. I picked them up at the Frankfurt Airport, taking them to my apartment for the last time.

The next morning, we headed for the largest city in the German Black Forest, stopping at Vernheim, near Mannheim, to see another friend of the girls. She was married and had a couple of children. I was anxious to leave for our final destination.

We found a place in the middle of the city of Freiburg where we bought flowers for the Scharf Family whom we would be visiting. We followed the direction given us at the flower shop and were able to find the house we were to visit which was less than ten minutes away. I met the mother and father of the girl whom we were visiting. The girl was dressing. I sat in the corner of her room, which is often the custom in Germany.

I saw a large picture of a super beautiful young lady on the wall. I asked one of my Berlin friends, "Who is that?" "She is our girlfriend," one of them answered. I said to myself, "That's her! That's her! She is the girl that I have been looking for the world over. She is the one I cannot say no to." After two hours, she came out give me a warm greeting. I did not change my mind. She was still the one. Now it was necessary for me to woo her my way.

I was very receptive to her parents who had very good feelings about Americans. Both of them worked at an American Officers' Club in a place called Hof an der Saale (Hof on the Saale River) which was located on the East German-Czechoslovakia borders with West Germany. Her father graduated from the University of Leipzig, one of the world's most famous music universities from which Bach, Beethoven, Mozart, and just about all of Germany's most famous musicians graduated. Her mother came from Elbing, West Prussia, near Danzig, just north of Warsaw in Poland. She left East Germany ahead of the Russian advance. They moved to Hof for safety, and it was not far from her father's home in Leipzig.

The daughter was born in Hof where her father needed a clarinet so he could earn some money. He took some of the old German Riechmarks, which was in silver. He took it to a man who made instruments. He melted those silver coins and made a clarinet for her father, which he used to play at the U.S. Army Officers' Club where his wife worked. Both of them credit their survival to the United States Army. They had good reason to feel good about me because I was a retired major, I taught school at Princeton, New Jersey, and I had a good job in computer-related maintenance.

That night, I took my dates, three beautiful young ladies, to a nightclub in Freiburg. While those two Berlin foxes were floating around dancing from one man to another, I held tightly to Evelin, the name of the daughter whom we were visiting. I was dancing close, and she was not pushing me away. I asked her, "Will it be all right with your parents if I visit you sometime?" She gave me the impression that she thought it would be acceptable. We continued all that evening doing the same until closing. We ate and drank and had a very merry time. I took the girls to Evelin's house, and then I went to a very small hotel nearby where a reservation had been made for me.

The next morning I got up and had breakfast, I believe, at Evelin's house. With my white four-door Oldsmobile, we drove up the mountain into the Black Forest, stopping at one place before we began our climb and taking a few pictures. My first stop on the mountain was at Lake Tittisee. We lay under the sun, swam in the lake, ate, and drank. I stayed ever so close to Evelin without the two Berliners knowing what was going on. After staying there for several hours, we climbed higher and onto the other side of the highest mountain, Feldberg, stopping at a flat place in one of the green valleys, where I demonstrated how to hit golf balls, hitting a few balls which I did not bother to find. We drove further on the east side of Feldberg, stopping at Schluchsee the largest lake in the Black Forest, which was man made. We stopped there for some refreshments. Then we drove further eastward to St. Blasien, a city in the county, which bordered with Switzerland. We had dinner there and looked at some of the sights in this beautiful old city. Evelin had a cousin there, but we did not visit him. After this, we headed back to Freiburg; this time we did not stop.

Evelin had agreed for me to visit her in three weeks. We thanked Evelin and her parents for receiving us and making our visit there so wonderful.

Rosy, the blonde girl from Berlin, was beginning to fall in love with me and put a make-shift engagement ring on my finger. I was saying to myself, "It's too late." All the way to the Frankfurt Airport she was showing feelings which she had not shown in the almost eighteen months which I had known her. When she got to Berlin, she wrote me and called me, saying that she was sorry that she tried to make a fool out of me. I said, "You did not make a fool out of me." She even invited me to visit her in Berlin, which I did not accept.

During the third week, I received a letter from Evelin telling me not to come this week, but the next week. The next week, she said do not come this week, but the next week. The next week I wrote her a letter that I was going to Garmisch and that I would drive to visit her from there. I made my last visit to my old girlfriend there, but I did not tell her that I would not be back. I planned to spend that Friday in Munich. Then on Saturday, I planned to drive to Freiburg. I stopped by the Garmish Golf Course, where I saw the lady owner of the Golf Hotel, having coffee with some other lady bigwigs around Garmisch. While she was having her coffee, she gave me the snob treatment. When everyone left, we had our last chat. Whether she knew it or not, she was number two on my list for marriage, if things did not work out with Evelin.

As planned, I spent the night at the U.S. Army Columbia Hotel in Munich and drove the next day to Freiburg. When I arrived in Freiburg, Evelin and her mother were surprised to see me, because she had written me another letter, telling me not to come this week, but the next week. I wrote her that I was going to Garmisch, so that I would not get a letter from her, telling me to come the next week, and not this one. Her reason for sending the last letter for telling me not to come was because she had a cold. She soon found out that my being there helped that cold to go away. I assumed that the other letters were to give her an opportunity to drop some of her boyfriends.

We went to a very nice restaurant about ten miles outside of Freiburg, where we hit it off good, having a romantic good time. I even talked about marriage so she would not get the impression that I was down there to love and leave her. She did not think so. She said that because I was a black man, she did not think I would marry a blonde. I said, "I will marry you on Monday, if you want proof." We had a 'wine-and-dine' good evening together alone for the first time. The next day we drove to some of the nearby places where our romance would continue to grow. We always went to the nicest restaurants and the nicest places. With the exchange rate being four marks to a dollar, I could have the best of time for about $30 per day. I also wooed her parents, as well as Evelin, with some nice gifts.

During this period I stopped by the Officers' Club at Heidelberg with a young lady that I met in Mannheim. I met an old friend, Lieutenant Colonel Frank Plummer. I met Frank first when we was student at the Officers' Advance Course, at the Infantry School at Fort Benning, Georgia, in 1951. Frank was a lieutenant, and I was a Captain then. We had 5 black officers in this class and about 145 white officers. We black officers considered Frank to be the nicest white officer in the class, although all of them acted nice. This was the first time that I had seen him since then. He informed me that he was on the list to make full colonel. When he received his promotion, he said that he would invite me to a steak dinner. To my surprise, he made colonel and became commanding officer of the First Parachute Brigade at Lee Barrack in Mainz where I lived. This was July 1969.

I was teaching a TAERS class the week he arrived there. I invited him that Friday to give out certificates to the graduating class. When he arrived, we embraced each other. I congratulated him for his promotion and on his new command assignment. He told the class about the history of our relationship and then he announced that he had just received a superior rating in maintenance. He quizzed the people responsible as to what they attributed this superior rating. They said to these classes. Then he gave out the certificates.

He invited me that evening over to his house for that promised steak dinner. His driver picked me up at my quarters and took me to Frank's house. I met his second wife who was from Boston and his two children. Then I told him about my expected marriage to a German Girl who lived in Freiburg in the Black Forest near Switzerland and France. I departed his home, thanked him for the nice evening, and his driver drove me back to my quarters. I also told him that I would send him an invitation to the wedding.

The following week I had a TAERS class at Spangdahlem Air Base near Luxembourg. On Thursday of that week, I got a call from the Secretary of the Education Center at Lee Barracks in Mainz telling me that Colonel Plummer had canceled my TAERS class scheduled for the following week and asked me if I knew why. I said no, but I suspected that he did it because of my forthcoming wedding with a German girl. He was not hurting me; he was hurting himself. This just gave me a week's worth of vacation to be with my future bride.

I continued to visit Evelin every three weeks until Christmas 1968, at which time I went to the States to see my mother and family. I bought her a Christmas present and told her I would write her from the States. I believe I wrote her every day, using my Fort Dix post office box, which I'd had since before my retirement. My nieces criticized me for writing every day, but I continued to do so. When I went to Fort Dix on my way back to Germany, I had a stack of letters with a photograph having lots of kiss impressions on them. I showed her photograph to a German wife who was a friend of mine. She wrote Evelin a letter telling her what a nice person I am. That helped.

I arrived back in Germany on New Year's Eve 1968. I drove to Mannheim, which was about 75 miles closer to Freiburg than my home in the city of Mainz. I had planned to go to the New Year's Ball at the Rosengarten there. I decided to call Evelin from the Officers' Club at Benjamin Franklin Village. When I called, she said, "I am waiting for you. Didn't you get my letter inviting you to take me to the New Year's party?" I said, "No, but I will be there in two hours."

Although lots of ice was on the ground and I had about 130 miles to go, I did make it in two hours. Her father and mother were waiting for us to join them. Now I was pretty sure that we would have wedding bells sometime in the not too distant future. When I got there, we embraced as if we were already engaged. As we joined her parents at the ball, we continued to act as if we were engaged. This was truly the most enjoyable New Year's or any other event of my life up to this time.

One week later, I put a diamond engagement ring on her finger. I had one major problem, which might kill my hopes for marriage. I was 47 and my bride-to-be was 21. I looked so much younger than my age. I could have claimed 30 or younger and gotten away with it. I said I was 36, which was acceptable. I figured my best hope was for her to know me better; then my age difference might be more acceptable. I did not know exactly how I would come to explain it to her. To my surprise, I left my identification card (ID card) in the middle of the summer of 1969 at the German hotel where I was staying. The hotel owner gave it to Evelin's father, who called her at my quarters in Mainz, where she was visiting me. She was quite shocked and disappointed. Her father thought a lot of me; but in the best interest of her future, he recommended that she should break our relationship. She decided against her father and held on to our engagement. Her Father was polite but cool to me after that.

In Germany, a girl over eighteen has authority over her relationships. Although Evelin respected her father, she did not accept his recommendation. She did it, knowing that her father could be right. I said, "If I give you 30 or more years of a happy marriage, it will be worth it because so many young people never get that many happy years of matrimony." We had to decide on a wedding date. Evelin had just accepted a job as a draftsman with an engineer firm, doing most of the engineering work for the City of Freiburg. She did not tell the firm about her marriage plans. If she had, she would not have gotten the job. For that reason, we decided against an early marriage. We set September 25, 1969, as our wedding date.

The photograph in which I fell in love with her, saying that she was one when I first saw it, was made in conjunction with her being a candidate for Miss Germany. The pageant was held in February or March 1969. Evelin invited me to stay at the same hotel where the competition was being held. I did not want to go or stay at the same hotel, but she insisted that I should. The rules at the pageant as to what contestants could or could not do were not spelled out. If they did, we did not know about them. Often when the events were judged, Evelin and I went to the nightclub in the hotel, waiting for the next scheduled event. Apparently, the managers of the event did not want that, or they did not want a Miss Germany having an engagement to a Black American.

Evelin was not too excited about being Miss Germany, being satisfied with the prizes and the vacation. I lived on the first floor of the Bayerischer Hof in Munich, Germany, where the pageant was being held. She and the other contestant stayed on the eighth floor. When Peasant was over, Evelyn want to move to my room on the first floor, the hotel manager would not allow it, but when Evelin showed the manager on the desk her engagement ring, it was permitted. When a couple is engaged in Germany, they usually have full freedom with each other. I did not take these privileges unless she was visiting me at my home. In Freiburg, I stayed at my hotel and she stayed at her home.

I remember taking her to the golf club at Heidelberg, where I bought her a set of golf clubs even before she had ever been on a golf course. I did that so I would not have any problem playing golf.

The U.S. Army Commander for Europe was from South Carolina, and was rated to be so prejudiced that his own chief of staff reported him to the NAACP. I paraded my future bride right before him. I was surprised when he shook our hands and greeted us very politely. This was a real shocker, because his race relations program was the worst.

The next U.S. Army Europe Commander was the best that ever served in this position since the establishment of U.S. Army Europe. He was General Michael Davidson. He put teeth in human relations and the civil rights program. When senior commanders thought he was playing, they got relieved. He had two black major generals on this staff, a first for Europe. When I was there with my wife at the golf club, he introduced us to his brother-in-law who was visiting him.

About July 1969, the Department of Defense was trying to cut the budget by $5 billion. The maintenance program, which I was a part of, was heading for the axe. This program was so valuable. I didn't think it would ever be cut. The Colonel who was the secretary to the chief of staff, U.S. Army Europe, was over the Education Agency and Secretary-Custodian of the Heidelberg Golf Club, and a pretty good golf friend of mine. I gave him a report showing how much we had helped maintenance in Germany, probably the best it ever had and probably the best it will ever be. I pointed out that we were saving the Army millions and maybe billions in maintenance funds, plus the combat readiness was over 70 %, and that was not falsified data. I indicated that if this program is terminated, maintenance will drop to the 30 percent level, making it necessary to falsify reports, because no commander can afford to report combat readiness at a 30 percent level.

The reason being that motor officers and motor sergeants were not proficient in the TAERS -- MIL-STRIP aspect of maintenance. They needed formal instruction. I contributed it to the low literacy of the warrant officer, motor officer, and motor sergeant. Every commissioned officer who graduated from the Maintenance Supervisors' Course became highly proficient motor officers.

The Chief of Staff, U.S. Army Europe, would not allow my report to be given to the Board, which was preparing the budget cut. The Chief said my report was too convincing, stating that the maintenance program could be restarted at a later date, which never did take place.

The case in point was my friend Frank Plummer who canceled my TAERS Classes and PLL paid a dear price for his prejudice. His maintenance people worked around the clock, late at nights and on weekends, and still flunked the CMMI inspections.

When I was complaining in Mannheim, Germany, in 1957-59, while I was in the l3th Infantry, I stated that racism was driving the best people out of the Army. When I started teaching these maintenance courses in 1966, all the units in Germany were failing in maintenance because motor officers (who were warrant officers and motor sergeants) could not read any of those technical manuals sufficiently to handle computer-related maintenance. Some of these officers were saying, "These technical publications were written by PhDs to be read by PFCs." Others said, "These books are written by geniuses to be read by idiots." The best motor officers were the commissioned officers with college degrees who knew very little about maintenance and the Germans working for the U.S. Army who could read the publications.

My wife's father found that we were going ahead with wedding plans in spite of his caution about it due to our age difference. When he was convinced that we were going to get married anyway, he arranged for a formal engagement party. Afterward, he made all the plans for the wedding reception, dinner, evening buffet and wedding dance. The reception was planned at the Freiburg Castle high up on the side of the mountain overlooking the city of Freiburg, which had been modernized for this type of reception, convention, and major events of all kinds. The owner was the father of a student in a class of my wife's father. At the base of the mountain were cable cars, which transported family and guests to and from the castle.

We began sending our invitations six weeks or so before the wedding. We sent one to our girlfriend, Rosy, in Berlin. We sent one to Frank Plummer, whom I knew would not show up. My wife sent invitations to relatives, family friends, school friends, and the like. Rosa tried to discourage it.

Chapter 15
LOVE, MARRIAGE, AND FAMILY

On the day of our wedding, a four-seated buggy drawn by two horses, picked me up from my hotel, and drove me to the home of my future bride. There I picked up her and her father and drove to the Marriage Bureau at the City Hall in Freiburg. We drove through one of the old famous gates to the city and through the middle of the city where we were waved at by cheering crowds alone the way. The majestic marriage building was one of the most beautiful, artistic, old buildings in the city. As we came out, going to our buggy, spectators with motion picture cameras were winding along all over the place. We drove back along the city walls, which my bride had drafted for the engineer firm to install. Workers along this main thoroughfare to the center of the city stopped to cheer us.

This time we went to the church where it was pretty close to being filled with relatives and friends. My bride and I paraded to the altar, with the tail of her wedding gown being held by her two first cousins and two of her closest friends. When the ceremony was over, we went back to our buggy, this time with my mother-in-law and father-in-law. He drove to the cable car station, where we released the buggy and rode up the mountainside on cable car seven. The large dining room was arranged to seat about fifty or more guests, relatives, and lifelong friends of the family. First we had drinks--champagnes, wines, soft drinks, and all bar drinks found at such an entertainment centers. Congratulatory toasts, hand shaking, and meeting and talking to guests prior to lunch were the activities of the time.

The menu was of the highest quality of good and tasty food, which magnified the occasion. After our meals, my wife and I went to one of the best photo houses, where we took our wedding photos. Then we drove up the mountain with my car so that it would be available when we took off for our honeymoon. About four in the afternoon, it was time for coffee, tea and desserts--cakes, pies, drinks, and the like.

At about the end of coffee, my father-in-law detained me, after which my wife disappeared. This what is called stealing the bride, and it became my duty to go looking for her and bring her back. After searching some fifteen restaurants in the downtown area, I found her. Now we must get the cable car back up the mountain to the castle where we had the evening buffet waiting with all kinds of meats, ham, salamis, just about every kind of cold cuts and cheeses that could be imagined, with wines, champagne, beers, and cognacs. I believe I stuck to wine and champagne, because we had to drive to Mainz, to our home later--about 185 miles--and to catch the airplane the following morning for our honeymoon. We wined and danced until two in the morning, when we took off leaving the castle full of guests.

We left at two in the morning and arrived in Mainz a little before 5 a.m. At 10 a.m. we were scheduled to take off on the Iberian (Spanish) Air Lines to Tenerife, one of the Canary Islands off the coast of Africa in the Atlantic Ocean, which is supposed to have the best climate in the world and maybe the one of the best places to have a honeymoon.

My bride did not want to leave the Castle in Freiburg where the orchestra picked by her musician father was playing such beautiful dance music. She wanted to see all the beautiful flowers that were at her home. Her mother promised to photograph them, which we could see upon returning from our honeymoon. The dance, we were told, lasted until four in the morning, a little before we arrived at our new home in Mainz Gonsenheimer Spiess l0. This would be the first time that we slept in our new apartment.

Before we married, we had bought and installed our furniture. My wife's mother and father had slept there; Evelin and I stayed in my military quarters, promising not to sleep in our apartment until we got married. We did not get much sleep, because we had to be at the airport at ten o'clock the next morning.

We flew first to Madrid and then to Tenerife. We were taken from the airport located on a long plateau high above the waters of the Atlantic. We drove down the side of that plateau, seeing banana trees everywhere. We arrived at our hotel, the Grand Hotel, which we acquired through the American Express office. This was one of the oldest and most exclusive hotels on the island. We arrived, showered, and maybe we had our afternoon or evening meal. Then it was time to relax and make babies. I was not so sure whether we made babies or not. My wife wanted to wait for two years, but we made no specific effort to wait that long.

During the day my wife lay in the sand on the beach eating up the sun and trying to get a suntan. I stayed in the nice hotel because I already had my tan since birth. In the afternoon, we looked around, buying souvenirs and other things that fascinated us. We even went for a ride on a couple of camels. I did not go into the ocean because the water current was pretty strong. We did our swimming in the hotel swimming pool. We danced every night by band at the hotel. We met lots of nice people who found my pretty wife charming to look at. I enjoyed the pretty picture we presented everywhere we went.

Our first weekend there, my wife and I were strolling in the shopping area of the city, when a north African whom we bought quite a few things from, wanted to take us to a fiesta in the villages with natives. We drank red wine, one pitcher after another one. Our driver was so drunk that I told him to put us out at a hotel where we said we lived, but we did not. We got a taxi to our hotel. I was pretty tipsy from all of that red wine. My wife said that I was so tipsy that I urinated all over my bed.

The Canary Island is just one big mountain, with other mountains springing up from the main ridge. We decided to take a tour on the lowest elevation, which was located on the east side of the Island. The east side is a little arid, and the west side is very green. Because the rain comes from the west and the rain clouds do not rise above the mountain ridges to provide adequate rainfall for the east side, much of the water for the east is piped in from the west. Even the soil on the east side must have small walls to prevent the wind from blowing it away. We took a tour on this side where the steep slope dropped down to the ocean. The slope angle is about eighty degrees. As the tour bus went along the side of the mountain and up and down the slope on the road, the bus looked like it would not make it. Then here came another bus in the opposite direction, which did not seem to have enough of the road for passing. If the bus going in the opposite direction should not make it, it seems like it would slide all the way into the ocean, because there were no barriers. The drop looked to be two to three thousand feet. Going out, we were on the mountainside of the road. Coming back, we were on the ocean side. I was nervous enough going out, but I was scared in advance knowing that I would be looking down those steep slopes on our way back. I promised myself that I would not take another tour on this island. We made it both ways, and I was as happy as could be when that tour was over.

The highest peak on the mountain is about 17,000 feet. Snow is on it year around. This is straight up from the ocean. Many tourists come to the island to go to the top of that mountain to take pictures. I get pretty scared just thinking about it. My wife's cousin, with her husband, went to the highest point of that mountain and took some pictures. I got nervous just looking at the pictures. I remember as a small boy how nervous I got when I went down the steep grades going from Selma to Birmingham, Alabama, which was almost no mountain at all.

My wife and I went to the city on the east side, where it was much hotter and much dryer. It was interesting to see the climate pattern so different from one side of the mountain to the other. On the west side, it might rain a couple times per day for about an hour, then the sun came out again. Should I go to the Canaries again, I would go the Island called the Grand Canary, where the sand is white and the beaches are flat and much wider. Mountains are also there, but the island is not just a mountain.

All good things must come to an end, just like our honeymoon. We collected lots of flowers, which most tourists do, that weren't found in Germany. We caught our plane, headed to Madrid and then for Germany. But we had to stop at the International Airport in Paris because the fog was too heavy at Frankfurt. Iberian Air Lines put us up at the Paris Hilton on the Seine, near the Eiffel Tower. This was a nice way to end our honeymoon, at the Paris Hilton. We strolled through the City of Paris, which was close to the hotel, taking some more pictures, going into the restaurants, and stopping at some of the entertainment spots.

The next morning we got back on our airplane and flew into Frankfurt Airport. Then we got our car out of storage and drove to our new apartment in Mainz. This night was the second time we slept in our new place and the first time that we slept the whole night there. I did not have a job because the budget cut had eliminated my position and all the other positions associated with TAERS and MILSTRIP programs. I felt more sorrow for the Army than I did for myself. The Army was headed back where it was three years earlier, where it had to lie about the condition of its maintenance. None of the motor officers and motor sergeants, unless they had our training, were going to function efficiently without the input that we provided.

A week or so after we returned, my wife and I were visiting at the Lee Barracks sponsored German American Friendship Festival. I spotted Frank Plummer for the first time since I had the steak dinner at his house. Even though my maintenance business was no more, Frank did not know about it. I asked him why he canceled the TAERS class that I had scheduled for his unit. He said he was doing pretty well in maintenance and that he had something else he wanted me to do. He did not have the ability or the means to hire me because I had become a private contractor during my last eighteen months with the program. I said, "Frank, I am an authority in this program. No one associated with the Army can match me in my knowledge of this program. I could help make you make General." He did not believe me, of course. I knew his maintenance people. I saw them falling down and down. He soon reached the point, as I had predicted, that he could not pass his unit's maintenance inspections.

Some of his soldiers said Frank was so prejudiced that when the black soldiers of his unit were fighting white soldiers of another unit, he was pulling for the white soldiers. I said he is not fit to be a general. Had he been as nice as he was when I knew him at Fort Benning in 1951 and '52, I would have taught his classes for nothing. But after hearing that about him, I would not help him under any circumstances.

Little by little, some of my old students began to complain that they were getting instruction from 8th Division Headquarters requiring them to change their maintenance reports because the reports were too low. The battery commanders were forced to falsify them. A new Lieutenant Colonel came to Dexheim, Germany, as the 8th Infantry Division Engineer Battalion Commander. He was complaining at the Education Center that he had been instructed to falsify his maintenance report. I said, "Colonel you better do it, because everyone else is doing it." I went to the 8th Division Headquarters, G-4 Section, where a W-4 Warrant Officer had made out his combat readiness report which was going to the Pentagon. His maintenance report showed 85 percent proficiency. Then I looked at the spare parts supply at TASCOM, which had spare parts for maintaining at 70 percent zero balance. That meant 70 percent of their spare parts that were supposed to be in stock for maintenance were 70 percent zero. I said to the Warrant Officer, "This cannot be. Even if all the spare parts were everywhere they were supposed to be, the ability of the maintenance personnel wasn't efficient enough to achieve that high level of maintenance. "

Even during the time when the maintenance was at the highest efficiency level, it was not 85 percent. If it were 75 and it was elevated to 85, it could be tolerated, but from 30 percent to 85 percent was criminal. The Warrant Officer agreed with me and also knew I could not talk about this highly classified document. I said, "It's the Army's fault. It does not have a way of knowing what is good or bad when it comes to maintenance."

Later Frank Plummer was relieved from his command because of his maintenance failures. While he was in the transient billets suite at King Village in Mainz with his wife, he invited me over. I came with my wife. I told him that I had been to the United States with my wife. He acted as if he was surprised to see me back alive. He wanted to know how black people accepted my blonde wife. I said, "Fine; they like her." He asked me, "Can you still help me make general?" I said, "Frank, I cannot because I am out of politics." He was headed to V Corps as its new G-2, and no promotions. He was finished as far as promotions were concerned. It was good for the Army, because he would not have made a good general.

Because I was out of work, I planned to extend my honeymoon another two months and not start looking for work until the New Year. In the meantime, my wife began to think that she was pregnant, but she was not sure. We went to Freiburg to get the news on how our wedding party ended after we left for our honeymoon. We were told that the party did not end until four in the morning. Everyone had a great time. So many flowers were given that my mother-in-law's house looked like a flower shop. My father-in-law began walking around like a camel with a hump in his back when my wife said she was pregnant. He was walking liking an old grandpa and laughing. Tears begin to drop to my wife's cheek because she did not want a baby so early in our marriage. "I did not want a baby before two years," she said. It was too late, because the baby could not wait that long.

We begin retracing our steps of September 25, our wedding day, and seeing close friends and relatives, telling them how much we appreciated their presence at out wedding and showing them pictures of the wedding and honeymoon. We had to visit my wife's great aunt who lived not far away in a village called Kollnau. She was in her 80s and was very close to my wife. She was one of the first to see the diamond engagement ring that I gave Evelin the past January and one of the first to give her approval. This old aunt in her 80s, celebrated by giving us some ham, cheeses, bread and a hafer drink made from fruits, clear like vodka, but better and just as strong. Her drinks were always the best.

We went to visit a Norwegian lady friend of my wife's mother and a friend of the family who attended the wedding. She told us that our wedding photograph was in the showcase of the biggest photo house in Freiburg. We went by to see it. Then we talked to the manager about buying it, but he told us to let it stay in the window a few more days and then he would give it to us. He did give it to us, and it became our most famous collector's item, mounting it in our bedroom.

We visited St. Blasien where we went the second day after I met Evelin. This time we visited her cousin there and his wife Elizabeth; both were at the wedding. When we were in the village the first time, we did not stop by; but this time we did, as husband and wife. We made the customary toast of the occasion, a cognac, champagne, then coffee, and a variety of sweets. This visit to and around Freiburg was like a second honeymoon. We had to visit the castle on the mountain overlooking the City of Freiburg, where all the celebrations began following the wedding ceremonies. Mister Datler, who owned the facility, gave us his warm greeting, which he extended to us each time we visited his magnificent old place that he made into a modern-day jewel while maintaining its old artistic wonder.

We went by Schuster where I always stayed in Freiburg before I got married. It was from there that I departed by buggy on my wedding day. It was there where I went to my first New Year's ball when I decided to buy that diamond engagement ring the following week. It was there where my father-in-law often went in the evening to have his beers and wines with his friends while relaxing from a day's work and talking about old times and telling the latest jokes.

The City of Freiburg was good to me, giving me my bride and treating me always like a celebrity, which came so natural to this University City. France could be seen from our wedding castle, and Switzerland is only a few miles down the road. Italy, Liechtenstein, and Austria were close by. Students at the University are from every continent, which makes the City of Freiburg feel so much like home for all who visit there. As before our marriage, we visited our favorite eating and drinking establishments both with my wife's parents and alone. We tried to visit all of those in City who attended our wedding before heading home. Later we thanked the rest of those witnessing us taking our vows and giving them an accounting of our brief wedding history.

Now I was back in Mainz where our new neighbors noticed the new family on the block, where we got the usual congratulations and best wishes given to all the newly married couples. I began taking my wife to all of those places I went looking for a wife, but did not find one. Oh, how glad I was! Now all of those chicks that looked the other way could see that I did even better. Even my old girlfriends in Berlin were mad and jealous. I said, "That's the way the ball bounces." My wise old Aunt Willie in the United States, in her 80s, said that because I was so nice to my mother, God found a wonderful wife for me. And that's all I have to say about that.

I was determined to honeymoon through the Thanksgiving and Christmas and New Year's seasons and my wife's twenty-third birthday on January 4, and do nothing else. I was able to get away with it. I looked for and got a job as a substitute teacher in the Department of Defense Dependent School System in the City of Wiesbaden, just across the Rhein River from Mainz where I lived. I was over-employed as a substitute teacher, substituting almost daily and managing student dormitories two or three nights per week. I always enjoyed teaching and being around teachers. I was well liked by the principal, secretary, teachers, and students--which was enough to make me like the job. I stayed there doing this work until the end of the school year and was invited back for the following year, but I decided to go into private business.

Every weekend I was down in Heidelberg playing golf. My wife was pregnant and was not happy waiting in the clubhouse all day while I played golf, but she put up with it. I was a scratch golfer then playing for a little money. The rule was that one had to shoot 75 on a 72-par course to break even. Anything over was the score of the losers. Making money became a little hard, but I generally broke even, which was worth the effort because of the fun I had.

Both my wife and I loved the Von Steuben Hotel and Air Force Officers' Club. There we could wine, dine, and dance daily. Lobster dinners were available there, and we ordered it at least once per week. Down the street was the Park Cafe, one of the nicest clubs in Germany where good music was played and the bar services were the best. There were no shortages of nice places to go. The closer we got to June 6, the less my wife could do. That was the day my son was born, the product of the Canary Island.

I was allowed to observe the birth of my son. The first thing I saw was a head full of black hair and then a crying baby. Then the nurse took him away. I do not remember what happened after that. I must have kissed and congratulated my wife. They must have shown my wife the baby, but I do not remember that either. The next day when my wife breast fed the baby, she said how sweet the baby was.

I could not figure how she could tell; because when I saw him, he did not look so sweet to me. But, I knew he was. He did not seem to have much color or personality, but that changed in a hurry to being one of the most beautiful babies ever.

During this period, correspondence courses were king, and LaSalle University dominated that business in Germany. I did not work for LaSalle, but I worked for a former LaSalle sales manager who set out to go on his own with other correspondence schools. We marketed a variety of courses in drafting, building construction, electronics, art, and writing. Then we took on RCA, which had a variety of electronics, to include black-and-white and color TV, with kits to build both. This was a fascinating program that was fully funded by the GI Bill. This program was so popular that we were allowed to enroll the students at U.S. Army Education Centers. We even employed instructors to assist students in understanding the program and overcoming problems. I remember enrolling sixty students in one month, the highest of any salesman.

Our competitors went to the Veterans Administration stating the RCA course was licensed to be for home study and not for classroom instruction. The salesmen were paying for instruction and not RCA, which did not violate anything; but because of the propaganda, we no longer were allowed to operate at the Education Center and RCA did not fight for our rights to continue as before. After that we made a settlement with RCA. It stopped marketing its home study programs.

Then we went to ICS, which was the finest correspondence school in the world. About that time, the Veterans Administration came out with a requirement, requiring all of our students to be counseled by the Education Centers. When our students went before the Education Center counselors, the counselors talked them out of taking correspondence courses and enrolled them in their newly acquired opportunity colleges. This became a no-win war for correspondence schools, with only the best salesmen being able to survive. I was always able to make it; but because so many others were not, the schools could not survive because the sales force became too weak. This was about 1978.

In September, 1970, my son was less than three months old, and my mother became critically ill. I had to go to Selma, Alabama, on an emergency leave with my blonde wife and brown baby. I bought a black wig for my wife because I did not want to run into any trouble. We flew to Montgomery, Alabama, where my first cousin, Frank H. Blevins, Jr., picked us up.

We arrived in Selma finding my mother very ill, and we were not expecting her to live very long. She was staying with her sister, my Aunt Mable (the Aunt Mable I boarded with when I was in the seventh grade). We were given the same bed and same room that I used then. My mother got all excited when she heard my baby crying. My wife got nervous because she thought that her presence there was causing problems for my mother. She was about ready to go back to Germany. Whatever I did to calm her did not help. My sister Erin, an Associate Professor from the University of Illinois, was able to calm her and make her understand what my mother was going through.

In a day or so one of my nieces wanted to take my wife downtown for shopping. I told her to wear the wig, and my niece said, "She don't need to wear that thing." She went without it, but I was concerned. They had a nice shopping trip, but I was happy to see her back. All of my mother's children showed up with the exception of my brother Ed who lived in Ohio. We were thinking about selling the 80 cows that my mother owned. I think we sold one or two and then decided against it. Our mother did not want it because the cows were her life. She loved them, and they loved her. We did all we could for her, and we were not sure how she would do; but I had to head back to Germany where my correspondence business with RCA was booming.

We borrowed the car from my niece Mable, which we used to drive to the Montgomery Airport. On our way there the car had a flat tire near Haynesville, Alabama. This is where a Klu Klux Klansman killed a lady from Detroit during the Civil Rights March by Doctor Martin Luther King to Montgomery in 1965. I told my wife to stay down while I fixed the flat. I did it very quickly and drove to the airport, leaving my niece's car there, and caught an Eastern Airline flight to Newark, New Jersey. The stewardess on the airplane walked around like she had an ant in her pants. She had never seen and African-American man with a blonde wife and a brown baby get on a plane in Alabama before. I had to tell her who I was, why I was there, where I was from, and where I was going. That calmed her down. We landed in Newark where we were met by my Niece Mary who lived in Fort Lee, New Jersey, on the Hudson River, a short distance from the Hudson River Bridge. We could cross over it to Manhattan.

The next day, my niece gave us her car so I could show my wife New York City. She took care of our baby while we drove around most of Manhattan, down the West Side Drive along the Hudson River to the end of Manhattan, then up the East River by the UN Building and down the Harlem River to 125th Street, by the Apollo Theater, to the Central Park to downtown Manhattan where we parked the car and ate a steak sandwich. Then we went to the Rockefeller Center and to the Theater were we saw the Rockettes.

After leaving Rockefeller Center, we did a little window shopping, going by Tiffany's. We were so well dressed that one of the men there was not going to let a millionaire pass the store without an invitation. We informed him that we were not in a jewelry-buying mood that day. Anyway, we looked like millionaires. The last stop before going back to my niece's and the baby was to the Empire State Building. I am a licensed pilot, but I have always been afraid of the ground-connected heights. When I reached the 110th floor of that building, I was a nervous wreck. It did not bother my wife at all, and it didn't bother me either when I got back on the ground. My wife enjoyed her Manhattan tour, and we were happy again to be back holding our baby and thanking our niece for keeping him and loaning us her car.

The next day we went to Willingboro, New Jersey, where we visited and stayed with my old friends, John and Eva Greens. I had known them since 1960 when I was stationed at Fort Dix, New Jersey. We visited an old lady friend in Philadelphia, the widow of the late Lieutenant Colonel Miller, who passed away before my retirement at Fort Dix. We just had a wonderful time during that visit. My wife and I will always remember it with great joy. We returned to Frankfurt, Germany, with an airline flight from Kennedy International Airport.

In April 1972, my mother became ill again. I flew to New Jersey, just outside of Fort Dix. This time we stayed with the Greens again, whom we visited during our first trip there in 1970. I contacted a retired sergeant who worked for me when I was on active duty at Fort Dix, New Jersey. He was a Buick automobile salesman. He loaned me a new Buick, which I used to drive my family to Selma, Alabama, with a disconnected speedometer. I had a Gulf credit card for gasoline and hotel accommodations at Holiday Inn, which was just perfect for us. I headed south, spending my first night at a Holiday Inn at Richmond, Virginia. Then we took off for Alabama the next day. On the throughway, not too far from South Hill, Virginia, I was stopped by the highway patrol for speeding (going 85 miles per hour). He took us to the Justice of the Peace at South Hill, which was known as a redneck town. I was a little concerned with my blonde wife and almost two-year old son, as I waited for the judgment being made, which took about two hours. I was issued a $49 bond and released. My wife did not know whether I got lynched or not, but was quite relieved when I showed up to head further south.

We drove through North Carolina and into South Carolina when another highway patrolman stopped me again for speeding. I told him that I was on emergency leave from Germany to visit my mother who was very ill in Alabama. He acted as if he did not quite believe me, but I offered to give him the telephone number. He gave us a $25 fine and let us go. We did not get caught any more, but we were running behind time due to all those run-ins with the highway patrolmen. I was determined to drive through to Opelika, Alabama, where my sister Jean and her husband lived. We made it about eleven o'clock that evening, driving all the way from Richmond, Virginia. I do not believe that I was ever so happy to see my sister as I was that evening. We were wined and dinned. My sister's daughter was close to the age of my son, and her two boys were older. We all had much fun together.

The next day we took off for Selma, Alabama. We stopped by Tuskegee to see Mrs. Patterson, the mother of the girl that I was engaged to when I went to Germany in 1948. We were still good friends. She was very elated to see that I had gotten married and had very handsome baby son. We left for Selma where I stopped by my sister Geneva's house to say hello and to find out about my mother before heading home to see her. My mother was not required to stay in bed, even though she was quite sick. I tried to put her in the hospital, but a German doctor from Calogne, who was the head doctor there, would not allow her to stay because she felt that my mother's condition could not be helped. We took her home and cared for her. But she still got around and fed her cows and hogs. My young son had a wonderful time. Every time we looked for him he was upon the fence being entertained by the hogs.

My wife bathed and took good care of my mother, which made her very, very happy. Even though she was my wife, my mother never before had a white woman to care for her and show so much love. That, I believe, meant more to my mother than I could imagine. She had faced so much racism during her lifetime. She loved my wife. More than anything, she enjoyed hearing my son's voice again. The black people of our Pernell Community had been chased from their homes because they marched with Doctor Martin Luther King and had built a new community near my mother's house. I took my wife to visit some of them. They were very nice, establishing a nice relationship with my wife.

I did not want to stay too long as I was a little cautious because of my white wife, not knowing what might go through the minds of some of the local rednecks around there. I did not carry a weapon for protection. My mother's condition was stable; and my sister Geneva, her two daughters, and her son were 15 to 20 minutes away by car. My sister Jewel, although handicapped, could cook, telephone, and help my mother until some of the other family members came to provide more help.

At this time my mother was 76 years of age. Her brother, my Uncle Arthur, was in a nursing home in Marion, Alabama, about 15 minutes away. My wife and I were on our way to Jasper, Alabama, to see my oldest brother, W. Clarence White, and his family before going back to New Jersey and home. My mother asked me to stop by and see my uncle because Marion was on the same route that I would take traveling to my brother's hometown. I found my Uncle Arthur in very bad shape with a stroke, unable to move, and having heavy pains. He was pleased to see me, but his suffering was too great for him to enjoy my presence. Tears came to my eyes, as I was helpless to do anything for him. In about six weeks he passed away.

My wife and my brother's wife hit it off better than she had with any of my relatives. My sister-in-law played piano for her church and the choir. My wife's father was a music professor in Germany who managed bands, played in symphony orchestras, and taught and composed music. My wife plays the piano, also. My father-in-law loved Mahalia Jackson music, which he collected. My wife liked her music also, plus Negro spirituals. My wife and Mary had a good time, going to her church where she played and they sang church songs.

My brother and I played golf. I do not know who won, but he is pretty hard to beat on his home course. I visited his two sons and daughters. I also visited the wife and children of my deceased brother, Frank H. White. It is always so pleasing for me to visit with my family.

After spending several days there, we headed north through Birmingham and Atlanta. From Atlanta we took the same route that we used coming south. This time I was a little wiser, avoiding highway patrols. I tried to figure out all the places along the way where they could hide. When there were no hiding places, I kind of put my foot in the gas tank. I believe I stopped at Atlanta and a Holiday Inn near Greensboro, North Carolina, for our meals. We bought some souvenirs that were made by American Indians in North Carolina. We spent the night at the home of Mrs. Turner in Lawrenceville, Virginia, who was wife of the deceased Mr. B. C. Turner. Mr. Turner was the father of my commanding officer when I was on ROTC at South Carolina State College. He was a very rich man who made his money on the stock market. When I last saw him in 1956 or '57, he was already in his 80s. When we arrived at his home, we found only the maid there. Mr. Turner was no longer alive, but his widow was on vacation in South Carolina. The maid called her on by telephone, and I talked with her. She told the maid to give us the guest room and invited us to come again when we returned to the States.

The late Mr. Turner was kind of an authority on stock market. He still had General Motor stocks from the Depression years when he bought them at $1.50 per share. The same stock must have been worth well over $1,000 per share when I was there. He never needed to sell them or other valuable high quality stock. He lived off the dividends and used them to buy other stocks.

His beautiful brick house was surrounded by high quality flowers, which required a salaried gardener to take care of them. To my wife, this was the most beautiful place that she had seen in the United States. It certainly was one of the highlights of a somewhat somber trip. We had breakfast the next morning, and drove to the home of our friends, Lieutenant Colonel and Mrs. John Green, in New Jersey. This was the third time that we resided with them. The first time was when we visited them in September 1970 when my son was about three months old. It was just another good get-together between old friends. This would be the last time that we would see them until I visited Mrs. Green with my son in the summer in 1986, when my son was sixteen years old. At this time Eva and John Green were divorced. My wife and I do recall the joy of our last visit with them in 1972.

We went back to Germany by space available flight from McGuire Air Force Base in New Jersey. My stay in Germany did not last long because I had to return to Alabama within six weeks because my mother had passed away. This again was a sad time for me because I had lost a mother who had given her whole life for her children, just as my father did. There were great parents, but my parents were the greatest. They set the stage for a great heritage. Six out of nine of us became college graduates. Two are doctors or equivalent, two have masters, and two have BS degrees. One married during World War II after high school, and four out of five of her children finished college. More than 70 percent of her grandchildren were college graduates. She left us 250 acres of land and some cash. She passed away 24 years after my father. No child on God's Green Earth could ask for parents so wonderful as we were blessed to have had. Like my father, if God judges them by their works, which the Bible says he does, my parents should be right up there with the best of them. My mother's wish was for all of nine of her children to meet her in Heaven.

Uncle Arthur passed away about a week before my mother. Even though we did not tell her, she said, "Arthur's suffering is over." Before his children could go home as far away as California, all of them attended the funeral of my mother. The Tate and White families, from which my parents are a part, should be a legend for goodness for the large family. We try to remember it each year when we have our family reunion.

I returned to Germany to my wife and my son, almost two years old. I began my work in correspondence course education with RCA, which was booming during this time. My district was in the Rhineland-Pfalz area of Germany. I remember traveling through the world famous jewelry city, Idar Oberstein, Germany, where I could not pass a toy store without stopping to buy toys for my baby son. I bought him a number of airplanes, which were rather large and operated by batteries. With lights flashing, the airplanes taxied like real airplanes. My son now works in a management position at the Frankfurt International Air Port. He worked in five departments there as a University student. Because of strong recommendations by the department directors where he worked, his position as Project Manager was created to keep him at the Air

Port after he graduated from the University in Business Management and Economics. I often wonder if those airplanes I bought for him when he was two and three years of age, even though they were too advanced for his age, created in his subconscious a love for his managerial work dealing with the airline industry.

He is now developing a collection of different types of commercial airplanes and airplanes with the colors representing the airlines of different countries.

My son started kindergarten when he was three years of age. He went to a special kindergarten with handicapped children. This was a research project designed to help normal children to help and understand children who were less fortunate. When normal children began treating handicapped children as normal, the objective of the program was accomplished. Normal children who went to this school were selected from parents who were well educated and had professional careers. My son and later my daughter were selected by a teacher there who lived in the same apartment building as we. My wife and I were not only close to the teacher, but with her mother also.

We also sent our son to swimming school at the same three years of age as when he went to kindergarten. He soon became the best student swimmer in the kindergarten swimming pool. Our son did well in the kindergarten, mixing well with the handicapped children, treating them as normal, which was the objective of the program.

We had to transport our son by car because it was a little too far, and he was too young for walking. Shortly after school started, we established a car pool with two other families who lived in the same neighborhood. One of the boys became a classmate and close friend of my son for seven years. The closeness of our sons, and because we shared the car pools, caused us to develop close social relations, especially with the family whose son had a seven-year classmate relationship with our son.

As my son started elementary school after three years of kindergarten, my daughter began kindergarten. She followed the same procedure as my son.

She learned to swim from my son, and she to became the best swimming student there. For two years we had to drive our daughter to school. During her third year we established a car pool with another family.

I had a little fear for my son because he would probably be the only non-white student in his class. For that reason, I gave him some boxing lessons to help him protect himself; and I also drove him to and from school. It took only a few of those round trips before my son said he did not want to be driven to and from school. Two of his kindergarten classmates were still his classmates in the first grade. This school was located in the area near the university and most of the students came from this environment where law and order existed at the highest level. My son had no problems at all in school or when he traveled to and from school.

One of my son's schoolmates was a next-door neighbor who wanted to dominate him. In order to do that, he had to fight my son and win. My son was not the kind of boy who picked fights, and his playmate knew that he had to make my son real angry for him to fight. So he started calling my son names. He said his brown skin was S--- color. My son did not fight him about that. Then he called him a 'N'. This time my son did it to him, and I think my son did it to him three or four times. This boy's mother asked my wife why our son was always beating on her son. My wife said it was because her son called my son a 'N'. She said that she did not know where her son learned such a name. She kind of felt my son was justified. In spite of their hostile encounters, they continued to play together.

Anyway, this boy did not give up. He got a friend to help him take on my son. My son beat both of them. Then he got a third boy who was two years older. My son beat all three of them. By this time the word got around that my son began to be respected like superman. One of my son's friend from kindergarten told all the boys around the school that Cecil was stronger than they and none of them could beat him. The students there must have believed him, including my son.

Much later my son ran into a boy who had Judo training. This boy broke his nose. I told him after that he had better go slow. There will always be someone out there who can beat him. My son was not a bully, but he had confidence that he could protect himself. He traveled with the friends he developed in school and on his soccer team. Lots of boys did this as a matter of custom. Companions were not necessary, but they did come in handy once in a while.

After ten years in our luxurious apartment in the university area of Mainz, Germany, we bought a new house in a farm village, which is a part of the City of Mainz, on a nice hill were we can overlook the cities of Mainz and Wiesbaden and the Rhein River which runs between them. There are lots of fruit orchards and vegetable farms between the city and us. This Village of Finthen is loaded with restaurants and "Gast Haus" where people come from all around to enjoy themselves. We like both the village and its people. We soon became a part of it.

My son began school in Finthen in the third grade, and my daughter had one more year in kindergarten. It was from our new home where my daughter had a car pool with another family. My son soon began playing on the children's soccer team, which was quite convenient because the field was only 200 yards from our house. This allowed me to watch him from time to time. He became so well known that people in the village became to know us because of our son.

As my son began his fourth grade class, our daughter began her first grade at the school. My wife and I began to be disappointed because our children's grades were too low. We did not like the teachers because they appeared to be quite cold and unhelpful to the student development. They left it up to the children and the parents. German teachers were well educated, but they seemed to have had no sympathy for the children. At the end of the fourth grades, which was the end of elementary school, the best children went to the Gymnasium. The next best went to the Real Schule (School), and the worst went to Hoch Schule. After the eighth grade, the Hoch Schule student learns a trade. If they are good enough, they may go to Real Schule or even Gymnasium. In the Real Schule (School), the student graduates after the ninth grade. They are able to qualify for better trades or a professional school. The best students in the Real Schule are able to go into the Gymnasium in the tenth grade were they may qualify for the University.

Upon completing Gymnasium, students can select university courses based on their grades. In medicine, I believe, student must have a straight 'A' average to qualify.

Professors in the University required near-perfect performance from their students. Students who do not measure up to the highest standards are dropped. This is true almost without exceptions. Students who do not make it may take the course over. Two strikes and they are out. Students may take another course in the University or go to Fach Hoch School, which is a four-year college in the same or different program, which they took in the university, which will be equally as tough as at the university.

A neighbor of ours, who is a Doctor and Professor in Dental School at the University of Mainz, has two children fourteen and twelve years of age. She employs two university students to help her children with their schoolwork daily and employs a teacher to teach them on the weekend. Many parents make this kind of preparation, or similar preparation, to insure the success of their children in the university and in Gymnasium in preparation for the university.

Many of the best students who graduate from the Gymnasium may select careers in the military where they can train to become officers, or the police corps, in chemical industries, medicine, electronics. Many of the bright students take professional training within the industry where they work and take college or university courses in the industry where they work. Most of the highest job positions are held by men with doctorate degrees and who have been elevated to the status of professors.

Every professional in Germany must be trained, tested, and certified before he can get a license to serve the public. A person cannot fix bicycles for pay unless he is licensed to do so. Such repairman must prove himself professionally qualified before a licensed will be given. Every certified professional can be counted on to do a professional job. Germany bases its survival on having high-quality people doing high-quality work.

My wife and I were worried because our children were performing at a level below the middle of their class. I blamed it on my lack of proficiency in the German language and my wife for not coaching my children sufficiently. We blamed the teachers also. German teachers do not help students like American teachers. Upon completion of the fourth grade, my son had to either go to the Hoch Schule, the lowest level, or the Real Schule, the middle level. We found a Real Schule in one of the adjacent villages in the City of Mainz that accepted him. He did lots of fooling around with his friends and did not take his work seriously.

When my daughter finished the fourth grade, she had performed at about the same level as her brother. We sent her to the same Real Schule, where her performance was about the same level as her brother (which was unsatisfactory to us).

In 1986, I brought my sixteen-year old son to the family reunion in Selma, Alabama. This was the first time that he had been in the United States since he was one year and eleven months old. I considered this one of my best vacation trips with him. I was able to take him to the community where I was born. He lived with his aunts, uncles, and cousins that showed so much family love, it just engulfed him. Such love from families, he had never experienced in Germany. This made a great difference in his life. When he returned to Germany, he took an entirely different attitude toward his education.

My son's grades improved to the extent that he was able to enroll in the Gymnasium and later qualified for enrollment in the University of Mainz. While at the University, my son was able to get a student job at the Frankfurt International Air Port, where he worked in baggage control, later in information and courtesy, then in the ground comptroller division, and then in airport management. It was in this last job when he finished the University and his student job contract ended at the airport.

My son placed his name for twelve management-training positions. Over 1,200 applications were submitted for these twelve positions. This list was reduced to 50 with my son included. Because my son had been so strongly recommended by the five departments where he had worked, he was given a management job over all the applicants, based on his five years' experiences.

My next best vacation trip was when I traveled to the United States alone with my daughter, Vivian, in 1991. We flew into Atlanta and were picked up by my nephew and taken to my sister Jean's beautiful home in Opelika, Alabama. They had four bedrooms and a big swimming pool resting on nearly a quarter acre of land. This had to impress my daughter, because that much land in Germany could cost a half million dollars. She just had a wonderful time with her two cousins who were about four and eight years older. At the family reunion, she was showered with love, as my son had been five years earlier.

My daughter and I left the family reunion with two nieces for Atlanta, Georgia, where the elder niece lived. From there, I rented a car to show my daughter a little of the Middle Atlantic and the Northeast, United States. We drove first to Durham, North Carolina. My nephew (the father of the two daughters and son that I traveled to Atlanta with) invited us for dinner as we headed to New Jersey and Pennsylvania. He stopped by the grocery store and bought the choice item of foods that the store had. He prepared us the best possible meal, after which we moved happily up the highway to Washington, to Georgetown, where my daughter started buying things for her brother.

We left there after spending several hours, stopping at a Chinese restaurant for another meal. Then we headed for New Jersey. By this time, I was getting a little tired. I spent about one-third of the night at one of the Howard Johnson rest areas on the New Jersey Turnpike.

I contacted my old friend and next bunk mate in OCS, Doctor Marshall Vaughters, who invited me and my daughter to stay at his mansion in the mountainous woods just outside of Philadelphia in the direction of Valley Forge. He gave each of us a room with private baths. My biggest problem there was trying the find the place. If finding his place had been a course in map reading when I was in Officers Candidate School, I am not so sure that I would have passed it. But I did find it, even at midnight, when I overshot my mark by ten miles.

My daughter just shopped all the times. We spent two days at a mall in a city over in New Jersey. She even bought a bicycle at Sears and Roebuck, to take back to Germany. We went downtown Philadelphia where we went on a tour at Independence Hall. Then we started shopping again. We had left our car at the Pennsylvania Railroad Station. Then we shopped on our way back as close to the railroad station as the stores allowed. We got a taxi back to where our car was parked.

Our last day there we drove to New York City. I had planned to take my daughter on a boat ride around Manhattan as I did with my son, but the wife of my friend wanted me pick up her niece who was living on Fifth Avenue and we could see the City together. We went to Lincoln Center to pick up the niece's daughter, where we took up too much time. We shopped and ate before that. I wanted to show my daughter the Apollo Theater, which she saw on TV in Germany. Then we had to pick up someone near Central Park, which took up too much time again.

We took them back home and put them out. Then my daughter and I went down to look at the Trade Center building and the Battery where the ferries take off for Governors Island, Staten Island, and the Statue of Liberty. We took pictures of the Statue and ourselves. Then we left Manhattan by way of the Lincoln Tunnel. The time that we got back to Philadelphia was around midnight. By listening to my daughter as to where to turn off to go to my friend's house, we missed my mark by ten miles, going all the way to Villanova. After checking about twenty entries to the forest looking for the road to my friend's house, I stopped at a service station and found that the next road on the left side of the street was the right one. Once I got on it, I found my friend's house with ease.

My daughter's name is Vivian, and my friend's wife is also named Vivian. They both had the right names, a strong will; and they did not get along too well. I told my daughter, "Before you put your bicycle in your room, you should get permission." My daughter, thinking my friend's wife might say no, put it in her room without asking. Because it was already in her room, she was not going to tell her to take it out. It worked anyway. Since we were heading for Virginia Beach the next day to spend the last portion of our vacation with my nephew there, everything stayed as they were.

It was a long drive down the coast from Philadelphia to Virginia Beach. We left about nine o'clock in the morning, and it was night when we got there. We stopped to eat twice. The drive over the bridge tunnel across the bay from the eastern shore of Virginia to Virginia Beach (which was twenty to thirty miles across) took us about an hour. After we got across, I did not know which way to turn. A man at a service station told me which way to go. After we passed one street on the right, I had to travel a long way before I could go right again because of all of that water. I just kept on going right when I could. I drove five or six miles, stopping at a little shopping area. I was very close to where my nephew lived. I followed directions and spotted his house. I had been there before, but by his car. He was waiting for a call from us when I knocked on the door. During my next visit to Virginia Beach, it took me two hours to find his house.

I was interested in golf, and my daughter was interested in the beach. My nephew and I played golf the next day, and my nephew's daughter took my daughter to the beach. My daughter and my niece did not get along very well because my niece did not like the beach as much. In order to save money, I turned in my rental car. It was getting close to my daughter's birthday, and she was not happy. She wanted to cut her vacation short and head for home. I had to get that bicycle packed so it could go on the bus and on the airplane. This was the biggest problem I had on that vacation, dealing with that bicycle.

We went back on Iceland Air Lines out of Baltimore to Iceland, then to Luxembourg. We changed planes in Luxembourg for Frankfurt. This was my daughter's first trip to the United States. We arrived home the day before her eighteenth birthday, completing her first visit to the United States. My son, her brother, picked us up, including the bicycle, at the Frankfurt International Airport

When my son went to the United States, he got along with the men and women of the family; but my daughter did not make it too well with some of the women with which she had dealings.

Like my son, I believe this trip turned my daughter around from a German environment, to a more American one; and she began to take family advice more seriously. Her life became more focused in the right direction. It was my hope that family contact and family love in the United States would and did make a difference in the right direction.

My three lifetime objectives included economic independence, civil rights for black people, and a good family life. When I found my wife, I had retired, the anti-discrimination law had passed, and the voters' right act was the law of the land. Discrimination laws preventing mixed marriages had been removed. I got married September 25, 1969, at 48 of age. My final objective was achieved. For a person who worked so hard to achieve his lifetime objectives, my last one was the most difficult one. Like I felt when my life was given back to me on April 5, 1945, I said that I felt that God owed me something. He helped me to find my wife. I was 48 when I got married, and my wife's age was 22. In spite of my natural age, I looked the right age for my wife. Even at 78, people think I am about 58; and I feel that way. On my 75th birthday, my pastor said before our congregation that I did not look my age. I never did. I said before people in my church that I believe God had extended my life to be with my young wife, whom he gave me for my effort during the war, my subsequent participation in the civil rights movement after the war, and for advancing integration within the Armed Forces and democracy within the United States of America.

My life, a little bit like Job in the Old Testament of the Bible. I have been awarded with youthful health, and relatively stress free life for sacrifices, with two fine children, a son and a daughter. Because God gave me my wife, after having lived a Casanova free life for nearly thirty years, I have shown my appreciation by being faithful to her since our marriage.

I have two hobbies which have contributed to a good life--golf and dancing. I started playing golf when I was eleven years of age. I bought my first two golf clubs when I was fifteen. Before I went to college at eighteen, I bought a second hand set of left-handed golf clubs. Golf was the only varsity sport I played in college. During my second year in college, I became captain of the golf team. I received a letter in golf as a result of my being a member of the golf team. While I was in the military, I played golf as often as I could, depending on my military assignment and duties.

During this period and for six years after I retired from the military, I had a scratch handicap for about twelve years. Being retired and single, I worked, played golf during the day, and went dancing during the evenings. I traveled widely in Europe, playing golf in all the countries I visited. I went to many places because of the opportunity to play golf there.

After I got married, three years after I returned to Europe, golf and dancing became my family hobbies. I joined the United States Air Force Golf Club in Wiesbaden, Germany, thirty minutes from my family home in Mainz, Germany. My wife learned to play golf and became a good tournament winner in her flights.

When U.S. Air Force Headquarters moved to Ramstein, Germany, in the early '70s, I became a member of the Army Golf Council. I was able to bring about German membership in our golf club because of the reduction in military membership when the Air Force left the Wiesbaden area. For about ten years, I was chairman of the tournament committee where we scheduled one international Invitational tournament each year, one Pro-Am Tournament, Inter Club Tournaments, and an Inter-City Golf Tournament, with four golf clubs participating.

In the inter-city golf club tournament, I won the senior tournament for six consecutive years. My last one was won when I was 68 years of age, with senior age limit starting at age 54. At age 77, my handicap is fourteen. My putting is much better. I am hopeful of winning the senior this year, which will be during the month of my 78th birthday. My wife and I are usually the life of the party in the many balls and dancing events.

Chapter 16
RACISM IS OUR GREATEST SIN

Doctor Billy Graham stated on TV in London, England, on Christmas 1996, that racism in the United States was too deep for the possessor of racism to remove it alone. He stated that he needed help from God to free him of his sins of racism. He stated on Christmas Day 1998 that racism is an inherited sin, which is passed on to first, second, third, and four generations according to the Bible. Even if the inheritor thinks he is not a racist, he is until he asks God's forgiveness for his possession of the sins of his forebearer that are passed on to him. If the inheritor became a racist on his own, he became a transmitter of his sins to his offspring, which will also go to the first, second, third and fourth generations, causing a racist chain reaction. Such a chain reaction of racism caused our United States Civil War, producing great punishment on part of both sides. Each side had racist guilt--one was on the side of the slave owners and the other on the side for permitting it for so long.

When the Constitution was drafted, slavery was permitted and tolerated to the point that God had enough. It was for punishment for the sins of slavery that caused the U.S. Civil War. I believe the United States and Colonies were the only white western civilized nation that owned black slaves within its own borders. It became a proud institution in the South where it existed until 1863, and it is still looked on as a part of the glorious past by too many of the offspring of ancestors of slave owners. It is the slave owning history of our country, which makes it extremely difficult for white people to accept black as their social equals to the extent that it is done in Canada and Western Europe. I have felt more comfortable with Europeans whom I had never seen before than I have with some of the white Americans with whom I have worked side by side on a daily basis because I could feel their racism. Such racism did not bother me; I just felt it as being there.

So long as the inheritors possess and worship the sin of slavery or the racist sins of their ancestors and practice them, we (and they) will pay the price of God's revenge for participating in, tolerating, or doing nothing. We are guilty when we allow all the racism about us to be ignored or try to hide from them. Joe Louis once said to his opponents in the boxing ring, "You can run, but you can't hide." I say to the racist, "You can hide, but you can't run. When you do, you will be seen for what you are."

God places the responsibility upon the good people to correct the bad people to the extent of their ability just like he expected the haves to help the have nots. He will do the rest when we have done our best. The non-forgiven sins of slavery are still with us in too many high places, which is the background of our racism.

While I was chopping cotton on our cotton farm in Southwest Alabama, I became aware of racism as a ten-year-old boy. It was exposed when four black men were charged with raping two white women. A young man working for my father explained it to me. He stated that the black men would probably be hung; but if four white men raped two black women, nothing would happen to them. That to me just had to be racism. This situation caused me to focus my life on education as a means of correcting it. These black men were never hung and believed to have been conveniently allowed to escape from prison and were pardoned some thirty years later. Most black people believe that rape never occurred. Because of my becoming aware of the sins of racism, I wanted, first, to protect it from my sisters; and then I wanted to protect it from my family and to black people of my community; and then I expanded it to include everyone because it looked so wrong to me. I felt that education was the only straw that could keep us afloat in the high waters of racism.

From that moment on, I made myself the example by educating myself, my family, and as many others who would follow it by the way of example. I predicted at this time to my father that racism (which we were facing) would be corrected in the 1960s. It was a hope, of course; but it was a hope I would try to make into a reality. I had everything to gain and nothing to lose. This seemed so impossible to me that I never talked about it. I just kept making one step after the next along this thousand mile journey for achieving my civil rights goals, not knowing where each step would lead me. I defined my actions and their accomplishments in Appendix A of this book as Silent Power. While I was doing my best, I believed that God would be with me.

It is not enough to glorify our accomplishments of the 1960s. This should be the beginning for ending the slavery-inherited racism in our land. Doctor Billy Graham was right when he stated the first step in overcoming the sins of racism begins with prayer. Prayer can advance us from a physical integrated society to a spiritual integrated society. We must search our soul to see the extent of our racism. Then ask God to free our souls from our acquired or inherited racist sin, regardless from whatever source they came. When we achieve this, we will be blessed beyond our greatest dreams. When we are free ourselves from the sins of racism, we will think more clearly, our brainpower will increase, and our potentials as a people and a nation will be increased to an unlimited degree. These blessings are not available in the atmosphere of hate.

Black people have asked white people to apologize for having been enslaved by them for nearly 250 years. Many reactions of whites are: "I have nothing to apologize for. I did not own any slaves. I am not a racist." Maybe their ancestors were. If such a person is not a racist, he has nothing to apologize for because God has removed racist sins from his soul; and he will not be held accountable for them. Such a person must give a sincere evaluation of his dealings with black people. In doing so, can he pass the test of one verse in The Ten Commandments, "Do unto others as you would have them to do unto you," in a manner acceptable to God? If he can pass that test, he can claim himself to be a non-racist. If he is a racist, God will forgive him if he asks him in the right way.

When he is free of this sinful burden, he is willing to apologize to anyone. The most important apology is by doing it with his acts and deeds. Then words of apology will not be necessary.

In the country community where I was born, every white man was a racist. Most of them thought they were supposed to be or had to be that way. All of them did not possess the same level of racism. They accepted the racist statutes that existed. A high percentage of racism was due to tradition, ignorance, and propaganda.

The disadvantage of all of this racism is that everyone is a loser. Booker T. Washington once said, "You can't keep a man in the ditch unless you get into the ditch with him."

If one is on a baseball, basketball or football team, he is expected to work together in order to have a winning team. The same is true with a military team. When a military team is divided when it goes to war, it can cause lots of unnecessary misfortunes. To win requires the best and closest team effort, which must be obtained before it goes to war. If it is divided along racist lines, it reduces its winning chances; greater casualties will result; and in some extreme cases, members may turn on each other.

I always considered Fort Bragg, North Carolina, to be a base that possessed lots of racism, surpassing Fort Benning, Georgia; Fort Hood, Texas; and Fort Riley, Kansas. The most ambitious officers were found in combat units there, the place where high ranks are made, a place where a high degree of racism existed. Most of the commanders were southerners from West Point and regular Army appointees. In such units, if a black officer danced with white women, it would be a kiss of death to their careers.

When those four white soldiers undergoing a Ku Klux Klan initiation killed the black couple in order to qualify for membership in this hate organization, it made me aware that the racist atmosphere that existed in such a military environment played into the hands of soldiers who are gullible to the pressure of hate group. A man who was one of the closest relatives of one of the men facing the death sentence, made a statement. He said, "The Army is partly responsible for the troubles which his son or nephew was facing." When I heard this over AFN here in Germany, I thought about all the warnings I gave to my commanders for giving command sanctions to racism in Germany and elsewhere. Anyway, I thought the Army did a bungled up job in investigating this case by not checking on the racism in the military environment at Fort Bragg, which I believe was in the command structure there. Racism almost always explodes when black officers dance with white women. I always integrated dances to expose racism and to try to eliminate it.

During the same timeframe, I was visiting my daughter who lives in Virginia Beach, Virginia. A lady friend of hers who is also from Germany came to my daughter's apartment with her man friend, a businessman and a veteran of the Gulf War. He served with the 82nd Air Borne Division there. My daughter was complaining to me that he never talks, that he was anti-social. I said to her, "If he was in the military, he will probably open up and talk to me." I introduced myself, and he seemed to feel very comfortable by talking with me about his military service. Then he said, "In the Gulf War, white soldiers shot black soldiers in the back. After that, many soldiers left the Army." Tears came into my eyes. I asked him, "Are you sure?" "Yes, I am sure," was his reply.

The next day I played golf with my nephew who is a retired lieutenant commander from the U.S. Navy and a nuclear engineer with General Electric. I told him about this statement from this Gulf War Veteran. He acted like this was no big deal. "In Vietnam black soldiers and white soldiers killed each other. When commanders have the freedom to toy around with integration in the Armed Forces, based on their inherited racism, they can do lots of damage to the integration of the military. The great danger is many of our very high commanders do not seem to realize how to deal with true integration in the military."

President Roosevelt, at the time we were sending Lend-Lease supplies to Russia during World War II, said, "Damn the torpedoes, full speed ahead." He was referring to the threat of enemy submarines. He also said, "The only thing we have to fear is fear itself." Every time the U.S. Senate took up civil rights legislation when I was a small boy, the racist elements in the South where I lived spread fear among the whites saying, "Do you want your daughter to marry a N---?" I do not think many white people thought this to be a possibility, but great fear was generated because of the thought of it. Even after all the civil rights achievements of the '50s and '60s, the fear created in the past was not justified. The racist elements did not mention or criticize all the integration that the white man was guilty of with black women. . .

The white racists where I lived talked about black men mixing the races. I have a white grandfather on my father's side and a white great grandfather on my mother's side. My mother and father had nine children. All of our colors range from white to middle brown. The Ku Klux Klan never said a word about that and the many other families, which were so mixed. This gave me the impression that mixing the races was no problem as long as it was performed by the white man. Mixing the races probably began when the first black woman came to America or shortly thereafter.

I have watched politics in the United States since the election of President Franklin D. Roosevelt in 1932. Some eight months before his election, I had already started working to end the segregated society in the South as a ten-year-old boy. Many black and white people at that time were more concerned about their survivability and had great hope under our new President that he would bring an end to the great Depression. With the exception of me, racism took a back seat to efforts being made to correct the economy.

One of the most pleasing steps the President made toward black people was when he selected Henry Wallace to become his Vice President during his second term. Mister Wallace had served during the President's first term as Secretary of Agriculture and had made some improvements in the economic life of farmers. This made him a politically acceptable Vice President. The next pleasing move of the President was his Supreme Court appointments.

Mr. Henry Wallace and Mrs. Eleanor Roosevelt became a great civil rights team. The Roosevelt administration caused many black people to switch from the Party of Abraham Lincoln to the Democratic Party of Franklin Roosevelt. This was the first time that black people had joined the party of the "Solid South" which had some of its most racist members like Senator Bilbo of Mississippi; Senator Cotton; Ed Smith of South Carolina; and Representative Rankins of Mississippi, who was trying to be more racest than Senator Bilbo.

During the Presidential Campaign for his fourth term, Roosevelt had to drop Mr. Wallace as his Vice President because the "Solid South" considered him too liberal. For this reason, President Roosevelt chose Senator Harry S. Truman as his running mate. Because Mr. Truman was considered a Southerner and a racist, liberal Democrats and minorities were opposed to his selection.

The death of President Roosevelt in May 1945, a few months after his fourth term election, occurred while I was in the Army General Hospital in Naples, Italy, during the beginning of May 1945. My girlfriend in Chicago, the daughter of an Illinois State Representative, wrote me stating that she was afraid that the civil rights gains and hopes for Black Americans went away with the death of President Roosevelt.

President Truman took over, surprising black people when he ordered the Armed Forces to be integrated in 1948. The fact that President Truman was elected as President in his own right later that year, showed that the American people accepted the integration of the Armed Forces. This would later play a role in the Supreme Court's decision to integrate public schools in 1954. The integration of the Armed Forces brought Black People more solidly into the Democratic Party and began to crack the walls of the "Solid South," causing the more racist element of the Democratic Party to seek refuge into the Republican Party. This became even more so when General Eisenhower who spoke against integrating the Armed Forces ran for and got elected President in 1952.

I explained in Chapter 4 how I believed integration of the Armed Forces occurred. The first person to get credit for should it be Mr. A. Phillip Randolph, the President of Sleeping Car Porters and later the Vice President of the AFL-CIO. He tried in 1942 to get President Roosevelt to integrate the Armed Forces for fighting in World War II. When Mister Roosevelt rejected the idea, Mr. Randolph threatened to march on Washington as a protest to the President's decision. In order to maintain national unity, Mr. Roosevelt issued an Executive Order establishing fair employment in business and industry doing business with the U.S. Government and stated that he would look into integration of the forces after the war. Two black combat divisions and the Tuskegee Airmen were established. I believed the forces, at that time, would be integrated if black combat troops performed reasonably equal to white combat troops. As a ten-year-old boy, as I explained in Chapter 1, Miss Lou Crenshaw, stated: "Every time there is a war, things get better for us." I was an ROTC student at Tuskegee University looking for evidence to see how World War II would make things better for us. I saw this focus on integration of the forces as a means of making Miss Lou's prediction that things would get better for us coming to pass. I came to believe General Marshall made himself the Research Director of the Integration Project. My explanation of this is covered in Chapters 4 and 17 of this book.

The major contributors to the integration of Armed Forces in my opinion are: Mr. A Phillip Randolph, President Roosevelt, Mrs. Roosevelt, General Marshall, President Truman, and myself. The combat units making the integration decision possible were The United State 92nd (Buffalo) Division and the Tuskegee Flyers.

Because the integration effort following World War II was not moving, Mr. Randolph threatened to march on Washington as he promised in 1942. Mr. Truman let it be known that he would not be intimated, but he did begin to make the move to integrate the Armed Forces. I believe he had to break his friendship with Secretary of States Jimmy Burns of South Carolina. General Marshall had collected enough evidence because of the performance of the Buffalo Division, Tuskegee Flyers, and smaller black combat units to recommend to President Truman that the Armed Forces was ready for integration.

It was the integration of the Armed Forces that created a chain reaction for the Civil Rights movement which really began when I solved the morale problem at Camp Patrick Henry in September 1944. I stated at that time that the racial segregation which existed at the base had killed the fighting spirit of the Buffalo Division. I said that the integration of that base by the President gave the black soldiers their spirit back and that their combat performance will cause the Armed Forces to be integrated." When I took Hill Z on April 5, 1945, the final spearhead objective which initiated the final campaign to end the war in Italy, I said, "We have passed the Test which General Marshall gave us." I was sure then that the Armed Forces would be integrated at that time, and I said as much.

Integration of the Armed Forces and all of the civil rights laws of the '50s and '60s will not kill the sins of racism in our country, but it will help. It will help some to realize that there is no such thing as a superior race and that we should work together for the benefit of the country and the world.

Doctor King was given the Nobel Peace Prize after his victory in Birmingham. During the following year, the final major civil rights campaign took place in my hometown of Selma, Alabama. This campaign led to the passing of the Voters Rights Act of 1965. This Voters Right Act, plus gains in education and economic growth, put power in the hands of black people and minorities, enabling them to bring about continuous changes in civil rights and reduce the influence of racism on a permanent basis.

After these two civil rights achievements, the United States was no longer considered a racist State, externally, leaving only South Africa in this category. Internally, the legal aspect of civil rights had changed, but the spiritual aspect of civil rights will continue to be with us. Externally, the civil rights victories took a lot of punch out of the Soviet Union's racist propaganda war against the United States, helping to win the cold war.

President Clinton has, on the other hand, done more by way of example to correct the sins of racism by showing that he does not have any of it. Each Democratic President since President Roosevelt has made major contributions to the civil rights of minorities, and in turn, increasing civil rights for all Americans. Not one Republican past president made any visible stand against racism. In fact, they have contributed to it. President Clinton has demonstrated by leadership more in the United States and around the world the importance of a non-racist society than any of our previous Presidents. I believe that nearly 100 percent of all black American have judged the President to be free of the sins of racism. Only God is a better judge of racism than black Americans. They have had over 400 years of experience with it; they are next to God in identifying it. I believe the President's success have been due to God blessing him by the way his non-racist attitude has influenced his judgment. I believe history will consider President Clinton as the greatest President we have ever had."

The United Sates has been blessed by God to have the strongest economy ever. It has been continuously outperforming all predictions. In spite of the economic downfall in Asia, Russia, and South America and the less than robust economies of the Third World, as well as in Europe, the economy in the United States of America continues to boost the stock markets higher and higher. The President's adversaries do not want to give him credit, but all who support him give him credit. If the economy was bad, he would be blamed. His adversaries say the economy is great because of Mister Greenspan. Mr.Greenspan has been there under five Presidents. I believe Mr. Bush blamed Mr. Greenspan for losing the 1992 election. I think God just blessed Mr. Clinton and Mr. Greenspan at the same time because of the President's non-racist attitude. God sees and knows what he is trying to do, and He is blessing him in his effort to do so.

The military is the strongest supporter of our foreign policy. The military must have a strong internal spiritual relationship within itself in order for it to do its best job for supporting external relationships with friendly nations and allies around the world. The military personnel come from our civilian environments, and they bring into the military their attitudes and prejudices from their home communities. Unless they are properly trained and supervised, our soldiers may retain as many attitudes and prejudices as their numbers are in the military. Military leaders seem to lack the courage necessary to get involved with pushing the spiritual aspect of integration to match the physical, nor does it wish to invite professionally trained people to do it for them. We must not be afraid to talk about our democracy and Constitution as it relates to individual members of the Armed Forces. Commanders who possess the sins of racism (by inheriting or by acquiring them) do not have the know-how to correct weaknesses which are a part of them. For example: When the Buffalo Division had lost it morale due to racism, not one white commander recognized it. They were concluding that black soldiers were cowards and were afraid to fight. If I had not explained how racism had destroyed the division's morale, it would have been deactivated; and I am sure the Armed Forces would not have been integrated immediately following World War II.

In 1984, I was requested by the Equal Opportunity Non-Commissioned Officer for the Mainz Germany Military Community to give the Black History Talks and The Martin Luther King speech that January. I had known the Master Sergeant for about ten years who asked me to speak. He knew that I was a certified history teacher in U.S. and World History, and I had played a role in Army integration and was involved in the Civil Rights Movement and that I had a good background in black history. Knowing how sensitive the military is about racial matters, I chose subjects which were not controversial. I chose to talk about Booker T. Washington and George Washington Carver, because I am a graduate of Tuskegee University where these two great men served. I could speak with a bit of authority on them. I spoke first at a battalion commanded by a black battalion commander. He had no objection to the subject matter, but he did not want to spare his men from training to participate in the program.

My next talk was for a battalion which had a white commander. He attended, as well as his entire battalion. This talk was better than the previous one, because this was the second time that I gave it. I left with the impression that I had done a superb job. The next morning I checked in with the Equal Opportunity NCO. He said, "Mr. White, the battalion commander called the Community Headquarters and told them that he did not ever want you to come back to his battalion again. He said the talks were an insult to his white soldiers." I said, "I was supposed to talk about black history, not white history. That battalion commander is nothing but a 'redneck,'" I said.

My next talk was for the brigade. This time I had the Deputy Community Commander (a colonel) and two lieutenant colonels in attendance. I changed the subject and talked about the Army education mission and the educational opportunities for members of the military. This was nothing about black history. All the commanders liked it.

I was really ready for my Doctor Martin Luther King talk. I read all the books which he had written, plus I had followed in great details all his campaigns. I had in some way been connected to his biggest one. The community commanding general had asked the Community Chaplain to interview me before I delivered the talk. I told him I was going to cover the high points of Doctor King's successes, that I had read his books, and that I already had pretty detailed knowledge of his accomplishments." If the general wanted me to write out what I was going to talk about, I would give it to him. "That won't be necessary," the Chaplain said. I had already sensed that I would not be delivering the address. I was notified the general had invited a black major general from Heidelberg who had received a Congressional Medal of Honor in Vietnam to give the talk. He turned out to not be available because he was in Washington, D. C. A black colonel chaplain gave the talk. I later found out the General who had rejected me was Brigadier General Norman Swartzkopf.

It is not enough just to place black and whites in the same barracks, the same dining facilities, side by side in military formations, or in the same military clubs, and let integration take care of itself. It can be corrected only when there are positive commands or interest to do so, such as we did in Wiesbaden, Germany, on January l4, 1999, during the Doctor Martin Luther King holiday event where we use a brotherly love approach. There we stressed how the civil rights movement advanced the cause of democracy in the United States and brought more respect for the United States around the world. We also stressed how the civil rights progress helped us to win the cold war by showing to the world that we are not a racist country. Doctor Martin Luther King's civil rights victories, which were honored by his receipt of the Nobel Peace Prize, helped a lot in winning the Cold War successes by blunting communist propaganda branding the United States as a racist State.

Is the Army better today? Maybe. If it is, it is because the Army is a little less racist than before because all of the present military personnel joined the Armed Forces since integration was established. With so much inherited racism in our society and the military and because the Army has never had any program installed dealing with racism and promoting the ideals of an integrated Armed Forces, little progress can be made. Racist polices have been left up to whatever commanders want it to be, within such guidelines he chooses. Under such loosely guided policies, racism will not go away. A high percentage of our military people are from the South, and it is from the South where most of the inherited racism exists. With less than the highest quality personnel in the military, commanders can get away with almost anything they want. An old saying in the military, "Soldiers do well in things which the commanders check. I am pretty sure that segregated policies are put under the rug or table, but they still exist. It is not the kind that can be touched, but it can be felt. When it is closely checked, we can find that the military is just as racist spiritually as it ever was.

One reason why I integrated dances was because I felt that the Army would never be successfully integrated until it had an open dance policy, allowing those to dance with whomever they chose. The silent segregated dance policy damages the spirit of the military as a career professional organization to a highly unknown degree. It has caused the low retention rate of high quality personnel, violence, and many other unknown indiscretions. Somehow the military does not know how to deal with it. Treat whites and blacks exactly the same. I always applied the Biblical Rule: "Do unto others as you would have them do unto you." It will never fail. There must be a continuous program with teeth, supervised by those who have the guts and who believe in a strong integration program and have the power to make it work.

This past January 14, 1999, I was invited to be one of the guest speakers at Doctor Martin Luther King's National Holiday Anniversary. I told the Equal Opportunity Non-Commissioned Officer who invited me that I would speak quite frankly about the role I played which contributed to Doctor King's Civil Rights successes. He told me to go right ahead, which I did. It was attended by all the top commands in the Wiesbaden Germany area. I was quite pleased, because this was the first time to my knowledge that the military let uncontrolled speakers speak on such occasions. In fact, the civilian guest minister spoke more freely than I did. This may have been an isolated command supporting the Martin Luther King celebration, but it was right on target as I saw it. Judging by all the congratulations which we received, it was on target for all of those who were in attendance.

In the past, commanders have had a hard time dealing with racial issues, afraid of the reactions of black and white soldiers. I somehow feel that the soldiers and low-ranking officers can deal with the race issues better than the more senior commanders. I have always felt that the best way to deal with race issues is to be realistic and truthful about it, the sooner the better. In August 1996, I asked a white major with whom I play tournament golf if he danced with black women at his command dances. He said, "We are doing fine, and I don't want to talk about it." I said, "Until we can talk about it, laugh about it, and joke about it, you are not doing fine." It was about three months before we got chummy again. He was also from Alabama. I believe that this a good explanation as to the status of integration of the Army. To be able to talk about it, laugh about it, and joke about it can only come when we no longer have the sin of racism.

We need to talk about brotherly love in a manner which Doctor Martin Luther King expressed during his anniversary program, during black history month, in the chapels and periodically throughout the year. The chaplains should be taking the lead in integration matters, but they do not seem have the guts to deal with it. We need to educate our soldiers out of racist molds, not by just hoping that it will go away and that the soldiers will make it work. That approach helps a little, but it needs command emphasis also. Until the Chaplains Corps are independent of the commanding officer, they can have little influence on changing moral standards of the military beyond the concepts of the commanding officers.

Back in the early 1970s, General Michael Davidson, U.S. Army European Commanders developed a strong equal opportunity program, setting up an Equal Opportunity School in Garmisch, Germany, requiring units' equal opportunity officers and non-commissioned officers to attend this program. The General visited this school often making sure that all commanders got the words on his equality opportunity policy. This program had teeth, and it worked as long as he was in command. When he left, the program for all practical purposes went with him and so did a continuous improvement in race relations and a positive attitude by commanders to promote racial harmony within their command after his departure. He was the one who invited the NAACP to Germany. Subsequent commanders failed to use the standards which he set effectively and ignored his advice to do so.

During February 1998, I gave my Silent Power talk, Appendix A, at a local installation in the military community in the Mainz-Wiesbaden, Germany, area where I live. The battalion commander was there with less than 20 of his low-ranking black and white enlisted male soldiers. There were no officers, no enlisted women, or non-commissioned officers. This was a little bit of an insult talking to so few people in a military theater to a battalion with a population of over 500 members. I talked as if the whole battalion was there. When I finished talking, all of the soldiers stood up giving me applause for my talk, and they expressed an interest in my autobiography, which I told them that I am writing. The Battalion Commander thanked me for my talk, stating, "This shows that one man can make a difference." Then he gave me a nice plaque showing the commander's appreciation to me for speaking on this occasion. I would have been happier if he had invited me back to speak to the rest of the battalion. I have found that the military commanders are afraid to talk about race or try to enhance a more enlightened racial understanding. The Battalion Commander's expression of appreciation was one thing, but his action gave me a different feeling. Either he was a little racist, or he was afraid to deal with the issue of race. Commanders need to give Martin Luther King Holiday Activity and Black History Month the same kind of attention they give to the war in the Balkins. Attending to morale issues make soldiers more effective when we engage in conflicts.

A couple of days ago, eleven months later, I saw the Equal Opportunity Sergeant who invited me to give the Black History talk. I asked him if he still had the same job. He said no. I asked him if he lost the job because he invited me to talk. He did not give me a clear answer on this question. I asked him if he thought that the battalion commander was a racist. He could not say yes or no. When I get such an answer, I judge the commander to be a racist or a little weak on the race issue and the sergeant as being a "yes man," which is the type of equal opportunity sergeant a racist commander wants to manage his equal opportunity program. The action of this battalion commander is typical of the equal opportunity interest which I have observed during the last 30 or more years in Germany, with the exception of the one which was held on January 14, 1999.

On February 23, 1999, a young black soldier came to me at the same installation where I gave my February 1998 Black History Talk. He said, "Sir, are you going to give us another Black History talk this year? I was at the one you gave last year. That's the kind of Black History talk we need. The Battalion Commander had only about fifteen or seventeen of us there. That was bad. That is nothing but racism. He just sweeps it under the rug." This Battalion Commander is from Chicago. I was happy to get these remarks from this young soldier who I judged to a high-quality person. He helped me confirm the racist views which I have found to exist in the military in Germany during my 33 years here since my retirement. I think the military needs to get jumping on taking racism out of its integration from the highest commander to the lowest-ranking soldiers.

The military can get any kind of people it chooses--those who will put up with anything and say nothing and those who will leave the military because they cannot serve voluntarily under racist integration policies. Several black and white officers have approached me and stated that I should head the NAACP in Germany. I said to them, "The NAACP is under the Commander-in-Chief, U.S. Army, Europe. Nearly all of them, I have judged to be racists. I will work with them as an equal, but not as a subordinate. I believe my patriotism to be greater than theirs, because I am not a racist. When it comes to dealing with racist matters, I consider myself to be a four-star general or higher. "

My approach to correct the sins of racism is covered in this book. My mission started as a ten-year-boy to correct racism as I saw it then and predicted that it would end in the 1960s through education. This was both a physical and a legal accomplishment. The accomplishments by many civil rights participants over a long period of time, with God's help, brought about an integrated Armed Forces, U.S. Supreme Court decision to eliminate public school segregation, the Anti-Discrimination Act of 1964, and the Voters Right Act of 1965. The United States Supreme Court decision of 1969 to nullify state laws banning interracial marriages gave black Americans their full legal constitutional rights. These were great accomplishments. I visualized then that it not only took educated people to bring civil laws, it will take educated people to make them work and to realize the benefits made available because of the Civil Rights revolution.

A backlash took place in the black communities after the end of the Civil Rights victories, because uneducated black people did not see any benefits. Because I used education as my mission to correct racism, my family was educated prior to, during, and after the Civil Rights Revolution, and was therefore able to participate fully in its benefits. Although many black people have been integrated into the work force, the uneducated black people will be those most affected by racism which continues in our society.

We have made great progress under these civil rights laws in education, economically, politically, and spiritually; but we still have a long way to go, especially in the spiritual aspect of integration. Progress will continue through moral pressure, economic pressure, education, and political power. There are still lots of racist sins out there. We saw a lot of it in the impeachment process of President Clinton.

Races were not classified by God. I think it was a classifying process developed by the British Empire, and racism was developed because of it. After that race became whatever racist people said it is. Most of the wars in this century, and maybe the last century as well have been in some way related to racism. Racism is one of the most unjustified evils ever crafted by mankind. We cannot justify and classify that which is created by God. Every human kind is a creation of God and must be accepted by man as a human equal.

Because slaves and racism did not fit into our Constitution in the United States, the slave owners tried to justify slavery by trying to make it like the Ancient Greeks and Romans that had both slavery and democracy. Neither the Greek nor the Romans had slavery and Christianity. The U.S. Christian had to create propaganda and lies that were not found in the Bible to try to live with and justify the sins of slavery. Blacks were denied their own history. Slavery against black people was the meanest kind of slavery. The Southern Christians during the time of slavery--or now the Christian Coalition and Moral Majority, groups which most black Christians will not have anything to do with--find their morality in abortions and infidelity, but never take a stand against racism in our society, our greatest sin, which infests high percentages of their membership

I believe that President Clinton's successes in the economy and his popularity on the world stage is because God has blessed him for his strong stands against the sins of racism. His brilliancy in selecting and utilizing cabinet members and appointees with similar racist views makes him a trusted and respected world leader. When King Hussein, sick with cancer, said that he had known all of our presidents since Eisenhower, and he considered President Clinton to be best of them. Clinton received the highest possible endorsement from Nelson Mandela. All the great leaders of the free world, I feel, have equal praise for President Clinton.

My objective as a ten-year-old boy in 1932 was to educate my family. When my youngest sister, Jean, graduated from college in 1956, my education objective for my family had been accomplished, raising the college level of my family 70 percent, which enabled it to make a major contribution to the Civil Rights movement of the '50s and '60s. Because of this, my family members became professional and were able to participate equally with whites and to be treated as equal to whites in accordance with anti-discrimination laws. This was the way forward from the past, and it will continue to be so in the future for all of us. Educated black people have reached a status where racist whites can no longer determine their destiny in the United States. It is the uneducated black people who are most hurt by racism, and the uneducated who are the victims in our advanced society. Racism, even for educated black people, causes promotion problems in and out the military. There are conspiracies to determine positions blacks will hold. Glass ceilings are too often established. Education, politics, economic power, and a watchful eye can help lift the infraction to our equality in all areas of our economy and put political power in the hands the non-racist members of our society.

I don't believe God permitted so many black people to come to this new world just for the convenience of white people, any more than he permitted the Israelis to be slaves to the Egyptians for over 400 years. I feel that we have a divine purpose of purifying our democracy and to prove that all people can overcome their racism and can live together in a non-racist environment and take our prosperity and democracy throughout the world. This may sound too ideal, but I believe black Americans have the hearts and the souls to lead the United States of America down this path. And, I believe that President Clinton has that vision. Black Americans, other minorities, and the good white people of the United States have a commanding lead to take the country from its racist past to reaching its destiny in accordance with the Constitution.

God has given us a promised land bordered between the world's largest oceans, with mountains, plains, deserts, fertile soil, and a climate pattern enjoyed by only a few countries in this world. He has also blessed us with people consisting of every race, color, and culture group in the world. As all of our people receive reasonable equality in our land, we will receive more and more respect from the countries from which our racial and culture groups came which will give us greater power to bring underdeveloped economies and democracies more in line with democracies of the United States and Western Europe. Because we have a greater number of racial and cultural groups, we are in a better position to do so. As we correct our own racial image at home, we will be in a better position to spread our image abroad. Our different races and cultures are our blessing and not our liabilities.

The civil rights victories have placed the destiny of the civil rights of each individual in his own hands. There are evil forces around to discourage, intimidate, frighten, and cause setbacks, but none can stop a well-educated, determined, ambitious person. The more the number increases, the easier our objectives for world peace and prosperity will become. Equality cannot be achieved on drugs, school dropouts, and welfare; but it can be done when each person takes advantage of his educational opportunities to achieve the goals he sets for himself and the country. Racism, in spite of its sometime viciousness, will advance the cause of civil rights instead of retarding them. In the words of President Franklin D. Roosevelt, "Damn the torpedoes, full speed ahead. The only thing we have to fear is fear itself."

God will always bless America so long as it carries out its duties of world leadership which He has provided and work to end racist sins at home and abroad.

APPENDIX

Appendix A: Silent Power
Appendix B: The Power of Education
Appendix C: The Big Surprise of February 17, 2001
Appendix D: The Big Red One

Appendix A:
SILENT POWER

One morning in 1932, a young man who was working for my father, Clarence White, picked up our local newspaper, The Selma Times Journal. When he did not sound off about the major league baseball results before he got where I was standing, I figured something was wrong. Therefore, I asked him, "What's the matter, Elzey?" "Four black men have been charged with raping two white women," he replied. "What will happen to these men?" I asked. "They will probably be hung." "What would happen if four white men raped two black women?" I asked. "Nothing," he said. To me, this was not right according to the Ten Commandments in the Bible. Later I said to my father, "In the 1960s, all of this will end." My father said, "It may happen in your lifetime, but not in mine." I said to myself, "If my father lives to be 75, he will see it."

I made the above statement while giving a Black History talk at a U.S. military installation in Mainz, Germany, on February 10, 1998.

On January 16, 1995, I spoke to General Couch, the new Commanding Chief of the U.S. Army Europe after he delivered his talk at the Martin Luther King Village in Mainz, Germany, on the occasion of Doctor Martin Luther King's National Holiday. At the conclusion of his address, I introduced myself to him and said, "Sir, you may not believe it, but I believe I planted the seeds which led to the integration of the Armed Forces of the United States following World War II." He said, "Maybe I will. Why don't you tell be about it." I did. "I would like for you to put that in writing, just what you told me, and send it to me at my Headquarters in Heidelberg, Germany." I sent it to him, but I did not get a reply.

In November of the same year while I was in the auto hobby shop here, I said to a fellow military retiree, "If it had not been for me, you may not have ever heard of Doctor Martin Luther King." I said, "I am writing my autobiography, the title of which is Give Me My Spirit Back. In this book I will ask the President to give me The Distinguished Service Medal for the role I played in the integration of the Armed Forces of the United States of America following World War II. I am also asking him to give me a Silver Star Medal for each of the offensive battles in which I was involved as a member of the 92nd Infantry (Buffalo) Division in Italy on November 27, 1944, and on February 14 and 15, 1945. I am asking that I will be given a Congressional Medal of Honor for the role I played in seizing the final spearhead objective in the final campaign which ended the war in Italy on April 5, 1945."

Between 1932 and January 1995, I did not say another word about the goals I set for myself sixty-two years earlier. In 1963 when President Johnson signed into law The 1964 Anti-Discrimination Bill; in 1965, he signed into law The Voters Rights Act; and in 1969, the United States Supreme Court abolished state laws forbidding interracial marriages, all of my predictions had been fulfilled. My father passed away in 1948 at 61 years of age. As he predicted, desegregation laws would not be eliminated in his lifetime, but maybe in mine.

Today I want to talk to you about how all of this was accomplished. I joined the Buffalo Division on or about August 15, 1944, at Fort Huachua, Arizona. Everyone was packing for shipment to the port in Virginia for further movement to Italy where we would go to war. In two weeks we left for Newport News, Virginia, to an installation named Camp Patrick Henry, Virginia. I found the morale of the soldiers within the division at that time to be very high. I felt comfortable going to war with troops who were so well trained and highly disciplined. After a week of hard work, we were ready to ship out, but we had to wait for a large number of ships which would form the convoy for sailing across the Atlantic. I was given a five-day leave. Upon returning, the convoy still had not been formed. A week or ten days later, I was given another five-day leave. I returned this time about a week before the end of September 1944.

On Sunday evening, September 27, 1944, we had a company meeting. I thought this was the time we would receive our orders to ship out. Instead, the Company Commander read a message coming from the Pentagon and from the War Department, signed by the Chief of Staff, General George C. Marshall, and the Secretary of War, Harry L. Stemson. The message read, "The morale of the Buffalo Division had dropped to an unacceptable level for combat and that it could not be understood why the best trained division of the war had lost its morale at the water's edge." We were given 24 hours to find the causes and solutions to the morale problem.

This was a larger shock to me, bringing back one of the revelations I received at the well house on the farm where I lived when I was ten years old. One of my friends said, "I hear black soldiers don't fight well. They are cowards and they run away in battle." My response was, "I don't believe that. The way we fight at the Jook every Saturday night, I think we can fight as good as anyone. If I ever go to war, I will show everyone that we can fight as good as anyone else."

Another revelation was given by an old lady, Miss Lou Crenshaw, when I asked her what she thought about the black and white problem. She said, "It is not right the way we are treated. Every time there is a war, things get better for us." I remember saying to her, "It looks like we are going to have to wait a long time because there is no war in sight."

A retired Master Sergeant who lived two houses from where I was boarding during my last four years of high school assured me that black soldiers fight as well as anyone. He joined the Army in 1906 and retired in 1936. He was a member of the famous 10th Cavalry which was one of the two cavalry regiments organized by General Sherman in 1868. These Cavalry Regiments were organized to protect white settlers in the West when white soldiers were used for occupation of the South during the reconstruction period following the United States Civil War. This regiment was one of the two original Buffalo Soldier Cavalry Regiments. It was also commanded by General Pershing in war with Mexico during World War I. Master Sergeant Davis fought with General Pershing during that war.

All of these revelations flashed through my mind as we attempted to solve the morale problem. It began to look like The 92nd Infantry Division was going to be deactivated.

In 1942 the Pentagon organized two black divisions, the 92nd and 93rd for the purpose for providing justification for the integration of the armed forces after the war, provided they measured up to the standards of white divisions. General MacArthur had already deactivated the 93rd because he said it would not fight, It was beginning to look as if the 92nd was heading for the chopping block because the morale problem began to indicate that it would not fight well either.

I was very concerned because in 1942 President Roosevelt promised to look into integrating of the Armed Forces after the war and that these divisions would provide data supporting that decision, based on how well they performed in battle. It began to look like all of this hope was going down the drain, but we did have 24 hours to solve this problem.

Five officers and five senior sergeants in our company, H Company 371st Infantry, were assembled for the purpose of solving this or these problems. Approximately 40 other companies in the Division were meeting for the same purpose. The company commander, the only white person in the unit, was from either Minnesota or Iowa: He felt that this was a black problem, and he didn't have the slightest idea what the morale problem could possibly be.

The discussion began with the executive officer, the second-in-command first Lieutenant Henderson. He said, "Our soldiers are going overseas for the first time and some feel that they will not see their families again, and they are a little sad about that. Once they are out in the middle of the ocean, the morale problem will be over." I was Junior because I was the most recent arrival and commissioned officer to the unit. Therefore, the other officers and sergeants were called on to give their response ahead of me. The two other black officers and the five sergeants agreed with the answer provided by the Executive Officer.

As I listened to them, I began to feel that they saw a chance to avoid the war, or they did not know the answer, or they were afraid to give it. As a 23-year-old second lieutenant, it looked as if the whole world was resting on my shoulders. I too considered agreeing with the others and avoiding the war, but I had an objective of eliminating legal racism in the 1960s. The Buffalo Division was our last hope. My mind was split between telling the truth and evading it. I decided to put my life on the line by telling the truth and putting the whole situation in God's hands.

When it was my turn to speak, I said, "I do not agree with the answers which I have heard. We are going overseas to fight for democracy. On this base are the worst examples of democracy that I have seen anywhere. I am from Alabama, and I have not seen anything there so bad as I have seen at this place. It is true that some of us will be killed when we go to war. This is the last bit of American soil that some of us will ever see again. We need to see here some of those democratic principles that we are going to be fighting and dying for." For example: "The first night after I arrived here, I went to the Officers' Club and ordered food and a drink from the service window but I was not allowed to eat it in the Officers' Club." I said to myself, "I am not going back into that place again. I noticed in the Sergeants' Club about 25 white sergeants; some were accompanied by their ladies. There are approximately 500 black sergeants here in our division. They are not allowed to use the white club, and there is no club here for them to go to. There are more than 20,000 low-ranking enlisted black soldiers here who do not have a service club and they are unable to visit the service club here which is used by the white enlisted soldiers."

"The Army," I said, "does not have the power to correct what is wrong in Alabama and Mississippi, nor does it have the power to correct what is wrong outside the gates here in Virginia; but it does have the power to correct things which are wrong here on the base. If it does, there will be no morale problem." "JUNIOR IS RIGHT! JUNIOR IS RIGHT! JUNIOR IS RIGHT!" were the loud responses coming from all those who had previously given their answers. I began to feel like I had just made the winning touchdown at a homecoming football game. The white commander, who previously didn't know anything about black problems, now knew them as well as anyone; and he would now be the delivery boy to send the message forward.

I believed the Lord had prepared way. The company commander's father-in-law, a brigadier general, was second-in-command of the division. The Division Commander was the brother-law- of the Chief of Staff of the Army. I knew that I had given the correct answer and I could live with it. When I told two senior retired sergeants about my answers for the morale problem here in Germany in 1985, they said to me, "It's a wonder that you were not put out of the Army for what you said." I said, "I would not have cared. They asked for the truth and I told it to them. I believed they wanted my answer. If there had not have been any black U.S. combat troops fighting for the country during World War II, it would have been very embarrassing to the Nation and the black people of the United States. The President had authorized these divisions against the advice of some senators and congressman, who said it was a waste of time and money because these people will not fight, or words to that effect."

The next morning, Camp Patrick Henry was completely integrated and the Division shipped out on October l, 1944, as scheduled. Not one word about morale was ever mentioned again.

The Buffalo Soldiers had gotten their spirit back. This was my greatest victory ever for democracy. Not only did I solve the morale problem, but also in doing so, I pointed out to all concerned that managing black soldiers was the same as managing white soldiers. If black soldiers are treated like white soldiers, they will perform equally to white soldiers. I believe only the President could have integrated Camp Patrick Henry.

I will talk about three battles in which I was involved because I believe they were quite significant for a small unit of thirty-six. Maybe the Lord planned it that way. I believe it to be so.

My unit was the second machine gun platoon, H Company, 37lst Infantry. My company was a unit of the second battalion. We occupied the south end of a mountain ridge with peaks getting higher and higher as it extended north toward the Po Valley, which was over a hundred miles away. We defended from the top of the mountain ridge along one of its finger ridges which extended westward toward the sea. About 2,000 yards from our position in the direction of the sea were about ten miles of beaches. The Division Headquarters was located at a city on the beach, Viareggio, Italy, some 15 or 20 miles to the rear.

On these grounds where my battalion was located, the weather was much warmer and there was less snow than the eastern regions occupied by the other two battalions of our regiment. It was easier for the brass, VIPs, and the press to visit us and observe my battalion more than the other battalions of the division. It was also safer to get to it. Therefore, my battalion became more of a show battalion than the others.

The first show for my battalion took place on November 27, 1944. My machine gun platoon had the mission of supporting F Company in an attack on a Hill called Georgia. My mission was to fire support from Hill Florida, starting at H-10 to H hour, and then to shift my fire to the enemy's position behind Hill

Georgia. H Hour was the time of the attack.

While briefing my platoon on its mission, I said, "Statistics show that the life of machine gunners in offensive combat is about five minutes. Because of that, I will rotate you on the guns in order for everyone to have an equal chance at survival." When H-10 came (meaning 10 minutes prior to the attack), I gave the order to commence firing. Nothing happened. I gave the order the second time. Nothing happened again. When I gave the third order, no one fired the guns. About two minutes had past. It was beginning to look like I was not going to do all of which I previously said I would do.

The Lord knew how much I wanted to show that black soldiers could fight as well as anyone else. In a situation like this, I was the one whom I could make to fire those guns. The gunners' hands were frozen with fear. I got on one gun and started shooting. My firing was right on target. Then I ordered one of my sergeants to shoot one of the other guns. We both were on target. Then I ordered the four gun crews back on their guns. This time they did a perfect job, enabling F Company to take Hill Georgia with little resistance.

The enemy had a tank buried into the mountain to the rear of Hill Georgia, and he used it to fire at point blank range at F Company's men, forcing them to move to the reverse slope of Hill Georgia. Taking advantage of the tank fire against F Company, the enemy counter-attacked. My machine gunner engaged the counter-attackers, wounding and killing some of them and forcing the rest to withdraw. After about 20 minutes, my company executive officer ordered me to cease fire. Then he said, "Good job".

I thanked my men for doing a good job and said nothing to them for failing to carry out my initial orders, to commence firing. When I told them that statistics indicated that the life of machine gunners in offensive combat was only five minutes, it scared them to death, so to speak. I took the blame for it. Because of the way it worked out, I was more elated over the accomplishment than I would have been if it had gone perfectly in the beginning. I believe these mishaps were lessons which would prove helpful to me in the future. More importantly, I had lived up to the promises which I made when I was ten years of age..

The next morning when I went into the company command post, the Company Commander said to me, "Lieutenant White, the Division Commander saw your platoon in action yesterday. He said that it was the best machine gun fire he had ever seen, including World War I and World War II. I have been authorized to recommend you for a Silver Star medal (the third highest combat award), or promote you to first Lieutenant, give you a Combat Infantry Badge and a R&R (leave) to Rome." I said, "I like the second part better."

I went to the rear, took a shower, got my dress uniform, and went to Rome with my Combat Infantry Badge and my new rank of first lieutenant.

I stopped by Leghorn, Italy, to see my brother Clarence en route to Rome and to show him my awards-the combat badge and my promotion. He was quite proud and wished me a safe drive and a good time in the Holy City. It was about 300 miles drive in an open jeep on this cold early December night. Nothing was going to stop me from making the trip. Even though I had been on the front line less than a month, this early break in the war was good for me because it enabled me to mature a little by letting me gain confidence, by letting me see how my military training proved itself in combat. It was a little bit like graduating from high school, basic training, or Officers' Candidate School. I grew as a man as I absorbed how I achieved success in battle.

When I returned to my unit, I was considered the hero of the first battle. The Division Commander had made me a hero when he stated that my platoon had done an outstanding job. When he made it known to all the regiments and battalions, my hero status became well established. A Tuskegee University classmate of mine, Lieutenant Harvey Thomas, who was in another battalion some 10 or 15 miles away, located me to tell me to take it easy and not to get myself killed.

I was lucky that the Division Commander saw my unit, and I was fortunate that things went so well. I always figured that God was with me and my objectives. He had helped me come up with the right answers for solving the morale problem in Virginia, and he had helped to set the right example for my platoon during its first combat mission. I always believed that God would help those who try to help themselves. I also felt that if I had not deserved God's help, I probably would not have gotten it.

I could never come to visualize myself as a hero, but I found it to be useful because others did. Shortly after I returned from Rome, the company commander asked me to leave my second platoon and take over the first platoon because its performance was below what he considered to be adequate in the last battle. My initial reaction was to object, but I realized the company commander had to do that which was best for the company. So I took the good soldier's attitude and accepted it.

I immediately became more impressed with the first platoon than I was with the second platoon which I left. I considered it was due in part to my new hero status and the probable dissatisfaction my commander had with the previous platoon leader. I found soldiers want proven leaders who have both the courage and ability to lead them, especially in combat. I began to feel that they found in me a kind of savior. I must admit that I was enjoying this royal treatment I was receiving, and I was determined to live up to their expectations of me.

I had a well-constructed three story stone house with a big cellar which provided good protection from enemy fire. In the cellar were barrels of Italian vino (red wine) which we drank more than we did water. My platoon had cooking facilities which enabled us to eat warm meals most of the time. The crews on our machine guns worked 24 hours per day. We had a rotation system during our defensive period (which occurred more frequently during the winter period when offensive combat was limited mostly to patrol activities and small units in combat).

On February 14, 1945, I went into offensive combat with my first platoon. We were getting ready for the spring offensive for ending the war in Italy. This was a battalion two-company size attack involving E and G Companies. I was assigned to support G Company. The attack took off in the early morning of February 14, 1945. We had to travel about 1,500 yards to our objective which was called Ohio Ridge. This was a downhill sloping ridge, connected to Hill Georgia which was where I was involved in my first offensive engagement on November 27. Ohio was the main ridge extending west toward the sea. After three hours, with little resistance, we along with E Company to our left occupied Ohio Ridge and begin digging in to defend our take, just in case the enemy wanted it back. Our units were not expecting to stay up there because this was a training mission. Higher command could order us back the same day or the next. We did not know that because it was their decision to determine when our units would withdraw.

About two o'clock in the afternoon I saw Captain Cook of G Company talking very excitedly on the phone to the Battalion Commander. I went to him to see what was the problem. At that time, I felt dirt disappearing from under my left boot. I looked to the east about 300 yards, and because the sun was shinning from the west, I was able to spot the enemy firing at me with a machine gun. I quickly fired one shot with my rifle, and I was sure it was a bull's eye. I kept my eye on the enemy just to make sure. He ran about five steps without his machine gun, and he fell. I observed him (using my field glasses) and assumed he was either dead or was dying, I felt killing him once was enough. Then I asked Captain Cook, without telling him that I had just saved both of our lives, "What's happening?" He said: "Our Navy wanted to get into the act with their big guns. Their rounds fell short, killing eleven of my men. I just told the battalion commander if the Navy kills any more of my men, I will march my company off this hill." I said, "I am sure the battalion commander will take care of it." I went back to my position.

Some 20 or 30 minutes later, I saw the Captain marching his company off the hill. I said, "What are you doing?" "The Navy killed eight more of my men." I knew if he withdrew that I was supposed to withdraw with him. Because he was withdrawing without orders, I considered it to be an unacceptable combat mistake; and I decided not to go with him. I said, "Tell the Battalion Commander I will try to hold the objective until he sends some reinforcements." He said he would. This situation reminded me of the one which my friend talked about at the well house in 1932, when he said black soldiers were cowards and they ran away in battle. Captain Cook was neither a coward, nor was he running away from battle; but he was making a mistake.

I guess the enemy must have been laughing his heart out, saying, "We do not have to kill the Americans. They are doing it for us." In any event, I redeployed my platoon to defend the ridge. I also judged that our adversaries were going to give the Captain a hard time when he showed up at Battalion Headquarters, treating him as if he was a coward running away from battle.

I got a little nervous when no reinforcement came because I knew we were quite vulnerable to a night attack. I believed that the Lord was with us again, because it rained very hard that night, making it difficult for the enemy to send his patrols on the slippery mountain. The next morning I told my platoon sergeant and section leaders, "If the enemy wants us, he can get us; but we will all fight until we are dead, because no one in this platoon will surrender. If anyone does, the enemy will take him over there on the side of the mountain and line him up and kill him before a firing squad. That's a hell of a way for a soldier to die." I am sure they knew I meant business; they knew I meant what I said.

To make life easier by helping them forget their fears, I issued a half gallon of Sicilian whiskey to the Platoon Sergeant. I told him to make sure everyone got a "shot" of it. Whiskey was only issued to officers. When all the men got a little, they said it was better than a turkey dinner.

The enemy did not attack, but he dropped a few mortar shells at us, without any of my men getting hit.

Later that afternoon on February 15, I had my Platoon Sergeant lay a wire to my Company Commander because I did not want to spend another night up on Ohio. When I talked to him, he was surprised that we were still alive. He said he thought that the Navy had wiped us out, too. I assured him that none of my men had a scratch. Captain Cook did not tell him anything about my platoon holding the objective and my request for reinforcements. E Company had also withdrawn, which meant that my platoon was on that mountain ridge alone. I was ordered to withdraw at first dark.

When I returned, I was a hero again by holding the line and not coming back without being ordered to do so.

Members of the U.S. press came from Rome to see the Buffalo Soldiers in action. I did not know it. They gave it to us and to the whole division. It was published everywhere in the States. Even the black people in the States thought we had messed up. According to the newspapers, it was all the fault of black people; white people were not accused of doing anything wrong. I really believed that if a white division had done exactly what we did, the Navy would have investigated, the battalion commander would have been criticized for not controlling Navy fires, and the withdrawal of the company which had suffered extremely heavy casualties, as a training mistake, especially since the enemy did not take advantage of the situation.

I saved the battalion and the division because I held the line and did not withdraw until I was ordered to do so. This made the newspaper report of our mission inaccurate, misleading, and destructive to the reputation of a great division. Captain Cook's company consisted of less than 200 men in a division of 40,000, and the reputation of the division as a whole should not have been down graded by the action of a commander of such a small unit.

I was recommended by my Battalion and my Company Commanders to be promoted to captain, after being first lieutenant for only two months and an officer for nine months, but the Regimental Commander said no because he thought I was too young. He decided that I needed another R&R to Rome.

After my first offensive battle, I was given R&R to Rome and now after my second one, I was given another one. I was equally as happy to go this second time. Again I went to the rear area of the division to the shower unit to get cleaned up and to be issued a set of clean clothing. This time I had an unexpected surprise at the shower unit. While taking my shower, the Chief of Staff of the Army came to look at the shower which I was using. The General who commanded U.S. Forces in Italy, the Fifth Army Commander, the Corps Commander, the Division Commander, and three or four one-star generals were with the Chief of Staff. This was the first time I had seen a five-star general in person, General of The Armies George C. Marshall. I was more excited with all that brass than my previous fights with the enemy. The bad publicity, which was given to the division by the press back home, brought the Chief-of-Staff to Italy to investigate this for himself. For the Chief-of-Staff of the Army to come to Italy on top-secret mission to investigate a Black Division showed to me how significant this division performance was to him in order to help him, in my opinion, to make a determination about the integration of the Armed Forces. This was an area of his research, in my opinion, which he would not delegate. I was happy to see the Chief of Staff, and I had a good idea why he was there.

Ever since I solved the morale problem of the division in Virginia, I felt General of The Armies George C. Marshall and I were on the same wave length with respect to the future of the integrated Army.

This time I went to Rome by day, and it was quite comfortable. I knew Rome better, and I had a nice time dancing and dating with the girls. My battlefield maturity grew as a result of this vacation and my recent offensive combat engagement. I did not see how I could have done my jobs any better up to this time in combat. When it becomes spring, the two Armies in Italy, the U.S. Fifth, and the British Eighth will take off in offensive combat to end the war in Italy. Our Division's objective was Genoa, the beginning of Po Valley on the northwest. It was 100 miles away, and the Italian Alps over which we must travel to get there are among the highest and most rugged in Italy.

I stopped by to see my brother Clarence on my way back to the front. I told him about my Rome visit and not to worry about me on the war front because I could take of myself. After leaving him and returning to my unit, I found that my battalion had pulled back for training as a result of the errors made on February 14.

A few days later, I was transferred to another regiment, 370th Infantry, which was considered the best regiment in the division. To me, it was apparent that General of The Armies Marshall had given the 92nd Division a clean bill of health and a vote of confidence after investigating the U.S. Press report about the performance of my Battalion on February 14, 1945, by giving it the mission of spearheading the Fifth U.S. Army's spring offensive. The 370th Infantry was chosen to be the spearhead regiment, and the best officers of the division were authorized to be transferred to this unit to give it the best chance for success. I felt that my wave length connecting me to the Chief of Staff of the Army was telling me that this was the test to determine whether the armed forces would be integrated. If we become successful in the forthcoming attack, if would be.

I was assigned to D Company, First Battalion, 370th Infantry and was given the first machine gun platoon. My hero status in this regiment was not as well known as in my previous regiment, but they knew that I was considered one of the best in the divisions. Therefore, I had nothing to prove in my new unit. I knew that we had a long fight ahead, and I was as determined as ever with my new platoon to prove that black soldiers were as good as the best fighters. For my satisfaction, I had already proven so. The big test would be the coming campaign of sustained warfare--not like the past fighting of one or two days of it and then pulling back for a break. It was the campaign that we were all waiting for, because we wanted to get the war over with and go home.

My previous company commander, Captain John Runyon, was also transferred to my new battalion. He was made the new commander of C Company, 1st Battalion, 370th Infantry Regiment. For the forthcoming spearhead mission, he requested that I be assigned to support his company because he knew he could depend upon me. His company would be in the third wave. The battalion commander denied his request because he wanted me to be in the first wave which would initiate the spring offensive.

It was hard to figure out how my reputation in this new regiment was so well known. I had been given the first platoon because my commanders wanted me to be in first wave. Maybe someone thought I was better than I thought I was. In any event, I was in the first wave.

On the morning of April 5, 1945, the spring offensive for ending the war in Italy, began with the first wave, consisting of A Company, 370th Infantry and the First Machine Gun Platoon, Company D, 370d Infantry. A heavy volume of artillery and mortar fire fell on the spearhead objectives--Hills X, Y and Z. Company A took off at full speed to our first objective, Hill X. Under the cover of long-range friendly fire, we forced the enemy to stay underground. My machine gun platoon provided direct fire, which could be observed by the gunners of my platoon. When my platoon could no longer fire as it would endanger Company A, I took off with it for Hill X at full speed under the protection of Company A's assault fire.

When I reached Hill X with my platoon, I saw only five men from Company A, even though I believe it was less than 15 minutes since we launched the attack. I asked those five men, "Which way did the

Company Commander go?" They pointed to Hill Y, our second objective. I looked around and did not see any dead bodies. I was surprised that the men of Company A had disappeared so quickly. Because I did not see any dead bodies, I assumed that members of the Company were alive and fighting. I placed my machine guns on the most dominant part of Hill X, where they would be in position to fire on all three objectives--X, Y and Z.

Upon observing all three spearhead objectives from my platoon's new position on Hill X, I still was unable to see Company A, I decided to move to the final objective, Hill Z, thinking initially that I would find Company A there.

It was not the duty of a machine gun platoon to take ground. This was the job of the rifle company, like Company A. My mission was to provide a heavy volume of supporting fire to make the job easier for the company which I was supporting to seize ground. I headed for the final objective, Hill Z, hoping to find the company commander there. When I got to the base of Hill Z, I began to have second thoughts; maybe Company A is not around. I did not want to take any chances. I was planning to prevent any surprises which the enemy might attempt by catching us by surprise and without us being ready for him if he were on that hill. I took the machine gun from one of the gunners and cradled it around my neck with my left hand on the pistol grip and my right hand on the trigger. This is a case where one must act within a split second, and I was not trusting my men to react correctly. This was based on my experience on November 27 when my gunners were at first afraid to shoot. I only knew myself. As we approached the crest of the Hill, the enemy threw open the tops of his bunkers and threw a bunch of grenades; but they did not show their heads initially. They threw these grenades so hard that they went over our heads down the mountain.

They were apparently waiting for the grenades to go off before coming up. My men hit the ground, which was what they were trained to do on grenade ranges. I dropped to my knees and placed machine gun fire over the opened bunkers, catching the enemies when they came up to attack us. In a matter of seconds, the final objective, Hill Z, the final spearhead objective, belonged to us.

In nothing flat, we had seized all three spearhead objectives, which were part of the enemies' defensive which had held us up for six months. What happened? We caught the enemy by surprise because of the rapid speed which followed our supporting fire. His position had been shelled off and on all winter without any attempt to take these hills. When they were shelled on this day, the enemy apparently thought we would not attack as before; and he stayed underground for protection from our fire. When we caught the enemy underground, he chose to stay there or be killed. He stayed there, becoming a victim of our surprise and fast-moving attack. This was a perfect execution of offensive combat.

The fact that I went to Hill Z was because I thought initially I would find Company A there. When it occurred to me that Company A may not be there, I just prepared to engage the enemy. If he showed up, I would get him. My comment was, "Nothing succeeds like success."

When I stood on Hill Z in less than two hours after the attack began, I said, "We passed General Marshall's test and now the Armed Forces will be integrated."

When I telephoned my commander that I was on the final objective--in less than two hours--he did not believe this to be possible. I believed everyone from the Pentagon right down to my company commander had to be shocked with this unbelievable surprise accomplishment that we had seized all the objectives in such a short period of time, and with such a small force. I believe the Chief of Staff of the Army had a hotline connection to Italy following this spearhead attack which he approved n February. This, to me, was classic combat. Many great objectives in warfare are taken without the intent of the taker to do so; but they do happen, and I was pleasantly surprised that we did it, without losing a man.

I was ordered to pull back, disengage from the enemy, because my unit was scheduled to spearhead another breakthrough the next morning on the central front to the east. B Company, the second wave, passed through my position to continue the attack northward. This permitted me to pull back.

On the way back, I noticed those five stragglers which I found in the morning had drifted into the mine field which I marked when I moved to Hill Z. I went in there to get them out. They failed to follow my instructions causing one of the mines near me to go off. I was blown unconscious, I believe, for a short time. Then I began to feel for my feet and legs, because I had no feeling in them. I found that they were still there, only the seams of my trousers had been blown loose. I had some abrasions on my left thigh and hand. I could not see because the explosion was against the front of my body. When I stood, I fell immediately to the ground. I believed that I felt myself dying. I was ready and not afraid to die because I felt God was with me and that I was doing his work. I had done all that I set out to do. Then I felt my life coming back. I said, "Maybe God owes me something."

During the next eight months, I was in a hospitalization rehabilitation status before I returned to full duty at Tuskegee University on the ROTC Staff there in November 1945. I had every right to feel good about my accomplishments.

In 1946, the Senate began hearings on the integration of the Armed Forces. In June of that year, the President recommended me for a permanent commission in the Regular Army; and it was approved by the U.S. Senate.

The President had the authority to integrate the Armed Forces without Congressional approval. Senate hearings were held anyway. I was sure that General Marshall and President Truman would have the final word on it. When he integrated the Armed Forces in 1948, I was sure that integration of the services would work. I believed then, as I did when I stated to General Couch in 1995, that I planted the seeds which led to the integration of the Armed Forces. I felt then that this integration would be the first link in the chain of events that would correct the civil rights problems in the United States.

The President gave me an appointment as a commissioned officer in the Regular Army of United States with the same status as those commissioned from West Point. I was one of six black combat arms officers so honored and the only one from the Buffalo Division.

When I told my Father in 1932, that the race problems would end in the 1960s, I did not visualize that I would help to do it with the role I would play during the war. I planned to do it through education. I was planning to set myself up as an example in education for my family and for my family to be an example for the community. After about 30 years of this, there would be enough educated black people to figure out a way to correct the civil rights problem. I had to work hard for my education. I had to work hard to help to educate my sisters and brothers who were older and to help the younger ones as well, three sisters and two brothers, in a family of nine children.

Integration of the services would be the beginning for civil rights achievements. The major forces behind any meaningful civil rights accomplishments must be made by black people who are educated. Not only was it necessary for well-educated black people to bring pressure against the barriers to civil rights, but they must also to use the opportunities made available when the barriers are eliminated. Military integration and the education of black people would put them in a position to take advantage of the opportunities available in a desegregated society.

My family began making preparation for our education prior to 1920. During the '40s and '50s, six out of eight eligible sisters and brothers in my family were college graduates. Later they would achieve two doctorate degrees or the equivalent, two masters degrees, and two bachelors degrees. This 70 percent college education level for my family would continue during the next two generations, and I am sure it will continue in subsequent generations. At the present time, the third generation has a 100 percent college level education achievement. Those who are old enough to have finished college have done so. Those who are of college age are in college, and those who are in high school are preparing for college.

As a result of my family's educational achievements, we have been able to participate in a variety of professional positions--two as Army officers, two as Air Force officers, and two as Naval officers, one who is a medical doctor in the Air Force. Other positions include high school principal, university professor, associate professor, school teachers, business executives, and elected officials, lawyers, nuclear engineers, actors, writers, graduate nurses, etc.

My father passed away in April, 1948. As the only unmarried brother, I assumed the role as head of the family. I continued to push education as a must in my family. I took financial responsibility for the education of my two youngest sisters and one nephew. This was a continuing process to use my family to help others by setting examples in educational achievements which I started as a ten-year-old boy in 1932. I believed God provided education as a means of achieving equality in our society.

My other financial support was for my mother and my sister Jewel who remained at home with my mother. I remodeled the family home where my mother and sister lived. All the modern conveniences were installed: electricity, hot and cold running water, water closets, gas heat, refrigeration, television, telephone, all of which were never before available in our country home. When I told my nephew one or two years ago that I believe that I contributed over $50,000 supporting and educating my family, he said, "I believe it was more than that."

While I was on ROTC Duty at Tuskegee University between 1945-48, I saw many of my former classmates return there to finish their education, interrupted by the war. Most of them would now have their education financed by the GI Bill of World War II. I saw this mass education of black veterans as a means to further ensure the achievements of civil rights for everyone. Additionally, people would receive education benefits as a result of the Korean War.

I went to Germany in 1948. I served in segregated military units during my three-year tour there in spite of the fact that President Truman ordered the Armed Forces to be integrated in 1948. Toward the end of my tour in July 1951, however, some units started integrating their soldiers.

I returned to the United States in July 1951 for the purpose of attending the Advanced Infantry Officers Course at Fort Benning, Georgia. While I was there, integration on the civilian front was part of the news on the radios and in the newspapers. Integration of public schools was before the Federal Courts

The next major move in the civil rights field took place in May 1954 when the U.S. Supreme Court ruled that segregated public schools were unconstitutional. This put an end to the Pressy vs. Ferguson equal-but-separate ruling of the Supreme Court in 1896, making it null and void and provided the legal basis for ending all segregation in public schools and businesses serving the general public. This decision brought tears to my eyes and joy to my soul as it looked as if my predictions and dreams were becoming more of a reality. Now more than ever, I began to realize how important education would be in helping to bring legal equality in our society.

In October 1954, I was transferred from South Korea to South Carolina State College, Orangeburg, South Carolina. I was disappointed because I wanted to go to an infantry division, feeling the need to advance my military career. To facilitate this, I was planning to go to the Pentagon and try to change it. On the way there, I stopped at South Carolina State College and found my first commander as an officer, Lieutenant Colonel Lofton, as commander of the ROTC Detachment. He said he needed my help because the ROTC program there was in its last year of probation. Because we got along so well before, I cancelled my vacation and went to work and saved the program by getting the University to finance an education reinforcement program for students who wished to enroll in the advanced classes that permitted them to become commissioned officers in the U.S. Army upon graduation from the university.

It began to look more and more like I had to do some more work for the Lord. All kinds of activity were going on in the State of South Carolina concerning public school integration. Everyone was a bit nervous about the forthcoming Supreme Court decree, which was expected in 1955. In the meantime, conservative elements exerted pressure forcing the Reverend Delaney of Clarenden County, South Carolina (who had initiated the major civil rights case leading to the desegregation decision) to leave the State for fear of his safety. Federal Judge Wates Warren (who was the only Judge of the three white Federal Judges panel who made up the Federal Regional Court) voted in favor to integrate public schools and was forced to leave Charleston, South Carolina, for the same reason as the Reverend Delaney.

Every time I had a chance to join the NAACP (National Advancement of Colored People), I did so. I joined the organization in Orangeburg in 1954. At that time no civil rights activity was planned as the organization was waiting for the Supreme Court's decree, which came in May 1955. For civil "righters," the Supreme Court rendered the best possible decision when it stated that public school integration would proceed with all deliberate speed. The segregationists just about went out of their minds over the decision, but the black people jumped for joy.

152

The summer of 1955, I went to Fort Benning, Georgia, for the ROTC Summer Camp. During the month of August, while I was away, five members of the NAACP petitioned the Board of Education of Orangeburg County to integrate their children into the public school in the fall of 1955. The answer was "no." A White Citizens Council organization was established to oppose the integration process. The Council consisted of one-half of the businesses in the City of Orangeburg, and they listed themselves in the Orangeburg newspaper as Charter Members. They began immediately to make economic pressure against the petitioners. The NAACP Secret Civil Rights Planning Committee, of which I was a part, put the word out for black people to trade with their friends, which meant that the chartered members of the White Citizens Council were not their friends.

The first casualties of the counter economic pressure were the White Citizens Councils who depended on business from black people in this county where blacks out-numbered whites by a large margin. A high percentage of black teachers who taught within a 50- to 100-mile radius of Orangeburg lived there. There were two black universities in Orangeburg. The White Citizens Council did not subject teachers, staff members, and students at these two institutions and public school teachers to economic pressure. This gave black people a vast economic edge in this economic warfare. The White Citizens Council took on the worst possible targets, exerting their scare tactics against the black community which no longer worked.

The mayor of Orangeburg who had the Coca Cola franchise, refused to deliver Coca Cola to the ESSO Service Station that was partially owned by one of the petitioners. Students on the campus at South Carolina State College began to smash any Coca Cola containers in the possession of students. This started a spontaneous boycott of Coca Cola products nationwide. Coca Cola stocks began to fall on the stock market. Look and Life magazines stated that the Civil Rights revolution had begun in Orangeburg and that they expected it to be fought out there.

Orangeburg businessmen who were charter members of the White Citizens Council, facing bankruptcy, called on the State for help. State officials in Columbia began to sound the alarm: "Communists are down there in that State College." State highway patrol began to patrol the campus, and the student body at the college went on strike.

I was on the faculty council, and I made suggestion to the president on how to manage the strike without surrendering the rights of black people. He eventually bent under the pressure of white newspapers by expelling student leaders. The faculty, however, drew up a proclamation that was sent to the Governor and state legislators declaring that if they believed the faculty at South Carolina State College were infested with Communists, that it was their duty to close down the college and transfer its students to the University of South Carolina and Clemson.

This proclamation caused the Governor and members of the State Assembly to give the "silent treatment" to the integration fight, as the school integration petition remained in place.

As the publicity generated at Orangeburg begin to spread, the civil rights movement followed elsewhere--first, in Rock Hill, South Carolina, and second, in Greensboro, North Carolina, where students there began sit-ins at Woolworth department store lunch counters. Then, in November 1945, the Bus Boycott in Montgomery, Alabama, began when Mrs. Rosa Parks refused to move to the back in the city bus. This situation at Montgomery, Alabama, established Doctor Martin Luther King as the ultimate civil rights leader. I said as a ten-year-old boy that through education a black leader would emerge to bring about civil rights changes in the 1960s. This leader came to be Doctor Martin Luther King.

The civil rights movement going to Montgomery, Alabama, was the end of the beginning for ending the legally segregated society in the South.

I traveled to Birmingham during 1956 and 1957 to visit a young lady friend who was a student at Tuskegee University. Across the street from where she lived was the residence of Lawyer Showes, the Civil Rights attorney for the NAACP. I told him about my military service with the Buffalo Division and its success during World Ward War II; and that my involvement in it had led to the integration of the Armed Forces of the United States. I told him that the Supreme Courts decision of 1954 and 1955 to integrate the public schools was a part of the chain reaction grown out of the integration of the Armed Forces.

I pointed out that these decisions and accomplishments have given us a legal basis for pushing for our constitutional rights. This was our time, and we must make the most of it. He explained some of the civil struggles which they had in Birmingham, insuring me that they were not giving in to the racist elements there. He even pointed out some physical encounters in which they had gotten the better result.

When I went back to Germany in September 1957, public facilities on the highways of South Carolina were denied to black people. But when I returned Stateside in July 1960, all of these facilities were open for everyone. This achievement was reached after Doctor King and his civil rights organization won a decision to outlaw bus discrimination in Montgomery, which occurred before I departed to Germany. As a result of this decision, the Interstate Commerce Commission ruled that all facilities engaged in interstate commerce must end all forms of discrimination.

After the Supreme Court outlawed bus transportation in the city of Montgomery, Alabama, Doctor King moved to Atlanta where his headquarters remained during the three years I was in Germany.

Upon my returning in July, 1960, I did enjoy having breakfast at a desegregated restaurant on Highway 30l, just outside of Orangeburg, South Carolina. It was hard to imagine what would have happened to me if I had tried the same thing three years earlier. Only businesses engaged in Interstate Commerce were forced to end discrimination, but it was a good end.

After leaving Montgomery, Doctor King's civil rights movement was largely concentrated in and around Atlanta. Later, in 1960, he broke probation in Decatur, Georgia; and the judge threw him into a maximum-security prison with inmates on death row. The segregationists hoped that the prisoners would kill him. This was a case similar to Daniel in The Lion's Den. The prisoners had great admiration for him. Senator Kennedy, running for President against Vice President Nixon, asked the Judge to release Doctor King, for an alleged promise of promotion if he made President. Many believe that this release of Doctor King from prison was the reason for the narrow victory John F. Kennedy had over Richard M. Nixon to become President of The United States.

Doctor King wasted no time using his Presidential connection to take his movement outside of Atlanta, when he joined forces in Albany, Georgia, which was already in progress. As I observed it from my Fort Dix, New Jersey, quarters, I judged it as not going well. A young lady whom I dated during the Christmas holiday of 1960 in my hometown in Selma, Alabama, was one of Doctor King's followers. She called me just about every evening at my quarters at Fort Dix, New Jersey, and gave me a report on activities in Albany. I told her during her last call, "Tell Doctor King that he is in a no-win situation there, a movement which he did not organize and one which was not well supported. Tell him to go back to Atlanta, assess the lessons learned in Albany, profit from them, and to take his next movement elsewhere." She never called me after that, but the movement there was terminated; and he returned to Atlanta.

His next movement, two years later, was Birmingham. Alabama. I would have never advised him to go there because I considered Birmingham to be about the meanest and most racist city in the United States. His campaign there was the most brilliant one in civil rights history anywhere. I was hoping that my visits there in 1956 and 1957 had helped. It was unfortunate that it took this extraordinary campaign of Doctor King and the death of President Kennedy for President Johnson to ram the Anti-Discrimination Act of 1964 through Congress. One of my predictions of 1932 had come to pass.

When Doctor King took his Voters Rights Campaign to my hometown of Selma, Alabama, I had a hidden feeling that maybe God was saying thanks to me for my effort for more than 30 years to bring so much good to our society. Birmingham and Selma were the perfect cities for launching the most important campaigns in the civil rights movement. Birmingham was the best place to end discrimination.

Selma, surrounded by five black belt counties, was the best place to fight for voters' rights.

No one in Selma would ever give me credit for anything of a civil rights nature. I left there in 1940 and went to college. I became a licensed pilot in 1941 and the first black commissioned officer for the city. I had gotten much publicity in the White Section of the Selma paper that was not seen previously by black people. I even wondered myself if anyone there ever followed my examples. A friend of mine, Bill Johnson, who was a GS-l4, a top official in the Army and Air Forces Exchange System Europe, asked a

Major General Ernest Harrell, U.S. Army Engineer Commander for Europe, who was from Selma, Alabama, did he know me. He said, "Yes. It was because of me that he went to Tuskegee University, took ROTC, and became an officer in the Army." My first objective as a ten-year-old boy was to be an example for my family and for my family to be an example for the community. I was happy to know that someone whom I did not know had used me as an example to reach such a high position in the Army. I knew I had a great impact on my nieces, nephews, and other relatives; but it was hard to gauge how many people would say that they followed my examples or the examples of my family. The most important satisfaction for me was that the goals, which I had set more than 30 years earlier, were accomplished in my hometown of Selma, Alabama.

The Campaign in Selma, which covered five black belt counties, was well organized and was well supported. The people in the Pernell rural community where I was born had been afraid of a white man's shadow when I was a small boy. They rose up and followed Doctor King, even when they were force to move from the land of their ancestors dating back to 1844. I was proud of the Selma Campaign and the people of my home community. Four of my nieces and one nephew were up front with Doctor King all the time and collectively had been in jail over 20 times. They were proud of it and were happy to tell me so.

A new village, which I called Doctor Martin Luther King Village, was built for the people in the Pernell Community where I was born after they became refugees for following Doctor King. Their home had all the modern conveniences, which my sister, Mable, and I provided for my mother. They had helped to make for a desegregated society, to achieve their rights to vote. More importantly, they were free and independent. I was most happy because if was for them that I initiated my civil rights movement in 1932.

The campaign to include the march to Montgomery gave President Johnson the "something spectacular" similar to Birmingham which he requested in order for him to push the Voters Rights Act through Congress. After the Voters Rights Act of 1965 was passed, my mission established as a ten-year-old boy had been accomplished. I retired from the Army in September 1, 1965.

I moved to Germany in 1966, looked for and found a wife, and have raised two wonderful children.

I have tried to be a true and faithful husband for my wife and father for my children. God would not allow me the blessing of my last mission, to find a wife, until I had completed the first one or seen the first one completed--removing legal racial barriers--a mission which I believe He gave me to as a ten-year-old boy. Finding the girl when and whom I married was worth the wait. He gave me a girl to marry that I could not say "no" to.

I was asked, "If you had to live your life over again, would you do it differently?" I said, "Yes, I would have invested in two stocks on the stock exchange, which I failed to do in 1965 or '66. If things had been different, my life would have been different. My life was one of reactions. I reacted to each situation that I faced as correctly as I knew how, with little regard to the consequences caused by my reactions. Whenever I have to give an accounting for my decisions, I want to be able to justify them. To me, this is what life is all about.

I am happy to have talked to you about black history--my black history, the black history that I was a part of, and the black history which all Americans and, to some extent, the world can be proud ... a black history that has helped to shape the character of America.

The power of my accomplishments and the accomplishments of the Civil Rights Movement was due to education and the opportunities opened up because of education. My mission was to eliminate the legal barriers which prevented black people from enjoying equal rights under the law. Education helped me to develop leadership, because I had to work in order achieve it. It helped me to become a commissioned officer, which helped me to take advantage of opportunities to enable the services to become integrated. Without my pursuit of education, I would not have been able to do what I did. I was silent because my objective was not a sure thing. I had faith, hope, and determination and, with the help of God, all things are possible. Talking about it may have done more harm than good. Therefore, being silent and doing those things that I took to bring about Civil Rights changes can best be defined as SILENT POWER.

Appendix B:
THE POWER OF EDUCATION

I believed when I told my Father that the racial segregation would end in the 1960s that it would be accomplished by the power of education. I did not tell my father that my plans to accomplish this task would be done though the education of black people. My father had previously told me that education made every person better at what he planned to do. I, therefore, concluded that education was some kind of miracle that God created to enable one person to become equal to another. Through education, the poor could become equal to the rich; the "down and out" could become equal to the high and mighty. The black could prove his equality to the white.

When I was in Rome in December 1944, I said to myself, "When the War is over, I want to return to Tuskegee University and complete my senior year of college while serving as a member of the ROTC Department there while I am still on active duty. My dream came true when I went there in November 1945. I was assigned to the ROTC Unit at Tuskegee University. Already education had played a major role in my life. Because of my education, I became a licensed pilot, a commissioned officer in the United States Army, and a certified schoolteacher in American and World History. Education put me into a position as an officer to solve the morale problem of the 92nd Infantry (Buffalo) Division in September 1944, which prevented its deactivation and became the basis for integrating the previously segregated base there. As a result, the Division went to war as scheduled.

The success of the Division in combat paved the way for the Armed Forces to be integrated. Even though I would have had the same desire to do this without having gone to college, I would not have had the power to do so without the education which permitted me to become an officer.

When I returned to Tuskegee after the war, I did not have any plans to make the military a career. It was my desire to go into business. Even after the President had given me a regular Army commission, I gave some thought of not accepting it. I was persuaded to do so by the Assistant Dean of Men who was a retired disabled veteran of World War I, a U.S. Army Captain who stated it was too great an honor to turn down. I thought it would give me the opportunity to marry a young lady whom I was interested in at the time. I accepted the commission, but she did not accept me. With an opportunity to retire in 20 years, I would still be young enough to go into business. I, therefore, decided to make my career in the military.

The Army gave me the permission to take college classes that did not interfere with my military duties. During the last two years of my three-year assignment, I completed my senior year and graduated just before I departed for military reassignment to Germany.

My original mission to educate my family as a means of correcting the race problem had not changed. My brother Edward, who had been drafted during the war after he finished high school, got married and enrolled at Tuskegee University under the GI Bill. My sister Geneva got married during the War after finishing high school and became a mother, thus preventing her from going to college. My next sister, Jewel, was handicapped and was unable to be educated academically. My two youngest sisters, Mable and Jean, became my responsibility to educate because my father passed away in April 1948, five months before I was reassigned to Germany. I was the only single brother and had to become the "Daddy" of the family and assume majority support for my mother and my handicapped sister. This family daddy role I accepted gracefully, without asking for assistance from other family members.

My sister, Erin, who married after her junior year in college, worked in her family's business in Pine Bluff, Arkansas. I prevailed on her behalf that she be allowed to finish college, because she was quite brilliant. She not only finished college, but both she and her husband got their doctorate degrees and retired as professors from the University of Illinois at Carbondale. My brother Clarence received his Master's Degree and became a high school principal. My brother Edward graduated from Tuskegee University and made the United Air Forces his career as a commissioned officer through the Air ROTC program.

My sister Mable graduated from Tuskegee University as a graduate nurse. She worked at the United

States Veterans Hospital there until she married a dentist and moved to Louisiana, where her husband established a business. My youngest sister Jean finished Tuskegee University as a teacher and became a public school counselor, achieving academic credit required for a Ph.D. degree. Out of a family with eight children eligible to go to college, six graduates--two with BS degrees and four with graduate degrees--and only one member of my family was a high school dropout.

My objective as a ten-year-old boy was to have all members of my family to become college graduates. This has been accomplished to a 70 percent level, which is acceptable.

Not only was I the father of the family after my father passed, I was a kind of silent family ambassador checking on the effort of my sisters and brothers in sending their children to college. I was always checking on the grades of my nieces and nephews in high school, which was necessary for them to go to college. I paid for four years of college for one of the sons of my brother who was the only high school dropout in the family. Because I was a military hero to my nieces and nephews, I had great influence over them and was able to encourage them to pursue college careers. When I told one of my nephews that I spent at least $50,000 educating and supporting my family, he said, "I think that you spent more than that." I said, " I have no regrets."

As a ten-year-old boy, I set myself up as a silent education example for my sisters and brothers. I worked hard on our farm to help and to encourage my father to continue to educate us. I worked in high school, providing some support for my sister and brother who were in college, and became economically supportive of my personal needs. This was a great inspiration to my father and made him more ambitious for supporting the education of the family.

My second education mission was for my family to be an education example for the black community. It's a little hard to measure it; but when neighbors observe one of them move away to high school and college, they have to see it, even if they try not to. They were impressed when I came home in an Army officer's uniform. When news about me was carried in the newspaper, in the section usually reserved for whites, black and white people were impressed with the fact white people talked about it to black people, making my achievements better examples for the black in my community. When a black Major General who commanded the United States Army Engineers, Europe, said to a friend of mine that it was because of me that he went to Tuskegee, joined the ROTC, and became an Army officer, I did not know him, which made me feel that my example set in practice worked in Selma, Alabama.

Economically, my family has been 100 percent professionally employed due to their education. All of those who wished to own their own homes have them. Out of three generations, only four have divorces, and not more than one of them are due to the misconduct of my side of the family. Out of eight married members of my sisters and brothers, only one I believe was guilty of cheating on his mate. No member of my family was ever on welfare.

Members of my family are law abiding, and we monitor each other to make sure that it remains that way.

We help each other in emergencies and provide educational assistance when it is necessary for any member of the family who are worthy and in need of assistance for education. My 85-year-old brother, W. Clarence White, who is a retired high school principal, teaches school every day for the purpose of educating his grandchildren. In addition, he manages the account for the golf course where he has played for over 20 years. My second oldest sister and her husband, in addition to sending all of their four daughters to college, have paid for the college of one granddaughter, are sending a grandson to college, and are preparing another one for college who is still in high school.

I feel that African-Americans have the greatest natural responsibility for correcting the sins of racism in the United States, because the sins of racism are more directed at them than other cultural groups. When I was preparing for the final campaign for helping to end the war in Italy in the spring of 1945, I said to my men, "We have two wars to fight. We have to fight to win the war here, and we must go home and win the war there for our civil rights. If you fight well here, you will fight well there. If we do so, no one can stop us. The Constitution is on our side. The leadership must come from black people. White people cannot stand for whites fighting for the rights of black people. Blacks must do it and then the people who believe in equality under the Constitution will join us.

The power of education must be used to expose racism in our churches, in our political parties, in our public schools, wherever it exists. Black Americans have the best eyes and spirit of seeing and feeling racism than any other Americans. It is their duty to use the power of education, politics, economics, and morality to expose and eradicate it for the benefit of all Americans.

My family not only believed in educating us; they taught us good manners as well. We were loved, and we were disciplined. Both to educate and to discipline are difficult. Both my wife and I have done our best to pass on to our children the examples set for us by our parents. I do not smoke, and my wife does not smoke. My twenty-eight year old son does not smoke. My twenty-five year old daughter does not smoke. We never did have to tell our children not to smoke. They just did not smoke, even when most of their friends do. One of us was always home for our children. We are not only proud of our children because they are our children; we are proud of them because they are the best that we could make them. They are educated, have good jobs, and they are a credit to civilization. Education, when it is used with love, discipline, and responsibility, is a credit to humanity. It will help us to advance the cause of democracy at home and abroad. We have a responsibility to man, but more importantly, to God.

Thanksgiving weekend, 1994, my college class, which started at Tuskegee University in September 1940 and went into the Army on June 9, 1943, had a reunion, some 51 years later. Some of us had not seen each other in 51 years. Naturally, we wanted to know what had happened in all of those years after we finished three years of college. We were all members of the advance ROTC class who went to Officers' Candidate School at Fort Benning, Georgia. Most of us graduated and served during World War II as commissioned officers, and returned to college after the war under the GI Bill to pursue our education. Fifty-one years later, fourteen accepted invitations to attend, but only nine of the fourteen who agreed to come appeared at the reunion. Thanksgiving weekend 1994, five of those who agreed to come didn't show up. One had a heart attack, one's wife was ill, and the others had legitimate business reasons for not coming.

The following is the status of the nine who appeared there:

Mister Charles Brown stated that he came to Tuskegee University with $5 in his pocket to get a college education. He became a commissioned officer during the war. He returned to college after the war and graduated. He is a retired Army Colonel living in Florida.

Mister Booker Conley, our host, is a retired Architecture Engineer from the Department of Engineers, Tuskegee University.

Mister Cecil B. Keene, a retired high school principal, Saint Petersburg, Florida. He served on the College and University Board of Regency for the State of Florida under three Governors, Republicans and Democrats. At the time of the reunion he was running for County Commissioner for Saint Petersburg, Florida.

Doctor Charles Lang, Professor at the University of California at Los Angeles, was one of the nine.

Judge Robert W. Penn, Municipal Judge, Toledo, Ohio.

Doctor Jean Peters, my old roommate, was an authority on world poverty. He was Consultant to the U.S. State Department on Poverty and did great work in solving poverty situations for the City of Detroit.

Attorney Stanford S. Smith of Cleveland, Ohio, and member of the staff of Congressman Stoke, member of the U.S. House of Representatives, was one of the nine.

Doctor of Dentistry, Harvey G. Thomas, of Muncie, Indiana, was there.

Major Cecil W. White, Selma, Alabama, who lived in Mainz, Germany, and who claims to be the father of the integrated Armed Forces of the United States of America, the author of this book, completed the nine in attendance.

Five of the fourteen who accepted the invitation to come, but were unable to do so were:

Doctor William W. Bearden of Frankfurt, Kentucky

Major General James F. Hamlet, Trenton, New Jersey

Mr. Theodore R. Johnson, Los Angeles, California,

Mister James B. Huntley, Architecture Engineer, Washington D. C.,

Colonel (US Army Retired) Crawford D. Russell, Atlanta, Georgia.

General Hamlet and I were supposed to drive south together, but he had a heart attack and was in critical condition during that time. He has since recovered and continues to be in good health. General Hamlet is the only African-American to command a division in combat, a cavalry division (helicopters) in Vietnam. He is listed in the Hall of Fame at the Army Aviation Center, Fort Rucker, Alabama.

At the time of the reunion, ten of our original thirty-four ROTC classmates were deceased. Since the meeting, three have died. My old roommate, Doctor Jean Peters, who had been suffering over two years with bone cancer, died one year after the reunion. Lieutenant General Jesse Brewer retired Deputy Police Chief for the City of Los Angeles, California, retired colonel from the United States Army, and later President of Los Angeles, Police Commission, died December 1996. My good friend, Doctor Harvey Thomas, passed away December 1997.

Six of the thirty-four were not there. Three did not respond to the invitation, and the whereabouts of the other three were unknown.

Four who were contacted who were unable to attend for business or health reason were:

Doctor L. Albert Scipio retired Professor of Howard University, Washington. D. C.

Mr. Jesse A. Brewer, Lieutenant General, Police Department, Los Angeles, California, retired colonel, U.S. Army, retired President of the Police Commission, Los Angeles, California.

Mister William A. Craig, Los Angeles, California,

Mister George Sims, Utica, New York.

I regret that we were unable to give a full accounting of all of the 34 members of our class, those who are still living and some of those who were deceased. We are scheduled to have our next reunion on Thanksgiving weekend 2000. I will be 79 then--some will be my age, some a year younger or a year older. I hope that the 21 whom we believe to be alive will be there.

We were honored to have our R0TC Professor who was our commander and who sent us into the Army on June 9, 1943, to be our guest speaker, Colonel U.S. Army (Retired) John A. Welch. He was a great Professor and his examples inspired all of us to be great achievers. I believe that he was in his nineties in 1994. If he were not, I am sure that he is now and is in good health, according to my latest information about him. It will be an even greater honor in 2000 than it was in 1994 if he is able to be our guest speaker again.

Each member of this Advanced ROTC Class in my opinion has measured up to any such class anywhere in the world. Nearly all of them came from poor Southern Black families who worked their way through college. Collectively, they have made a great impact on the United States and the world. It was the power which education was able to generate in these great classmates of mine, which made them such great people. When I look at our class photo, listing each of us by names, some were ages 20, 21, 22 (college boys) in 1943, before going into the Army. When I see how great these boys became 51 years later, it makes me proud to be one of them. Then I remember when I was a ten-year-old boy I said education was created by God to make us all equal. Now, I believe it more now than I did then.

The power of education helped to make Doctor Martin Luther King one of the greatest civil rights leader of all times. He may have been a great civil rights leader without so such much education. In the eyes of the world, his brilliancy demonstrated by his achievement in education gave him unparalleled civil rights' leadership everywhere in the world.

My father said when I was a small boy, "Education will make a person better or worse, depends on how he uses it." I believe it will make most people better. I stayed in touch with God; and I am sure that everyone who keeps God in his life as he acquires his education will be a much better person for taking on positions of leadership. I believe all of our problems--morale, economical, racial, political, and others--can be solved though the power of education with the help of God.

Appendix C
THE BIG SURPRISE OF FEBRUARY 17, 2001

I was traveling from Washington, DC, to Norfolk, Virginia. There were two or three empty seats on the flight. One was occupied by an African-American lady who did not look to impressive to me. It is difficult for me to sit next to someone without having some kind of conversation, especially on one of these small planes which carries about twenty nine passengers, with everyone sitting so close together.

I believe our conservation related to her traveling from Washington to Norfolk, Virginia, or whether her origin was from some other place. She indicated that she had been to some type of education conference in Northern, Virginia. I realized that I was traveling with someone quite special. I showed her my autobiography. She got pretty excited when she saw that I am a Buffalo Soldier. There was a black sailor sitting in a seat in front of us. She said excitingly, "He is A Buffalo Soldier! This young sailor jumped up, and was almost about to stand at attention, until, perhaps he realized that he was traveling on an airplane.

I felt honored to be getting all of this attention and sitting next to such an elegant lady. She indicated that she was the assistant to the Superintendent of Education of the Norfolk Virginia's Public School District.

My book was put together hurriedly, and I wanted her to act as a critic of my book, helping me to purify it, especially after she said that she had to check all the papers going to her boss office. She indicated that she wanted to acquire my book. She gave me her address and telephone number. I picked up some of my books from my publisher, contacted her, and took it to her house. Her husband indicated that he wanted my book also. He was a black man with an accent, indicating that he wasn't born and raised in the United States.

She had a gorgeous old three story southern homes, perfectly manicured. She gave me an invitation, after I told her I would like for her to meet my daughter. I took my daughter there. She was astound when she saw the beautiful interior of her house. She showed us around, and served us a very nice meal. My daughter was greatly impressed and she promised to come back again. Neither my daughter nor I could figure out where her husband came from. My daughter believed he came from Africa. I later found out that he was from Nigeria

I became interested in talking to her about speaking to four classes in her district about my book, during the month of February, Black History Month. My lady friend placed me in contact with the lady responsible for arranging such classes I sent her a copy of my book, called her when I was in the US and from my home in Germany. The best she could do was to arrange one class. I told her that I would not travel from Germany to the US for one class. My lady friend form the Superintendent's office insisted that I keep my promise to participate in the Black History Program at her house on February 17, 2001, telling me that a lot of people would acquire my book. I gave in and told her that I would come. I thought that this would be a good opportunity to speak to an integrated audience consisting of people from the Norfolk School District. I invited my publisher, who is white, a friend of mine who is the Vice President of the Chesapeake, Virginia, Regional Hospital, who was also white. Neither of these gentlemen could come.

My instinct told me to call her about the agenda of the Black History Program the day before the program began. After talking to her, I asked her if this program is restricted. She said, "Sort of." meaning that only black people would attend. Then I was glad that my white friends chose not to come.

I arrived at the home of my friend the next morning shortly after the program began. The house was filled with black people. I was given a program which I did not look at, believing that within three hours or so the people would be checking what the venders had to offer relating to Black History.

A tall black man began to talk giving me the impression of being a preacher. Then he began talking about the evil of Zionism, the rights of the Palestine, supporting the Arab causes. I began to look around and feel that I was the only one there who was not a Moslem. Then he begin to talk about how the white people had snatched black babies from the African mothers arms and brought them to the United States to be slaves, packed them like sardines in a can. If one got sick or cause trouble, he would be thrown overboard to the fishes. I saw the film called Roots, and I am a certified teacher of American and world history, and that I didn't need to be told that over, over again. I was there to market my books.

I like Jews. The best white friends which black people had in Selma, Alabama, were Jews. We bought our clothing from a store called Lilienthals and Bartons. I bought my first bicycle from Bendusky, a light hardware store. I caddied for him at the Selma, Alabama, Country Club and he always tipped me, even when it was written on the score card, please don't tip caddies.

I know the Biblical story how the Israelites had been enslaved in Egypt for four hundred and twenty years, how Moses emerged and brought them out of Egypt, kept them in the Wilderness for forty years. With the help of God they moved into the Land of Canaan, The Promised Land and formed the State of Israel. Because of their sins, not keeping Covenant with God, He told the Israelis that they had to share the land with the Philistines (now the Palestine).

I believe that the Israelis had a right to return to their homeland after being forced to leave by the Romans. I thought trading land for peace with the Palestine was a good idea. I didn't agree with the high handed way the Israelis built settlements on the West Bank. I get the impression that the Palestine leaders will not be happy with any settlement that the Israelis would make.

I was not impressed with this kind of talk and I did not know where it would lead to. Because of my book and the role I played in bringing about civil right changes, they, perhaps, felt that I would support them. I didn't know what they were all about, but I was beginning to feel good because I was there. It would enable help me to know more about Moslem and the role that they would play in the United States. I was not impressed with his speech and it was beginning to look like he was going to talk for ever.

I said, "Why don't you shut-up, and let somebody else talk because you are not talking about anything any way". Very politely, he said, "I will stop in a few minutes and let you talk." He kept on talking and I interrupted him again. He said, "I will stop talking and let you talk for five minutes." I said, "I didn't come all the way over here from Germany to talk five minutes.' He said, "OK. I will let you talk for ten minutes. " I talked `for forty minutes."

I Said, "The white man didn't bring the black man to America as slaves. I said that God sent the black man to American as slaves because he wanted a large number black people to come to America, and the only way a large number could come was through the institution of slavery. I wanted to say that the black man slavery was similar to the Israelites. When the Israelites population grew big enough to form a nation, Moses grew up to take them away." I did say, "When the black people population became ten percent of the white population, the Civil War came to free them. When black people get their Spirit Back, overcoming the racial propaganda which has held them back and allow them to believe in their God given abilities", they will be able to use their moral, economic and political power to help to purify the democracy within this country, In fact, the civil right changes which we have made already are due to these powers which were because they were authorized by the US Constitution. The powers are still there to make further changes.

"We are intended to be an integrated multi-Cultural Society, made up of people from the whole world. We have some way to go, but there are no obstacles big enough to stop us from building a more perfect democracy. We are not intended to have separate black states. This would be a step backward, even if it were possible. I got almost a standing ovation from the none hard core Moslem there, and the young ones, and the new recruits.

The person who spoke after me began to talk about the main purpose of the conference, Reformation, sue the United States for Slavery.

The lady of the house invited me to dinner. I said, "I don't want any reformation because slavery was sin which must be forgiven by God, which include inherited sin which has its roots in slavery". She said, "Give me your part. How does the food taste. Here is an African dish, let's see how you like it. She was trying to keep me entertained to stop me from interrupting this Reformation Conference. She took me up stair where the women were preparing a fashion show wearing Moslem clothes. I was not interested in this because I like clothes where I can see who are wearing them.

I knew that no one would be buying my books. The people would be concentrating on the fashion show, Moslem art, etc., and would not be coming to the room where my; books were located. I was considering not selling them my books anyway because we were moving in different directions.

She took me to a quiet room where one couple was eating and watching TV. I played the game by taking a pause from the conference.

I did not stay away very long before rejoining the conference. A couple from Philadelphia appeared to be the architect of this reformation plan, spoke. They wanted to raise two hundred and fifty million dollars to sue The United States for the sins of slavery, and the suit would be introduced at the International Conference on World Racism in Durban; South Africa, in June or July, 2001. I wasn't very much concerned about this because I didn't think this case was going anywhere anyway. He was encouraging as many Moslem as possible to show up in Durban to support the Reformation Suit.

My daughter was supposed to pick me up at three o'clock this afternoon. I was on the look out for her because I didn't want her to enter the house.

While I was waiting, a young Moslem stated, "I don't have a job". He was sitting next to me. I said, "How much education do you have"? He said, "I have a friend who has a good job". I took that to mean that his friend had the same amount education as he.

I said, "Your friend is lucky. When you are not educated, you have no qualifications, and you are at the mercy of the employer. If he is white, and he thinks a white person is better for the job, right or wrong, he is going to give the job to the white person. If you are educated and the employer gives some one else the job who is less qualified than you are, then you have a justifiable complaint. My family is eighty percent college graduates. Not one member of my family has ever been unemployed nor has one of them complained about his salary. We live in many different places in the US. I got another big applaud. All of my applauds were bigger than that of any of the high powered Moslem who were speaking there.

The people were not talking about how to help black people to get out of poverty; but embracing them in it, blaming the white man for causing it; and proving a safe haven of those in it. In this way, they can bring the poorest of the poor, and the neglected into their membership. This give them more power to expand their membership, and their leaders will use the well disciplined members to support their agenda, for good or evil.

No one is better than good Moslems, but it is the bad Moslems which run the show.

About this time, I spotted my daughter drive up in front of the house. I met her coming up the steps. I said, "Go back to the car. I don't want you to come into this house." She couldn't understand that because she was there before and had such a nice time. I said, "I will explain it when I get into the car". Reluctantly, she returned to the car. I went up the stairs and got my books, and told everyone that my daughter was scheduled to pick me up at this time. "Thanks for inviting me here." I left. I explained to my daughter why she should not come into the house. She still makes jokes about the exciting way I told her not to come into the house.

I left so quickly that I forgot my eye glasses. I called the lady of the house asking about my glasses. She said she had them. I said, "I will come over tomorrow to pick them up". I was hoping the next day that all the people attending the conference would be gone.

To my surprise, when I went there the next day they were all there, having slept on floor, on the couches and the like. They had eaten or were eating breakfast and they seemed to have been recovering from a restless night.

I talked to the lanky Moslem preacher who was the master of ceremony that I told to sit down and let someone else talk, the day before. He said that he had been in the US Air Force in England and he was now working with the American Indians in Nebraska. He had a copy my book in his hand, borrowing it from my lady friend. I was not interesting in selling him one. If, however, he had asked me, I would have made one available. He wanted me to stay there and chat with them. I told him that I had my daughters car and that she wanted me to bring it back as soon as possible. I am sure that I would have maintained my position had I stayed and that they were not going to change theirs either. I left politely, thanking everyone for the experience

I said that God always put me in difficult positions that caused me to fight my way out.

Now it became necessary to access my opinion about religion, and religion and politics. I am a Baptist, and I always plan to be one. The Baptist is not perfect and neither are the others religions in the application of their faith. Baptists may be the poorest organized and less disciplined, but they are the freest. I go to church to learn how to improve myself, learning what the preacher says that I can accept, because they are not perfect, either. God holds me responsible for my own decision and action. That which I accept have to make sense to me.

I believe in democracy and the separation of church and state. I believe in religious freedom. I believe in democracy knowing that it is not perfect, but it is the most perfect form of government when it operates freely. With the press exposing the bad guys, they can be removed through the election process

William Jennings Bryant said dictatorship is the best form of Government., but the biggest problem is that no one is good enough to be one. It also includes dictatorial political parties, clubs, churches, etc. This is a fact of history.

With my first exposure with the Moslem religion, I decided that it is not for me. All of the Moslem which I met are nice people but its religion has produces dictatorial leaders, bad guys, terrorists, and the good Moslem cannot not control them. They blame the West for their situation. It is caused by the church over the state. Church over the State didn't work with Catholic, it want work with the Protestant, and it is not working for the Moslem.

Their religion wont allow them to blame church, but the church is the blame. They have to blame somebody. They could blame the British Empire and Western Europe, but they blame the US and keep Europe in hostage, so that the terrorist won't hit them. Divide and conquer is a sure way to enable the terrorist to succeed. The terrorist feed on Israel crisis. They feed on it and stay in power because of it. The Moslem countries are held in hostage also, and they are afraid to speak out against the terrors so that they can be spared from being attacked by them

Somebody has to be strong.. The terrors use The United States and the Palestine-Israel Crisis as a shield to control its people and to hide their aggressive intent. None of these countries would be willing to take a large number Palestine as refugees in their countries. These terrorist countries or terrorist groups do not wish for Israel-Palestine crisis to be solved. They use this crisis to shield their intent, to get support from the Arab people, fuel their ability to keep them in power.

The Moslems at this conference did not talk about the Moslem terrorists, Iraq, Iran, Libya. I could not respect their views because they didn't deal fairly with the middle east situation.

I am not so sure that they figured that they would win the Reformation Suit, but it is an issue that lot of people support; win are loose, the Moslem win. They will continue use the reformation issue to increase their popularity and increase their followers because reformation appeal to lots of people who are not Moslems.

The terror crisis is both international and domestic. To deal with this situation, we have setup our home land security. The Department of Home Land Security uses agencies of the Federal, State, County and City governments, to include the US Armed Forces and Coast Guard. In order for these agencies to succeed, they need all the cultures groups of the US to be involved in a patriot way.

A true democracy is the best way to insure home land security. Our agencies will not succeed without feed back from the people. To prevent the rise of Moslem in the United States, which maybe the weak link in our home land security, we must be less racist. Already, white and black Moslem who are United Sates Citizens have been supporting Moslem related terrorism. I am not opposed to anyone's religion, so long as it remain religious.

My hometown of Selma, Alabama, is the last place where the last Civil Right Bill of the Civil Rights Revolution of the l960s took place. The Voters Rights Act of 1965 became a federal law because of it. This Voters Rights Law gave the black people of Selma, Alabama, voting power sufficient to elect a black mayor at the next election. Thirty five years later, a black mayor was elected.

For thirty five years, three black candidates and one white candidate ran to become mayor. The Black Candidates cut each other out, and the white one always won, the same White Mayor who was mayor when Doctor King conducted his Civil Rights Campaign in Selma. This White Mayor knew that in a matter of time a black man would become mayor. In Year 2000, the same white mayor who had been mayor for forty years or more, was opposed by Black Protestant and Black Moslem candidates. This timed I knew that Selma would have a black mayor In August 2000, I called my brother-in-law, Fred Martin, in Selma, Alabama, to congratulate him and Selma on electing its first black mayor.

What surprised me most was that the Moslem population in Selma had grown strong enough for Selma to have a Moslem running for mayor. I am not so sure when I grew up there if I had ever heard of the word Moslem.

I visited Selma in November 2000, one month after I had written the first edition of my book, three months after Selma elected its first black Mayor. When ever I am there I always want to know how race relation is going. I ask my brother-in-law, a veteran of World War II, a retired Life Insurance Executive who sent four of his five children to college, aided in the college education of all of his grand children who were old enough for college, a solid citizen, respected by both black and white people, "How is school integration going." He said, "The only thing integrated here is the teachers, and the white teachers are not interested in the education of black students". He has a grand son living with him in high school and is preparing for college.

My niece took me to her house which she bought from the last white mayor of Selma, a super home fitting for a mayor.

The ex-Mayor packed up and moved out of town. It appeared me that it would have been nice for him to remain in Selma to advise the black inexperience mayor in the job which he had held and loved for forty years. We talked about the rise of white private-tuition assisted schools . To black people, its just another way of maintaining segregated schools. This became an issue in the last presidential election and will continue to be a factor in future elections.

About eighty percent of my family are college graduates. We all went to or are attending public schools which are the foundation of our democracy. The black and white children should go to school together which will prepare them to work together as grown-ups. We must work together to make our public schools succeed and not run away from our responsibility to help them do so.

Every sin has with it own seed for its destruction The sin of slavery brought on the United States Civil War. World War I was a war between the haves and the haves not nations. All of these were caused by race related sins. It took World War II to finish what World War I started. The unfinished sins of World War I brought on Communism, Nazism, Fascism, and Imperialism. The sins of Colonialism created Nazism, Fascism, and Imperialism. The sins of Communism also helped to created Nazis. The sins of Nazism were too evil to survive. The sins of Communism and Nazism were so great that they crashed into each other like two runaway trains. The Russians lost about twenty five million dead, the Nazi about five million. The Colonial powers did not lose the war but they lost their possessions. Colonized nations around the world became free and independent. It brought about civil rights changes in the United States. Japan and Italy lost the war. The sins of racism made everybody pay a dear price.

The sins of racism, which remains, have brought on the sins of terrorism. Terrorism has no boundaries, not even barriers of the oceans will keep them away. The rise of Moslem in the United States are caused by racism. There have already been white and black US citizen who are Moslem that have terror connections. I don't think many Moslem will aid terror, but it will only take a few.

As I have already stated our best defense is our democracy. White people and black people must work together to take away conspirator racism, which produces conspirator terrorism.

A friend of mine who works here in Germany returned from a visit to our hometown, Selma, Alabama. He said, "White people in Selma have moved out side of the City limits, west of the Selma, Alabama's Country Club, and built a white neighborhood". I said, "Getting away from those "N," I said, "Racism is going to kill the white man"". They don't get the message. The Mayor is black, the Chief of Police is black, and the Fire Chief is black. They did not leave town when the mayor was white." This is not the way to bring about a closeness between black and white people which is necessary in the age of terrorism, White people should not wait until they are hit by terrorist before they start making love with black people. We should be united to prevent it. Every sin which is not forgiven creates its own seeds for its destruction. It is the sins of racism which have created world wide terrorism.

People of the United States must use the weapon of unity to win the war against terrorism. We must not be a victim of the sins of the past . A verse of The Tenth Commandment "Do Unto Others As You Would Have Them To Do Unto You is the basis of our Constitution and it is The Commandment of God. When we follow that Commandment we should have no grounds for fear, but a basis for love for one another. Love will last for ever. Fear and hate will fade away. This is a sure way to stand up to terrorism and defeat it.

Appendix D
THE BIG RED ONE

In January 2002, SFC Reata Owens, contacted me for being the guest speaker for the lst US Infantry Division during the Doctor Martin Luther King Holiday-Birthday commemoration events. She contacted me the previous year, but the date she wanted me to come had already been scheduled. I told her that she had first priority this year for Doctor Martin Luther King's birthday memorial celebration and for the Black History month as well.. Because the Division Chief of Staff had such an interest in the program, she wanted me to provide as much information about the message which I would be presenting to the division as soon possible. I told her that I would send her a biographic summary of my book and a copy of my auto-biography.

I sent her ten copies of my book which she requested for those who were interested in acquiring it prior to Doctor King's birthday. This material could not get there fast enough because of the intense interest in the program. I also had eye surgery schedule at the Walter Reed Hospital in Washington, DC, in January 2002, also. Because I did not want my eye operation to interfere with the Doctor King anniversary event, I got permission from my doctor at the Landstuhl Regional Hospital here in Germany to arrange an early January 2002 eye operation at Walter Reed which would permit me to be able make my speaking engagements.

I told Sergeant First Class Owens about the operation which had been arranged for early January and that I would be back in Germany in time for the week of the 22d of January, 2002, for paying tribute to Doctor King.

My eye operation which was schedule for the first week in January ceased to an emergency and was therefore postponed to the second week because the medical surgical team would be together on that date. The operation was successful, and I was released at my request with the doctors permission the second day after the operation to my Landstuhl Doctor.

I called SFC Owens that I was back and that I could do the Doctor King speaking engagements.

I believed I was picked up Monday at my home in Mainz, Germany, 22 January by Master Sergeant Eric Nelson and Sergeant First Class Reata Owens on this day which President Bush proclaimed as Martin Luther King Birthday holiday. It took about two and a half hour in the Army Sedan to make the trip from Mainz to Wuerzburg, Germany. To my surprise, I was placed in a VIP Suite room no. 1, reserved for General Officers. Natural I was honored. This was the first time I was placed in celebrity status. My friends said I deserved it.

When much is given, much is expected. I felt good about the arrangement and I was determined to give it my best. Major Randy Clements, the Division Equal Opportunity was the architect of the program, Master Sergeant Nelson was the manager of the program. SFC Owens was the assistant, Sergeant First Class Darren Branham was my escort. This would proved to a perfect team. My scheduled was perfectly arranged and carried out between Master Sergeant Nelson and Sergeant First Class Branham. Sergeant Branham is very intelligent and a first class non-commission officer. I enjoyed talking to him going to and from the various installation where I would be speaking.

My speaking engagements were done at four installation during a three day period.. The first day, Tuesday, I spoke at the lst Infantry Division Headquarters in Wuerzburg at a prayer breakfast. In the afternoon, I spoke in Bamberg. The second day I spoke in Schweinfurt, and the third day, I spoke in Ansbach. My speech was general the same, all from memory, with the exception of my biographic summary, the blue print for the civil rights corrections which I developed as a ten year old boy in l932. I will read it.

Ladies and gentlemen, I feel honored to have been asked to come here to speak to members of the lst United States Infantry Division on the occasion of the Doctor Martin Luther King birthday celebration. I am sure that you feel number one in every way. I also feel that you have set up the Martin Luther King Program which is number one and that it will be an example for the Armed Forces of The United States of America.

I want to thank Sergeant First Class Reata Owens who tried last year to get me here, but was unable to do so because I already had scheduled a Black History speaking engagement. This year she was the first to call me. She said she wanted me for a whole week. I had to think about that because I speak without compensation. I cave in and said that I would do it.

I had to arrange for some emergency surgery on my eye. I arranged to go to The Walter Reid Hospital the first week in January . My operation was on January 8, and I got cleared on January 10 to return to Germany. My Doctor at the Walter Reid wanted me to stay longer, but at my request, he released me my eye Doctor at Landstuhl Regional Hospital who was aware of my speaking engagement here. All of this was coordinated with Sergeant Owens. I want to thank her and Master Sergeant Nelson for picking me up, bringing me here, taking me to very nice VIP quarters and arranging my schedule. I want to thank Major Randy Clemens, the Division Equal Opportunity Office for developing this program. I want to thank the Division Commander and the Division Chief of Staff for placing the highest level of interest in honoring Doctor Martin Luther King, on this day and week which was scheduled by The President of The United States, President Bush. I want to thank Mister Leinberger for his opening remarks, Chaplain (LTC) Nichols, the First Infantry Division Chaplin, for his opening invocation, Chaplain(Cpt) Taylor of the 101 Military Intelligence Battalion for his remarks, "I Have A Dream". I want to thank the Giebelstadt Gospel Chorus for it musical selection, I want to thank 1st Sergeant of Headquarters and Headquarters of The First US Infantry Division for introducing me.

The title of my talk today will be illustrated by selecting three Civil Right Rivers which flood to The Sea of Civil Right Success for The United States of America which established a higher level of civil rights for all America. It made America a more successful world power. It enabled The United States to bring down the racist government of South Africa. It helped to prevent France and Italy from becoming communist states. It established the beginning of the down fall of The Soviet Union, and it may have prevented World War III.

The Three Rivers theory which I said that I will illustrate to show how the post World War II civil rights achievements were accomplished began with Military River. It was the Military River which make it possible for the other two rivers to flow. The integration of the armed forces enabled the United Sates Supreme Court to declare that segregation in public schools was unconstitutional; this would also apply to all types of public facilities and services. The public school desegregation suit was initiated by the NAACP which established the NAACP River but the NAACP River would not have flooded if the America people had not elected President Truman in 1948, after he had integrated the US armed forces. Chief Justice Earl Warren stated that the American people elected President Truman after he integrated the armed Forces. This showed that the American People accepted the Integration of the armed forces and he believed that they would accept the integration of the public school

The resistance to the public school integration ruling caused the other two rivers to come together to form the third river, The King River. The force of these river brought about changes as they flooded to the sea of civil rights successes.

My talks will give more details about how theses rivers developed and brought about the Civil Rights successes of the 1950s and 60s.

In 1932 I developed this blue print for the purpose desegregating the south in the 1960s. I wrote it as a biography, and I will read it to you:

Cecil Ward White established an education plan as 10 year old boy in the cotton fields of Alabama in 1932 for correcting the civil rights problems facing African Americans

His plans to do so would be made possible by the education of himself and his family which would give incentives to black people to do likewise over a 30 year period. He visualized that a better educated black environment would cause a well educated black person to emerge as a civil rights leader to bring about changes in the civil rights laws.

He believed that God created education to be an equalizer that would help the down and out to rise up and be equal to the high and mighty. It would help the poor to become equal to the rich, and it would help black people to be equal to the whites people.

As a result of this education of the White Family, Mr. White education enabled him to become a commissioned officer in the United States Army during World War II and to become a member of 92nd Infantry Buffalo Division which went to war in Italy. The fighting achievement of Mr. White and the Buffalo Division provided sufficient evidence to enable the Armed Forces of the United States to become integrated in 1948. The integration of Armed Forces together with the Black Veterans of World War II and the Korean War who became educated under GI Bill enabled them to create the environment which led to the emerging of Doctor Martin Luther King. Together with the effort of Mr. White, they were able to bring about the changes in the civil right laws which he predicted as a ten year old boy. The forces which brought about these changes remain in effect to bring about continuous improvements in racial and human relations.

Mr. White believes that he did more to change the Civil Rights within the United States than all the US Presidents since Abraham Lincoln.

I will talk about how the three rivers made my blue print a reality, and bringing Doctor King into the civil rights movement. It begin with the Military River in February, 1942, when President Roosevelt under pressure by civil rights leaders to integrate the military services to fight the war. The President said no, but he would look into the integration situation after the war. In June of that year plans were made to establish two black infantry divisions, The 92d Infantry Division, the 93rd Infantry Division and the 99th Percuit Squadron(The Tuskegee Airmen}. I was a college student then. It appeared to me at that time that the Services would be integrated if these units fought on the same level as white units.

I joined the 92nd Infantry (Buffalo) Division on or about the middle of August 1944. I went there from Camp Breckinridge, Kentucky. Officers who were senior to me left earlier than I plus some younger ones who volunteered to join the division. I said to myself, "I am not going to volunteer, but if I am order to go, I will know that God sent me. If God sent me, I know that He is expecting me to do a good job". This was the force behind my motivation to keep a promise which I made as a ten year old boy in 1932.

Right away, after I joined the division, I started running and training my platoon for battle. In two weeks we were at the Port of Debarkation, Camp Patrick Henry, in

New Port News, Virginia heading for war in Italy. Because we were traveling with 25 - 30,000 soldiers, lots of ships had to be assembled to form the convey to take us across the Atlantic Ocean. I felt quite pleased going to war with such a well trained and highly disciplined division.

We were in Virginia close to thirty days. Four days before the end of September 1944, units of the division received an electronic message from the Pentagon stating that the morale of the division have fallen below the level required for combat and that it cannot be understood why the best trained division of the war had lossed its morale at the waters edge. We were given 24 hours to find the problems which caused the low moral and the solution to it.

The 'first thing which came to my mind was what my friend said when I was ten years old. "Black Soldiers do not fight well. They are cowards and they run away in battle."

I didn't believe it then and I didn't believe it at that time. The morale of the division was very high when we arrived at the port, and there must to have been something going on at the port since we arrived which caused this low morale. I was afraid that the division would be deactivated. If it were, my prediction that a civil rights correction in the 1960's would not be realized. Because General McArthur had already deactivated the 93d Division because he said it would not fight. The only hope for bringing about an integrated armed forces rested with the Buffalo Division.

Ten senior men of our company were assembled to comply with the message from the War Department. The company commander, 1st Lieutenant John Runyon, was the only white person in the group. There were four black officers, two 1st Lieutenants and two 2nd Lieutenants; 1st Sergeant, three Platoon Sergeants, Sergeant First Class, Supply Sergeant, Staff Sergeant.

The company commander was from the northwestern part of the United States and he didn't know a great deal about black people. He, therefore, asked the Executive Officer, Lieutenant Henderson to conduct the conference His answer was, "Our soldiers are going overseas for the first time. They feel that they may not see their loved ones again; and they are a little sad about that. Once they get out in the middle of the ocean, every thing will be all right." He called on the two officers who were senior to me, skipping me because I was new to the unit. The two officers and the five non-commissioned officers all agreed with the answer of Lieutenant Henderson. I judged the two first lieutenants and four of the non-commissioned to have given Uncle Tom answers. The other second lieutenant and my platoon sergeant gave their answers with the hope of avoiding the war. These were my opinions of course.

I was the only remaining African-American who had not given an answer. Lieutenant Henderson, said, "Junior, What do you think"? I considered giving the avoid the war answer, but this would have killed all of my hopes and predictions about civil rights changes in the 1960s. I decided to tell the truth and put the whole matter in God's Hands.

I said, "We are going overseas to fight for democracy. Here at this base is the worst example for democracy that I have seen anywhere. I am from Alabama, and I have not seen anything there so bad as it is here. It is true that if we go to war some of us will be killed. This is the last bit of American soil that some of us will ever see again; therefore, we need to see right here at this base that which we will be fighting and dying for". For example, I said: "The first night after I arrived here, I went to the service window at the officers club and ordered food and a drink. I got it, but I was not allowed to eat it at this club which was reserved for white officers and there were no club for black officers. There is a very nice non-commissioned club, but it to was reserved for the white NCOs. For the five hundred or more black NCOs, there was no club. Over 20,000 low ranking enlisted black men of the division has no service club. They to were not allowed to attend the service club which was reserved for white low ranking enlisted men. We all have been here nearly one month."

I said, "The Army can't correct the racial wrongs in Mississippi, Alabama, and those which exist outside the gates of this installation here in Virginia. The Army can correct the racial wrongs at this base. And if it does, there will be no morale problem". JUNIOR IS RIGHT! JUNIOR IS RIGHT! These were the yell given by all black people there.

Now the white commander, from Iowa or Minnesota, knew the answer as well as the rest of us. He dashed off to his father-in-law with the answer who was a general and assistant division commander. From there the answer was presented to the division commander, to the War Department and to The President of the United States.

I told this to two retired senior non-commission officers in 1985 here in Germany. One said, "It's a wonder that you were not put out of the Army for what you said". I said, "I would not have cared. If they didn't want the right answer they should not have asked for it. I would have gone back to Tuskegee and sold my news papers because I was making more money selling news papers than I was making as 2nd Lieutenant in the Army. Most of the times when white people ask black people questions, they want Uncle Tom answers, and they had gotten them from the other officer and non-commissioned. I knew that the military was serious about having the correct answers because The President and the War Department had been criticized for setting up the Black combat units. The critics were saying, You know those "N" can't fight. If those critics had studied a little history, they would have found out that those uneducated ex-slaves fighting saved the Union during the Civil War according to General Grant. The Buffalo Soldiers established in 1866 were veterans of the Civil War. The black soldiers of the Civil War received 24 Congressional Medals of Honor and the Buffalo Soldiers of 1866 to 1896 fighting to protect White settlers, earned 17 Congressional Medals of Honor".

A retired white brigadier general in July 2002, also said he agreed with those retired NCOs. I said to myself, "If I had been from New York, Chicago or Los Angeles, I probably would have gotten in trouble. I am from Alabama. Down south when a black man has the courage to say what I said, white people listen. The division commander was from Alabama and he knew me because I am from Alabama.

About six hours later, The President of The United States integrated that base. The black soldiers got their spirit back, causing their morale to shoot up like a rocket. They fought successfully, helping to win the war in Italy, and enabling the United States Armed Forces to become integrated.

I made the promise when I was ten years old that if I go to war, I will show every one that black soldiers can fight as good as any body else. I kept that promise, enabling me to play a major role in bringing about the integration of the US Armed Forces. The details of my combat role can be found in Chapter 4 of my autobiography, World War II and Me.

In my first battle the division commander said my machine fire supporting a rifle company in offensive combat was the best that he had seen in World War I and World War II. I was recommended for a silver star medal or a promotion to 1st lieutenant, a combat infantry badge and a RR (rest and rehabilitation) to Rome. I took the latter. In our second battle, my battalion received some criticism. I was the only hero. Instead of giving me a silver star medal, I was recommended for promotion to Captain at 23 years of age by my company and battalion commanders, both of whom were white officers. At that time I had been 1st lieutenant for only two months and an officer for only tem months. I didn't get it because the regimental commander said, " I am too young.".

In the final campaign to end the war in Italy, the best officers in the Buffalo Division were sent to the 370th Infantry Regiment whose mission was to spearhead the final campaign to end the war in Italy I was assigned to the 1st Battalion, Company D, 1st Machine Gun Platoon. The Regiment was organized into nine offensive waves. I was in the 1st wave that went against the Gothic Line which Hitler had ordered that this line must be held at all cost. In less than two hour, with one section of my machine gun platoon, I seized the final spearhead objective, penetrating the Gothic Line. I said at that time that the division had passed the test that the Chief of Staff of the US Army had given to the it and that the Army would now be integrated. Three years later, in July 1948, President Truman integrated The Armed Forces of the United States.

From the civil rights point of view, this established the Military River.

The next river was the NAACP (The National Association For The Advancement of Colored People) River. This organization start working in 1910 to end segregation laws which discriminated against black people. Progress was from slow to almost none. Its major efforts were to get federal civil rights laws passed. Filibustering in the US Senate blocked every effort.

Because of this, the NAACP begin to direct its civil rights push through the federal courts. In the late 1939 and early 1940, integration of graduate law schools began with University of Texas and Oklahoma. After World War II, in the late forties, college integration took place. The greatest amount of publicity took place over the integration of The University of Alabama. A little of this was shown in the movie Forest Gump.

The biggest integration cases dealt with the integration of public school. It was in South Carolina where it took place. A Reverend Delaney who was the principal of a school in Clarendon County, South Carolina, requested the school superintendent to provide a school bus, any kind of bus, for his school because busses were provided for white school children;. He did not make any progress. The superintendent said, "The white children were getting busses because the white people were paying more taxes".

Mr. Delaney requestd the NAACP to take the case. The NAACP was trying to get the federal courts to enforce equal but separate segregation law which existed throughout the south. A white federal judge by the name of Waites Warren told Thurgood Marshall, the Chief Attorney for The NAACP, that he should go after school integration. Mr. Marshall decided to do so realizing that he had little chance of winning such a case. Taking the advice of Judge Warren and going after school integration, over the advice of the NAACP Executive Committee, Mr. Marshall went for integration of the public schools. The court had a split decision on the Public School Integration Suit. Two of the Federal Judges voted against school integration, with Judge Warren supporting it. The Case went before the United States Supreme Court.

At that time the Chief Justice of the US Supreme Court `was Carl Vincent of Kentucky. He had written, but had not announced the decision against school integration when he died very suddenly of a heart attack. Now, Mr. Marshall, Attorney for the NAACP, hope went up, waiting for President Eisenhower appointment for the position of Chief Justice of The US Supreme Court. He was Earl Warren, the former Governor of California. Initially, Chief Justice Warren planned to go along with decision of the late Chief Justice Carl Vincent of Kentucky.

After becoming more enlighten about the injustices facing black people, he asked the other justices to go along with him in the writing of the decision to declare that the segregation of public school was a violation of the l4th Amendment of the Constitution of The United States of America. This Decision was made in May l954. I read about this decision in The Stars and Stripes in South Korea were I was stationed. One year later, May 1955, the US Supreme Court decreed (ordered) that The US Public Schools would integrated with all deliberate speed. This decision established the second river, The NAACP River

In November l954, I was transferred from South Korea to South Carolina State University for a ROTC duty assignment. This University was located in Orangeburg South Carolina. In August 1955, five members of the NAACP petitioned the Board of Education of Orangeburg County to integrate the public schools. As a result of this petition, the biggest half of the white businesses in Orangeburg formed an organization called The White Citizen Council. This Council, speaking for the County, rejected the petition, and brought economic pressure against those who made the petition.

I was one of the top secret planners of the NAACP. Our Organization passed the word to black people of the community to trade with your friends, meaning not to trade with members of the White Citizen Council. black people Orangeburg in County out numbered whites and had lots of economic power which the white businesses depended on. Two black universities existed there black teacher living within one hundred miles of Orangeburg had residence there. The loss of these customers, brought the business of the Chartered Members of The White Citizens Council to near bankruptcy. Publicity by radio, television, news papers, national magazines, and a boycott against Coca Cola, caused the civil rights movements to spread, first to Rock Hill, South Carolina, sit-ins at the Woolworth lunch counter in Greensboro, North Carolina. These movements created the environment which caused Mrs. Rosa Parks not to give up her bus seat to a white passenger on December l, 1955, in Montgomery, Alabama. This situation would bring an unknown Doctor Martin Luther into the Civil Rights Movement The well educated Black person who I predicted that would emerge as the civil rights leader when I was a ten year old boy in 1932. This would be the beginning of the third river, The King River.

The King River which was made possible by the Military and The NAACP Rivers.

Doctor King was born in Atlanta, Georgia, a city which I considered to be The Civil Rights Capital of The United States. Five black colleges and universities are located there. In l910, The National Association for Advancement of Colored People (NAACP) was organized there. His grand father helped to organize this civil rights organization and made a Civil Rights March on the City of Atlanta, Georgia, in l910. His Father marched on Atlanta in 1925, four years before young Martin was born.

Martin was an inherited Civil Right Leader. He graduated with honors at all levels of his educational training. In college, he considered at first to be a lawyer. Then he decided to be a minister of the gospel while attending Morehouse College in Atlanta, Georgia. He graduated from there with honors. He took his graduate studies, first at the Theological University at Springfield, Pennsylvania, where he graduated with honors. He delivered the students' commencement address at this graduation exercise. He was the first black person to be given that honor.

He studied both at Boston University and at Harvard University. He graduated with his doctors degree from Boston University. He felt that his calling would be in the South. He became the pastor of a relatively small Baptist Church, Dexter Avenue Baptist Church in Montgomery, Alabama. When Mrs. Rosa Parks got in trouble for not moving in the back of the bus and giving up her seat to a white person, the better educated black people selected this well educated man to be the Civil Rights leader as I predicted when I formed my Civil Rights Blue Print in l932. Doctor King would lead the bus boycott until he was tried and convicted, getting a fine and a suspended sentence. He appealed it and it was upheld by the United States Supreme Court causing the public bus service in Montgomery, Alabama, to be integrated. This would truly cause the King River to flow.

Doctor King's would leave his church in Montgomery, and would join his father as his assistant pastor at a Baptist Church in Atlanta, Georgia, This would free Doctor King to be more active in civil right matters. He worked in and around Atlanta until 1961, engaging in sit ins at public facilities, making speeches at racist trouble spots.

On or before l960, The US Interstate Commerce Committee required all public business engaged in inter state commerce to integrate their facilities, which included busses, trains, restrooms at services station, restaurants, motels, hotels, and the like. Public business operating within the southern states would remain segregated.

In 1960, A judge in Decatur, Georgia, sentenced Doctor King to a maximum security prison where death row intimates were being held, because he violated a court injunction. Many people felt that the Judge hoped that the death row intimates would kill him. Instead, they treated him with great respect.

In l960, Senator John F. Kennedy was running for election for President of the United States. He and Vice President Richard Nixon were running a close race. Senator Kennedy was alleged to have called the Judge in Decatur, Georgia, to release Doctor King from prison, with a promised that he would give him a federal Judge position, if he became President. Doctor King's release from prison, according to many, gave Senator Kennedy the edge in winning the presidential election

After President Kennedy became inaugurated as President in January 1961, Doctor King would get more involved in the civil rights movements, which would be the beginning of the Civil Rights Revolution. To black people with a President as a friend in the White House, the time was right to make a move to integrate the South.

The first step in this direction would occur in Albany, Georgia, where some preachers there moved to integrate public facilities. They need a little help, initiating a call to Doctor King for that purpose.

During the Christmas of l960, I met and dated a young lady in my home town, Selma, Alabama, who demonstrates with Doctor King. When Doctor King went into Albany, this young lady called me at my Fort Dix's New Jersey quarters ever night to tell me what they were doing. I was following the activities there also on television, radio and news papers I saw that Doctor King was not winning

Sheriff Prichard was outsmarting the demonstrators. He would arrest the marchers, keeping them in jail for four or five days, then he would release them. He would continue to do this. If he tried and convicted them, the marchers would appeal the case and the Supreme Court would integrate the public facilities of the city. When older people got tired on going to jail, the crowds got smaller and smaller. The last time my girl friend called me, I told her to tell Doctor King to leave Albany and that he was in a no win situation there. He went to Albany upon request of the civil rights leaders. Support was going down hill as the crowds were getting smaller and smaller. Tell him to go back to Atlanta, plan his next move else where, profiting by his mistakes there. He left and I did not get any more phone calls.

In l963, the Civil Rights Revolution began in Birmingham, Alabama. Doctor King was invited to come there to manage the campaign to integrate public facilities

In January l956, I met a young lady who was a student at Tuskegee University who became my young lady friend. She was from Birmingham, Alabama. Across the street from her home was the residence of Lawyer Shores who was the Attorney for the NAACP. When I went to visit her, I also visited him. I told this civil rights lawyer about the role which I played which helped to bring about the integration of the US Armed Forces, and the role I played in initiating the civil rights movement which started in Orangeburg, South Carolina, in August 1955.

I told him that the civil rights movement would come to Birmingham in the l960's and if they fail to be ready to deal with it, our civil rights would be delayed thirty years. We talked about the foes which they would have to deal with it. I said, "They are not so tough as the enemy we faced to bring about the integration of the armed forces in Italy. We penetrated The Gothic Line which Hitler ordered to be held at all cost, advancing up the west coast of Italy through the Italian Alps. We moved through Genoa a hundred miles away then to the Switzerland and French borders which were more than fifty miles away in twenty eight days to end the war in Italy.

In 1963, Doctor Martin Luther's campaign initiated the Civil Rights Campaign in Birmingham, Alabama. The people in Birmingham was ready to support Doctor King. The lambs went against the beasts and won. They had God's blessing to help Doctor King and the people of Birmingham to tame the most racist city in the United States. Doctor King was the only person who I can imagine who had the qualities to take on The City of Birmingham and win. I am glad that I contributed to it.

The final campaign would be in my hometown of Selma, Alabama. I believe that the inlightenment which I brought to Selma, plus Doctor Kings victory in Birmingham prepared Selma and the surrounding counties to bring about the campaign which would end the legal racist segregated south. As a result of the successes of the Selma civil right movement, The Voters Right Law of 1965 was enacted. In 1969, the United States Supreme Court declared that law which prevented interracial marriage were unconstitutional. After this decision, all racial discrimination with in the UnIted States came to an end.

These civil right Laws gave more freedom to both black and white peoples. Black people may have gotten one hundred percent benefit. White people got at least sixty percent. Booker T. Washington, the founder of Tuskegee University in Alabama stated, "You can't keep a man in the ditch unless you get into the ditch with him." The whites were on top but they were both in the ditch. White juries were not allowed to find a white man guilty for murdering a black man. White plantation owners were required to chase black people off their lands when they marched with Doctor King. When white peopled didn't want black people to get educated; they set the example by not getting educated themselves. When white people did not follow these southern traditions, they were subjected to the same terrorism as black people. The civil right revolution demobilized the Ku Klux Klan from being a political force to the rank of a terrorist organization, some of whom have been put to death for their crimes against black people. To a greater degree we are all got out of the ditch, even though we have a little more climbing to do.

The fighting ability of the black soldiers are handicapped by the racism which they faced both at home and in the military. Racism takes their spirit away. A man cannot fight without his spirit. Here with the Big Red One, the Martin Luther King and Black History Programs have heightened the spirit of all its people. The spirit of white soldiers are elevated by the spirit of black soldier which let both of them know that they can depend on each other. I have judged the spirit of integration here as high as it was in September 1944, when President Roosevelt integrated the base at Camp Patrick, Virginia, which gave the Buffalo Soldiers their Spirit Back which enable them to fight and help to win the war in Italy.

These programs are a credit to the outstanding leadership of this Division from the top to the bottom.

Each of the five communities of this Division where I have spoken and been involved have shown the highest level of professionalism and commitment to equal opportunity, and the integration of the armed forces.

God have given us the greatest land on this earth and a constitution which is second to none, filled with emigrant who came to this Promise Land to find a better life. This is the last frontier. We will be measure by God on how well we manage our blessing.

I have written; this chapter on behalf of the Big Red One which have made Doctor Martin Luther King Birthday holiday and the Black History Month's events not just for black people but for all people of the division. Members of this division have shown the highest level of satisfaction and enthusiasm in the division's human relation commitment as demonstrated in these black history events.

The Three Rivers civil rights successes which brought major civil rights changes within the United States must be compared to some extent with The American Revolutionary War and Civil War, which have kept the Ship USA on course for reaching it constitutional destiny for all the Citizens of The United States of America.

There is a saying, "I will forget what you said. I may forget what you did, but I will never forget how you made me feel."

PHOTOGRAPHS

Merry Christmas
and
A Happy New Year

Cecil

Kitzingen · Germany 1949

Serving on the Berlin Airlift

My Brothers in 1947 on our family farm at Marion Junction, Alabama.
From left to right: Edward, Clarence, Frank, Cecil

Photograph at Tuskegee University, Spring 1946

The Education Father. This picture of my Mother and Father was taken during World War II (I believe in 1944), perhaps after church, praying for their four sons and two sons-in-law, all who were in the Armed Forces.

TUSKEGEE UNIVERSITY

FIRST YEAR ADVANCED CLASS R. O. T. C.
DECEMBER 1942

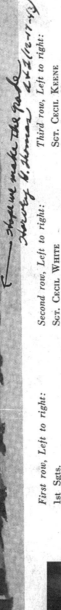

Louis A. Scipio
Regtl. Sgt. Maj.

1st Lt. J. H. Hurd
Instructor

First row, Left to right:

1st Sgts.
Chester L. Kemp
Theodore Gipson
William Bearden
James Hamlet
Harvey Thomas
Sgt. James Shuford
Sgt. William Dobson
1st Sgt. Charles Brown
1st Sgt. Fred Brown Booker Conley
1st Sgt. Louis A. Scipio

Second row, Left to right:

Sgt. Cecil White
Sgt. William Craig
St. Sgt. Stanford Smith
St. Sgt. Jean Peters
St. Sgt. Benton Barlow
St. Sgt. Harry McClasky
Sgt. Charles Lang
St. Sgt. James Roberts
St. Sgt. Crawford Russell,
St. Sgt. John Suggs
St. Sgt. Theodore Johnson
St. Sgt. Harry B. Harris

Third row, Left to right:

Sgt. Cecil Keene
Sgt. James Huntley
Sgt. Lorenzo Robinson
Sgt. Adolphus Rogers
Sgt. Jesse Brewer
Sgt. George Sims
St. Sgt. Edward Horton
Robert Penn
Not on picture:
St. Sgt. Lewis Crawford
Sgt. Earl Youngblood
Sgt. Larry Lee

68

Military Retirement Photo.   September 1, 1965

CERTIFICATE OF RETIREMENT
FROM THE ARMED FORCES OF THE UNITED STATES OF AMERICA

TO ALL WHO SHALL SEE THESE PRESENTS, GREETING:
THIS IS TO CERTIFY THAT

Cecil W White   038 208

Major   Infantry

HAVING SERVED FAITHFULLY AND HONORABLY,
WAS RETIRED FROM THE

UNITED STATES ARMY

ON THE   first   DAY OF September
ONE THOUSAND NINE HUNDRED AND Sixty-five

J. C. Lambert

MAJOR GENERAL, UNITED STATES ARMY,
THE ADJUTANT GENERAL

WASHINGTON, D. C.

At the faculty club, Tuskegee University, 1946.

*Doctor Frederick Douglas Patterson,
President of Tuskegee University presenting
awards to ROTC on ROTC day, 1948.*

*ROTC Duty at Tuskegee University from 1945
to 1948. Lieutenant Colonel Barrow
and I, 1947.*

*Major Cleve L. Albott, Athletic Director of
Tuskegee University, presenting the Cadet of
the Year Award to the most
Outstanding ROTC Student, 1947.*

TUSKEGEE UNIVERSITY

*Graduation from college in September 1948,
prior to departure for Germany.*

*Kitzingen Training Center, Germany.
The first Post World War II
non-commissioned
officer school, 1949.*

*United Negro College Fund Campaign, 1950,
Kitzingen, Germany.*

*Kitzingen, Germany, November 1951,
from left to right: Chaplin Beasley,
Frederick D. Patterson, President Tuskegee
University, Colonel Bigelow, Comander,
Captain Cecil W. White.*

Major Cecil W. White G2, G3 advisor to the 3 rd Republic of Korea Infantry Division.

Up Front with General Maxwell Taylor in Korea.

Christmas 1953. A visit by General Kim, the 3rd Korean Infantry Division commander and staff to his American Advisors.

Christmas 1955. ROTC banquet at South Carolina State University. From left to right: LTC Lofton, PMS&T, President Turner, Mrs. Turner, Colonel Singleton, Military District Commander. My guest and I.

The First Battle Group, 13th Infantry, Mannheim, Germany, 1958. Colonel Ellis Williamson and Staff. Colonel Williamson is the third from the right.

The First Battle Group, 13th infantry, Mannheim, Germany, 1958, Colonel Chiccolella, Staff and Commanders

My American winning soccer team receiving a plaque from the Village Mayor, Germany, 1958

I am leading the parade with the Village Mayor.

Perfect German-American Friendship. I took approximately fifty soldiers to this German village at their invitation to participate in its annual fair. All of our soldiers were invited guests in the villagers' homes.

My Unit's Winning Soccer Team

Colonel Chiccolella meeting the German press

*Special Services Officer, Nuernberg, 1958.
Passing the winning prizes to Lieutenant
General Farrel, The Seventh US Army
Commander, for presentation to the event win-
ners.*

*Special Services Nuernberg Germany.
I am presenting this soldier the first prize
in the Art and Craft Contest for his creativity
in Bust of President Eisenhower, 1959.*

*Chain of Commander Photograph Fort Dix,
New Jersey, December 1961.*

*Me with one of the company commanders of
my battalion with platoon leaders.
Fort Dix, New Jersey, 1961.*

*Celebrating Christmas 1960
in Selma, Alabama.*

My Mother, Jennie T. White, in the middle;
my sister Jewell White is on the left; and my
sister Geneva White Martin is on the right.
The photo is taken during the 1960's.

SHE IS THE ONE!

The Berlin girls

Wedding Day, Freiburg, Germany,
September 25, 1969

My bride and I are on cable car 17 to the
castle on the mountain for the reception,
dinner, tea, buffet, and wedding dance.

One of my lifelong friends Leo Kaufmann,
his wife Marliese, and his daughter Cecile
leading the buffet line.

Reception and dinner; to our left is the
bride's Aunt Freedle.

Waiting at the cable car station with in-laws
Lotte and Werner Scharf .

Honeymoon at the Grand Hotel, Canaria Island, September 30, 1969

Honeymoon, Tenerife, Canaria Islands October, 1969

Honeymoon ends in Paris

Cecil Ward White, Junior, The first born will be given to God at my wife's Protestant Church, Freiburg, Germany, July, 1970.

Second Honeymoon, Spain, 1971. From left to right, my mother-in-law, Lotte Scharf, Me, and my wife Evelin.

At my Alabama home in 1972. My son and me standing by the car.

*My daughter at
two years of age.*

My first school day

My son at five years of age.

*My favorite first cousin Lucy Burt and
her husband, Bill, visiting my mother
doing her last days, Spring 1972.*

*From left to right: Me; Cecil White, Jr., son;
Frank H. White, Jr., nephew,
Virginia Beach, Virginia 1986.*

*With Members of my family.
Chicago, April 1999.*

192

Christmas 1999
Left to right: Me; mother-in-law; wife, Evelin;
son, Cecil Jr.; daughter, Vivian.

My wife, son, and daughter,
1998

Son and daughter,
Christmas 1998

Wife and daughter, by the bay,
San Francisco, March 2000

My wife, Evelin

Bull's Eye

193

The Education Class. From left to right: Doctor (Professor) Charles Lang; Doctor Jean Peters; Major US Army (Retired) Cecil W. White; Mr. Booker T. Conley (Architecture Engineer); Colonel US Army (Retired) John A. Welch (Architecture Engineer); Judge Robert W. Penn; Attorney Stanford S. Smith; Colonel US Army (Retired) Charles H. Brown; Mr. Cecil B. Keene, High School Principal (Retired); Doctor Harvey G. Tomas (Dentist). Doctor Peter and Doctor Thomas are now deceased.

The Educated Family. The Sixtieth Wedding Anniversary, four generations of the Moore Family. Malvin E. Moore III and Erin White Moore are both Doctors of Education, Professors and retired from the University of Illinois at Carbondale, residing in Louisville, Kentucky. Each of the adults in this photo are university graduates, making this a one hundred percent university educated family. The grand-daughter, middle rear, Erin Moore, after her grandmother, is studying for her Doctorate Degree from Temple University, Philadelphia, Pennsylvania. She is a graduate from Spelman College, Atlanta, Georgia, Masters Degree from Ohio state, and one year as an invited student to the London School of Business.

EDUCATION SISTERS

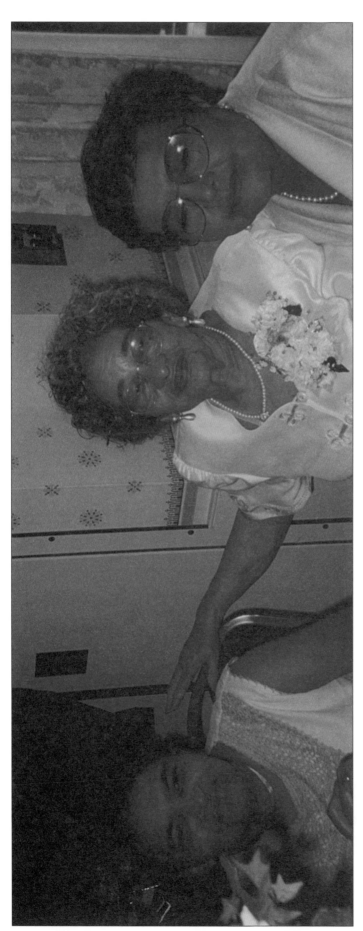

Jean White Gunn, the fifth member of The White Family to graduate from Tuskegee University, Alabama, achieved the Academic requirement for her Doctorate Degree, is retired from Columbus, Georgia, Public School District along with her husband Walter who achieved his Masters Degree in Physical education. They reside in Opelika, Alabama.

Geneva White Martin, married her high school boyfriend, Fred, when he was drafted in the Navy after they both finished high school. The four daughters are university graduates; the son who did not go to college is a retired master sergeant from the US Air Force. Her children were participaants along with other young people during Doctor King's Civil Rights Campaign in Selma, Alabama. Collectively they were locked-up between twenty to twenty-five times.

Mable White Henderson is a Graduate Nurse from Tuskegee University. She and her Doctor of Dentistry husband have three children. The oldest, a daughter and lawyer, is a member of a law firm in Atlanta, Ga. Her son is a medical doctor and Lieutenant Colonel in the USAF, stationed at Andrews Air Force Base, Md. The youngest daughter is an entertainer, actress, writer, producer, and is now working on her doctorate degree.

A visit by Governor Thompson of Wisconsin at the US Berlin Aircraft Memorial in Wiesbaden, November 1998
From left to right: Governor Thompson's Aide, Governor Thompson, Me, SMS Sheehan, Colonel Lloyd Waterman (now General).

The 50th Anniversary of the ending of the Berlin Airlift, May 13, 1999.
Conversing with Admiral Abbott, Deputy Commanding Chief U.S. European Command.

Wiesbaden, Germany, July 4, Commemoration of the 50th Anniversary of the beginning of the Berlin airlift

Tegel See (Tegel Lake) Berlin, 12 May 1999. A city-sponsored boat ride during the commemoration exercise 9-13 May 99. My wife Evelin on the right with one of our friend's wife.

Colonel Gail Haverson US Air Force retired was the candy bomber during the Berlin Air lift 1948-49.

The lady on his left was one of the children who received the candies which he threw from the plane in Berlin during the 1948-49 Berlin Air Lift.

HAPPY REUNION

Book signing at **HOCHLER**, *West Germany*

Weihnachts-Markt 2000 bei HOCHLER

President William Jefferson Clinton and Vivian White,
September 06, 1999
Labor day, Norfolk, Virginia, School System

Vivian White receives VIP invitation to attend Labor Day
speech delivered by the President to Hampton Roads educators.

My only photo of the Berlin Airlift 1948-49